Marylanders to Ohio and Indiana

Migration Prior to 1835

INDIANA & OHIO

Henry C. Peden, Jr.

HERITAGE BOOKS
2020

HERITAGE BOOKS

AN IMPRINT OF HERITAGE BOOKS, INC.

Books, CDs, and more—Worldwide

For our listing of thousands of titles see our website
at
www.HeritageBooks.com

Published 2020 by
HERITAGE BOOKS, INC.
Publishing Division
5810 Ruatan Street
Berwyn Heights, Md. 20740

International Standard Book Number
Paperbound: 978-1-68034-491-2

CONTENTS

Foreword v

Marylanders to Ohio and Indiana: Migrations prior to 1835 1

Index 215

FOREWORD

There were many Marylanders who migrated to Ohio and Indiana "in the early days" by way of Pennsylvania, Virginia and Kentucky and this book is the sixth in a series about Marylanders "on the move." The previous five books on the subject are *Marylanders to Kentucky, 1775-1825* (compiled in 1991), *Marylanders to Carolina* (compiled in 1994), *More Marylanders to Kentucky, 1778-1828* (compiled in 1997), *More Marylanders to Carolina* (compiled in 1999), and *Marylanders to Tennessee, 1775-1835* (compiled in 2005), which are available from Colonial Roots, Inc.

Travel westward prior to 1800 was initially by foot on Indian paths and then by horse and wagon on trails cut through the wilderness. This subsequently led to the creation of the old National Road from Baltimore through Western Maryland, the building of the Chesapeake and Ohio Canal which reached Harpers Ferry, VA in 1833, and the Baltimore and Ohio Railroad which reached that place in 1834. Some travelers migrated via Pennsylvania and went by boat down the Ohio River, settling in Kentucky (which became a state in 1792) and Ohio (which became a state in 1805) and later moving to Indiana (which became a state in 1815). Early travel was inherently dangerous due to bad weather conditions, mountainous terrain, flooded rivers, unexpected illnesses and accidents, and Indian uprisings that constantly plagued the earliest settlers. Without a doubt, our ancestors who traveled west during those perilous times were indeed a hardy lot to endure such hardships.

This book, like the others in the series, has been compiled in an effort to identify as many early Marylanders as possible in order to assist researchers in finding their elusive ancestors. We have all at one time or another wondered where they went and from whence they came. Hopefully, this book will be of some value in that regard, realizing of course that not all of them could be identified and presented within this one volume. Therefore, I plan to compile and publish more material in another volume to be titled *More Marylanders to Ohio and Indiana* in the very near future.

As will be seen, a variety of sources has been used in this compilation and each one has been identified within the text. A plethora of information was gleaned from pension and bounty land applications of veterans of the Revolutionary War and the War of 1812, and their widows' applications, as well as church records, county histories, newspapers, and family records. It must be noted that the author assumes no responsibility for error of fact or the opinion expressed or implied in each source, or the accuracy of the material published by others. One should always be aware of family tradition and undocumented statements.

v

I want to express my sincere appreciation to Jane F. Burgess of Rockville, MD, E. Claire Albert of Columbia, MD, and F. Edward Wright of Lewes, DE, for their generous contribution of information for this book.

Henry C. Peden, Jr.
Bel Air, Maryland
January 11, 2006

MARYLANDERS TO OHIO AND INDIANA: MIGRATIONS PRIOR TO 1835

ISAAC ACKRIGHT

Isaac Ackright was born circa 1738 and enlisted at Baltimore, MD during the Revolutionary War. He applied for a pension in Wayne Co., OH on 26 May 1824, aged 86, and his son **John Ackright** stated that his father's house had burned down on 15 Mar 1824. {Ref: *Genealogical Abstracts of Revolutionary War Pension Files*, by Virgil D. White (1990), Application R22}

JOHN ADAMS

John Adams was born in Somerset Co., MD on 5 Mar 1763 and served aboard a privateer during the Revolutionary War. He married **Sophia Smith** in 1805 and applied for a pension in Ross Co., OH on 16 Oct 1833, aged 70. John died on 19 May 1835 and **Sophia Adams** died in Fayette Co., OH on 9 Nov 1847. In 1852 their surviving children were as follows:
1. **Josiah Adams**
2. **Celia Adams** married **Mr. Moomaw**
3. **Elizabeth Adams** married **Mr. Kerr**

{Ref: *Genealogical Abstracts of Revolutionary War Pension Files*, by Virgil D. White (1990), Application R83; *Revolutionary Patriots of Worcester & Somerset Counties, Maryland, 1775-1783*, by Henry C. Peden, Jr. (1999), pp. 2-3}

THOMAS ALBERT

Thomas Albert and **Catherine Saylor**, of Maryland (county not stated), married in Ohio (county not stated) after 1815. {Ref: *Maryland Revolutionary Records*, by Harry Wright Newman (1938), p. 109}

WILLIAM ALEXANDER

William Alexander was a lieutenant in the 5th Maryland Line during the Revolutionary War and served from 10 Dec 1776 until 27 Aug 1777 when he died of wounds received in battle. He had married **Elizabeth Cruthers** and it was noted in the pension record that she was last heard from around 11 Aug 1813 after starting on a trip south. An **Elizabeth Alexander** subsequently applied for a pension in Union Co., OH on 11 Aug 1857, aged 80, but her application was rejected. {Ref: *Genealogical Abstracts of Revolutionary War Pension Files*, by Virgil D. White (1990), Application R58; *Archives of Maryland*, Volume 18, p. 182}

ZACHARIAH ALLBAUGH

Zachariah Allbaugh (sometimes spelled Albaugh), son of **Zachariah and Susannah Allbaugh**, was born on 31 Oct 1758 in Frederick Co., MD and served as an Associator during the Revolutionary War. He also took the Oath of Allegiance in 1778. After the war he lived in Maryland for 8 years, then moved to Pennsylvania for 36 years, and then moved to Ohio. He applied for a pension in Licking County on 29 Oct 1832, aged 74, and died on 8 Nov 1857. {Ref:

2

Genealogical Abstracts of Revolutionary War Pension Files, by Virgil D. White (1990), Application S2902; *Revolutionary Patriots of Frederick County, Maryland, 1775-1783*, by Henry C. Peden, Jr. (1995), p. 3}

THOMAS ALLEN

Thomas Allen was born on 17 Mar 1749 in Maryland (county not stated) and married **Rhoda Cares** (b. 15 Jul 1748) on 22 May 1770. He served as a private in the 3rd Company, 3rd Battalion, under Capt. **Benjamin Price** during the Revolutionary War and was last reported as sick in Annapolis on 1 Jan 1782. The children of **Thomas and Rhoda Allen** were as follows:

1. **Martha Allen** (b. 1771) married **Vincent Brown**
2. **Thomas Allen, Jr.** (b. 22 May 1775) married **Katherine Myers**
3. **Mary Allen** (b. 1779) married **Mr. Fiscus**
4. **Hutchins Allen** (b. 1781)
5. **Robert Allen** (b. 1783) married **Mary Allen**
6. **John Allen** (b. 1785) married **Nancy A. White**

Rhoda Allen died on 15 Sep 1816 and **Thomas Allen** died on 4 Jul 1825 in Brown Co., OH. {Ref: DAR Application 165501; *A Roster of Revolutionary Ancestors of the Indiana Daughters of the American Revolution* (1976), p. 12}

AQUILA AMOS

Aquila Amos, son of **William Amos** (sometimes spelled Amoss) and **Mary Sinclair** of Baltimore Co., MD, was born on 20 Feb 1774 in Harford Co., MD and married **Elizabeth Montgomery** (b. 29 Jul 1778) on 1 May 1804. They subsequently moved to Meigs Co., OH by 1828. Elizabeth died on 22 Sep 1863 and Aquila died on 12 Feb 1866. Their children were as follows:

1. **Thomas Montgomery Amos** (6 Mar - 21 Mar 1806)
2. **Meranda Emaline Amos** (20 Oct 1807 - 12 Jan 1858) married **Leonard Chalk** (1807-1873); they had a daughter **Julia H. Chalk** (1829-1909) who married **Corbin Clark Amos** (1810-1883) and died in Brownsville, OH
3. **William Bradford Amos** (b. 27 Dec 1809) married **Eliza Warren** on 31 May 1835
4. **Elizabeth Jane Amos** (b. 25 Oct 1812) married **Rev. Isaac Kimber** on 15 Sep 1830
5. **Orpha Ann Amos** (b. 29 May 1816) married **Elisha Irvin** on 31 May 1835
6. **Sarah Louise Amos** (b. 7 Nov 1818) married **James Ward** on 10 Dec 1835
7. **James Montgomery Amos** (b. 13 Dec 1821) married first to **Hannah Smith** on 23 Oct 1849 and second to **Hannah Kirkbride** on 1 Dec 1852
8. **Mary Louisa Amos** (30 Jun 1824 - 11 Mar 1908. Athens Co., OH)
9. **Alonzo Aquila Amos** (11 Sep 1828, OH - 3 Nov 1828)
10. **George Washington Benjamin Franklin Amos** (22 Mar 1832, Meigs Co., OH - 13 Sep 1889, Trimble, OH) married **Rachel Davis Drake** (1837-1916) on 15 Apr 1855

{Ref: *Children of Mt. Soma*, by Gertrude J. Stephens, pp. 511-512}

DITTO AMOS

Rev. Ditto Amos, son of **Nicholas Day Amos** and **Christiana Ditto**, of Harford Co., MD, moved with his family to Washington Co., MD prior to 1790 and about 1795 they moved to Bourbon Co., KY. Ditto married **Martha "Patsy" Neale** and was an ordained Methodist minister. He was the first member of the Amos family to purchase land in Rush Co., IN on 27 Dec 1825 and 16 Nov 1826. By 1834 they had moved to the northern part of Shelby Co., IN. Around 1839 they moved to Clinton Co., IN, near Kirklin, and **Ditto Amos** died circa 1842. Their children were as follows:

1. **Aquilla Amos** (26 Mar 1808, KY - 1 Aug 1850, Indianapolis, IN) married **Nancy Jones** (1810-1880) in Rush Co., IN on 15 Oct 1828; their children were as follows:

1-1. **Elizabeth Amos** (28 Jan 1829, Rush Co., IN - 22 Dec 1882) married **Uriah Lane** on 27 Dec 1845

1-2. **Thomas D. Amos** (25 Nov 1830, Rush Co., IN - 1908) married first to **Sarah R. McGuire** on 18 Feb 1851 and second to **Huldah A. Cowan** on 8 Sep 1864

1-3. **Martha Amos** (20 Jan 1832, Rush Co., IN - 28 Dec 1860?) married **Jonathan Davis** on 18 Feb 1852

1-4. **James Amos** (5 Nov 1833, Rush Co., IN - 14 Jan 1890, Indianapolis, IN) married **Lydia Wolfe** on 15 Feb 1859

1-5. **Margaret Amos** (25 Aug 1835, Shelby Co., IN - 3 Dec 1858) married **William Henderson** on 12 Dec 1856

1-6. **William Hayden Amos** (b. 1 Jul 1837, Shelby Co., IN) married **Eliza Conover**

1-7. **Lucinda Amos** (24 Feb 1839, Shelby Co., IN - 1912) married **George W. Moore**

1-8. **Joseph Amos** (24 Nov 1840 - 31 Jul 1842, Clinton Co., IN)

1-9. **Isaac Neale Amos** (24 Nov 1842, Clinton Co., IN - 24 Oct 1900, Clermont Co., IN) married **Sarah A. Conover**

1-10. **Samuel Amos** (b. circa 1844) married first to **Frances E. Cosler** on 18 Mar 1864 and second to **Emma J. Shields** on 3 Nov 1867

1-11. **Nancy Jane Amos** (18 Feb 1848 - 3 Jan 1849)

1-12. **Aquilla "Ditto" Amos** (18 Dec 1849 - 10 May 1873) married **Mary Carr** on 22 Sep 1869

2. **Asbury Amos** (circa 1809, KY - 1856, Clinton Co., IN) married **Mary Ann Lines** on or about 29 Jun 1830

3. **Nancy Amos** (22 Sep 1812, KY - 9 Oct 1873, Clinton Co., IN) married **John Lewis Reeves** on 3 Jul 1838

4. **Christiana Amos** (b. circa 1814, KY) married **William H. Endaly** on 6 Jun 1833

5. **James H. Amos** (24 Aug 1816, KY - 1 Apr 1853, Clinton Co., IN) married **Mary Ann Boyle** (b. 1821, VA, d. 1896, KS) on 26 Sep 1839

6. **Sarah Amos** (b. circa 1818, KY) married **Peter Moore** (b. circa 1797, NC) in Clinton Co., IN on 21 Mar 1843

7. **Thomas Amos** (22 May 1822, KY - 29 Dec 1908) married **Demarue C. Thurman** in Clinton Co., IN on 30 Sep 1843

8. **William Amos** (8 Sep 1828, Rush Co., IN - 5 Dec 1908, Kirklin, IN) married **Julia Catherine Walker** (1830-1898) on 10 Feb 1848 in Indianapolis, IN

9. **Elijah Neale Amos** (13 May 1832, Rush Co., IN - 23 Sep 1903, Clinton Co., IN) married **Lydia B. Epperson** (1842-1886)

{Ref: *Children of Mt. Soma*, by Gertrude J. Stephens, pp. 342-371}

ELIJAH AMOS

Elijah Amos, son of **Nicholas Day Amos** and **Christiana Ditto**, of Harford Co., MD, moved with his family to Washington Co., MD prior to 1790 and about 1795 they moved to Bourbon Co., KY. Elijah married **Rebecca Neale** and they moved to Rush Co., IN by 1827. Some of their children were already married, but all of them went with them with the possible exception of their son Thomas who owned land in Indiana in the 1830's, but apparently never actually lived there. **Rebecca Amos** died prior to 1840 and **Elijah Amos** married **Cassander Cullison** on 23 Jun 1840. He died by 1863 and **Cassander Amos** married **Samuel Seawright**. The children of Elijah Amos were as follows:

1. **Thomas Amos** (circa 1801, KY - 1886, Bourbon Co., KY) married **Susannah Crump** on 27 Dec 1821 (no children)

2. **Ditto Amos** (14 Aug 1803, KY - 1879, Laurel, IN) married **Rebecca Crump** on 17 Nov 1824 and moved to Rush Co., IN; their children were as follows:

2-1. **Cassander Amos** (b. 30 Sep 1825) married **George Pennington** on 25 Sep 1843 and moved to Iowa

2-2. **Thomas J. Amos** (b. 3 Jan 1827, Rush Co., IN) moved to Tennessee and married **Sarah Paul** (b. circa 1837)

2-3. **Granville Amos** (b. 18 May 1828, Rush Co., IN) moved to Tennessee, married (wife's name unknown) and died after 1880 in Arkansas

2-4. **Susannah Amos** (14 Dec 1830 - 29 Jan 1921) married **William Alfred Williams**

2-5. **Polly Amos** (13 Jul 1832 - 8 Sep 1834)

2-6. **William Harrison Amos** (b. 23 Mar 1835, Laurel, IN) married first to **Matilda Isabella Paul**, second to **Polly (Kearns) Ponton**, and third to **Eliza Ann (Craft) Fisher**

2-7. **Rebecca Jane Amos** (17 Apr 1837 - July 1838)

2-8. **Emmaline Conwell Amos** (31 Mar 1840, Laurel, IN - 13 Jan 1933) married **Henry L. Wann** (1828-1910) in Franklin Co., IN on 30 Oct 1870

2-9. **Martha Jane Amos** (2 Jan 1842, Laurel, IN - circa 1926, California) married first to **James S. Smith** and second to **Mr. Dion**

2-10. **Amanda Amos** (2 Apr 1853, Laurel, IN - 27 Sep 1943) married **J. B. Allen** in South Dakota and later returned to Indianapolis, IN

3. **Martha "Patsy" Amos** (1805, KY - 26 Jun 1894, Shelby Co., IN) married **Rev. Thomas S. Jones** (1806-1868) in Rush Co., IN on 25 Jan 1828; their children

were as follows:

    3-1. **Elijah Jones** (11 Mar 1831 - 12 Aug 1903, Madison Co., IN) married first to **Sarah Catherine Wagoner** in 1854 and second to **Susannah Marshall** in 1862

    3-2. **Sarah Jones** (10 Aug 1832 - 18 Aug 1908) married **William A. Wagoner** in 1852

    3-3. **John Jones** married **Electra Grubb** in 1851

    3-4. **Harrison Jones** (1834 - 16 Jun 1908, Shelby Co., IN) married **Hulda D. Farrow** in 1856

    3-5. **Mary Ann Jones** (1 Mar 1836 - 16 Sep 1908) unmarried

    3-6. **Louise Jones** (no further information)

    3-7. **Rebecca Jones** (1843 - 22 Oct 1917) married **Tilson Wheeler Marshall** in 1866

    3-8. **Melissa Jones** (1846-1928) married **James Madison Tillison** in 1883

    4. **Cassana Amos** (15 Sep 1808, KY - 28 Nov 1889) married **Charles T. Thompson** (1810-1892) in Rush Co., IN on 16 Dec 1830

    5. **Harrison Amos** (9 Jan 1813, KY - 27 Apr 1893, Fountaintown, IN) married first to **Hannah Jones** (of Clermont Co., OH, died before 1850 in Shelby Co., IN) and second to **Elizabeth Jane Seely** (1826-1884) in Hancock Co., IN

    6. **William Amos** (30 Jun 1816, KY - 7 Jul 1893, Shelby Co., IN) married first to **Mary Ann Trees** (1816, OH -1869, IN) and second to **Mary (Cherry) Wood** (1834, OH -1920, IN)

    7. **Elizabeth "Betsy" Amos** (1 Oct 1817, KY - 17 Jun 1887, Greenfield, IN) married **Elijah Boling** (1815-1867)

    8. **Caroline A. Amos** (b. circa 1842, IN) married **Rice W. Robertson** in Shelby Co., IN on 28 Jul 1861

    9. **Hester J. Amos** (1844, IN - 10 Jan 1877, Middletown, IN) married **Alfred M. Poundstone** on 1 Sep 1867

    10. **Mary A. "Molly" Amos** (b. circa 1849, IN) married **William D. Robertson** in Shelby Co., IN on 3 Oct 1867

{Ref: *Children of Mt. Soma*, by Gertrude J. Stephens, pp. 302-315, citing research by Maurine Schmitz, Mabel (Wood) Swaim and Glendola (Amos) Peck}

FREDERICK AMOS

    Frederick Amos was born circa 1762 in Baltimore (now Harford) Co., MD, son of **Joshua Amos** (1725-1779) and **Martha Bradford**. He married **Naomi Alderson** and her brother **Abel Alderson** married **Ann Amos**, daughter of **Benjamin Amos**. Around 1824 Frederick moved to Cumberland Co., PA and by 1836 they moved to Richland Co., OH; their children were as follows:

    1. **Joshua Amos** (no further information)

    2. ---- **Amos** (daughter; no further information)

    3. **Thomas Alderson Amos** (1797, Harford Co., MD - 1 Apr 1994, Mansfield, OH) married **Sarah Chatham**

    4. ---- **Amos** (daughter; no further information)

    5. **Abel B. M. Amos** (b. 1802) married **Lydia ----**

6

6. **John G. Amos** (28 Feb 1802, Harford Co., MD - 25 Jan 1892, Darlington, Richland Co., OH), unmarried
7. **Caroline D. Amos** (12 Mar 1804, Harford Co., MD - 16 Aug 1889, Richland Co., OH), unmarried
8. **William Amos** (no further information)
9. **Fred T. Amos** (b. 1809, Harford Co., MD and died in Knox Co., OH, date not given) married twice: first wife's name unknown and second wife was **Margaret Shafer**
10. **Ellen Amos** (b. 1814, Harford Co., MD)
11. **James M. Amos** (b. 3 Jan 1816, Harford Co., MD, lived in Richland Co., OH, and died 31 May 1890 in Noble Co., IN) married **Margaret Weaver**

{Ref: *Children of Mt. Soma*, by Gertrude J. Stephens, pp. 511, 530-532}

MORDECAI AMOS

Mordecai Amos (sometimes spelled **Amoss**), son of **James Amos** and **Hannah Clark**, was born in 1753 in Baltimore (now Harford) Co., MD and served as a lieutenant in the 8th Battalion of the Harford County militia during the Revolutionary War. He appears to have married **Martha Ann Richardson** circa 1780, but some family members indicate he married **Margaret** ---- while others indicate it was **Susanna** ----. This issue will not be resolved here and will require additional research. Be that as it may, the children of **Mordecai Amos** were as follows:

1. **Rachel Amos** (b. c1781) married **Benjamin Standiford** on 9 Jan 1798 and lived on "My Lady's Manor" in Baltimore Co., MD. Their children were as follows:
    1-1. **William (Amos?) Standiford**
    1-2. **James Adolphus Standiford**
    1-3. **Sarah H. Standiford**
    1-4. **Benjamin Standiford, Jr.**
2. **Henry Richardson Amos** (b. 13 Apr 1783 and died circa 1856/1860 in Carroll Co., OH) married **Mary M. Streett** on 17 Mar 1803 in Harford Co., MD; their children were as follows:
    2-1. **John Streett Amos** (b. 23 Feb 1804, Harford Co., MD, and died 27 Apr 1847, Washington Co., PA) married first to **Elizabeth Rampley** (b. 28 May 1803, d. 10 May 1843, Harrison Co., OH) and second to **Mary Fullerton** in Washington Co., PA. **John and Elizabeth Amos** moved to Harrison Co., OH around 1828 with their oldest child and their other children were born there:
        2-1-1. **William Rampley Amos** (1824-1876)
        2-1-2. **Mary Ann Amos** (1829-1922)
        2-1-3. **John Mordecai Amos** (1831-1906)
        2-1-4. **Darcus Amos** (1833-1835)
        2-1-5. **James R. Amos** (1835-)
        2-1-6. **Nicholas D. Amos** (1837-1917)
        2-1-7. **Thomas Amos** (1838-1840)
        2-1-8. **Abeth Amos** (1842-1843)
    2-2. **Mordecai Amos** (b. 20 Feb 1806, Harford Co., MD, d. 5 Mar 1873

at Malvern, Carroll Co., OH) married **Lucy Ann Wayne** in Baltimore Co., MD on 8 Dec 1829. Their children were as follows:

2-2-1. **John Wayne Amos** (1831-1903)

2-2-2. **Louisa Ann Amos** (1832-1858)

2-2-3. **Mary Amos** (1834-   )

2-2-4. **Charlotte M. Amos** (1836-1860)

2-2-5. **Olivia Amos** (1839-1908)

2-2-6. **Caroline Amos** (1842-1859)

2-2-7. **---- Amos** (1844-1859)

2-2-8. **Mordecai Streett Amos** (1846-1923)

2-2-9. **William Amos** (c1848-   )

2-3. **Martha Amos** (b. 1 Jul 1808) married **John Watt** on 9 Jan 1828 in Harford Co., MD; their known children, born between 1828 and 1850, were as follows:

2-3-1. **Ann E. Watt**

2-3-2. **Mary M. Watt**

2-3-3. **Charlotte Watt**

2-3-4. **Caroline Watt**

2-3-5. **John H. Watt**

2-3-6. **David T. Watt**

2-3-7. **William O. Watt**

2-3-8. **---- Watt** (female)

2-4. **Ann Amos** married **Samuel B. Parker** on 24 Mar 1835

2-5. **---- Amos** (no further information)

2-6. **Charlotte Amos** (b. 1814) married **George Swain**, of Baltimore, MD, on 6 Nov 1834; their daughter **Mary M. Swain** was born in Ohio; **Charlotte Swain** lived with her brother **Abraham "Abram" Amos** in Tuscarawas Co., OH in 1860

2-7. **Ariel Amos** (b. 24 Apr 1818 and died 15 Jul 1896, Douglas Co., KS) married **James Harper** (1813-1873) on 27 Jun 1837 in Carroll Co., OH; their children were as follows:

2-7-1. **Mary Catherine Harper**

2-7-2. **Lecky Harper**

2-7-3. **Amanda Harper**

2-8. **Amanda Amos** married **Robert Gibson**

2-9. **William H. Amos** (b. 14 Oct 1827 and died 10 Jun 1901, Saline Co., KS) married **Nancy Isabella Watt** (1828-1905) on 3 Oct 1848 in Carroll Co., OH; their children were as follows:

2-9-1. **Mary Cordelia Amos**

2-9-2. **Ariel Amos**

2-9-3. **Henry Amos**

2-9-4. **Amanda Amos**

2-9-5. **Elizabeth Amos**

2-9-6. **Sophia Maud Amos**

2-10. **---- Amos** (son; no further information)

2-11. **Abraham "Abram" Amos** (b. 5 Mar 1832 and died 2 Jan 1894) married **Mary Watt** on 5 Nov 1855 in Carroll Co., OH; their children were as follows:

    2-11-1. **Mary M. Amos**

    2-11-2. **Josie Amos**

    2-11-3. **Albert W. Amos**

    2-11-4. **Edwin M. Amos**

3. **Mary Amos** (b. circa 1784; nothing further)

4. **Robert Amos** (b. circa 1786) married **Martha Johns** on 31 Mar 1808 in Harford Co., MD, and moved to Kentucky in 1816; their children were as follows:

    4-1. **Sarah Ann Amos** married **Benjamin Quigg**

    4-2. **Mary Amos** married **William Crull**

5. **John Archer Amos** (b. 1790 and died testate in 1851) married **Sarah Ann Wayne** on 27 Dec 1814 in Baltimore Co., MD. Their children were as follows:

    5-1. **Sarah Margaret Amos** married **James Worthington**

    5-2. **John M. Amoss** married **Mary Jane Glenn**

6. ---- **Amos** (female, b. circa 1792)

7. **Thomas Amos** (b. circa 1794; nothing further)

8. **William Amos** (b. 1797 and died after 1880) married **Susannah Richardson** on 1 Nov 1815 and lived in Harford Co., MD

9. ---- **Amos** (female, b. circa 1800)

10. ---- **Amos** (female, b. circa 1802)

11. ---- **Amos** (female, b. circa 1804)

Mordecai Amos (b. 1753 as cited above) applied for a pension in Harford Co., MD on 25 Sep 1832, aged 79, and moved to Harrison Co., OH in 1835 to live with some of his children. He died prior to 18 Aug 1842 and one of his sons, **William Amos**, signed a power of attorney in Harford County on 22 Feb 1853. {Ref: *Children of Mt. Soma*, by Gertrude J. Stephens, pp. 380, 466-484; *Genealogical Abstracts of Revolutionary War Pension Files*, by Virgil D. White (1990), Application S2034; *Revolutionary Patriots of Harford County, Maryland, 1775-1783*, by Henry C. Peden, Jr., p. 5}

PETER ANDERSON

A certificate of removal was received by the Milford Monthly Meeting in Wayne Co., IN on the 18th day of the 11th month, 1830 for **Peter Anderson** from the Northwest Fork Monthly Meeting in Caroline Co., MD. On the 17th day of the 5th month, 1838 **Peter Anderson** was reported for *"marrying contrary to discipline"* and was disowned. {Ref: "Migration of Caroline County Quakers to Indiana," by F. Edward Wright, *Maryland Genealogical Society Bulletin*, Volume 34, No. 3 (1993), p. 282}

WILLIAM ANDERSON

William Anderson, a man of color, served in Maryland during the Revolutionary War and subsequently moved to Ohio where he applied for a pension in Warren County on 15 May 1818. {Ref: *Genealogical Abstracts of Revolutionary*

9

War Pension Files, by Virgil D. White (1990), Application R203}

WRIGHT ANDERSON

A certificate of removal was received by the Milford Monthly Meeting in Wayne Co., IN on the 18th day of the 3rd month, 1830 for **Wright Anderson** and his children **William Anderson, Mary Elizabeth Anderson, Ann Anderson, Jane Anderson, John Anderson, and Margaret Anderson**, from the Third Haven Monthly Meeting in Talbot Co., MD. **Mary Elizabeth Anderson**, daughter of **Wright Anderson** and **Margaret** (deceased), of Fayette Co., IN, married on the 28th day of the 10th month, 1841 to **Jesse Heacock**, son of **John and Christiana Heacock**, of Henry Co., IN, at the Milford Monthly Meeting House in Wayne Co., IN. {Ref: "Migration of Caroline County Quakers to Indiana," by F. Edward Wright, *Maryland Genealogical Society Bulletin*, Volume 34, No. 3 (1993), p. 282}

ADAMANERS ANDRES

Adamaners Andres and family moved from Maryland (county not stated) and settled on the east bank of the Whitewater in Harrison Township, Dearborn Co., OH in 1813. They were accompanied by the Mettler family. One of Adamaners' sons was **James Andres**. {Ref: *History of Dearborn and Ohio Counties, Indiana* (1885), p. 526}

NOBLE ANDREW

Noble Andrew served on active duty in the War of 1812 as a private in the company of Capt. **Peter Willis** in Caroline Co., MD from 16 Aug to 30 Aug 1813. He subsequently moved to Ohio where he applied for bounty land (warrant number not given) in Delaware County on 30 Mar 1855, aged 60. {Ref: *Maryland Militia, War of 1812, Volume 1, Eastern Shore*, by F. Edward Wright, p. 106}

SAMUEL ARNETT

Samuel Arnett served in Maryland during the Revolutionary War and married **Nancy ----** on 8 Dec 1788. They lived in Maryland for 8 years and then moved to Washington Co., PA for a few years, then to Columbiana Co., OH, and then to Richland Co., OH. Their daughter **Nancy Arnett** married **Solomon Culver**. Samuel filed for a pension in Richland Co., OH on 31 Oct 1832, aged 86, and died on 28 Jun 1837. **Nancy Arnett** filed for a widow's pension in Richland Co., OH on 3 Aug 1850, aged 85. The application was rejected because his entire service during the war was as a waiter or a wagoner. {Ref: *Genealogical Abstracts of Revolutionary War Pension Files*, by Virgil D. White (1990), Application R262; *Rejected or Suspended Applications for Revolutionary War Pensions* (1852), p. 337}

GEORGE ARNOLD

George Arnold served as a private in a German Regiment of the Maryland Line during the Revolutionary War and was discharged on 22 Mar 1779. He applied for a pension in Somerset Co., PA on 16 Dec 1818, aged 67, having lived in that county for 30 years. In 1820 his wife (name not given) was aged 65 and two daughters lived with them, one of whom was blind. George married **Eve Plumb** on 20 Jun or 2 Jul 1831 in Millersburg, OH. **Eve Arnold** filed for a widow's pension in Medina Co., OH on 3 Mar 1855, aged 85, and stated George had died in Holmes Co., OH on 21 Jun 1836. Her son **Jacob Plumb**, aged 70 in 1856, stated he was a son of Jacob Plumb and Eve Arnold, formerly **Eve Plumb**, and his father Jacob had died in December, 1817. He was a Revolutionary War pensioner and lived in Somerset Co., PA until 1816 when he moved to Wayne Co., OH. Jacob, the son, stated **George Arnold** died on 22 Jun 1835. {Ref: *Genealogical Abstracts of Revolutionary War Pension Files*, by Virgil D. White (1990), Application W25356; *Archives of Maryland*, Volume 18, p. 184}

THOMAS ASHTON

Thomas Ashton, of Harford Co., MD, enlisted in the War of 1812 and served on active duty as a private in Capt. **Joshua Amos'** Company from 29 Aug to 26 Sep 1814. He also served in Capt. **Frederick T. Amos'** Company, 42nd Regiment, from 12 Oct until 27 Oct 1814 when he was discharged at Baltimore. He subsequently moved to Ohio and died in Fairfield County on 19 Mar 1845. **William Ashton** and **E. P Bull** stated they attended the funeral. **Laura Ashton**, widow of Thomas, resided in Fairfield Co., OH on 19 Jul 1853, aged 65. She stated that she and **Thomas Ashton** were married on or about 25 Feb 1828 by **Nathan Beals**, a Justice of the Peace, and her previous name was **Laura Swan**. On 20 Oct 1853 **Laura Ashton** stated she married **Thomas Ashton** in Licking Co., OH and **Sephrona Bull** stated she attended the wedding. **E. P. Bull**, who lived in the immediate neighborhood of **Thomas Ashton**, stated that soon after the date of the marriage **Laura Ashton** *"removed to the residence of said Thomas Ashton in Fairfield County."* Affidavits dated 13 Aug 1853 from Harford Co., MD were made by **Lloyd Martin** and **Barret Johnson** who served in the same companies as **Thomas Ashton**. On 30 May 1855 **Laura Ashton**, aged 63, resided in Fairfield Co., OH when she applied for bounty land (warrant 55-120-56666). **Chenowith Ashton** and **Joseph Ashton** were acquainted with her. {Ref: *Maryland Militia, War of 1812, Volume 3, Cecil & Harford Counties*, by F. Edward Wright, pp. 20, 29, 39}

JOHN AYRES

John Ayres served in the Delaware and Maryland Lines during the Revolutionary War and applied for a pension in Clark Co., OH on 24 Mar 1824, aged 70. He had no family with him at the time, but two daughters (names not given), aged about 20 and 22, lived in Maryland. {Ref: *Genealogical Abstracts of Revolutionary War Pension Files*, by Virgil D. White (1990), Application S45226}

ELLEN BAGLEY

Ellen Bagley, youngest daughter of the late **William Bagley**, of Deer Creek, Harford Co., MD, died at Cincinnati, OH in 1832 (exact date not given in newspaper). Her mother **Susan Bagley** had died on 20 Mar 1831 in Harford County. The will of **Susanna O. Bagley**, of Harford Co., MD, was written on 17

Aug 1830 and probated on 24 May 1831. She bequeathed her farm and all of its contents to her daughter **Elizabeth H. Bagley** and $1 to each of her children, viz., **Samuel H. Bagley, Susan O. Routh, George W. Bagley, Mary Ruth, John O. Bagley, Ann Ramsey, Catherine A. Bagley, Ferdinand Bagley, Ellen S. Bagley, and William Bagley**, and $1 to her grandson **Richard Sappington**. {Ref: *Baltimore American*, 14 Apr 1831 and 2 Aug 1832, abstracted by Lorrie A. E. Erdman; Harford County Will Book SR No. 1, p. 535}

HENRY BAGUN

Henry Bagun served in Maryland during the Revolutionary War. He was born on 27 Feb 1761 in Lancaster Co., PA and lived in Washington Co., MD at the time of his enlistment. In 1788 he moved to Huntington Co., PA, in 1803 to Fayette Co., PA, in 1806 to Westmoreland Co., PA, in 1811 to Wayne Co., OH, and in 1822 to Stark Co., OH, where he applied for a pension on 8 Aug 1832. aged 72. {Ref: *Genealogical Abstracts of Revolutionary War Pension Files*, by Virgil D. White (1990), Application S5269}

EMMOR BAILY

Emmor Baily requested a certificate of removal on the 8th day of the 6th month, 1815, from the Baltimore Monthly Meeting, Western District, to Short Creek Monthly Meeting in Ohio for himself, his wife **Elizabeth Baily**, and their ten minor children, **Henry Baily, Mary Baily, Abraham Baily, Jacob Baily, Ezra Baily, Hannah Baily, Phebe Baily, Emmor Baily Jr., Martha Baily** and **Ann Baily**, having already removed there. **Margaret Baily** and **Elizabeth Baily**, being about to remove to settle with their parents (not named) within the verge of Short Creek Monthly Meeting in Ohio, also requested a certificate of removal at that same time. {Ref: Baltimore Quaker Monthly Meeting Minutes}

JAMES BALCH

James Balch was born on Deer Creek in Baltimore (now Harford) Co., MD on 25 Dec 1750 and around 1772 he married **Susanna Lavinia Garrison** (b. 13 Feb 1758). Their children were as follows:
1. **Amos P. Balch**
2. **Ann Wilkes Balch**
3. **Martha Balch**
4. **Mary Balch**
5. **Elizabeth R. Balch**
6. **Ethelinda Balch**
7. **Albinda Bloomer Balch**
8. **Calvin Balch**
9. **John C. Balch**
10. **Jonathan Edward Balch**

James Balch was licensed to preach by the Presbytery of Abington in 1787 and he was still a member there in 1798, but by 1803 he had transferred to the

Presbytery of Cumberland. He was one of the first trustees of Greenville College in Tennessee. He later moved to Sullivan Co., IN where he died on 12 Jan 1821. Over his final resting place in the Presbyterian Cemetery near Graysville is a square pillar of marble with this inscription: *"Sacred to the memory of Rev. James Balch, who departed this life January 12th, 1821, aged 70 years and 18 days."* Below this inscription are these words: *"Removed from near the site of Hopewell Church, west of Turman's Creek, by a Committee of the Vincennes Presbytery, October 19th, 1880."* **Susanna Balch**, widow of **Rev. James Balch**, died in 1834. {Ref: *Balch Genealogica*, by Thomas Willing Balch (1907), pp. 373-374}

CHARLES BALDWIN

Charles E. Baldwin enrolled in a company of light horse during the War of 1812 at or near Ellicott Mills in Anne Arundel Co., MD around August, 1814 and participated in the Battle of Bladensburg. Although the name of his captain was not remembered by his widow, Maryland military records indicate that Charles was first sergeant under Capt. **Charles A. Warfield** and served on active duty in Col. **Frisby Tilghman**'s Cavalry Troops from 22 Aug to 24 Sep 1814. He married **Elizabeth White** on 31 Aug 1817 in Maryland (by **Parson Richards** of the Baptist Church) and subsequently moved to Ohio where he died on 8 Aug 1851 at McConnelsville in Morgan County. **Robert A. Pinkerton** and **Milton Seaman**, acquaintances of the family, attested to a bible entry that *"Charles E. Baldwin, second son of Joseph and Rebecca Baldwin, of Chester County, Pennsylvania, was married to Elizabeth White, daughter of Thomas and Elizabeth White, formerly of Derbyshire, England, on the 31st day of August 1817."* **Elizabeth Baldwin** applied for bounty land (warrant 55-rej-272416) on 1 Apr 1857, aged 57. {Ref: *Maryland Militia, War of 1812, Volume 4, Anne Arundel & Calvert Counties*, by F. Edward Wright, pp. 48, 61}

JOHN BALDWIN

John Baldwin was born in 1757 near Princeton, NJ (one source stated Frederick Co., MD) and lived in Frederick Co., MD at the time of his enlistment in the Revolutionary War. He served as a private for four months in 1776 in the company of Capt. **Jacob Good** (one source spelled his name Goodie), two months in 1777 and 1778 in the 6th MD Line, and participated in the Battle of Germantown. He married **Mary Curry Barker** (b. 1757, Ireland) in 1779 and moved to Kentucky in 1791. They lived in Washington and Mason Counties until 1796 or 1797 wand then moved to Adams Co., OH. Their children were as follows:
1. **Mary Baldwin** married **Joseph Wade**
2. **Keziah Baldwin** (b. 1 Jan 1783) married **William Moore**
3. **James Baldwin** married **Rachel Perry**
4. **Elizabeth Baldwin** married **David Robe**
5. **Ann Baldwin** married **William Newell**
6. **Matilda Baldwin** married **Charles Smith**
7. **Sarah Baldwin** married **Thomas Wright**
8. **Elijah Baldwin** married **Larisa Jolly**

John Baldwin applied for a pension at Liberty Township, Adams Co., OH on 6 Oct 1832, aged 75. **Mary Baldwin** died on 15 Nov 1834 and John died on 14 Oct 1848. They are buried in Kirker Cemetery. {Ref: *Archives of Maryland*, Volume 18, pp. 46, 83; DAR Application 579540; *Genealogical Abstracts of Revolutionary War Pension Files*, by Virgil D. White (1990), Application S2364; *A Roster of Revolutionary Ancestors of the Indiana Daughters of the American Revolution* (1976), p. 29}

GEORGE BALITZ

George Balitz served in Maryland during the Revolutionary War and also served under Gen. Wayne in the Indian Wars that followed. He was subsequently a resident of Urbanna, OH and applied for a pension in Champaign Co., OH on 13 May 1818, aged 81. Although he stated in 1820 that he never had any children, his son **William Balitz** applied for bounty land (warrants 1843-100 and 2379-100) in Campbell Co., KY on 24 Dec 1831. He stated his father died on 10 Jul 1825 in Urbanna, OH, having lived with **William H. Fyffe, Sr.** for 11 years. Before he died he made **William H. Fyffe, Jr.** his heir and he gave William H. Fyffe, Sr. his bounty land claim. {Ref: *Genealogical Abstracts of Revolutionary War Pension Files*, by Virgil D. White (1990), Application S44349}

JOHN BANTHAM

John Bantham served in Maryland during the Revolutionary War, having enlisted in 1775, and applied for a pension on 2 Apr 1818 in Coshocton Co., OH. In 1820 he was aged 72 and his wife **Rachel** was aged 70. {Ref: *Genealogical Abstracts of Revolutionary War Pension Files*, by Virgil D. White (1990), Application S44344}

AQUILA BARBER

Aquila Barber served as a private in the War of 1812 and was on active duty in the company of Capt. **Charles Pumphrey** in Anne Arundel Co., MD for 15 days in September, 1814. He married first to **Rachel Watts** and later moved to Ohio where he married second to **Ellen Kerr** on 25 Dec 1834 at Appleton in Licking County. Aquila received bounty land (warrant 55-160-55283) and died on 25 Jan 1864. It is unclear whether he died in Harrison Co., OH or Harrison Co., MO. **Ellen Barber** applied for and received a widow's pension (WO-24361, WC-33748) and lived in Eagleville, Harrison Co. MO from 1878 until her death circa 1892. {Ref: *Maryland Militia, War of 1812, Volume 4, Anne Arundel & Calvert Counties*, by F. Edward Wright, pp. 33, 61; *Index of War of 1812 Pension Files*, by Virgil D. White, p. 95}

LYDIA BARCROFT

On the 10th day of the 8th month, 1815, a certificate of removal for **Lydia Barcroft** from the Gunpowder Monthly Meeting in Baltimore Co., MD was produced at the Baltimore Monthly Meeting, Eastern District. **Lydia Barecroft** *(sic)* requested a certificate of removal on the 5th day of the 6th month, 1816, from

14

the Baltimore Monthly Meeting, Eastern District, to the Plymouth Monthly Meeting in Ohio, having already removed there. **Lydia Barcroft** again requested a certificate from the Baltimore Monthly Meeting on the 8th day of the 5th month, 1817. {Ref: Baltimore Quaker Monthly Meeting Minutes}

JAMES BARKERS

James Barkers was born on 14 Mar 1760 and served in Maryland during the Revolutionary War. He subsequently moved to Ohio and applied for a pension in Jefferson County on 19 Apr 1833, age 73. {Ref: *Genealogical Abstracts of Revolutionary War Pension Files*, by Virgil D. White (1990), Application S2948}

ADAM BARNES

Adam Barnes volunteered around 12 Mar 1813 to serve in Anne Arundel Co., MD during the War of 1812 and was discharged at Fort Severn near Annapolis around 9 Sep 1813. On the day the British burned the U. S. Capitol he volunteered as a captain of his own company and served from 23 Aug to 27 Sep 1814. He marched to Washington City and from there to Baltimore where he served in the 32nd Regiment. He subsequently moved to Ohio and applied for a bounty land warrant in Monroe County on 20 Nov 1850, aged 70. He applied again in Belmont Co., OH on 9 May 1855, aged 76, and received bounty land (warrant 55-80-20037). Witnesses were **Jeremiah Hollister** and **William G. Perry**, residents of Monroe County. {Ref: *Maryland Militia, War of 1812, Volume 4, Anne Arundel & Calvert Counties*, by F. Edward Wright, pp. 42, 61}

DORSEY BARNES

Dorsey Barnes served as a private in the War of 1812 in the rifle company of Capt. **John T. Randall** in Baltimore Co., MD, from 26 Jul to 25 Aug 1814. He was noted as absent without leave from 25 Aug to 1 Nov 1814, but apparently returned to duty (date not given) and was discharged at Camp Hampstead on 1 Dec 1814 by Capt. **Benjamin Gorsuch** of the 2nd Regiment. Dorsey subsequently moved to Belmont Co., OH where he and **Ruth Barnes** conveyed their right to land called *Head Quarter* in Baltimore Co., MD to **John Brower** on 22 Feb 1819. {Ref: Baltimore County Deed Book WG No. 150, p. 399; *Maryland Militia, War of 1812, Volume 2, Baltimore*, by F. Edward Wright (1979), pp. 73, 88}

ELIJAH BARNES

Elijah Barnes, probably a son of **Nathan and Ellis Barnes**, was born circa 1755 and served in Anne Arundel Co., MD during the Revolutionary War, having enlisted in the Flying Camp on 20 Jul 1776. He married **Catharine Shipley** on 17 Aug 1784 in Baltimore, MD and a son **Absalom Barnes** was born there on 24 Aug 1786. They subsequently moved to Ohio and Elijah filed for a pension in Butler County on 16 Oct 1832, aged 77. He died on 13 Aug 1840 and **Catharine Barnes** applied for a widow's pension in Decatur Co., IN on 27 May 1843, aged 76. {Ref: *Genealogical Abstracts of Revolutionary War Pension Files*, by Virgil D. White (1990), Application W9717; *Archives of Maryland*, Volume 18, p. 40}

JOHN BARNETT

John Barnett was born between 1780 and 1790 in Chambersburg, PA and married **Bethia Amos** (daughter of **Nicholas Day Amos** and **Christiana Ditto** of Harford Co., MD) on 1 Oct 1803 in Bourbon Co., KY. They moved to Rush Co., IN by 1827 and their children were as follows:

1. **John Barnett, Jr.** (b. 5 Jun 1827) married first to **Nancy Jane Points** (1828-1868) on 19 Mar 1848 and second to **Mrs. Anna C. Major** in 1869

2. **William A. Barnett** married Mary **Ellen Hall** and lived in Johnson Co., IN {Ref: *Children of Mt. Soma*, by Gertrude J. Stephens, pp. 303-304}

JOHN BARRET

John Barret and **Sarah Cole**, of Maryland (county not stated), married in Ohio (county not stated) after 1805. {Ref: *Maryland Revolutionary Records*, by Harry Wright Newman (1938), p. 110}

MORDECAI BARRY

Mordecai Barry served as a private in Anne Arundel Co., MD in the 2nd Regiment during the War of 1812 and was stationed at Annapolis under Lieut. **Francis Bealmear** for 30 days from 26 Jul to 25 Aug 1813. **Elisha Barry** also served for 30 days, **Caleb Barry** served for 29 days, and **Joshua Barry** served for 21 days. Mordecai later served under Capt. **Thomas H. Hall** for 2 days on 21 and 22 Aug 1814. He married **Peninah Saxton** in Huntington Co., PA on 26 Sep 1822 (by **Rev. Smith**) and died at Northumberland, PA on 29 Jul 1823. **Peninah Barry** applied for bounty land (warrant 55-160-86612) at Saxton, Bedford Co., PA on 27 Aug 1857, aged 55. **David Black**, of Huntington County, and **Jacob Fockler**, of Bedford County, were acquainted with the family. A letter dated 19 May 1858 stated, in part: *"It appears there were three brothers, Barry, who served in the same company ... Elisha Barry, Caleb Barry, and Mordecai Barry ..."* The following is part of a letter from **Elisha Barry** to his sister-in-law: *"Cardington, Morrow Co., Ohio, March 13th 1858 -- Sister Peninah Barry ... In 1812 myself, Caleb and Mordecai were ordered out and drew our pay as privates. At that time us boys all lived at home with our father. So when one went all three went. In 1813 about the 27th or 28th of July the British fleet hove up in sight of Annapolis, and our company was immediately ordered out, and Mordecai Barry with the rest of us, and rendezvoused at Annapolis and put in under the command of Capt. Francis Bellmere ... the time we served under Capt. Bellmere was one month ..."* **John Arney**, of St. Joseph Co., MO, stated he was personally acquainted with **Mordeca Barra** *(sic)* and that said **Mordica Barra** *(sic)* died at the house of **Samuel Millend**. {Ref: *Maryland Militia, War of 1812, Volume 4, Anne Arundel & Calvert Counties*, by F. Edward Wright, pp. 15-16, 20-21, 62}

EDWARD BARTON

A certificate of removal from Northwest Fork Monthly Meeting in Caroline Co., MD was received by the White Water Monthly Meeting in Wayne Co., IN on the 18th day of the 9th month, 1824, for **Edward Barton** and his son **William Barton**. A certificate was also requested to White Water on the same day for **Anna Barton**; however, the certificate was returned to Northwest Fork on the 11th day of the 1st month, 1826, stating that it could not be received in consequence of her having had an illegitimate child after leaving the meeting in Federalsburg, MD and before arriving at White Water Monthly Meeting. **Edward Barton** died after the 7th day of the 8th month, 1834, and in his will he named **William Barton** as his executor and mentioned these children:

1. **Lydia Barton** (married **Mr. Clark**)
2. **Andrew Barton** (eldest son)
3. **Levin Barton** (next eldest son)
4. **Ann Barton** (married **Mr. Cornthwait**)
5. **Elizabeth Barton** (married **Mr. Sparkling**); died by 1834
6. **Mary Barton** (youngest daughter, married **Mr. Wasson**)
7. **William Barton** (youngest son)

In the 1830 Census of Wayne Co., IN, **Edward Barton** and **Andrew Barton** lived in New Garden Township. {Ref: "Migration of Caroline County Quakers to Indiana," by F. Edward Wright, *Maryland Genealogical Society Bulletin*, Volume 34, No. 3 (1993), p. 279}

BENJAMIN BASSFORD

Benjamin Bassford (sometimes spelled Basford) was drafted as a private in Anne Arundel Co., MD in the War of 1812 and served under Capt. **Thomas T. Simmons** in the 32nd Regiment in the spring of 1813. **Benjamin Basford** and **Richard Basford** served in said regiment from 22 Aug to 27 Sep 1814 and **Robert Basford** served from 22 Aug to 17 Oct 1814. **Benjamin Basford** and **Richard Basford** also served in the 2nd Regiment from 18 Oct to 1 Dec 1814 and were discharged at Baltimore (one source indicated 18 Dec 1814). Benjamin subsequently moved to Ohio and applied for a bounty land warrant in Monroe County on 29 Oct 1850, aged 58. **Elijah Basford**, of Noble Co., OH, appeared in 1851 and verified Benjamin's service. **Benjamin Bassford** applied again for bounty land (warrant 55-120-31665) in Noble Co., OH on 12 Apr 1855, aged 64. A letter dated 14 Feb 1906, from **Wallace Bassford**, 3411 Newark St., Washington, D.C., secretary to the Hon. **Champ Clark**, House of Representatives, stated, in part: *"My father, James C. Bassford, of Mexico, MO, who served in Company J, 25th Ohio Infantry, has written me to make inquiry to learn if his father, Benjamin Bassford (sometimes spelled with one "s"), of Anne Arundel County, ever drew pension for his service in the War of 1812 ... "* {Ref: *Maryland Militia, War of 1812, Volume 4, Anne Arundel & Calvert Counties*, by F. Edward Wright, pp. 28, 43, 63}

WILLIAM BATEMAN

William Bateman was born in 1757 in Pennsylvania, near Delaware, and later moved to Cecil Co., MD where he enlisted during the Revolutionary War. He also took the Oath of Allegiance in 1778 and he may have been the **William Bateman** who married **Sarah Pearce** on or about 14 Mar 1780 (date of license). Five years after the war he moved to Fayette Co., KY (the part that is now Jessamine County) and 19 years later he moved to Floyd Co., IN, where he applied for a pension on 11 Nov 1833, aged 76. {Ref: *Genealogical Abstracts of Revolutionary War Pension Files*, by Virgil D. White (1990), Application S32099; *Revolutionary Patriots of Cecil County, Maryland, 1775-1783*, by Henry C. Peden, Jr. (1991), p. 7}

SUSAN BAYLES

Susan Jane Bayles, wife of **Jesse Bayles**, of Urbana, OH, and daughter of the late **Lloyd Buchanan**, of Baltimore, MD, died on 4 Nov 1831, aged 25, in Urbana, OH. {Ref: *Baltimore American*, 15 Nov 1831, abstracted by Lorrie A. E. Erdman}

NATHANIEL BEALL

Nathaniel Beall, of Montgomery Co., MD, wrote his will on 29 Dec 1828 (probated 10 Jun 1831) and mentioned his brother **Jeremiah Beall**, of Ohio (county not stated). {Ref: *Abstract of Wills, Montgomery County, Maryland, 1826-1875*, by Mary G. Malloy, Jane C. Sween and Janet D. Manuel, p. 9}

NINIAN BEALL

Ninian Beall was born circa 1761 and served in Maryland during the Revolutionary War, having enlisted in Frederick County. He also took the Oath of Allegiance in 1778. Ninian married **Christiana Stull** in August, 1790, and applied for a pension in Frederick Co., MD on 5 May 1818, aged 57. In 1820 he was a resident of St. Clair Township, Butler Co., OH, with wife **Christiana Beall**, age 47, and the following children:

1. **Ninian Beall, Jr.** (b. 27 Oct 1792)
2. **Zephaniah Beall** (b. 10 Apr 1795)
3. **John Beall** (b. 1805)
4. **Joseph Beall** (b. 1808)
5. **Margaret Beall** (b. 1810)
6. **James Beall** (b. 1812)
7. **Sarah Beall** (b. 1815)

Ninian Beall died on 13 Jun 1836 and **Christiana Beall** applied for a widow's pension in Ripley Co., IN on 12 Nov 1839, aged 66. {Ref: *Genealogical Abstracts of Revolutionary War Pension Files*, by Virgil D. White (1990), Application W9722; *Revolutionary Patriots of Frederick County, Maryland, 1775-1783*, by Henry C. Peden, Jr. (1995), p. 24}

18

THOMAS BEALL

Thomas Beall was born in July, 1761 and served in Maryland during the Revolutionary War. He applied for a pension in Preble Co., OH on 28 Jun 1818. {Ref: *Genealogical Abstracts of Revolutionary War Pension Files*, by Virgil D. White (1990), Application S45270}

THOMAS BEALMEAR

Thomas Bealmear, physician, of Ohio (county not stated) and Susan R. Shipley, of Baltimore Co., MD, married on 24 May 1832. {Ref: *Baltimore American*, 26 May 1832, abstracted by Lorrie A. E. Erdman}

MOSES BEAMAN

Moses Beaman was born on 8 Aug 1757 in Cumberland Co., PA and lived in Bradford Co., PA at the time of his enlistment during the Revolutionary War. He also served one tour of duty as a substitute for his father William Beaman (sometimes spelled Beman). After the war he moved to Maryland and lived near Cumberland for 20 years and in 1827 he moved to Harrison Co., OH. Moses applied for a pension on 22 Oct 1833, aged 76, a resident of Stock Township. He died on 13 Dec 1842 and his widow (not named) remarried and moved to parts unknown, according to their son William Beaman, of Knox Co., OH, in 1856. Their children were as follows:

1. **William Beaman**
2. **George Beaman**
3. **Samuel Beaman**
4. **Moses Beaman, Jr.**
5. **Thomas Beaman**
6. **Mary Beaman**
7. **Margaret Beaman** married **Mr. Herching**

{Ref: *Genealogical Abstracts of Revolutionary War Pension Files*, by Virgil D. White (1990), Application S2970}

WILLIAM BEARD

William Beard was born on 27 Dec 1759 or 1760 in Frederick (now Washington) Co., MD and later moved to North Carolina. In May, 1779 he was drafted in Rowan County and in 1780 he moved to Lincoln Co., NC and enlisted there. In December, 1780 he returned to Washington Co., MD and also enlisted there. He later moved to Virginia and in 1810 he went to Ohio where he applied for a pension in Ross County on 11 Oct 1832, aged 72 on 27 Dec last. {Ref: *Genealogical Abstracts of Revolutionary War Pension Files*, by Virgil D. White (1990), Application S2370}

WILLIAM BEARD

William Beard was born on 10 Oct 1762 on Bell's Island, one mile below Coonrod's Ferry on the Potomac River, and lived in Montgomery Co., MD at the

19

time of his enlistment in the Revolutionary War. In 1799 he moved to Loudoun Co., VA and in 1827 he moved to Ohio where he applied for a pension in Belmont County on 15 Jun 1835, aged 72 on 10 Oct last. {Ref: *Genealogical Abstracts of Revolutionary War Pension Files*, by Virgil D. White (1990), Application R671}

HUMPHREY BECKETT

Humphrey Beckett was born on 24 Jun 1761 and served in Maryland during the Revolutionary War. He was a private in the 7th MD Line on 24 May 1778 and participated in the battles of Camden, Guilford Court House, Eutaw Springs, and the Seige of 96. He was promoted to corporal on 21 Dec 1780 and sergeant on 8 Sep 1781. He served as sergeant major, surgeon's mate, and quartermaster sergeant. Humphrey married **Mary "Polly" Shreves** (b. 15 May 1762 or 1768) on 22 Feb 1786 and their children were as follows:
1. **Elizabeth Beckett** (b. 1787) married **James Beckett**
2. **Benjamin H. Beckett** (b. 1793)
3. **Ann or Anna Beckett** (b. 21 Apr 1796)
4. **William Beckett** (b. 23 Nov 1798)
5. **Carle Beckett** (b. 24 Apr 1801)
6. **Eliza Beckett** (b. 11 Oct 1803)
7. **Marie or Maria Beckett** (b. 1807)
8. **Egbert Beckett** (b. 1809)
9. **Alfred Beckett** (b. 1811)
10. **Polly Beckett** (b. 1813)

Humphrey Beckett received a disability pension under the Act of 25 Apr 1808 due to wounds received in battle and applied again for benefits on 5 Jun 1818 in Pickaway Co., OH. In 1825 he moved to Warren Co., IN and died on 2 Apr 1830. **Mary Beckett** applied for a widow's pension on 14 Sep 1838 and died on 25 Dec 1839. Family records indicate an **Elizabeth Beckett** was aged 33 in 1820, having married **James Beckett** on 7 Jun 1812, and she was a widow with 3 small children. **Lucy Beckett**, daughter of James and Elizabeth Beckett, married **Sylvester Stone** on 11 Dec 1817. The only surviving children in 1852 were **Benjamin H. Beckett, Elizabeth Beckett, Maria Raney**, and all were living in Iroquois Co., IL. {Ref: DAR Application 488657; *Genealogical Abstracts of Revolutionary War Pension Files*, by Virgil D. White (1990), Application W9726; *A Roster of Revolutionary Ancestors of the Indiana Daughters of the American Revolution* (1976), p. 44}

JAMES BECKETT

James Beckett and **Elizabeth Beckett**, of Maryland (county not stated), married in Ohio (county not stated) on 7 Jun 1812. {Ref: *Maryland Revolutionary Records*, by Harry Wright Newman (1938), p. 110}

BENJAMIN BECKWITH

Benjamin Beckwith was born in 1760 about 12 miles from what is now Washington, D.C. He was an Associator in 1775 and served in the Maryland Line during the Revolutionary War, having enlisted in Frederick County. He took the Oath of Allegiance in 1778. He was also drafted on 12 Jun 1781, but provided a substitute. After the war he moved to Cumberland, MD for 10 years, then to Frankford, Hampshire Co., VA, and then to Newton Township, Muskingum Co., OH. About 10 or 12 years later moved to Morgan Township, Morgan Co., OH, and there he applied for a pension on 21 Jul 1832, aged 72. {Ref: *Genealogical Abstracts of Revolutionary War Pension Files*, by Virgil D. White (1990), Application S2063; *Revolutionary Patriots of Frederick County, Maryland, 1775-1783*, by Henry C. Peden, Jr. (1995), p. 31}

HARRIET BEECHER

Harriet Beecher, wife of **Rev. Dr. Beecher**, died at Cincinnati, OH on 7 Jul 1835. {Ref: *Baltimore American*, 15 Jul 1835, abstracted by Lorrie A. E. Erdman}

JESSE BENNETT

Jesse Bennett was born in 1759 and served in the Maryland Line during the Revolutionary War, having enlisted in Anne Arundel County on 5 Apr 1777. One source stated that he served in the 3rd MD Regiment until he deserted on 1 May 1879. A short time after the war he moved to North Carolina and in 1816 he moved to Brown Co., OH, where he applied for a pension on 22 Jul 1833, aged 74. {Ref: *Genealogical Abstracts of Revolutionary War Pension Files*, by Virgil D. White (1990), Application R759; *Archives of Maryland*, Volume 18, p. 85}

AARON BERGET

Aaron Berget and **Elizabeth Hodgkins**, of Maryland (county not stated), married in Ohio (county not stated) before 1831. {Ref: *Maryland Revolutionary Records*, by Harry Wright Newman (1938), p. 110}

JAMES BERRY (BARRY)

James Berry (or Barry) was born on 14 Oct 1759 on Deer Creek in Baltimore (now Harford) Co., MD and lived in Smyrna, DE at the time of his enlistment in the Revolutionary War. After the war he moved to Chestertown in Kent Co., MD, then to Cecil Co., MD, and then to Baltimore, MD. Around 1820 he moved to Cincinnati, OH and applied for a pension in Hamilton Co., OH on 2 Apr 1845, aged 85 *(sic)*. His application for a pension was rejected *"for further proof of service."* It should be noted, however, that Delaware records indicate **James Berry (or Barry)** enlisted as a private in the Continental Troops under Capt. **David Hall** on 17 Jan 1776 and was on duty at Lewes on 11 Apr 1776. He subsequently served in the company of Capt. **Charles Nixon**, 2nd DE Regiment, in 1780. {Ref: *Genealogical Abstracts of Revolutionary War Pension Files*, by Virgil D. White (1990), Application R796; *Rejected or Suspended Applications for Revolutionary War Pensions* (1852), p. 344; *Delaware Archives, Military*, Volume I, p. 42, Volume II, p. 645, Vol. III, p. 1089}

PURNELL BERRY

Purnell Berry received a certificate of removal to Milford Monthly Meeting in Wayne Co., IN on the 18th day of the 11th month, 1830 from the Northwest Fork Monthly Meeting in Caroline Co., MD. **Mary and Sarah Berry** also received a certificate at that same time. Purnell was reported on the 15th day of the 5th month, 1834 for *"marrying contrary to the rules of discipline"* and was disowned. {Ref: "Migration of Caroline County Quakers to Indiana," by F. Edward Wright, *Maryland Genealogical Society Bulletin*, Volume 34, No. 3 (1993), p. 282}

WILLIAM BERRY

William Berry, his wife **Sarah Berry** and their minor children **Elizabeth Berry, James Berry, and Mary Jane Berry**, received a certificate of removal to Milford Monthly Meeting in Wayne Co., IN on the 18th day of the 2nd month, 1830 from the Northwest Fork Monthly Meeting in Caroline Co., MD. Their other children, apparently born after the move to Indiana, were **Esther Ann Berry, Sarah C. Berry, Susan Berry, William H. Berry, Margaret Berry, and Lydia Ann Berry** (b. 11th day of 6th month, 1845). **Sarah Tomlinson**, formerly **Sarah Berry** (relationship to **William Berry** not indicated), was reported on the 16th day of the 5th month, 1833 for *"marrying contrary to rules of discipline"* and was disowned. **James Berry** was reported on the 15th day of the 4th month, 1847 for *"attending places of diversion and neglecting attendance of meetings"* and was disowned. **Mary Jane Berry** was reported on the 19th day of the 1st month, 1850 for *"attending places of diversion and neglecting meetings"* and was disowned. **William Berry** was reported on the 20th day of the 3rd month, 1851 for *"attending a marriage contrary to the rules of discipline at his own house and for neglecting meetings"* and was disowned. {Ref: "Migration of Caroline County Quakers to Indiana," by F. Edward Wright, *Maryland Genealogical Society Bulletin*, Volume 34, No. 3 (1993), pp. 282-283}

WILLIAM BERRY (BARRY)

William Berry (or Barry) was born in Maryland and served there during the Revolutionary War in both the army and navy. He married **Hannah Oldacres** on 26 Feb 1793 in Fauquier Co., VA and later moved to Ohio where he died in March, 1822 (county not stated). **Hannah Berry** moved to Scott Co., IN and died on 27 May 1845. **William H. English**, administrator of her estate, filed for a pension on 14 Aug 1850, indicating her children were as follows:

1. **John Berry**
2. **Seymour Berry**
3. **Isaac Berry**
4. **Andrew Berry**
5. **Abraham Berry**
6. **Catharine Berry** married **Mr. Hoagland**
7. **Sarah Berry** married **Mr. Babbitt**

In 1850 all of the above children lived in Scott Co., IN except Abraham who had moved away (place not stated). {Ref: *Genealogical Abstracts of Revolutionary*

War Pension Files, by Virgil D. White (1990), Application W9724}

JAMES BEVARD

James Bevard, son of **Charles Bevard** (b. 1722), was born in Baltimore (now Harford) Co., MD on 29 Nov 1762 and allegedly served as a private on 1 Apr 1776 in the company of Capt. **John Patrick** during the Revolutionary War. Since James would have been only 13½ years old at the time, there is an apparent mistake in his year of birth. Also, there was a **James Bevard** who signed the Association of Freemen in 1776 and he would have been at least 18 years old to do so, thus placing his year of birth at least by 1758. James married on 2 Apr 1795 to **Mary Shidle** (2 Apr 1779 - 7 Nov 1807) and they had the following children:

1. **George Bevard** (4 Jan 1796 - 14 Feb 1869) married **Mary Wallis** (6 Sep 1797 - 9 Mar 1860) on 23 May 1820 in Churchville, MD
2. **Charles Bevard** (b. 27 Feb 1798)
3. **James Bevard, Jr.** (b. 5 Nov 1799)
4. **John Bevard** (b. 7 Dec 1801)
5. **Elizabeth Bevard** (b. 12 Nov 1804)
6. **William Bevard** (b. 3 May 1807)
7. **Martha Bevard** (b. 5 Jan 1809)

James Bevard moved to Ohio and died after 1809. **Charles Bevard**, his brother, also served under Capt. **John Patrick** in 1776 and signed the Association of Freemen in 1776. He married **Amelia Chance** in 1798 in Harford Co., MD. Some researchers have confused Charles the son with Charles the father with respect to who married whom and which one died in 1817; therefore, additional research will be necessary to substantiate this undocumented piece of the family history as briefly presented here. {Ref: *Revolutionary Patriots of Harford County, Maryland, 1775-1783*, by Henry C. Peden, Jr. (1985), p. 19; Undocumented typescript entitled "Bevard Family" compiled by Anna Lee Kirkwood Smith, of Harford Co., MD}

JOHN BEVARD

The Irish-born Bevards came to America in the days immediately following the close of the Revolutionary War. One of these was **John Bevard** (b. 1762, probable son of **Charles Bevard** who was born in 1722 in Ireland) who married **Hester Smith** (b. 1766, MD) on 20 Nov 1787 in Frederick Co., MD. By 1795 John owned over 100 acres in Woodberry Township, Huntingdon Co., PA, and he was naturalized there on 26 Aug 1802. John and **Hester Bevard** had six children and the family gradually moved west from Maryland across Pennsylvania and into Ohio. The first three children were born in Maryland and the last three in Pennsylvania. The third child **Jacob Bevard** was born on 10 May 1791, married **Ann Buckalew** on 10 Jul 1817 in Muskingum Co., OH, and in 1820 they lived in Licking County. They had two sons, the oldest being **James Madison Bevard** (b. 1817) who married **Sarah Sparks** on 17 Aug 1840 in Ohio. {Ref: Information gleaned from *www.geocities.com/Heartland/Woods/7237/brevhist.htm* on the Internet}

HENRY BITZELL

Henry Bitzell was born in Germany in 1718 and married **Mary Margaretha Alexander** in Frederick Co., MD on 2 Nov 1760. He served as an Associator during the Revolutionary War and took the Oath of Allegiance in 1778. **Henry Bitesele** *(sic)* was a first lieutenant in the Catoctin Battalion, Frederick County Militia. He subsequently moved to Hamilton Co., OH and **Henry and Mary Bitzell** both died in 1821 in Sycamore Township. Their children were as follows:

1. **Henry Bitzell, Jr.** (b. 1762) married **Ann Bell**
2. **Peter Bitzell** (b. 1764) married **Saville Creps**
3. **George Bitzell** (b. 1765) married **Rebecca Honnell**
4. **John Bitzell** married **Catherine Kern**
5. **Samuel Bitzell** married **Mary ----**
6. **Joseph Bitzell** married **Sarah Kern**
7. **Mary Bitzell** married **John Line**
8. **Gustave Bitzell** (nothing further)
9. **Elizabeth Bitzell** married **Michael Boroff**
10. **Catherine Bitzell** married **Jacob Kern**

{Ref: DAR Application 556733; *A Roster of Revolutionary Ancestors of the Indiana Daughters of the American Revolution* (1976), p. 52; *Maryland Historical Magazine*, Volume XI, p. 164; *The Maryland Militia in the Revolutionary War*, by S. Eugene Clements & F. Edward Wright, p. 53; *Revolutionary Patriots of Frederick County, Maryland, 1775-1783*, by Henry C. Peden, Jr. (1995), p. 36}

WILLIAM BIVINS

William Bivins was born on 14 Apr 1748 in Somerset Co., MD and enlisted at Blackfords Town in nearby Sussex Co., DE during the Revolutionary War. After the war he lived in Maryland, Virginia and Indiana and he applied for a pension at Ripley, Montgomery Co., IN on 22 Sep 1834, aged 85 *(sic)*. It should be noted that, although his application was rejected, the name of **William Bevans** appeared twice on the muster rolls of the Worcester Co., MD Militia on 15 Jul 1780 and **William Beavens** was a corporal in the Worcester Militia in 1780-1781. {Ref: *Genealogical Abstracts of Revolutionary War Pension Files*, by Virgil D. White (1990), Application R876; *Revolutionary Patriots of Worcester & Somerset Counties, Maryland, 1775-1783*, by Henry C. Peden, Jr., pp. 18, 22}

HUGH BLACK

Hugh Black was born in 1737 or 1738 and enlisted at Baltimore, MD during the Revolutionary War. He married **Sarah ----** on 20 Jul 1779 and subsequently moved to Ohio. He applied for a pension in Pike County on 7 Jul 1818, aged 81, and in 1820 he stated he was aged 82 with a wife about his age and they were dependent on an only son who had a family (names were not given). **Hugh Black (or Blackwell)** died on 27 Nov 1835 and **Sarah Black (or Blackwell)** died on 13 Mar 1839, leaving children, but none were named. On 14 Feb 1851 **James K. Black**, aged 29, of Butler Co., MO, was administrator of Sarah's estate, but his relationship was not given. It should be noted that, although this pension was rejected, there was a **Hugh Blackwell** who served as a private in the 4th MD Regiment from 2 Apr 1777 to April-May, 1779, but *"not heard of"* afterwards. {Ref: *Genealogical Abstracts of Revolutionary War Pension Files*, by Virgil D. White (1990), Application R893; *Archives of Maryland*, Volume 18, p. 88}

JOHN BLACK

John Black was born on 13 Mar 1763 in Lancaster Co., PA and lived in Washington Co., MD at the time of his enlistment in the Revolutionary War. He also had two brothers **William Black** and **Samuel Black** who enlisted at Williamsport, MD. John moved to Berkeley Co., VA during the war, lived there 5 years before moving to Fayette Co., PA, then 13 years later he moved to Adams Co., OH and 24 years later he moved to Highland Co., OH, where he applied for a pension on 13 Mar 1833, aged 70. In 1839 he lived in Clermont Co., OH and in 1852 he lived in Union Township, Brown Co., OH. **Gabriel Black** also lived there, but no relationship was indicated. John died prior to 1856 at which time his son **William H. Black** lived in Brown County. His application was rejected and the reason was *"not military service."* It should be noted, however, that records do indicate that **John Black** was a private in the Washington Co., MD militia in the company of Capt. **John Reynolds** in 1776-1777. {Ref: *Genealogical Abstracts of Revolutionary War Pension Files*, by Virgil D. White (1990), Application R887; *Rejected or Suspended Applications for Revolutionary War Pensions* (1852), p. 337; *The Maryland Militia in the Revolutionary War*, by S. Eugene Clements & F. Edward Wright, p. 240}

JOHN BLACK

John Black enrolled as a private in Anne Arundel Co., MD in the company of Capt. **Roderick Burgess** during the War of 1812 and served on active duty from 22 Jul to 19 Sep 1814 in the 32nd Regiment. He stated that he was married on 1 Jan 1820 in Anne Arundel County, but the name of wife was not given (and no marriage license has been found in Maryland records). He subsequently moved to Erie Co., OH and applied for a pension (SO-19597, SC-24618) and bounty land (warrants 50-40-23650 and 55-120-48175). He died in Vermilion, OH on 18 Apr 1891. {Ref: *Maryland Militia, War of 1812, Volume 4, Anne Arundel & Calvert Counties*, by F. Edward Wright, pp. 42, 65; *Index of War of 1812 Pension Files*, by Virgil D. White, p. 174}

JOSHUA BLACK

Joshua Black volunteered in Anne Arundel Co., MD around 9 Mar 1813 and served as first lieutenant in the company of Capt. **Adam Barnes** during the War of 1812, according to his own statement; however, military records indicate he was appointed a lieutenant in the militia on 19 Sep 1812 and he served from 16 Apr to 31 Jul 1813 in Lt. Col. **Gassaway Watkins'** Regiment and from 23 Aug to 27 Sep 1814 in the 32nd Regiment, both times under Capt. **Adam Barnes**. He was discharged from the service at Baltimore around 15 Oct 1814 and subsequently moved to Indiana where he applied for a pension (SO-6, SC-1240) and bounty land (warrants 50-80-8978 and 55-80-7125). On 2 Apr 1855 he was a resident of Marion Co., IN, aged 66, and **P. S. C. Hunt** and **Edward Heizen** were acquainted with him. On 22 Feb 1871 he lived in Indianapolis, IN, aged 82, and **George W. Powell** and **Amos Hanway**, of Marion Co., IN, were acquainted with him. **Wilson A. Woollen** and **William W. Woollen**, residents of Indianapolis, stated they had known **Joshua Black** for 20 years and 30 years respectively. On 24 Oct 1933 **H. E. Eldredge**, 2205 South 10th St. East, Salt Lake City, UT, inquired to the U. S. War Department about the service of **Joshua Black** in the War of 1812 (nothing further). {Ref: *Maryland Militia, War of 1812, Volume 4, Anne Arundel & Calvert Counties*, by F. Edward Wright, pp. 9, 40, 42, 65; *Index of War of 1812 Pension Files*, by Virgil D. White, p. 174}

SAMUEL BLACK

Samuel Black was born circa 1762 and served in Maryland and Virginia Lines, and also in sea service, during the Revolutionary War. He subsequently moved to Ohio and applied for a pension in Adams County on 17 Jun 1826, aged 64, with a wife aged 58 and their children were all of age (names not given). {Ref: *Genealogical Abstracts of Revolutionary War Pension Files*, by Virgil D. White (1990), Application R892}

JAMES BLACKBURN

James Blackburn was born in 1752 and served in the Maryland and Virginia Lines during the Revolutionary War. He subsequently moved to Ohio and applied for a pension in Warren County on 14 May 1818. In 1820 he had a wife **Martha Blackburn**, aged 45, and two children, **James Blackburn, Jr.**, aged 19, and **Rebecca Blackburn**, aged 16, both suffering with consumption. He also stated he had lost two children (names not given) within a year and his son **William Blackburn** had died prior to 1820. **James Blackburn**, a Revolutionary War soldier, died at Lebanon, OH in 1825, aged 73. {Ref: *Niles Weekly Register*, 22 Oct 1825; *Genealogical Abstracts of Revolutionary War Pension Files*, by Virgil D. White (1990), Application S42619}

ELI BLADES

Eli Blades (sometimes spelled Blads) was born on 21 Feb 1764 in Somerset Co., MD and enlisted in Worcester Co., MD during the Revolutionary War. In 1789 he moved to Woodford Co., KY for 10 years, then moved to Clermont Co., OH for 3 years, and then to Clark Co., IN. He applied for a pension in Lexington Township, Scott Co., IN on 19 Feb 1841, aged 77. {Ref: *Genealogical Abstracts of Revolutionary War Pension Files*, by Virgil D. White (1990), Application R908; *Revolutionary Patriots of Worcester & Somerset Counties, Maryland, 1775-1783*, by Henry C. Peden, Jr. (1999), p. 24}

JOHN BLAIR

John Blair, son of **Andrew Blair** of Washington Co., MD, married first circa 1774 to **Martha Davis**, daughter of **David Davis**, and second circa 1785 to

26

Frances ---- (b. c1769, MD, d. 17 Aug 1860, Montgomery Co., OH). John died testate on 23 Nov 1799 and **Frances Blair** married **Jacob Lear** on 29 Sep 1801 in Washington Co., MD. The children of **John Blair** were as follows:

1. **Elizabeth Blair** (b. circa 1775, probably d. 1819) married **Hugh Brotherton** (d. 1830)
2. **John Blair, Jr.** (b. circa 1777, d. 1835) married **Sarah Bell** in Franklin Co., PA on 4 Aug 1812
3. **James Blair** (b. 22 Sep 1789, d. before 1804)
4. **Andrew Blair** (b. 5 Jul 1791) married **Sarah Litten** in Franklin Co., PA on 27 Jun 1815
5. **Samuel Blair** (b. 11 Nov 1792, Washington Co., MD, d. 5 Mar 1871, Montgomery Co., OH)
6. **Sarah Blair** (b. 9 Feb 1794, MD, d. 21 Feb 1867, Montgomery Co., OH) married **James Litten** (1789-1871) in Washington Co., MD on 2 Oct 1817
7. **David Blair** (b. 16 Apr 1797, d. testate in 1869 in either Franklin Co., PA or Washington Co., MD)
8. **Jesse Blair** (b. 31 Oct 1798, d. 1851, MD)

{Ref: "Andrew Blair of Washington County" by John H. Stutesman, *Western Maryland Genealogy*, Volume 4, No. 1 (1988), p. 5}

MERRIKEN BOND

Merriken Bond, of Cincinnati, OH married **Jane Bond**, daughter of the late **Dennis Bond**, of Harford Co., MD, on 10 Dec 1836. **Dennis Bond** had written his will in 1807 and final distribution of his estate was made on 24 Oct 1815 to his heirs, viz., wife **Mary Bond** and children **Harriott Bond, Jane Bond, Frances Bond, Eliza Bond, Nicholas W. Bond and Elijah J. Bond**. {Ref: *Baltimore American*, 13 Dec 1836, abstracted by Lorrie A. E. Erdman; *Heirs and Legatees of Harford County, Maryland, 1802-1846*, by Henry C. Peden, Jr. (1988), p. 24}

MORDECAI BOND

Mordecai Bond was born on 6 Jul 1770 and enrolled as a private in Cecil Co., MD during the War of 1812. He served on active duty from 12 Oct to 27 Oct 1814 in the company of Capt. **John Smithson**, from 28 Aug to 26 Sep 1814 in the company of Capt. **John Turner** in the 42nd Regiment, and was discharged at Baltimore. He subsequently moved to Ohio and applied for bounty land in Washington Township, Carroll County, on 13 Nov 1850, aged 80. He applied again on 18 May 1855, aged 84, in Carroll County (warrant 55-120-56528) and his claim was witnessed by **Robert Denniston** and **James R. Hackathorn**. {Ref: *Maryland Militia, War of 1812, Volume 3, Cecil & Harford Counties*, by F. Edward Wright, pp. 19, 28, 41}

SILAS BOND

Silas Bond, son of **Benjamin and Mary Bond**, and **Hannah Kennard**, daughter of **Ely and Elizabeth Kennard** (the mother being deceased) of Fawn Township, York Co., PA, married on the 4th day of the 2nd month, 1806, at the

Deer Creek Monthly Meeting in Harford Co., MD. They were the parents of the following:

1. **Benjamin Bond** (b. 30th of 10th mo., 1807)
2. **Eli or Ely Bond** (b. 24th of 12th mo., 1808)
3. **Silas Bond, Jr.** (b. 22nd of 1st mo., 1811)

On the 11th day of the 11th month, 1824, the Deer Creek Monthly Meeting in Harford Co., MD reported that *"Ely Bond, having so far deviated from the path of rectitude as to be guilty of fornication, is disowned."*

On the 14th day of the 7th month, 1825, **Eli Bond**, a minor, requested a certificate of removal from the Deer Creek Monthly Meeting to the Still Water Monthly Meeting in Ohio. On the 15th day of the 9th month, 1825, **Benjamin Bond** and **Eli Bond**, minor sons of **Silas Bond**, both requested a certificate of removal from Deer Creek Monthly Meeting to Still Water Monthly Meeting. {Ref: Deer Creek Quaker Monthly Meeting Minutes}

JOHN BONFIELD

John Bonfield moved from Baltimore, MD to the State of Ohio (county not given) in 1815. {Ref: Class Registers, East Baltimore Station (Fell's Point), Methodist Episcopal Church}

ADAM BOSS

Adam Boss was born in Bucks Co., PA in 1762 and at age 13 his father (name not given) moved to Baltimore, MD. He served during the Revolutionary War under his brother Lt. **Jacob Boss** and after the war Adam moved to Fauquier Co., VA. He married **Harriet Ransdell** on 24 Jan 1822 in Prince William Co., VA and then moved to Kentucky. Five years later they moved to Cincinnati, Hamilton Co., OH and he applied for a pension on 20 Sep 1832, aged 70. Adam died on 17 Jun 1833 and **Harriet Boss** applied for a widow's pension on 25 Oct 1856, aged 60 *(sic)*. {Ref: *Genealogical Abstracts of Revolutionary War Pension Files*, by Virgil D. White (1990), Application W10238}

JACOB BOWER

Jacob Bower was born on 11 Oct 1750 and served in Maryland and Pennsylvania during the Revolutionary War. He married **Anna Rohrer** (b. 1 Jan 1764, daughter of **John Rohrer**) on 14 Feb 1782 in Washington Co., MD. Their children were as follows:

1. **Christiana Bower** (b. 3 Sep 1782)
2. **Jacob Bower Jr.** (b. 1 Apr 1784)
3. **Anna Bower** (b. 26 Mar 1789)
4. **Susannah Bower** (b. 28 Oct 1790)
5. **John Bower** (b. 20 Jun 1794)
6. **Catharine Bower** (b. 10 Mar 1797)
7. **Frederick Bower** (b. 29 May 1798)
8. **Barbara Bower** (b. 13 Feb 1801)
9. **Elizabeth Bower** (b. 7 Oct 1803)

10. **Sarah Bower** (b. 25 Aug 1808)

Jacob Bower moved from Bedford Co., PA to Stark Co., OH around 1810 and applied for a pension on 13 Apr 1818, aged 69. He died in 1824 and **Anna Bower** applied for a widow's pension at Lake Township on 13 Sep 1839, aged 75. **Jacob Bower**, who was probably the father of Jacob Bower the soldier, died in Washington Co., MD before 29 Mar 1783 (date of entry in balance book) and his heirs were his widow **Magdalen Bower** and children **Jacob Bower, Barbara Bower, Catherine Bower, John Bower, Conrad Bower, Mary Bower, George Bower, Henry Bower**, and **Susannah Bower**. {Ref: *Genealogical Abstracts of Revolutionary War Pension Files*, by Virgil D. White (1990), Application W5227; *Washington County, Maryland Records, 1778-1801*, by Raymond B. Clark, Jr., p. 24}

ISAAC BOWMAN

On the 14th day of the 6th month, 1804, at the Baltimore Monthly Meeting, Western District, it was recorded that **Isaac Bowman**, a young man convinced of Friends' principles and who was received into membership about two years ago at Hardshaw Monthly Meeting, requested a certificate of removal to Philadelphia Monthly Meeting on the 25th day of the 8th month, 1803 (endorsements noted). On the 30th day of the 3rd month, 1804, said **Isaac Bowman** requested a certificate of removal to Baltimore Monthly Meeting from Philadelphia, having resided a short time with them. On the 14th day of the 6th month, 1804, said **Isaac Bowman** requested a certificate of removal from the Baltimore Monthly Meeting to Middlesex Monthly Meeting in Ohio, having resided a short time with them as well. {Ref: Baltimore Quaker Monthly Meeting Minutes}

PHILIP CASPER BOWMAN

Philip Casper Bowman was born on 25 Oct 1755 or 1756 at Little York in York Co., PA and married **Katie Fast or Faust** (b. 14 Aug 1753, Palse, Germany) in 1772 in Pennsylvania. They lived in Frederick, MD at the time of his enlistment in the Revolutionary War. He volunteered in June, 1776 and participated in the battles of Trenton, Princeton, Brandywine, Germantown, and Monmouth. After the war they moved to Fayette Co., PA and in 1806 they moved to Columbiana Co., OH, where Philip applied for a pension on 15 Aug 1832, aged 75. Their children were as follows:

1. **Elizabeth Bowman** (b. 12 Nov 1774) married **Daniel Stentz**
2. **John Jacob Bowman** (b. 23 Nov 1779) married **Elizabeth Stough**
3. **Christian Bowman** (b. 2 Feb 1781) married **Elizabeth Kreager**
4. **Joshua Bowman** (b. 9 Mar 1787) married **Lovina Jones**
5. **Kezia or Keziah Bowman** (b. 1788) married **James Webb**
6. **John Nicholas Bowman** (b. 22 Dec 1791) married **Catherine Altman**
7. **Charlotte Bowman** (b. 2 Mar 1794) married **Robert Gault**
8. **Sarah Bowman** (b. 19 Mar 1796) married **John Orr**
9. **Rebecca Bowman** (b. 18 Mar 1800) married **Theron R. Landon**
10. **Catharine Bowman** (b. 14 Jul 1802) married **John Krebs**

11. **Joannah Bowman** (b. 19 Sep 1804) married **Henry Goodman**

12. **Rachel Bowman** (b. 19 Feb 1807) married **Samuel Richards**

Katie Bowman died at Ellsworth, OH on 23 Nov 1826 and **Philip Bowman** died on 17 Jan 1845. {Ref: *Genealogical Abstracts of Revolutionary War Pension Files*, by Virgil D. White (1990), Application S2091; *Index of Patriots, Revolutionary War Heroes and Their Families, Cincinnati Chapter DAR, 1893-1981*, by Jeraldyne Beets Clipson and Katherine Brewer Brinkdopke (1983), p. 57}

JOHN BOYD

John Boyd was born in 1756 in Cecil Co., MD and served in the Maryland Line during the Revolutionary War. He also took the Oath of Allegiance in 1778 and he may have been the **John Boyed** *(sic)* who married **Mary McBurney** on or about 24 May 1778 (date of license). He subsequently moved Union Township, Belmont Co., OH and applied for a pension on 2 Aug 1832. {Ref: *Genealogical Abstracts of Revolutionary War Pension Files*, by Virgil D. White (1990), Application S2088; *Revolutionary Patriots of Cecil County, Maryland, 1775-1783*, by Henry C. Peden, Jr. (1991), p. 13}

JOHN BOYER

John Boyer was born on 18 Nov 1759 in Northumberland Co., VA and when he was young his father (not named) moved his family to Ninety-Six District, SC. John enlisted in the Revolutionary War and after the war he moved to Baltimore, MD for 19 years. He subsequently moved to Hamilton Co., OH, where he applied for a pension on 17 Sep 1832, aged 73. {Ref: *Genealogical Abstracts of Revolutionary War Pension Files*, by Virgil D. White (1990), Application S32125}

MARY BOYLE

Mary A. Boyle, youngest daughter of the late Capt. **Thomas Boyle**, of Cincinnati, OH, married **Joseph M. Williamson**, Esq., of Baltimore, MD, on 18 Dec 1833. {Ref: *Baltimore American*, 27 Dec 1833, abstracted by Lorrie A. E. Erdman}

SAMUEL BRADFORD

Samuel Bradford volunteered around 10 Aug 1814 as a private in Capt. **John Hall**'s Company in the 3rd Regiment of Cavalry commanded by Col. **Frisby Tilghman** at Annapolis, MD during the War of 1812. He married **Margaret Belt** in 1815 (by **Rev. Frederick Jones**, a Methodist minister) and subsequently moved to Ohio. Samuel died at Columbus, OH around 23 Nov 1851 and **Margaret Bradford** applied for bounty land (warrant 55-rej-133347) in Delaware Co., OH on 1 May 1855, aged about 65. **Augustus A. Welch**, aged 42, and **Braman Dickinson**, aged 51, stated they had known the Bradfords for 15 years. On 20 Jan 1871 **John Waddle** and **Jacob Hanner**, of Emmitsburg, MD, appeared and stated they were privates in the company of Capt. **Lewis Weaver** in Emmitsburg, MD during the War of 1812 and served at Baltimore where they became personally acquainted with **Samuel Bradford**. {Ref: *Maryland Militia, War of 1812, Volume*

30

4, *Anne Arundel & Calvert Counties*, by F. Edward Wright, pp. 45, 68}

CORNELIUS BRADLEY

Cornelius Bradley was born circa 1755 either in Ireland or in Cecil Co., MD and married **Mary Hogan** (b. 1755, Ireland) in 1775. Cornelius enlisted in the company of Capt. **Henry Dobson** in the 6th MD Regiment on 10 Jun 1778, participated in the Battle of Monmouth, and was discharged on 14 or 15 Mar 1779. He also took the Oath of Allegiance in Cecil Co., MD in 1778. Cornelius subsequently moved to Kentucky where **Mary Bradley** died (date and county not stated) and around 1806 he moved to Posey Co., IN. He was living with a son (name not given) when he applied for a pension on 28 Feb 1821, aged 66. His children were as follows:
1. **David Bradley** married **Elizabeth Brazer Kirby**
2. **John Bradley** married **Hannah McFadin**

{Ref: DAR Application 450394; *A Roster of Revolutionary Ancestors of the Indiana Daughters of the American Revolution* (1976), p. 69; *Genealogical Abstracts of Revolutionary War Pension Files*, by Virgil D. White (1990), Application S35798; *Archives of Maryland*, Volume 18, p. 187; *Revolutionary Patriots of Cecil County, Maryland, 1775-1783*, by Henry C. Peden, Jr., p. 13}

WILLIAM BRANDENBURG

William Brandenburg was born on 8 Oct 1758 in Middlesex Township, NJ and lived 3 miles from Middletown, Frederick Co., MD at the time of his enlistment in the Revolutionary War. He was in all likelihood related to **Samuel Brandenburg** who served as an Associator in Frederick CO., MD in 1775. In 1812 William moved to Fayette Co., PA and in 1816 he moved to Montgomery Co., OH. In the fall of 1817 he moved to Bethel Township, Clarke Co., OH, where he applied for a pension on 2 Oct 1832, aged 73. {Ref: *Genealogical Abstracts of Revolutionary War Pension Files*, by Virgil D. White (1990), Application S2405; *Revolutionary Patriots of Frederick County, Maryland, 1775-1783*, by Henry C. Peden, Jr. (1995), p. 45}

WILLIAM BRATTEN

William Bratten (sometimes spelled Bratton) was born on 5 Dec 1755 in Worcester Co., MD and lived there at the time of his enlistment in the Revolutionary War. He entered the service on 9 Aug 1776 for one year and boarded the ship *Virginia* which was lying in the Chesapeake Bay, near Baltimore, under Commodore **James Nicholson**. The ship remained in the bay, blockaded by the British for the whole 12 months. In 1797 William moved to Davidson Co., TN and in 1802 he moved to Smith Co., TN. In 1825 he moved to Brown Co., OH for one year, then went back to Tennessee, and in 1837 returned to Ohio. He applied for a pension in Brown Co., OH on 17 Apr 1838, aged 82. {Ref: *Genealogical Abstracts of Revolutionary War Pension Files*, by Virgil D. White (1990), Application R1168; Revolutionary War Military Collection, Manuscript MS.1814 (Box 12), Maryland Historical Society; *Revolutionary Patriots of Worcester & Somerset*

Counties, Maryland, 1775-1783, by Henry C. Peden, Jr. (1999), pp. 33-45}

FREDERICK BRENTLINGER

Frederick Brentlinger, a Revolutionary War soldier formerly of Hagerstown, MD, died at his residence near Mount Vernon, OH in November, 1825, in his 73rd year. {Ref: *The Torchlight and Public Advertiser*, Hagerstown, MD, 14 Feb 1826}

Frederick Brentlinger was undoubtedly related to **Conrad Brentlinger** (sometimes spelled Brendlinger and Brandlinger), a Revolutionary War soldier who died suddenly on 30 Mar 1829 in his 77th year, an old inhabitant of Hagerstown, MD. {Ref: *Marriages and Deaths from the Newspapers of Allegany and Washington Counties, Maryland, 1820-1830*, by F. Edward Wright, p. 107}

JOSEPH BREVETT

Joseph Brevett and wife **Cassandra Brevett**, of the Baltimore Monthly Meeting, were the parents of the following:
1. **George Fox Brevett** (b. 18th of 5th mo., 1806)
2. **Cassandra A. Brevett**
3. **Elizabeth Boraston Brevett**
4. **James M. Brevett**
5. **Ellen Isolobo Brevett** (b. 11th of 4th mo., 1818)
6. **Joseph Plummer Brevett** (b. 15th of 11th mo., 1820)

Joseph Brevett requested a certificate of removal on the 11th day of the 8th month, 1820, from the Baltimore Monthly Meeting, Western District, to the Miami Monthly Meeting in Ohio. {Ref: Baltimore Quaker Monthly Meeting Minutes}

JOHN BRILEY

John Briley was born in 1760 and enlisted in Anne Arundel Co., MD at the time of the Revolutionary War. On 29 Jul 1781 he was enlisted by Capt. Lynn to serve in the Maryland Line for the duration of the war. He later moved to Ohio and on 27 Jun 1818 he applied for a pension in Madison County. In 1820 he was aged 60 with a wife **Sally Briley**, aged 53, and the following children:
1. **John Jefferson Briley** (b. 1806)
2. **Samuel Briley** (b. 1808)
3. **Nelson Briley** (b. 1810
4. **Tite Briley** (b. 1813)

On 23 Nov 1837 **John Briley** was living in Fayette Co., OH. {Ref: *Genealogical Abstracts of Revolutionary War Pension Files*, by Virgil D. White (1990), Application S42631; *Archives of Maryland*, Volume 18, p. 401}

SOLOMON BRITTINGHAM

Solomon Brittingham, son of **Jeremiah Brittingham**, was born on 15 Apr 1765 *(sic)* and served in Maryland during the Revolutionary War. He was a private in the 2nd MD Regiment by 24 Apr 1780 when he was listed as a recruit entitled to clothing from the Commissary of Stores. He married **Leah Brown** (b. 4 Mar

1783, daughter of **James and Mary Brown**) on 25 Feb 1806 and their children were as follows:

1. **Lotty Brittingham** (b. 27 Aug 1806)
2. **Polly Brittingham** (b. 29 Nov 1807)
3. **Abner Brittingham** (b. 29 Aug 1809)
4. **Rieley Brittingham** (b. 2 Aug 1811)
5. **Hampton Brittingham** (b. 22 Jul 1813)
6. **Nancy Brittingham** (b. 9 Aug 1815)
7. **Martha Brittingham** (b. 25 Jul 1817)
8. **Betsy Brittingham** (b. 26 May 1819)
9. **Enoch Brittingham** (b. 30 Jun 1821)
10. **Hester Brittingham** (b. 19 Jan 1824)
11. **Celey Brittingham** (b. 17 Apr 1827)

Solomon Brittingham moved to Liberty Township, Fairfield Co., OH and applied for a pension on 29 Mar 1832. **Leah Brittingham** applied for a widow's pension in Peoria Co., IL on 19 Oct 1860, aged 77. Solomon was in all likelihood from Worcester Co., MD where the Brittinghams were prominent in the colonial era and many of them served during the Revolutionary War. He died on 11 Oct or 7 Nov 1835 (both dates were given) in Ohio. {Ref: *Genealogical Abstracts of Revolutionary War Pension Files*, by Virgil D. White (1990), Application W9754; *DAR Patriot Index*, p. 370; *Revolutionary Patriots of Worcester and Somerset Counties, Maryland, 1775-1783*, by Henry C. Peden, Jr., pp. 36-37; *Archives of Maryland*, Volume 43, p. 150}

R. S. BROOKE

R. S. Brooke, of Cincinnati, OH, married **Sarah McCulloh**, daughter of **Edward Pannell**, Esq., in the Chapel of St. Mary's Seminary on 20 Feb 1832. **Edward Pannell** died on 22 Feb 1835, aged 83. {Ref: *Baltimore American*, 24 Feb 1832 and 24 Feb 1835, abstracted by Lorrie A. E. Erdman}

JOHN BROOKOVER

John Brookover was born in 1760 near Bladensburg, MD and was an apprentice at Three Springs, MD at the time of his enlistment in the Revolutionary War. His father (not named) lived at Carroll Manor in Frederick Co., MD and died in Ohio in 1832. After the war John lived near Winchester, VA, then moved to Muddy Creek near Uniontown, PA, and around 1812 moved to Wood Co., OH. He applied for a pension on 4 Oct 1832, aged 72. {Ref: *Genealogical Abstracts of Revolutionary War Pension Files*, by Virgil D. White (1990), Application S5300; *Revolutionary Patriots of Frederick County, Maryland, 1775-1783*, by Henry C. Peden, Jr. (1995), p. 49}

ISAAC BROWN

Isaac Brown served in the 11th Virginia Line during the Revolutionary War and married **Esther Williams** on 22 Mar 1779 in Harford Co., MD. Their children were mentioned, but not named, in his pension application, including a daughter born in the fall of 1780 and a son born in December, 1781. **Isaac Brown** applied for a pension in Columbiana Co., OH on 9 Jun 1818, age 60; however, in 1820 he stated he was 66, a resident of Augusta Township, Carroll Co., OH, with a wife **Esther Brown**, aged 66, and a daughter **Rachel Brown**, aged 30. Isaac died on 26 Oct 1825 while visiting his sister (not named) in Belmont Co., OH. His brother-in-law **David Williams** lived in Fayette Co., PA in 1839. **Esther Brown** applied for a pension in Carroll Co., OH on 30 Jan 1840, aged 86. {Ref: *Genealogical Abstracts of Revolutionary War Pension Files*, by Virgil D. White (1990), Application W4415; *Historical Register of Virginians in the Revolution, 1775-1783*, by John H. Gwathmey (1938), p. 100}

JAMES T. BROWN

James T. Brown was born in 1795 in Kentucky of a Maryland family and moved to Indiana Territory in 1814. {Ref: *History of Dearborn and Ohio Counties, Indiana* (1885), p. 153}

JOSEPH BROWN

Mary Parker was born circa 1780 in Harford Co., MD, a daughter of **Aquilla Parker** (b. 3 Nov 1755, Baltimore Co., MD, d. 4 Dec 1834, Bourbon Co., KY) and **Elizabeth Amos** (b. 1762, Baltimore Co., MD). Mary married **Joseph Brown** (b. 22 Oct 1770, VA, d. 24 Oct 1861 in Miami Township, Clermont Co., OH) on 17 Feb 1799 in Bourbon Co., KY and they moved to Ohio by 1803. Their children were as follows:

1. **George Brown** (b. 16 Mar 1800, KY, d. 18 Jul 1843 in Clermont Co., OH) married **Martha Hopkins**

2. **Ruth Brown** (b. circa 1802, KY, d. 22 May 1854 in Milford, OH) married **David Smiser** (1795-1872) on 31 Aug 1819 in Clermont Co., OH

3. **William Brown** (b. 3 Jul 1803, OH, d. 13 Sep 1886 in Jackson Township, Clermont Co., OH) married first to **Eleanor Riggs** (died 1834), second to **Margaret McGinley** (died 1835), and third to **Sarah Strouder** (died 1885)

4. **Elizabeth Brown** (b. 1 Mar 1805, OH, d. 5 Oct 1851 in Clermont Co., OH) married **Hiram South** (1802, NJ - 1891, OH) circa 1823

5. **John Brown** (b. circa 1806, OH, d. 17 Jun 1879 in Shelby Co., OH) married **Mary Fitzwater** on 6 Aug 1829

6. **Thomas Brown** (b. 9 Nov 1808, OH, d. 30 Jan 1857 in Mercer Co., OH) married **Lydia McFarland** on 22 Nov 1832

7. **Cassandra Brown** married **Joshua Wright**

8. **Christena Brown** married **Samuel Fitzwater** on 21 Jan 1832 in Clermont Co., OH

9. **Aquilla P. Brown** (b. 2 Jan 1816, Mulberry, OH, d. 14 Jan 1884 near Loveland, OH) married **Sarah Motsinger** (1816-1891) on 9 Mar 1837

10. **Clemency Brown** (b. 12 Feb 1817, Clermont Co., OH, d. 2 Jan ---- [year not given], Olney, IL) married **Donald Bowlby** (1816, NJ - 1896, IL) on 6 Feb 1840

11. **Mary Ann Brown** (b. circa 1820, Clermont Co., OH) married **Philip**

34

Smiser on 5 Jul 1837 in Clermont Co., OH

12. **Joseph Brown** (b. 1822, Clermont Co., OH, d. 19 Aug 1830, Mulberry, OH)

13. **Henry P. Brown** (b. 28 May 1825, Clermont Co., OH, d. 31 Jul 1911, Milford, OH) married first to **Emma Smiser** and second to **Elizabeth Snyder** {Ref: *Children of Mt. Soma*, by Gertrude J. Stephens, pp. 86-100}

NICHOLAS BROWN

Nicholas Brown was born in Frederick Co., MD on 17 Oct 1765 *(sic)* and served as an ensign in the company of Capt. **Joseph Heister** in Berks Co., PA during the Revolutionary War. He married **Sarah Whitaker** (b. 12 Apr 1769, MD) in Washington Co., PA in 1792 and their children were as follows:

1. **Basil Brown** (28 Apr 1793 - 20 May 1854) married **Abigail Turner** on 9 Jan 1817

2. **Thomas Brown** (b. 21 May 1795)

3. **Nancy Brown** (b. 16 Jul 1797)

4. **Catherine Brown** (3 Jan 1799 - 29 Mar 1876) married **Eli Holmes** on 13 Nov 1817

5. **Asa Brown** (4 Jun 1801 - 26 Jun 1883) married **Hannah Comly** on 13 Dec 1827

6. **Betsy Brown** (b. 20 Jul 1803) married **Isaac Green**

7. **Rezin Brown** (b. 16 Jun 1805), unmarried

8. **Margaret "Peggy" Brown** (b. 30 Aug 1808, Madison Co., KY, d. 16 Jan 1892, Robinson, IL) married **John Callahan** on 24 Mar 1824

9. **Edward Brown** (b. 29 Sep 1811) married **Elmira "Myra" Owen** in 1838

10. **Sally Brown** (b. 11 Apr 1814) married **Rev. John Glaze** in 1830

Nicholas Brown died at Kirkersville in Licking Co., OH on 29 Jun 1858 and **Sarah Brown** died on 4 Jan 1859. {Ref: *Directory of Maryland State Society DAR, 1892-1965*, p. 182; DAR Application 248741; *A Roster of Revolutionary Ancestors of the Indiana Daughters of the American Revolution* (1976), p. 82}

SOLOMON BROWN

Solomon Brown was drafted in Anne Arundel Co., MD around 1 Jul 1814 during the War of 1812. He served on active duty in the 32nd Regiment under Capt. **Roderick Burgess** from 22 Jul to 19 Sep 1814 and was discharged near Baltimore around 1 Oct 1814. He married **Catharine Rider** in Baltimore Co., MD in January, 1810 (by **Rev. Charles Dorsey** of the Methodist Episcopal Church) and they subsequently moved to Muskingum Co., OH where Solomon died in Buskenick (Bruskeruk?) Township in November, 1833. **Catharine Brown** applied for bounty land (warrant 50-rej-80182) on 22 Nov 1850, aged 69. **Edward Sawens**, aged 88, of Muskingum Co., OH, stated in 1850 that he had known the Browns from the time they lived in Baltimore Co., MD within a mile of his residence and again when they became neighbors in Ohio, they having moved to Ohio three years before him. {Ref: *Maryland Militia, War of 1812, Volume 4, Anne Arundel & Calvert Counties*, by F. Edward Wright, pp. 42, 69-70}

WILLIAM BROWN

William Brown was born in 1743, probably in Maryland, and served in the Revolutionary War. He married **Elizabeth** ---- (b. 1767, probably MD) circa 1794 and their children were as follows:

1. **Mary "Polly" Brown** (b. 1795), unmarried
2. **Samuel Brown** (b. 1 Nov 1797) married **Jeanette Burrough**
3. **Bentley Brown** married **Nancy Williams** on 2 May 1833
4. **Matilda Brown** (b. 1800), unmarried
5. **Thomas Brown** (nothing further)
6. **Fanny Brown** (6 Jun 1811, Fredericksburg, VA - 8 May 1878, Putnam Co., IN) married **John Crawford Sellers** (1796-1874) in Kentucky on 1 Mar 1821
7. **Sarah Brown** married **Greenberry Bryant**
8. **James Brown** (unmarried)

William Brown died in 1829 in Putnam Co., IN and **Elizabeth Brown** died in 1852. {Ref: DAR Application 567111; *A Roster of Revolutionary Ancestors of the Indiana Daughters of the American Revolution* (1976), p. 83}

WILLIAM BROWN

William Brown, of Harford Co., MD, possible son of **John and Susannah Brown**, was commissioned a first lieutenant on 10 Jul 1812 and served under Capt. **Henry P. Ruff** in the 42nd Regiment during the War of 1812 from 30 Apr 1813 for 6 months. After the war he moved to Ohio and married **Hannah Brown** in Butler County on 23 Jun 1835. He applied for bounty land (warrants 50-80-10215 and 55-80-38197) and died on 17 May 1860. In 1880 Hannah lived at Fairfield, Franklin Co., IN. {Ref: *Maryland Militia, War of 1812, Volume 3, Cecil & Harford Counties*, by F. Edward Wright, pp. 2, 25, 76; *Heirs and Legatees of Harford County, Maryland, 1802-1846*, by Henry C. Peden, Jr. (1988), p. 6}

THOMAS BRYAN

Thomas Bryan was born in Waterford, Ireland on 17 Mar 1741 and lived in Baltimore Co., MD at the time of his enlistment in the Revolutionary War. He served as a private in the 4th MD Regiment from 8 May 1778 to 5 May 1780 and four years after the war he moved to Berkeley Co., VA. He lived there 4 years, then moved to Green Co., PA for 6 years, and then to Jefferson Co., OH. He applied for a pension on 27 Aug 1833, aged 92, and resided in Steubenville, OH. No information about his family was given, but a grandson (not named) was mentioned. {Ref: *Genealogical Abstracts of Revolutionary War Pension Files*, by Virgil D. White (1990), Application S3050; *Archives of Maryland*, Volume 18, p. 89}

ROBERT BURCHFIELD

Robert Burchfield was born at Pipe Creek in Baltimore Co., MD on 18 Dec 1759 and lived in Rowan Co., NC at the time of his enlistment in the Revolutionary War. In 1775 he served as a ranger and frontier guard against Indians. He enlisted in the militia in November, 1777 for 5 months, in November, 1781 for 1 month, and

36

in May, 1782 for 3 months. He married **Elizabeth Hill** (b. 1768, Burke Co., NC) in March, 1787 and moved to Ripley Co., IN where he applied for a pension on 13 Nov 1832, aged 73. He died on 29 Oct 1844 and **Elizabeth Burchfield** applied for a widow's pension on 26 Feb 1845, aged 77. She died on 20 Sep 1845 and their children were as follows:

1. **Mary Burchfield** married **Mr. Roberts**
2. **Sally Burchfield** married **Mr. Kelly**
3. **Betsy Burchfield** married **Mr. O'Neal**
4. **John Burchfield** (nothing further)
5. **Nancy Burchfield** married **Mr. Whittam**
6. **Kitty Burchfield** married **Mr. Smith**
7. **Robert Burchfield** married **Elizabeth Meredith**

{Ref: DAR Application 373606; *A Roster of Revolutionary Ancestors of the Indiana Daughters of the American Revolution* (1976), p. 91; *Genealogical Abstracts of Revolutionary War Pension Files*, by Virgil D. White (1990), Application R1444}

JOHN BURGES

John Burges, of Fawn Township, York Co., PA, son of **Joseph and Deborah Burges**, of Campbell Co., VA, and **Drusilla Morgan**, daughter of **John and Ann Morgan**, of Harford Co., MD (the father being deceased), married on the 28th day of the 10th month, 1795 at Deer Creek Monthly Meeting in Harford County. Among the witnesses were **Tacey Burges, Daniel Burges, Martha Burges, Hugh Morgan and Armfield Morgan**. {Ref: Baltimore Quaker Monthly Meeting Minutes}

On the 23rd day of the 5th month, 1811, **John Burges** requested a certificate of removal from the Deer Creek Monthly Meeting in Harford Co., MD to the Baltimore Monthly Meeting, Eastern District. After residing in Baltimore for a short time he requested a certificate of removal to the Plymouth Monthly Meeting in Ohio on the 12th day of the 9th month, 1811. The same requests were noted for **Joseph Burges** and his wife **Ann Burges** who also removed to the Plymouth Monthly Meeting in Ohio. {Ref: Deer Creek Quaker Monthly Meeting Minutes}

ROBERT BURGOON

Robert Burgoon was born in 1753 and enlisted in Anne Arundel Co., MD during the Revolutionary War. He subsequently moved to Ohio and applied for a pension in Morgan County on 1 Oct 1834, aged 81 years, 9 months and 15 days. He died on 4 Jul 1841, leaving no widow, but a son **Jacob Burgoon** lived in Laurel Township, Hocking Co., OH in 1854. It should be noted that, although his application was rejected, **Robert Burgoon** was enlisted by **John Worthington Dorsey** and passed by **John Dorsey** on 22 Jul 1776 in Anne Arundel Co., MD. He also took the Oath of Allegiance in 1778, as did **Jacob Burgoon, John Burgoon, and Jacob Burgoon, Jr.** (name sometimes spelled Burgoone and misspelled as Burgoe). {Ref: *Genealogical Abstracts of Revolutionary War Pension Files*, by Virgil D. White (1990), Application R1453; *Archives of Maryland*, Volume 18, p.

39; *Revolutionary Patriots of Anne Arundel County, Maryland, 1775-1783*, by Henry C. Peden, Jr., p. 24}

RICHARD BURKE

Richard Burke was born in 1756 and stated that he served in the Maryland and Pennsylvania Lines during the Revolutionary War. He applied for a pension in Preble Co., OH on 14 Sep 1820, aged 64, with a wife aged 60, a son aged 14, and a daughter aged 18 (no names given). {Ref: *Genealogical Abstracts of Revolutionary War Pension Files*, by Virgil D. White (1990), Application R1461}

JEREMIAH BURROWS

Jeremiah Burrows was born in January, 1752 in Queen Anne's Co., MD and his father (not named) died when he was 2 years old. Jeremiah lived in Maryland at the time of his enlistment in the Revolutionary War and moved to Delaware before the war ended. About 7 or 8 years later he returned to Queen Anne's County and around 1809 he moved to Virginia (county not stated) for about 10 years. He then moved to Ohio where he applied for a pension in Hamilton County on 1 Apr 1818. He reapplied on 1 Apr 1834, aged 82, and resided in Mill Creek Township at the time. {Ref: *Genealogical Abstracts of Revolutionary War Pension Files*, by Virgil D. White (1990), Application S8110}

JOSHUA BURTON

Joshua Burton enlisted at Frederick, MD during the Revolutionary War and applied for a pension in Franklin Co., OH on 9 Jun 1818, aged 69, and a resident of Pickaway Co., OH; however, in 1821, he stated he was aged 75 with a wife aged 70. {Ref: *Genealogical Abstracts of Revolutionary War Pension Files*, by Virgil D. White (1990), Application S42111}

JOHN BUSKIRK

John Buskirk was born in 1757 in Frederick Co., MD, of German descent (name was originally **John Van Buskirk**). He enlisted in Shenandoah (then Dunmore) Co., VA and served as a private, ensign and lieutenant in the Virginia and Pennsylvania militia during the Revolutionary War. His brother **Isaac Buskirk** served for him in one part of a tour of duty. After the war John lived in Hampshire Co., VA, then moved to Fayette Co., PA, then to Kentucky and in 1822 he moved to Indiana. He applied for a pension on 10 Oct 1832, aged 75, in Monroe Co., IN, but lived in Green Co., IN. His wife's name was not given, but their son **Abram Buskirk** was aged 49 in 1832. John lived with his son **Joseph Buskirk** in 1840 and died on 1 Dec 1840, aged 83. His known children were as follows:

1. **George Buskirk** (nothing further)
2. **Abram Buskirk** (b. 1783) married **Mary Ann Boswell**
3. **Hannah Buskirk** (b. 1796) married **John Cochran**
4. **Joseph Buskirk** (living in 1840)
5. **Alfred Buskirk** married **Lithia Dayhoff**

{Ref: DAR Application 69845; *A Roster of Revolutionary Ancestors of the Indiana*

Daughters of the American Revolution (1976), p. 94; *Genealogical Abstracts of Revolutionary War Pension Files*, by Virgil D. White (1990), Application S32148}

HENRY BUTLER

Henry Butler, son of the late **Samuel Butler**, of Baltimore, MD, died of cholera in Cincinnati, OH in 1832 (exact date not given in newspaper). {Ref: *Baltimore American*, 1 Dec 1832, abstracted by Lorrie A. E. Erdman}

JAMES CAHILL

James Cahill was born on 27 Jan 1749 in Queen Anne's Co., MD and lived there at the time of his enlistment in the Revolutionary War. After the war he moved to Kentucky and in 1814 went to Ohio. He applied for a pension in Brown Co., OH on 3 Apr 1834. {Ref: *Genealogical Abstracts of Revolutionary War Pension Files*, by Virgil D. White (1990), Application S8186}

DENNIS CALLAHAN

Dennis Callahan was born circa 1752 and served in Maryland during the Revolutionary War. He enlisted in Queen Anne's County in Capt. Emory's Co., 5th MD Regiment, under Col. Richardson in Gen. Smallwood's Brigade, and served from 6 Jun 1778 until 19 Mar 1779 when he was discharged. He subsequently moved to Ohio and applied for a pension in Adams County on 12 Aug 1821, aged 72, and stated that he had no family. {Ref: *Genealogical Abstracts of Revolutionary War Pension Files*, by Virgil D. White (1990), Application S42118; *Archives of Maryland*, Volume 18, p. 193}

Mary Callahan, who was in all likelihood related to **Dennis Callahan**, served on a Grand Jury on 26 Oct 1779 and took an oath *"to prevent the growth of Toryism"* in Queen Anne's Co., MD {Ref: County Court Minutes, 1779}

GEORGE CALLAHAN

George Callahan was born in Maryland (county not stated) on 27 Dec 1765 *(sic)* and died on 25 Feb 1839 in Licking Co., OH. His tombstone indicates he was a soldier in the Revolutionary War. He married first to **Mary Wells** (27 Dec 1774, PA - 23 Jul 1813, OH) at Uniontown, PA in 1792 and second to **Elizabeth Whitehead** in 1818. His son **John Callahan** (24 Nov 1801, PA - 12 Feb 1883, Robinson, IL) married on 24 Mar 1827 to **Margaret Brown** (30 Aug 1808, Madison Co., KY - 16 Jan 1892, IL). {Ref: DAR Application 248741; *A Roster of Revolutionary Ancestors of the Indiana Daughters of the American Revolution* (1976), p. 98}

GEORGE CALVERT

George Calvert and **Emma Hoskinson**, of Maryland (county not stated), married in Ohio (county not stated) after 1830. {Ref: *Maryland Revolutionary Records*, by Harry Wright Newman (1938), p. 111}

JOSEPH CAMPBELL

Joseph Campbell, of Harford Co., MD, enrolled as a private in the company of Capt. **Frederick T. Amoss** during the War of 1812 and was later discharged in Baltimore, MD. He subsequently moved to Indiana where he applied for bounty land (warrant 55-160-101418) in Brown County on 9 Mar 1851, aged 56. **Joseph Campbell**, aged 68, was still living in Brown County on 5 Feb 1862. {Ref: *Maryland Militia, War of 1812, Volume 3, Cecil & Harford Counties*, by F. Edward Wright, p. 43}

WILLIAM CAREL

William Carel (sometimes spelled Carrol and Carrill) was born in November, 1757 and lived in Frederick Co., MD at the time of his enlistment in the Revolutionary War as a private on 18 May 1778. **William Carrill** was also an Associator in 1775 and took the Oath of Allegiance in 1778. In 1822 he lived in Adams Co., OH and at that time a **George Carel** (relationship not stated) lived in Morgan Co., OH. **William Carel (or Carrill)** applied for a pension in Raccoon Township, Gallia Co., OH on 8 Aug 1832. {Ref: *Genealogical Abstracts of Revolutionary War Pension Files*, by Virgil D. White (1990), Application S2107; *Revolutionary Patriots of Frederick County, Maryland, 1775-1783*, by Henry C. Peden, Jr. (1995), p. 65}

BENJAMIN CARLISLE

Benjamin Carlisle was born in 1759 and enlisted in Montgomery Co., MD during the Revolutionary War. He served as a private in 1782 in the First Partizan Legion commanded by Brig. Gen. Armand, **Marquis de la Rouerie**, and was discharged on 15 Nov 1783. He subsequently moved to Ohio and applied for a pension in Fairfield County on 30 Apr 1818, aged 59. In 1820 he stated he was aged 61 with a wife aged 56 (name not given) and these children: oldest daughter (not named), aged 16, **Sarah Carlisle**, aged 13, and **Benedict Carlisle**, aged 8. {Ref: *Genealogical Abstracts of Revolutionary War Pension Files*, by Virgil D. White (1990), Application S42115; *Archives of Maryland*, Volume 18, p. 594}

GREENBERRY CARR

Greenberry Carr, of Anne Arundel Co., MD, married **Rachel Hobbs** on 10 Dec 1811 (by **Rev. Slingsbury Linthicum**) and in 1813 he was drafted into the War of 1812. He was on active duty for 20 days in July-August, 1813 and served in the company of Capt. **Henry Woodward** in the 22nd Regiment. He subsequently moved to Ohio and died in Clermont County in June, 1819. On 22 Sep 1855 **Rachel Carr**, aged 63, applied for bounty land (warrant 55-rej-218258). Witnesses were **Joseph Gwynn** and **Harry Garrett**, all of Clermont Co., OH. {Ref: *Maryland Militia, War of 1812, Volume 4, Anne Arundel & Calvert Counties,*, by F. Edward Wright, pp. 34, 72}

THOMAS CARR

Thomas Carr was born in Maryland (county not stated) on 23 Jun 1755 and died at Charlestown, IN on 26 Oct 1822. He served as a captain in the militia of Westmoreland Co., PA during the Revolutionary War and married **Hannah Coombs** (15 Jul 1766, PA - 3 Jun 1829, IN) in 1785 in Fayette Co., PA. Their children were as follows:

1. **Absolom Carr** (b. 12 Sep 1786) married **Jane Weir** in 1812
2. **Elizabeth Carr** (b. 28 Aug 1788) married **John Boell**
3. **Nancy Carr** (b. 20 Nov 1791) married **Enoch Parr** in 1812
4. **John Carr** (b. 6 Apr 1793) married **Mary Neal** in 1817
5. **Joseph Carr** (b. 7 Feb 1796) married **Nancy Drummond**
6. **Hannah Carr** (b. 4 Sep 1798) married **John Parr**
7. **Thomas Carr, Jr.** (b. 4 Apr 1800) married first to **Polly Robertson** in 1827 and second to **Elizabeth Robertson** in 1841
8. **Rachel Carr** (b. 23 Feb 1802)
9. **Jefferson Carr** (b. 14 Oct 1806) married **Mary Woodson** in 1837
10. **Rebecca Carr** (b. 16 Jun 1810) married Dr. **James S. Athon** in 1835
11. **Elisha Carr** (b. 12 Feb 1813)

{Ref: DAR Application 520020; *A Roster of Revolutionary Ancestors of the Indiana Daughters of the American Revolution* (1976), p. 105}

THOMAS CARR

Thomas Carr, of Frederick Co., MD, served as a private during the War of 1812 in the company of Capt. **Philip Smith** from 23 May 1813 to 8 Sep 1813. He married **Mary Caroline Hearn** on 20 Jan 1814 in Frederick County and subsequently moved to Chillicothe, Ross Co., OH where he died on 10 Dec 1860. **Mary Caroline Carr** applied for a widow's pension (WC-1872) and died circa 1878. {Ref: *Maryland Militia, War of 1812, Volume 2, Baltimore*, by F. Edward Wright, p. 72; *Index to War of 1812 Pension Files, Volume 1*, by Virgil D. White, p. 346}

RACHEL CARROLL

On the 23rd day of the 10th month, 1816, the Gunpowder Monthly Meeting, Baltimore Co., MD, recorded that **Rachel Carroll** (sometimes spelled Carrol), *"having her birth and education amongst Friends, gave written testimony that she had gone out in marriage to a man not in membership, for which she is sorry and asks to continued as a member."* On the 9th day of the 4th month, 1817 **Rachel Carroll** requested a certificate of removal to the Little Falls Monthly Meeting in Harford Co., MD. On the 5th day of the 8th month, 1817, the Little Falls Monthly Meeting received a certificate for **Rachel Carroll** from the Gunpowder Monthly Meeting. She later requested a certificate of removal on the 4th day of the 8th month, 1818, and again on the 8th day of the 9th month, 1818, to White Water Monthly Meeting in Indiana. {Ref: Little Falls Quaker Monthly Meeting Minutes}

WILLIAM CARTER

William Carter, of Baltimore Co., MD, served as third sergeant during the War of 1812 in the company of Capt. **Henry Snowden** in the 6th Cavalry District from 31 Aug 1814 to 19 Sep 1814. He married **Ruth Jean** on 23 Oct 1814 in Baltimore and subsequently moved to Jefferson Co., OH where he died on 7 Mar 1854. **Ruth Carter** applied for a widow's pension (WC-4936) and died circa 1878. {Ref: *Maryland Militia, War of 1812, Volume 2, Baltimore*, by F. Edward Wright, p. 75; *Index to War of 1812 Pension Files, Volume 1*, by Virgil D. White, p. 353}

JOHN H. CARVER

John H. Carver removed from Baltimore, MD to Cincinnati, OH on 4 Apr 1827. {Ref: Class Lists, Baltimore City Station, Methodist Episcopal Church}

SAUL CARY

Saul Cary was born in Worcester Co., MD in 1765 and enlisted there during the Revolutionary War. When he was aged 25 or 26 he moved to Piqua Co., OH and in 1827 he moved to Hamilton Co., IN, where he applied for a pension on 12 Oct 1839, aged 83. {Ref: *Genealogical Abstracts of Revolutionary War Pension Files*, by Virgil D. White (1990), Application R1684}

It should be noted that there was a **Solomon Cary, Sr.** and a **Solomon Cary, Jr.** (name sometimes spelled Carey) who took the Oath of Allegiance in 1778 and served in the Worcester Co., MD Militia in 1779-1780; however, since **Saul Cary** was too young to take the oath or to serve in the militia at that time, perhaps one of these men was his father. {Ref: *Revolutionary Patriots of Worcester & Somerset Counties, Maryland, 1775-1783*, by Henry C. Peden, Jr., p. 45}

For more detailed information about the early Carey (Cary) families in Worcester Co., MD, consult *Colonial Families of the Eastern Shore of Maryland, Volume 9*, by Henry C. Peden, Jr. and F. Edward Wright (2000)}

JACOB CASEY

Jacob Casey applied for a pension in Franklin Co., OH on 1 May 1818, age 62, and stated he served in the Pennsylvania, Virginia and Maryland Lines during the Revolutionary War. In 1822 he had a wife upwards of 60 years of age, two daughters aged 30 and 24, and a son aged 24 who lived 500 miles away (no names were given). {Ref: *Genealogical Abstracts of Revolutionary War Pension Files*, by Virgil D. White (1990), Application S42114}

WILLIAM CASH

William Cash was born in Maryland in 1756 and lived in Frederick Co., MD at the time of his enlistment in the Revolutionary War as a private under Capt. **Philip Meroney** on 5 Aug 1779. **John Cash** also enlisted on that same day. William subsequently moved to Richland Township, Belmont Co., OH and applied for a pension on 4 Sep 1833. {Ref: *Genealogical Abstracts of Revolutionary War Pension Files*, by Virgil D. White (1990), Application S3120; *Revolutionary*

42

Patriots of Frederick County, Maryland, 1775-1783, by Henry C. Peden, Jr. (1995), p. 66}

JOHN CAVENDER

John Cavender was born in 1760 at Newark, New Castle Co., DE and served in the Delaware Line at the beginning of the Revolutionary War. In May, 1778 he moved to Cecil Co., MD and also enlisted there, as did **James Cavender** (relationship not stated). **John Cavinder** *(sic)* took the Oath of Allegiance in Cecil County in 1778 and **John Cavender** received payment for providing quarters and firewood to the Delaware military in November, 1782. He married **Margaret ----** in August, 1784 or 1785 in Newark, DE and afterwards moved to Pennsylvania and then to Ohio. He applied for a pension in Crosby Township, Hamilton County, on 5 Sep 1832 and died on 12 Sep 1837. **Margaret Cavender** applied for a widow's pension in Brookville, Franklin Co., IN on 21 Aug 1843, aged 80. Their children were as follows:
1. **Easter Cavender** (died in infancy)
2. **John Cavender** (died in infancy)
3. **Alexander Cavender** (18 Sep 1788 - 1843)
4. **John Cavender** (b. 1 Jan 1791)
5. **Robert Cavender** (b. 22 Apr 1793)
6. **Polly Cavender** (b. 18 Sep 1795)
7. **Eliza Cavender** (30 Jan 1805 - 1839)

{Ref: *Genealogical Abstracts of Revolutionary War Pension Files*, by Virgil D. White (1990), Application W9776; *Revolutionary Patriots of Cecil County, Maryland, 1775-1783*, by Henry C. Peden, Jr., p. 19; *Delaware Archives, Military Records*, Volume II, p. 605}

JOSHUA CECIL

Joshua Cecil (sometimes spelled Sissill) was born circa 1730 in Prince George's Co., MD and was enrolled on 13 Jul 1776 as a private by Capt. **John H. Lowe** during the Revolutionary War. He married **Mary ----** circa 1760 in Maryland and after the war they moved to Jefferson Co., OH. Joshua died before 19 Apr 1814 and **Mary Cecil** died after 1814 in Harrison Co., OH. Their children were as follows:
1. **Joshua Cecil, Jr.** (b. 1762) married first to **Mary Reardon** and second to **Jane Cummings**
2. **Melinda Cecil** (b. 1764) married **Jonathan Andrews**
3. **Levi Cecil** married **Martha Toole**
4. **Jeremiah Cecil** (nothing further)
5. **Elizabeth Cecil** married **Jarrett Ball**
6. **Ann Cecil** married **Mr. Andrews**
7. **Brice Berry Cecil** (nothing further)
8. **Kinsey Cecil** (b. 1770) married first in Maryland (wife's name not known), second in Kentucky to **Luvana Helvey**, and third in Kentucky to **Elizabeth Muters**
9. **Hazel Cecil** (b. 1774) married **Lyde Ball**

10. **Adin Cecil** (b. 1780) married **Sarah Toole**
{Ref: DAR Application 446209; *A Roster of Revolutionary Ancestors of the Indiana Daughters of the American Revolution* (1976), pp. 109-110; *Archives of Maryland*, Volume 18, p. 35}

UNIT CHANDLER
E. C. Chandler, aged 27, wife of **Dr. Unit Chandler**, recently of Kent Co., MD, and daughter of **William R. Stuart**, Esq., of Baltimore, MD, died in Cincinnati, OH in 1834 (exact date not given). **Unit Chandler** and **Elizabeth D. Stuart** obtained a marriage license in Kent Co., MD on 17 Mar 1817. {Ref: *Baltimore American*, 15 Aug 1834, abstracted by Lorrie A. E. Erdman; *Kent County, Maryland Marriage Licenses, 1796-1850*, by Raymond B. Clark, Jr. and Sarah Seth Clark (1972), p. 5}

JOHN CHANEY
John Chaney (sometimes spelled Cheney) served in the War of 1812 in Anne Arundel and Calvert Counties, MD and was a substitute for his father (name not given). He was a private on active duty for 5 days in June, 1814 in the company of Capt. **William S. Tillard** in the 2nd Regiment and from 26 Jul to 1 Aug 1814 in the company of Capt. **Richard Ireland** in Calvert Co., MD in the 32nd Regiment. He subsequently moved to Ohio and applied for bounty land (warrant 55-rej-245227) in Belmont County on 12 May 1856, aged 56. Witnesses were **Stephen Wilson** and **Philip Hunt**. John also applied for a pension (SO-25238) and on 20 Mar 1873 he recalled that some of the men in his company were **Dora Hodgkins, William Fowler, Martin Wells, George Wilkinson**, and **S. Stamp**, all of Calvert Co., MD. On 15 Sep 1873 he resided at Barnesville, Belmont Co., OH and stated he served in the Hall's Creek Company commanded by Capt. **Richard Ireland** and Capt. **Mordecai Taneyhill's** Artillery Company. **Thomas Jones**, a resident of Calvert Co., MD, stated he served in the Lower Marlboro Company commanded by Capt. **Benjamin Leitch** and he was acquainted with **John Chaney** who served in the Hall's Creek Company at the same time. {Ref: *Maryland Militia, War of 1812, Volume 4, Anne Arundel & Calvert Counties*, by F. Edward Wright, pp. 29, 50, 73; *Index of War of 1812 Pension Files*, by Virgil D. White, p. 372}

LEWIS CHANEY
Lewis Chaney (sometimes spelled Cheney) served in the War of 1812 in Calvert Co., MD in the company of Capt. **Benjamin Leitch** and was on active duty on 6 and 7 Aug 1813 and from 2 Aug to 17 Aug 1814 and in the company of Capt. **Hillary Wilson** from 26 Jul to 1 Aug 1814. He subsequently moved to Ohio and applied for bounty land (warrant 55-rej-140942) in Clermont County on 28 May 1852, aged 77. He stated, in part: *"I belonged to a company of men employed in guarding the sea coast to prevent the landing of the British ... I was first called into service of Calvert County, Maryland in the spring of 1813 and that thence forward until the close of the war my company continued in actual service, one half of them serving a week and then returning home, their places being supplied by the other*

half ... I continued thus to serve every other week as long as said company continued in service, to wit, until the winter of 1814 when I was honourably discharged at Calvert County." {Ref: *Maryland Militia, War of 1812, Volume 4, Anne Arundel & Calvert Counties,* by F. Edward Wright, pp. 50, 51, 73}

JAMES CHAPLINE

James Chapline was born in 1750 and enrolled in the first militia company organized for the Revolutionary War in the Elizabeth Town District of Frederick County (now the Hagerstown area of Washington County) on 6 Jan 1776. He was a first lieutenant in the company of Capt. **Joseph Chapline** on 22 Jun 1778 and a lieutenant in the Select Militia on 20 Mar 1781. He served in the Maryland House of Delegates, 1779-1783, subsequently moved to Ohio and died in Jefferson County circa 1825. The Maryland Chancery Court case of **William Williams Chapline** vs. **James Chapline**, et al., dating back to 1790 and supplemented in 1809 by **William Price**, et al. vs. **Henry Neighkirk**, et al., was noted in *The Farmers' Register and Maryland Herald* in Washington Co., MD on 29 Dec 1829. It stated, in part, that **James Chapline** died several years ago, intestate and insolvent, and his children and heirs were as follows:

1. **Alitha Chapline** married **William Wallace**
2. **Romena Chapline** married **John Miser**
3. **Joseph Chapline**
4. **Heros Chapline**
5. **Atlas Chapline**
6. **Cyrus Chapline**

All of the above Chapline heirs resided outside of Maryland by 1829. {Ref: *Marriages and Deaths from the Newspapers of Allegany and Washington Counties, Maryland, 1820-1830,* by F. Edward Wright, p. 125; *Revolutionary Patriots of Washington County, Maryland, 1776-1783,* by Henry C. Peden, Jr., pp. 57-58}

AMELIA CHARLES

A certificate of removal was received at Milford Monthly Meeting in Wayne Co., IN on the 23rd day of the 12th month, 1826 for **Amelia Charles**, a minor under the care of **Hatfield Wright** and his wife **Mary Wright**. In the minutes it was later stated that **Amelia Charles** of Henry Co., IN, daughter of **Henry and Mary Charles** of Dorchester Co., MD, married **Thomas Butler** at the Bethel Monthly Meeting on the 13th day of the 1st month, 1828. {Ref: "Migration of Caroline County Quakers to Indiana," by F. Edward Wright, *Maryland Genealogical Society Bulletin*, Volume 34, No. 3 (1993), p. 283}

LEVIN CHARLES

A certificate of removal was received at Milford Monthly Meeting in Wayne Co., IN on the 27th day of the 1st month, 1827 for **Levicia Charles** and one was received for **Levin Charles** on the 27th day of the 10th month, 1827 from the Northwest Fork Monthly Meeting in Caroline Co., MD. Both had joined the Hicksite sect and were disowned by the Orthodox meeting. **Levin Charles,** son of

Henry and Mary Charles, of Dorchester Co., MD, was the brother of **Amelia Charles**, *q.v.* Levin married **Anna Williams**, daughter of **William and Hannah Williams**, of Madison Co., IN, at the Milford Monthly Meeting in Wayne Co., IN on the 23rd day of the 5th month, 1839. He died on the 6th day of the 10th month, 1853. {Ref: "Migration of Caroline County Quakers to Indiana," by F. Edward Wright, *Maryland Genealogical Society Bulletin*, Volume 34, No. 3 (1993), p. 283}

JOHN CHENOWETH

John Chenoweth served in Maryland during the Revolutionary War, having enlisted in Washington (now Allegany) County during the war. He later moved to Kentucky and married **Mary Buskirk**, daughter of **Michael Buskirk**, on 13 Mar 1792 in Shelby County. John died on 3 Mar 1820 and **Mary Chenoweth** moved to Indiana where she applied for a widow's pension in Vermillion County on 21 Jun 1842. A son, **Isaac Chenoweth**, aged 43 in 1843, lived in Perryville, IN. {Ref: *Genealogical Abstracts of Revolutionary War Pension Files*, by Virgil D. White (1990), Application W9787}

JOHN CLANCEY

John Clancey enlisted in the Maryland Line at Log Town, MD in 1777 and after the Revolutionary War he moved to Washington, D.C. where he applied for a pension on 6 Apr 1819, aged 65. On 24 Aug 1820 he resided in Jefferson Co., OH and died on 5 Jun 1841. {Ref: *Genealogical Abstracts of Revolutionary War Pension Files*, by Virgil D. White (1990), Application S42126}

ANTHONY CLARK

Anthony Clark was born in Ireland and immigrated to Baltimore, MD in 1776. He lived there at the time of his enlistment in the Maryland Line and during the Revolutionary War he moved to Berkeley Co., VA. Twelve years later he moved to Monroe Co., OH for 24 years and then moved to Windsor Township, Lawrence Co., OH. He applied for a pension on 28 Aug 1832, aged 74, and died on 23 Jul 1833. {Ref: *Genealogical Abstracts of Revolutionary War Pension Files*, by Virgil D. White (1990), Application S3156}

JACOB N. CLARK

Jacob N. Clark was born on 13 Oct 1754 and lived in Baltimore, MD at the time of his enlistment in the Revolutionary War. He later moved to Smithfield, Jefferson Co., OH and applied for a pension on 13 May 1833. {Ref: *Genealogical Abstracts of Revolutionary War Pension Files*, by Virgil D. White (1990), Application S15379}

JAMES CLARK

James Clark was born in 1743 in County Tyrone, Ireland and immigrated to America on 11 Jun 1767 or 1768, landing at Philadelphia on 25 Aug 1767 or 1768. Three months later he moved to Lancaster Co., PA, settled on Chickey's Creek, about 9 miles from the town of Lancaster, and lived there at the time of his enlistment in the Revolutionary War. He also served as a substitute for his brother-in-law **Alexander McGauchey** at which time they lived in York Co., PA, about 30 miles from Little York. He later moved to Baltimore, MD, lived there for 9 years and then moved to Columbiana Co., OH in 1829. He applied for a pension in New Lisbon, OH on 15 Aug 1832, aged 89, and died on 28 Dec 1836. {Ref: *Genealogical Abstracts of Revolutionary War Pension Files*, by Virgil D. White (1990), Application S2125}

JOHN CLARK

John Clark was born on 13 Aug 1747 and enlisted at Baltimore, MD during the Revolutionary War. After the war he followed the sea for 5 years and then was a pilot for 2 years in Baltimore. He later lived at various places in Maryland, Virginia and Pennsylvania and married **Sarah Louden** (b. circa 1774) on 7 Aug 1794 in Berkeley Co., VA. Their children were as follows:
1. **Joseph Clark** (b. 20 Jun 1795)
2. **Nancy Ann Clark** (b. 19 Feb 1797) married **Mr. Davis**
3. **John Clark, Jr.** (b. 7 Mar 1799)
4. **Catherine Clark** (b. 19 Jun 1801, d. before 1853)
5. **Sarah Clark** (b. 9 Aug 1804, d. before 1853)
6. **Elizabeth Clark** (b. 2 Jan 1807) married **Mr. Groves**
7. **Jane Clark** (b. 20 Aug 1811) married **Mr. Peltier**
8. **James Clark** (b. 1 Aug 1813, d. before 1853)

John Clark applied for a pension in Pickaway Co., OH on 4 Jun 1818, having lived there for 18 years. He died on 26 or 27 Jul 1833 and widow **Sarah Clark** married **Simeon or Simon Cochran** (who served in the Virginia Line during the war). Simon died in 1845 and **Sarah Cochran** died on 5 Oct 1853, survived by children **Joseph Clark**, **John Clark** (who resided in Franklin Co., OH in 1854), **Nancy Ann Davis**, **Elizabeth Groves**, and **Jane Peltier**. **Nancy Clark**, wife of **John Clark**, died on 5 Jun 1839 and **Joannah Clark**, wife of **John Clark**, died on 31 May 184-(?). {Ref: *Genealogical Abstracts of Revolutionary War Pension Files*, by Virgil D. White (1990), Application W6741}

JOHN CLARKE

John Clarke was born near Mt. Holley, NJ and was raised at Old Town in Frederick Co., MD. He lived in Maryland at the time of his enlistment in the Revolutionary War and subsequently moved to Ohio. On 5 Oct 1832 he applied for a pension in Deerfield Township, Warren Co., OH, and mentioned **Elisha Clarke**, but no relationship was indicated. {Ref: *Genealogical Abstracts of Revolutionary War Pension Files*, by Virgil D. White (1990), Application S3158; *Revolutionary Patriots of Frederick County, Maryland, 1775-1783*, by Henry C. Peden, Jr. (1995), p. 72}

JOSHUA CLEMENTS

Joshua Clements was born in Caroline Co., MD on 6 Aug 1795 and married **Maria E. Crain** on 25 Nov 1834 in Dayton, OH, having moved there circa 1813-

1814. During the War of 1812 he was drafted at Greensborough, Caroline Co., MD as a private and served in the company of Capt. **Andrew Baggs** from 15 Aug to 25 Aug 1813. Joshua was a physician and had an office on Main Street in Dayton, OH which burned down about 1 Jan 1836. His discharge paper was lost in the fire. He was still living in Dayton on 5 Jun 1871 when he applied for bounty land (warrant number not given), but his claim and his pension application (SO-18490) were rejected because of insufficient service. {Ref: *Maryland Militia, War of 1812, Volume 1, Eastern Shore*, by F. Edward Wright, p. 106; *Index of War of 1812 Pension Files*, by Virgil D. White, p. 410}

THOMAS CLIFTON

Thomas Clifton lived in Washington Co., MD at the time of his enlistment in the Revolutionary War. He enlisted as a private in the Washington Co., MD militia company of Capt. **William Heyser** on 3 Aug 1776 and appeared on the Continental Line muster roll of 23 Oct 1776. He served in the German Regiment under Lt. Col. **Ludwick Weltner** and was discharged at Fort Wyoming, PA on 26 Jul 1779. He subsequently moved to Ohio and applied for a pension in Ross County on 17 Jul 1819, aged 74. but on 18 Apr 1821 he stated he was aged 66 with a wife and a son aged 15 (no names were given). He died on 30 Sep 1832. {Ref: *Genealogical Abstracts of Revolutionary War Pension Files*, by Virgil D. White (1990), Application S42125; *Archives of Maryland*, Volume 18, pp. 264-265; *The German Regiment of Maryland and Pennsylvania in the Continental Army, 1776-1781*, by Henry J. Retzer, p. 96}

HENRY CLOSE

Henry Close, possibly of Baltimore or Harford Co., Maryland, married **Magdalene** ---- and moved to Richland Township, Belmont Co., OH circa 1802. They died in 1858 and were buried in the Methodist Cemetery at St. Clairsville. {Ref: *Trail Blazer*, Volume 4, No. 3 (1998), p. 68}

CASPAR CLUTTER

Caspar Clutter was born in New Jersey on 20 Sep 1745 and enlisted at Baltimore, MD during the Revolutionary War. **Gasper Clutter** enlisted as a private in Capt. Smith's Company No. 8 in Baltimore, MD on 27 Jan 1776. He subsequently moved to Ohio and applied for a pension in Knox County on 3 Aug 1832, aged 86. {Ref: *Genealogical Abstracts of Revolutionary War Pension Files*, by Virgil D. White (1990), Application S5010; *Archives of Maryland*, Volume 18, p. 18}

JAMES COBB

James Cobb died of cholera in Cincinnati, OH in the last week in July, 1833 (exact date not given in newspaper). {Ref: *Baltimore American*, 1 Aug 1833, abstracted by Lorrie A. E. Erdman}

SIMON COCHRAN

Simon Cochran and **Sarah Clark** (widow), of Maryland (county not stated), married in Ohio (county not stated) after 1822. {Ref: *Maryland Revolutionary Records*, by Harry Wright Newman (1938), p. 112}

EDWARD COEN

Edward Coen was born in Baltimore Co., MD on 22 Nov 1754 and lived in Harford County at the time of his enlistment in the Revolutionary War. He was also a signer of the Association of Freemen in Susquehanna Hundred in 1775-1776. Edward had a brother who lived in Tuscarora Valley, PA and he went to stay with him and also enlisted there. **James Coen** (b. 24 Aug 1752) was probably that brother. He had moved from Baltimore Co., MD to Cumberland Co., PA, served in the Revolutionary War, and then moved to Greene Co., PA where he applied for a pension on 10 Sep 1832, aged 80. After the war **Edward Coen** moved to the Monongalia River for 2 years, then moved to Washington Co., PA, then to Mason Co., KY for 2 or 3 years, then to Bourbon Co., KY, then to Maysville, KY, then to Hamilton Co., OH, then to Butler Co., OH, then to Switzerland Co., IN, then back to Hamilton Co., OH, and then to Clermont Co., OH, where he applied for a pension on 22 May 1833, aged 78. {Ref: *Genealogical Abstracts of Revolutionary War Pension Files*, by Virgil D. White (1990), Applications S17356 and S2139; *Revolutionary Patriots of Harford County, Maryland, 1775-1783*, by Henry C. Peden, Jr. (1985), p. 44}

JOHN WILLIAM COLBERT

John William Colbert was born in Dublin, Ireland in 1759 and immigrated to Baltimore, MD in 1773. He enlisted near Poplar Spring, MD during the Revolutionary War and subsequently moved to Ohio. He applied for a pension in Clermont Co., OH on 8 May 1832, aged 63. {Ref: *Genealogical Abstracts of Revolutionary War Pension Files*, by Virgil D. White (1990), Application R2110}

EZEKIEL COLE

Ezekiel Cole was born in Baltimore Co., MD on 8 Jan 1748 and lived at Baltimore at the time of his enlistment in the Revolutionary War. He subsequently moved to Ohio and applied for a pension at Salem Township, Jefferson Co., OH on 6 Sep 1834, aged 86. He stated his brother's widow (name not give) lived in Jefferson Co. and she had the family bible. Ezekiel's son **Thomas Cole** wrote a letter of inquiry from Richmond to the War Department on 7 Mar 1853. {Ref: *Genealogical Abstracts of Revolutionary War Pension Files*, by Virgil D. White (1990), Application R2127}

SAMUEL COLE

Samuel Cole was born in North Hundred, Baltimore Co., MD on 20 Sep 1762 and lived there at the time of his enlistment in the Revolutionary War. When he was 30 years old he moved to Ohio. He applied for a pension in German Township in Harrison County in 1835, aged 72, and died on 13 Mar 1842, leaving these children

(order of birth uncertain):
  1. **Thomas Cole**
  2. **Elijah Cole**
  3. **Meshac Cole**
  4. **Charles Cole**
  5. **Betsy Cole** married **Mr. Wright** who died before 1853
  6. **Juliana Cole**
  7. **Tensa Cole** married **Luke Tipton** and died before 1853
  8. **Sarah Cole** married **John Barret** and died before 1853

{Ref: *Genealogical Abstracts of Revolutionary War Pension Files*, by Virgil D. White (1990), Application R2142}

STEPHEN A. COLLINS

Stephen A. Collins, son of **Charles Collins** and **Elizabeth Chisley**, was born in Baltimore, MD on 9 Oct 1807 and married **Alpha Shion** (b. 23 Aug 1813, Brownsville, PA, daughter of **Ebenezer Shion** and **Jane Owens**) on 3 Jul 1830, probably in Fayette Co., PA. After the birth of their first two children in Pennsylvania, Stephen and Alpha moved to Steubenville, Columbiana Co., OH, in the early 1830's, where Stephen was a shoemaker by trade. Their other children were born there and in 1851 the family moved to Hanover Township, Shelby Co., IN. After Stephen's death in Rush Co., IN on 18 Jan 1879, **Alpha Collins** moved to Burden, KS where she married **Thomas Shelton**, a widower (b. 17 Jun 1796, Mercer Co., KY - d. 16 Mar 1890, KS) on 11 Jun 1884. She returned to Indiana and died on 13 Nov 1889. She is buried beside Stephen in the Asbury Cemetery, Morristown, IN. The children of **Stephen and Alpha Collins** were as follows:
  1. **Robert C. Collins** (18 Apr 1831, PA - 21 Sep 1831, PA, of a defective heart)
  2. **Melzena Jane Collins** (20 Apr 1833, PA - 28 Nov 1905, Jericho, Shelby Co., IN) married **Joseph Ralph** on 25 May 1868
  3. **George William Wallace** (7 Jan 1836, OH - 19 Jan 1914) married first to **Eveline Darmer**, second to Mrs. **Martha A. Talmadge**, and third to **Lucy Gillespie**
  4. **Anna Maria Collins** (21 Jul 1838, OH - 1924) married **John Milton Blackford**
  5. **Ebenezer Van Buren Collins** (22 Oct 1840, OH - 9 Feb 1883) married first to Mrs. **Elizabeth (Moss) McConnell** and second to Mrs. **Margaret (Lafollette) Michaels**
  6. **John Ogden Collins** (14 Apr 1843, OH - 30 Oct 1920) married first to **Sarah Ann Darmer**, second to Mrs. **Mary Ann (French) Railey Files**, and third to Mrs. **Susan Agnes (McMillen) Lazenby**
  7. **Edwill David Perkins Collins** (9 Aug 1845, OH - 3 Mar 1938) married **Pamelia Louise Tetree Cox**
  8. **Howard J. Collins** (21 Sep 1848, OH - died after 1924) married **Mary A. Boone**
  9. **Dearmond Leborn Collins** (25 Jul 1851, OH - 9 Apr 1929) married

50

Cyrelda Belle Anderson
{Ref: *Our Collins Family of Maryland, Pennsylvania, Ohio and Indiana*, by Maurine Collins Schmitz (1985), pp. 3-8}

CHARLES CONAWAY

Charles Conaway was born in Kent Co., MD on 30 Jun 1752. His father (not named) died before he was 2 years old and his mother (not named) moved to Queen Anne's Co., MD. Charles enlisted there during the Revolutionary War and also took the Oath of Allegiance in 1778. In 1787 he moved to Fayette Co., PA and in 1817 he moved to Adams Co., OH where he applied for a pension on 20 Oct 1834. In 1839 he lived at Archer, Harrison Co., OH and signed his name Charles Conaway, Sr. **Michael Conaway** also lived there, but no relationship was indicated. {Ref: *Genealogical Abstracts of Revolutionary War Pension Files*, by Virgil D. White (1990), Application S16087; *Revolutionary Patriots of Kent & Queen Anne's County, Maryland*, by Henry C. Peden, Jr. (1995), p. 54}

MICHAEL CONLEY

Michael Conley and **Rebecca Bradock**, of Maryland (county not stated), married in Brown Co., OH on 20 Apr 1825. {Ref: *Maryland Revolutionary Records*, by Harry Wright Newman (1938), p. 112}

THOMAS CONN

Thomas Conn, of Cecil Co., MD, volunteered during the War of 1812 and served as second sergeant in the company of Capt. **William Garrett** from 29 Apr to 28 May 1813. He was discharged at the headwaters of the Elk River in Elkton, MD (date not given) and subsequently moved to Ohio. He applied for bounty land (warrant 50-40-53909) in Tuscarawas County on 23 Aug 1851, aged about 76. {Ref: *Maryland Militia, War of 1812, Volume 3, Cecil & Harford Counties*, by F. Edward Wright, pp. 14, 44}

RICHARD CONWAY

Richard Conway was born in 1762 in Queen Anne's Co., MD and enlisted at Hampshire Co., VA during the Revolutionary War. He served for 6 months in 1781, 6 months in 1782, and was stationed at the Winchester Barracks. He married **Polly** ---- and their children were as follows:
1. **Michael Conway** (b. 1792)
2. **Miles Conway** (b. 1794) married **Dulcibella Berry**
3. **Charles Conway** (b. 1798)
4. **Richard Conway, Jr.** (b. 18 Nov 1806) married **Cinthia Ray**
5. **Jeremiah Conway** married **Mary Ray** (sister of Cinthia)

Richard Conway died after 15 May 1855 in Henry Co., IN. {Ref: DAR Application 363547; *A Roster of Revolutionary Ancestors of the Indiana Daughters of the American Revolution* (1976), p. 135}

THOMAS COTTINGHAM

In 1814 the mother of **Thomas Cottingham**, a widow with five children (names not given), from Maryland, settled on the Whitewater in what is now Harrison Township, Ohio Co., IN. {Ref: *History of Dearborn and Ohio Counties, Indiana* (1885), p. 526}

THOMAS COURTNEY

Thomas Courtney was born in 1759 in County Armagh, Ireland and lived in Maryland during the Revolutionary War. He later moved to Brown Co., PA and married **Catharine** ---- in April, 1792. They had children (no names were given) and the oldest was born on 18 Jan 1793. Thomas subsequently moved to Ohio and applied for a pension in Brown County on 29 Oct 1833, aged 74. He died in July, 1839 while on a trip to Cincinnati, OH and his widow was informed by her daughter-in-law (not named). **Catharine Courtney** applied for a widow's pension in Pendleton Co., KY on 20 Mar 1844, aged 79. {Ref: *Genealogical Abstracts of Revolutionary War Pension Files*, by Virgil D. White (1990), Application R2371}

COVINGTON FAMILY

The Covington family migrated to Indiana by way of Kentucky and in 1816 they settled at Rising Sun in Dearborn County. The brothers **Robert E. Covington** and **Thomas Covington**, of Somerset Co., MD, moved to Boone Co., KY about the time Gen. Harrison called on the governors of Ohio and Kentucky for reinforcements in the war with the Indians and the British in northwestern Ohio in 1813. They joined the Kentucky militia and served several months. Soon after the War of 1812, circa 1816, two of their sisters, **Eunice Covington** (wife of **Henry Hayman**) and **Polly Covington** (wife of **James Hayman**) moved from Maryland and settled in Rising Sun, IN. **Robert Covington** then made his home there as well and **Thomas Covington** settled near Hartford. Robert (b. 31 Oct 1789) married **Mary Fulton**, daughter of Col. **Samuel Fulton**, on 7 Jan 1819 and died on 26 Aug 1825. **Mary Covington**, his wife, died on 26 Jul 1875. Their sons were **S. F. Covington** and **John B. Covington**; one other child died in infancy. **Thomas Covington**, brother of Robert, married circa 1819 to **Polly Nichols** (daughter of Maj. **George Nichols**, b. MD, moved to Indiana, Washington Township, in 1808; served in the Indian Wars of 1791-1792 and in the War of 1812) and they had several sons. The eldest son, **George N. Covington**, died in infancy from a fever, as did his father Thomas shortly thereafter. Years later the Covington family moved to Illinois. {Ref: *History of Dearborn and Ohio Counties, Indiana* (1885), pp. 491, 662-664}

ISAAC COX

Isaac Cox was born circa 1755, enlisted in Frederick (now Washington) Co., MD during the Revolutionary War as a private in the Washington County militia company of Capt. **Bennett Johnston** in 1776-1777. He subsequently moved to Indiana and applied for a pension at Noble Township, Rush County, on 22 Sep 1832, aged 77. He stated that since 1816 he had neither a wife nor children. Also mentioned were **Jacob Cox** (of Hamilton Co., OH in 1826), **Daniel Cox** (postmaster at Pleasant Ridge, Rush Co., IN in 1828), and **Rev. Elmer H. Cox** (of Rush Co., IN in 1833), but no relationships were given. {Ref: *Genealogical Abstracts of Revolutionary War Pension Files*, by Virgil D. White (1990), Application S32186; *The Maryland Militia in the Revolutionary War*, by S. Eugene Clements & F. Edward Wright, p. 242}

NATHANIEL COX

Nathaniel Cox was born on 25 Oct 1759 and lived in Dorchester County on the Eastern Shore of Maryland at the time of his enlistment in the Revolutionary War. He subsequently moved to Indiana and applied for a pension in Tippecanoe Township, Tippecanoe County, on 14 Aug 1838. Nathaniel's application was rejected and he is not listed in "Muster Rolls of Maryland Troops, 1775-1783" published in Volume 18 of the *Archives of Maryland*. He may have been the son of **Nathaniel Cox** who was head of household in Transquakin Hundred in 1776, aged between 50 and 60, with two males aged between 10 and 16, one male under age 10, one female aged between 50 and 60, one female aged between 30 and 40, one female aged between 16 and 21, one female aged between 10 and 16, and one female under age 10. {Ref: *Genealogical Abstracts of Revolutionary War Pension Files*, by Virgil D. White (1990), Application R2411; 1776 Census of Dorchester Co., MD}

WILLIAM COY

William Coy was born on 10 Mar 1756 in Somerset Co., MD and lived in Montgomery Co., MD at the time of his enlistment in the Revolutionary War. He subsequently moved to Indiana and applied for a pension in Switzerland County on 18 Sep 1832. His children were as follows:
1. **Thomas Coy**
2. **Nancy Coy**
3. **Susannah Coy**
4. **Samuel Coy**
5. **Esther Coy**
6. **Elizabeth Coy**
7. **Ann Coy**
8. **William Coy**
9. **Sarah Coy**
10. **Mary Coy**
11. **Seely Coy**
12. **Frances Coy**

Maryland military records indicate that **William Coy** was a private in the Montgomery Co., MD militia in September, 1777 and a corporal on 15 Jul 1780. **William Koye** took the Oath of Allegiance on 28 Feb 1778. **William Coy** married **Mary Ann Dennis** on 25 Nov 1779 in Montgomery County and lived in Rock Creek Hundred. {Ref: *Genealogical Abstracts of Revolutionary War Pension Files*, by Virgil D. White (1990), Application S31614; *The Maryland Militia in the*

Revolutionary War, by S. Eugene Clements & F. Edward Wright, pp. 196, 202; *Maryland Records: Colonial, Revolutionary, County and Church from Original Sources*, by Gaius M. Brumbaugh, Volume 2, p. 518; *Revolutionary Patriots of Montgomery County, Maryland, 1776-1783*, by Henry C. Peden, Jr., p. 78}

WILLIAM CRAIG

William Craig was born in Baltimore Co., MD on 15 Jun 1755 and at age 5 or 6 his family moved to Cecil Co., MD. He lived there at the time of his enlistment in the Revolutionary War. **William Craige** *(sic)* took the Oath of Allegiance in Cecil Co., MD before the Hon. **John Veazey** on 13 Jan 1779. He later moved to Wellsburg, VA, lived there for 7 years, and then moved to Belmont Co., OH where he applied for a pension on 8 Mar 1833, aged 77. {Ref: *Genealogical Abstracts of Revolutionary War Pension Files*, by Virgil D. White (1990), Application S2479; Cecil County, MD Oaths, Maryland State Archives, Microfilm M3218; *Revolutionary Patriots of Cecil County, Maryland, 1775-1783*, by Henry C. Peden, Jr. (1991), p. 25}

JAMES CRAWFORD

James Crawford, son of **Josiah and Cassandra Crawford**, was born circa 1759 in Baltimore (now Harford) Co., MD and married **Sarah Jones** (b. 1762, daughter of **John Jones**). On the 6th day of the 2nd month, 1786 he was disowned by the Hopewell Monthly Meeting for marriage contrary to discipline of Friends (Quakers). The children of **James and Sarah Crawford** were as follows:

1. **Cynthia Crawford** (8 Feb 1786 - 16 Jul 1845) married **Richard Hawkins** (b. 25 Aug 1770, son of **Thomas Hawkins** and **Sarah Hargrove**) on 12 May 1803 and died at Beallsville, OH

2. **Benedict Crawford** (married **Sarah ----**)

3. **Cassandra Crawford** (b. 1790) married **William Growdy**

4. **Elijah Crawford** (1794-1868) married **Elizabeth Cooper**

5. **Ruth Crawford** (b. 1796) married **Robert Phillips**

6. **Elizabeth Crawford** (married **Mr. Harrison**)

7. **John Crawford** (b. 1799, became a minister)

8. **James Crawford, Jr.** (b. 10 Oct 1801, d. 23 Nov 1827) married **Anna Taylor** (12 Jan 1806 - 18 Mar 1884, daughter of **Edward Taylor** and **Elinor Hewitt**)

9. **Greenberry Crawford** (b. 17 Sep 1803) married first to **Rhoda Winters** and second to **Margaret Ecky**

10. **Abel Crawford** (18 Apr 1806 - 21 Apr 1871) married **Mary Winters**

11. **Josiah Crawford** (d. 1875) married **Nancy Cooper**

James Crawford moved to Jefferson Co., OH and settled in Island Creek Township around 1796, according to family histories. The earliest land patent for him there was a certificate dated 28 Dec 1805. He gave land for a cemetery to the trustees of Mt. Tabor Methodist Church in 1828 and he and his wife were buried there. **Sarah Crawford** died on 3 Feb 1839 and James died testate by 26 Aug 1844. {Ref: Information compiled in 1993 by Patricia Andersen, of Gaithersburg, MD, citing *Tombstone Inscriptions and Family Records of Jefferson County, Ohio*, by Esther Weygandt Powell, p. 47, and *20th Century History of Steubenville and Jefferson County, Ohio and Representative Citizens*, by Joseph B. Doyle, p. 851}

WILLIAM CRITCHFIELD

William Critchfield was born near Hancock, MD in 1763 and lived in Washington Co., PA at the time of his enlistment in the Revolutionary War. He later moved to Bedford Co., PA and also enlisted there. He subsequently moved to Ohio and applied for a pension at Danville in Union Township, Knox County, on 29 Sep 1832. His brother **John Critchfield** lived in Holmes Co., OH at that time. {Ref: *Genealogical Abstracts of Revolutionary War Pension Files*, by Virgil D. White (1990), Application S16091}

JOHN CROFT

Margaret Croft, wife of **John Croft**, requested a certificate of removal from the Baltimore Monthly Meeting, Eastern District, to the Plainfield Monthly Meeting in Ohio on the 10th day of the 8th month, 1809, having already moved there with her husband and their two minor children, **William Croft** and **Stacy Croft**. {Ref: Baltimore Quaker Monthly Meeting Minutes}

JAMES CROSBY

James Crosby was born in County Westmeath, Ireland on 25 Jul 1741 and at the age of 24 or 25 he immigrated to America. He lived about 2 miles from Hagerstown, MD at the time of his enlistment in the Revolutionary War. In 1791 he moved from Washington Co., MD to Bedford Co., PA for 25 years and then moved to Ohio. He applied for a pension at Clayton Township, Perry Co., OH on 8 Nov 1832, having lived there for 16 years, and died on 3 Jun 1835. {Ref: *Genealogical Abstracts of Revolutionary War Pension Files*, by Virgil D. White (1990), Application S11339}

MOSES CROSLEY

Moses Crosley was born on 2 Jan 1764 in Frederick (now Washington) Co., MD and lived there at the time of his enlistment in the Revolutionary War. He served as a drummer and private in the Washington County militia. Moses married **Rachel Powell** on 1 May 1784 in Washington County and subsequently moved to Ohio. He applied for a pension at Clear Creek Township in Warren County on 24 May 1833 and died on 13 Mar 1843. **Rachel Crosley** died on 8 Jan 1846 in Montgomery Co., OH and their only surviving child in 1855 was **William Crosley**, aged 70, of Montgomery County. The name was sometimes spelled Crossley and Crosely. {Ref: *Genealogical Abstracts of Revolutionary War Pension Files*, by Virgil D. White (1990), Application R2516; *Maryland Revolutionary Records*, by Harry Wright Newman (1938), pp. 17, 112}

WILLIAM CROSLEY

William Crosley (sometimes spelled Crossley and Crosely) was born on 5 Oct 1761 and enlisted at Shaftsbury in Washington Co., MD during the Revolutionary War. He married **Sarah ----** (b. 10 Nov 1762) at Hagerstown, MD on 27 Apr 1785. They later moved to Ohio and he applied for a pension in Brown County on 31 Mar 1834, aged 72. His brother **Moses Crosley** was aged 69 on 2 Jan 1834 and lived in Warren Co., OH. William died on 7 Sep 1839 and **Sarah Crosley** applied for a widow's pension in Shelby Co., IN on 10 Sep 1845, aged 82 years and 10 months. Their children were as follows:

1. **Catharine Crosley** (b. 31 May 1786)
2. **Mary Crosley** (b. 15 Jul 1788)
3. **Elizabeth Crosley** (b. 25 Nov 1790)
4. **George Crosley** (b. 15 Apr 1793)
5. **Sarah Crosley** (b. 29 May 1795)
6. **Rachel Crosley** (b. 4 Jan 1798)
7. **Moses Crosley** (b. 11 Jul 1800)
8. **Cynthia Crosley** (b. 22 Oct 1802)
9. **William Crosley, Jr.** (b. 27 Mar 1805)
10. **Anna Crosley** (b. 22 Oct 1807)

{Ref: *Genealogical Abstracts of Revolutionary War Pension Files*, by Virgil D. White (1990), Application R2517; *Maryland Revolutionary Records*, by Harry Wright Newman (1938), pp. 17}

GEORGE H. CROSS

George H. Cross served in Anne Arundel Co., MD during the War of 1812 as a private in the company of Lieut. **John Thomas** in the 32nd Regiment beginning 24 Aug 1814 until he was reported *"deserted Sep 19 with arms and accounts."* Also serving in the same company were **Adderson Cross** (*"deserted Sep 10"*), **Jeremiah Cross** (*"discharged by surgeon Sep 12"*), and **Leonard Cross** (*"deserted Sep 6"*). George subsequently moved to Virginia and married **Delilah Morton** in Hampshire County on 20 Mar 1820 (by **Rev. Arnold**, a Baptist preacher). They later moved to Ohio and George applied for bounty land (warrant 55-rej-222730) in Athens County on 16 Jan 1851, aged 66 *(sic)*. He died on 25 May 1855 in Bern Township and **Delilah Cross** applied for a bounty land warrant in Athens County on 26 Sep 1855. The witnesses were **Alphus Baker** and **A. B. Glazier**. She applied again in Fairfield County on 14 Jan 1857, aged 65. The witnesses were **George Bourne** and **Rebecca Bourne**. The Cross family bible stated **George H. Cross** was born on 20 Mar 1792, married **Delilah Morton** on 9 Mar 1820, and died on 25 May 1855. Their children were as follows:

1. **John Cross** (b. 17 Feb 1821)
2. **Jerry Cross** (b. 3 Oct 1822)
3. **Nancy Ann Cross** (b. 16 Aug 1824)
4. **Rachel Cross** (b. 31 Dec 1825)
5. **Jonathan Cross** (b. 16 Apr 1827)
6. **David Cross** (b. 16 Apr 1827, twin)

7. **Rebecca Cross** (b. 3 Dec 1829)

8. **Lydia Cross** (b. 20 Jan 1833)

{Ref: *Maryland Militia, War of 1812, Volume 4, Anne Arundel & Calvert Counties*, by F. Edward Wright, pp. 43, 76}

JOHN CROSS

John Cross served in Anne Arundel Co., MD during the War of 1812. He was drafted in Baltimore on 26 Jul 1814 and served in the company of Capt. **John R. Brown** in the 2nd Regiment. He also served in the company of Capt. **Charles Pumphrey** in the 22nd Regiment from 17 Sep to 23 Sep 1814. He subsequently moved to Ohio and applied for bounty land (warrant 55-rej-139763) in Fairfield County. The witnesses were **William Cross** and **Emily Tetman**, of Franklin Co., OH. {Ref: *Maryland Militia, War of 1812, Volume 2, Baltimore*, p. 87, and *Anne Arundel & Calvert Counties, Volume 4*, pp. 32, 38, 76, by F. Edward Wright}

WILLIAM CROUCH

William Crouch and **Lucinda Rollins**, of Maryland (county not stated), married in Indiana (county not stated) on 17 Oct 1819. {Ref: *Maryland Revolutionary Records*, by Harry Wright Newman (1938), p. 112}

ADAM CRUM

Adam Crum served in the Maryland Line during the Revolutionary War and subsequently moved to Monroe Co., OH where he applied for a pension on 12 May 1818, age 69. In 1820 his wife **Mary Crum** was aged 50 and the children living with them were **David Crum** (aged 20), **William Crum** (aged 17), and **Mary Crum** (aged 14). His son **Henry Crum** applied on 4 Jun 1852 for himself and the surviving children aforesaid. Henry stated his parents were married before 1800, his father died on 26 Feb 1831, and his mother died on 18 Jul 1851. **Henry Crum** was aged 53 on 29 Apr 1851, **David Crum** was aged 51 on 16 Jun 1851, **William Crum** was aged 49 on 7 Jun 1851, and **Mary Crum** was aged 47 on 3 Oct 1851. {Ref: *Genealogical Abstracts of Revolutionary War Pension Files*, by Virgil D. White (1990), Application W2068}

HUGH CULL

Hugh Cull was born in October, 1759 at what is now Havre de Grace, Harford (then Baltimore) Co., MD and moved when 4 years old with his father (not named) to Pennsylvania. In 1777 they moved to Kentucky and settled near where the present city of Lexington now stands. Hugh married **Rachel Meek** in Henry County in 1785 and they moved to Wayne Co., IN and settled is what is now Boston Township, about five miles below Richmond, near the Elkhorn. **Hugh Cull** was a Methodist local preacher and also a member of the convention which framed the first constitution of the state at Corydon, IN. *"His biographer, Rev. William C. Smith, dates his death August 31, 1862 and adds 'aged 104 years and 10 months.' If, however, he was born and died at the dates given, he would have been but 102 years and 10 months. As he is generally said to have been 105 years old, Mr. Smith* *probably erred in giving the year of his birth or that of his death."* {Ref: *History of Wayne County, Indiana*, by Andrew W. Young (1872), p. 159}

SOLOMON CULVER

Solomon Culver and **Nancy Arnett**, of Maryland (county not stated), married in Ohio (county not stated) before 1820. {Ref: *Maryland Revolutionary Records*, by Harry Wright Newman (1938), p. 112}

CAMPBELL DALE

Campbell Dale was born circa 1756 and lived in Worcester Co., MD at the time of his enlistment in the Revolutionary War. He served as a private in the militia company of Capt. **Josiah Dale** in the Sinepuxent Battalion, 1779-1780. Campbell later moved to Indiana and applied for a pension in Delaware County on 15 Jul 1835, aged 79. {Ref: *Genealogical Abstracts of Revolutionary War Pension Files*, by Virgil D. White (1990), Application R2630; *The Maryland Militia in the Revolutionary War*, by S. Eugene Clements & F. Edward Wright, p. 254}

WILLIAM DAMSELL

William Damsell, of Cecil Co., MD, served in the War of 1812, first in the company of Capt. **William Garrett** and afterwards as a sergeant in the artillery company of Capt. **John King** from 18 Apr to 21 May 1813. By July, 1814 he was captain of an artillery company and although he stated they were not attached to any particular regiment, his unit was in fact attached to the 1st Brigade under Major **James Sewall**. They were called out to man and garrison Fort Hollingsworth and Fort Defiance from 10 Jul to 19 Jul 1814 and again from 27 Aug to 6 Oct 1814 when he was discharged at Elkton, MD. William subsequently moved to Ohio and applied for a bounty land warrant in Richland County on 29 Oct 1850, aged 63. He died in Morrow Co., OH on 28 Aug 1854 and his widow **Katharine Damsell** applied for bounty land (warrant 55-120-69414) on 29 Aug 1855, aged 56, stating that she married William Damsell on 22 Oct 1853 and her previous name was **Katharine Patterson**. Included in his application file in 1850 was the following note: *"Capt. Damsel -- Lieutenant Buchanan and Harvey of the Artillery corps are ordered to take the command of the drafted, volunteers and levy en mass artillery and immediately proceed to Fort Hollingsworth at Elkton Landing to act under any artillery officer who may be there from the state of Delaware and in case no artillery corps should be there, Captain Damsel will take the command of the guns, always amenable to older officers on the station -- Captain King and Lieut. McClallan are discharged after the 8th instant and are now permitted to return home -- By order, R. W. Armstrong B. M."* (no date was given). {Ref: *Maryland Militia, War of 1812, Volume 3, Cecil & Harford Counties*, by F. Edward Wright, pp. 13, 17, 21, 45}

DAVID DANNER

David Danner (sometimes spelled Dannor) was born in March, 1759 in Frederick Co., MD and lived there at the time of his enlistment in the Revolutionary

War. **Jacob Danner** and **Samuel Danner** were fined as non-enrollers in Frederick County in April, 1776. At the age of 32 or 33 David moved to Westmoreland Co., PA for 8 to 9 years, then to Jefferson Co., KY for 3 years, then to Harrison Co., IN for 28 years, and then to Clay Co., IN where he applied for a pension on 29 Oct 1833. {Ref: *Genealogical Abstracts of Revolutionary War Pension Files*, by Virgil D. White (1990), Application S32208; *Revolutionary Patriots of Frederick County, Maryland, 1775-1783*, by Henry C. Peden, Jr. (1995), p. 92}

AUGUSTUS DARBY
Augustus Darby was drafted in Denton, Caroline Co., MD and served in the War of 1812 as a private in the company of Capt. **Peter Willis** in the 19th Regiment from 15 Aug to 30 Aug 1813. He subsequently moved to Morgan Co., OH where he applied for bounty land (warrant number not given) on 20 Mar 1855, aged 68, and received 160 acres. {Ref: *Maryland Militia, War of 1812, Volume 1, Eastern Shore*, by F. Edward Wright, pp. 82, 110}

ENOS DAVIS
Enos Davis was born circa 1761 and enlisted in Maryland during the Revolutionary War. He subsequently moved to Indiana and applied for a pension in Fontaine County on 4 May 1829, aged 68. Children were mentioned, but none were named, in his application. {Ref: *Genealogical Abstracts of Revolutionary War Pension Files*, by Virgil D. White (1990), Application S35877}

ICHABOD DAVIS
Ichabod Davis was born in Anne Arundel Co., MD on 15 Apr 1758 and lived there at the time of his enlistment in the Revolutionary War. He also took the Oath of Allegiance in 1778. Ichabod subsequently moved to Ohio and his wife (not named) died on 7 Nov 1819. He applied for a pension in Columbiana Co., OH on 5 Jul 1844 and died on 29 Jul 1845, leaving these children:
1. **Julia Davis** married **Samuel Koffel** and lived in Columbiana Co., OH in 1855
2. **Mary Davis** married **Josiah Gaskill** and lived in Columbiana Co. OH in 1855
3. **Amos Davis** (of Columbiana Co., OH in 1855)
4. **Isaac R. Davis** (of Columbiana Co., OH in 1855)
5. **John Davis** (of Crawford Co., OH in 1855)
6. **Ruth Davis** married **Mr. McChord** and died before 1855
{Ref: *Genealogical Abstracts of Revolutionary War Pension Files*, by Virgil D. White (1990), Application R2724; *Revolutionary Patriots of Anne Arundel County, Maryland, 1775-1783*, by Henry C. Peden, Jr. (1992), p. 43}

JAMES DAVIS
James Davis served as a private in Talbot Co., MD during the War of 1812 in the company of Capt. **Samuel Stevens** from 14 Apr to 21 Apr 1813 and 9 May to 10 May 1813 and for 11 days in August, 1813, in the company of Capt. **William**

Jordan in August, 1813 for 13 days, and in the artillery company of Capt. **Clement Vickers** in March(?), 1814 for 13 days. **James Davis** married **Margaret Pritchard** on 1 Mar 1814 in Talbot Co., MD (by **Rev. Mulliken**, a Methodist minister) and they later moved to Ohio. He died in Belmont County on 6 Aug 1837 and **Margaret Davis** applied for bounty land on 22 Mar 1855, aged 65, stating her husband had volunteered at Easton, MD in 1813. **John McKissan** and **William Wilson**, residents of Belmont Co., OH, had been acquainted with her for 4 or 5 years. She received a land warrant (claim 3679) for 160 acres. {Ref: *Maryland Militia, War of 1812, Volume 1, Eastern Shore*, by F. Edward Wright, pp. 86, 89, 99, 117}

LEVI DAVIS

Levi Davis was born in Hampshire Co., VA and at the age of 5 or 6 his parents (not named) moved to Frederick Co., MD. Levi lived there at the time of his enlistment in the Revolutionary War. In 1775 he was a sergeant in the militia company of Capt. **Samuel Plummer** in Frederick Co., MD. In 1813 he moved to Kentucky and then to Indiana. His brother **Ebenezer Davis** lived in Pickaway Co., OH and on 1 Jun 1847 stated that Levi died on 6 Mar 1846; however, Levi's son **James Davis** stated that his father died on 8 Mar 1847, leaving a widow **Hannah Davis** who had died before 1847. Their children were as follows:

1. **Irena Davis** married **John Hendrix**
2. **Rachael Davis** married **Solomon Ritchey**
3. **Sarah Davis** married **Shelby Harney**
4. **Stephen Davis**
5. **James Davis**
6. **Rebecca Davis** married **John Crider**
7. **Effee Davis** married **Aaron Gelstrap**
8. **Jane Davis** married **Samuel Starr** and he died by 1847
9. **Nancy Davis** married **John McNeeley** and both died by 1847, leaving children **Isaac McNeeley** and **Levi McNeeley**

On 10 Nov 1851 **James Davis** was the administrator of the estate of **Levi Davis** in Jackson Co., IN. {Ref: *Genealogical Abstracts of Revolutionary War Pension Files*, by Virgil D. White (1990), Application S32210; "Journal of the Committee of Observation of the Middle District of Frederick County, September 12, 1775 - October 24, 1776," *Maryland Historical Magazine*, Volume XI, p. 54}

REZIN DAVIS

Rezin Davis advertised in *The Maryland Herald and Elizabeth-Town Advertiser* on 25 Jan 1805 the sale at his residence on Ringgold's Manor [near Hagerstown, MD] of his entire stock of horses and cattle, 8 negroes (with the liberty of choosing their own masters), and 1,080 acres in Ohio (county not given). {Ref: *Western Maryland Newspaper Abstracts, Volume 2, 1799-1805*, by F. Edward Wright, p. 104}

60

THOMAS DAVIS

Thomas Davis was born on 8 Nov 1753, lived in Durham Parish, Charles Co., MD, and served in the 4th Maryland Line during the Revolutionary War. He was drafted on 27 Jul 1781, served as an Orderly Sergeant for Gen. **William Smallwood**, participated in the siege of Yorktown, and was discharged on 29 Nov 1783. He married **Johannah Whitten** or **Johanna Whitler** (b. 21 Feb 1764) on 2 Jan 1786 and subsequently moved to Ohio. Thomas applied for a pension in Perry Co., OH on 6 Nov 1832 and died on 22 Sep 1840 in Knox Co., OH. **Johannah Davis**, a resident of Clinton Township, applied for a widow's pension on 23 Nov 1840 and by 1846 she was living in Mount Vernon, Knox Co., OH. Also mentioned was **Isaac Davis** (Acting Justice of the Peace), **John W. Davis** (Clerk of the Court), and **H. M. Davis**, but no relationships were given. {Ref: *Genealogical Abstracts of Revolutionary War Pension Files*, by Virgil D. White (1990), Application W6974; *Revolutionary Patriots of Charles County, Maryland, 1775-1783*, by Henry C. Peden, Jr. (1997), p. 73}

WILLIAM F. R. DAVIS

William F. R. Davis was born on 14 Dec 1763 in Frederick (now Montgomery) Co., MD and lived there at the time of his enlistment in the Revolutionary War. In 1792 he moved to Fauquier Co., VA and in December, 1823 he moved to Greene Co., OH. William applied for a pension on 17 Sep 1832 in Sugar Creek Township, Greene Co., OH. {Ref: *Genealogical Abstracts of Revolutionary War Pension Files*, by Virgil D. White (1990), Application S3258}

JAMES H. DAWSON

James H. Dawson, of Wayne Co., IN, son of **Elisha Dawson** and **Lydia Dawson** (deceased) of Caroline Co., MD, married **Ann Wright**, daughter of **William and Celia Wright**, of Wayne Co., IN, on the 22nd day of the 2nd month, 1830 at the Fairfield Meeting House. On the 17th day of the 10th month, 1844 **James H. Dawson** was reported for *"marrying contrary to discipline"* for which he was condemned by the Fall Creek Monthly Meeting. On the 20th day of the 3rd month, 1847 **Lydia Dawson, Sarah Ann Dawson, and Celia Ann Dawson**, children of **James H. Dawson**, were granted a certificate of removal to the Fall Creek Monthly Meeting. **Sarah Thomas**, formerly **Sarah Dawson**, was disowned for *"marrying contrary to discipline"* on the 19th day of the 5th month, 1859 and was refused membership because she *"availed herself of the privilege of a divorce by law."* {Ref: "Migration of Caroline County Quakers to Indiana," by F. Edward Wright, *Maryland Genealogical Society Bulletin*, Volume 34, No. 3 (1993), p. 283}

JOHN DAWSON

John Dawson was born circa 1774 on the Eastern Shore of Maryland and was raised in Virginia. When a young man he moved to Tennessee, then to Kentucky, where he married (wife's name not given) and in 1799 they moved to Miller Township, Ohio Co., IN and raised a family (names not given). John died in 1848. See "John Jackson," *q.v.* {Ref: *History of Dearborn and Ohio Counties, Indiana*

(1885), p. 459}

W. H. DAWSON

W. H. Dawson, native of Baltimore, MD, resident of Cincinnati, OH, and an officer in the U. S. Army, died at Fort Jessup, LA of pulmonary consumption on 31 Jul 1835, aged 30. {Ref: *Baltimore American*, 9 Nov 1835, abstracted by Lorrie A. E. Erdman}

HENRY DEAL

Henry Deal (sometimes spelled Deale) was born in 1794 and volunteered at or near Baltimore during the War of 1812, but served in Anne Arundel County companies. He was 5 feet 7 inches tall, with brown hair, blue eyes, and a fair complexion. He served as a private in the company of Capt. **Benjamin McCeney** from 16 to 30 Apr 1813 and in the company of Capt. **Jacob Franklin** in the 2nd Regiment from 14 Apr to 15 May 1814 and 18 Jun to 22 Jun 1814. After his discharge he resided at Baltimore until 1818 and then moved to Knox Co., OH where he resided at Martinsburg. His first wife was **Elizabeth Baughman** and she died at Bladensburg, Knox Co., OH in April, 1845. His second wife was **Rhoda Ann Carmichael** and they were married at Martinsburg, OH on 5 Nov 1845 (by **A. C. Scott**, a Justice of the Peace). **Henry Deal** died on 11 Jun 1879. **William Stevens**, aged 77, and **Elias Hardman**, aged 70, both of Martinsburg, OH, stated that they had known him for 35 years and 25 years respectively. **Rhoda A. Deal** applied for a widow's pension (WO-42075) and in a letter dated 15 Feb 1884, she stated, in part, that *"Henry Deal was called on later at different times and his guardian Markey Jackson, I believe Jackson was his given name, thought he count not spare him any longer and got him discharged from the service."* **James Sims**, of Knox Co., OH, stated that he [Sims] had served under Capt. **Andrew Porter** during the War of 1812, was stationed at Fort Deposit around 1 Jun 1813, and had been acquainted with **Henry Deal** for about 40 years. {Ref: *Maryland Militia, War of 1812, Volume 4, Anne Arundel & Calvert Counties*, by F. Edward Wright, pp. 17, 18, 20, 78; *Index of War of 1812 Pension Files*, by Virgil D. White, p. 561}

NOBLE DEAN

Noble Dean wa born circa 1756 and lived in Dorchester Co., MD, about 1½ miles from the Delaware state line, at the time of his enlistment in the Revolutionary War. He served as a private in the 2nd Maryland Regiment under Capt. **John Eccleston** in 1778. His brother **Charles Dean** lived about 3 miles away in Delaware. Noble subsequently moved to Ohio and applied for a pension in Cincinnati, Hamilton Co., OH on 6 May 1834, aged 78. {Ref: *Genealogical Abstracts of Revolutionary War Pension Files*, by Virgil D. White (1990), Application R2805; *Archives of Maryland*, Volume 18, p. 294}

ABRAHAM DEAVER

Abraham Deaver was born in Frederick Co., MD on 13 Nov 1749 and served in Maryland during the Revolutionary War. He petitioned the Maryland General

Assembly under the Act of May 12, 1780, stating he had been a non-juror to the Oath of Allegiance in 1778 due to "ignorance" and now desired relief under the Act and to take the Oath. Abraham married **Ann Lakin** (b. 27 Sep 1762, Frederick Co., MD) on 25 Jun 1778. He died in Deavertown, OH in 1831 and **Ann Deaver** died there in 1842. Their children were as follows:

    1. **Levi Deaver** (b. 1782) married first to **Sophia Griffith** and second to **Nancy House**

    2. **Reuben Deaver** (b. 1784) married first to **Mary A. Rhodes** and second to **A. Moody**

    3. **Susannah Deaver** (b. 19 Apr 1786) married **Enoch Minshall**

    4. **Basel Deaver** (b. 1788) married **Mary Ann Eberhard**

    5. **Abraham Deaver, Jr.** (b. 1790) married **Margaret Matthews**

    6. **Walter Deaver** (b. 1792)

    7. **Nancy Deaver** (b. 1794) married **Mr. Hackney**

    8. **Sarah Ann Deaver** (b. 1798) married **Joseph Atkinson**

    9. **Eli Deaver** (b. 1800) married **Clarissa Thissel**

    10. **James Deaver** (b. 1805) married **Rebecca** ----

    11. **Henry J. Deaver** (b. 1808)

Abraham Deaver, of Muskingum Co., OH, made an affidavit on 8 Oct 1819 in support of the Revolutionary War pension of **Miscal Deaver** who had applied in Frederick Co., MD on 22 Jan 1819, aged 66. Abraham knew about the military service of Miscal, but his relationship to him was not stated. {Ref: *Genealogical Abstracts of Revolutionary War Pension Files*, by Virgil D. White (1990), Application S34738; DAR Application 359585; *Index of Patriots, Revolutionary War Heroes and Their Families, Cincinnati Chapter DAR, 1893-1981*, by Jeraldyne Beets Clipson and Katherine Brewer Brinkdopke (1983), p. 94; *Revolutionary Patriots of Frederick County, Maryland, 1775-1783*, by Henry C. Peden, Jr. (1995), p. 96; *Marriage Licenses of Frederick County, 1778-1810*, by Margaret E. Myers (1986), p. 36}

THOMAS DEFORD

Thomas DeFord was born on 9 Dec 1736 on the Eastern Shore of Maryland and lived near Taneytown, Frederick Co., MD, at the time of his enlistment in the Revolutionary War. In 1810 he moved to Pickaway Co., OH and in 1824 he moved to Delaware Co., OH, where he applied for a pension on 19 Nov 1832. {Ref: *Genealogical Abstracts of Revolutionary War Pension Files*, by Virgil D. White (1990), Application S2514}

ELIAS DELASHMUTT

Elias Delashmutt, son of Capt. **Elias Delashmutt** and **Elizabeth Nelson** of Frederick Co., MD, was old enough to serve as a private in his father's militia company during the French and Indian War in 1757. He married **Catherine Waugh** and their known children were as follows (order of birth uncertain):

    1. **William Waugh Delashmutt** (settled in Ohio Co., VA, now Tyler Co., WV)

2. **Peter Delashmutt** (lived in Frederick Co., MD in 1796; no further record)

3. **Sarah Ann Delashmutt** (b. 26 Jan 1773) married **Isaac Shimer** (1765-1848) in Frederick Co., MD on 16 Jan 1798 and moved to Marion Co., IN where she died on 23 Mar 1856

4. **Elias N. Delashmutt** (b. c1777) married first to **Elizabeth O'Harra** in Franklin Co., OH on 3 Oct 1809 and second to **Anne Waugh** in Mason Co., KY on 16 Mar 1819; he died in Madison Co., OH in July, 1823

5. **Elizabeth Delashmutt** (married **William Walling** in Frederick Co., MD on 27 Dec 1796)

{Ref: "Captain Elias Delashmutt of Frederick County" by George Ely Russell, *Western Maryland Genealogy*, Volume 5, No. 1 (1989), pp. 8-10}

THOMAS DELOUGHERY

Thomas Deloughery, physician,, of Baltimore, MD, died at Millerstown, OH on 15 Sep 1832, aged 38. {Ref: *Baltimore American*, 6 Nov 1832, abstracted by Lorrie A. E. Erdman}

JAMES DEVAUN

James Devaun served in the Maryland Line during the Revolutionary War and later moved to Ohio. He applied for a pension in Licking Co., OH on 5 May 1818, aged 66, but in 1820 he stated he was aged 70. He had a wife **Lydia Devaun**, but no other family lived at home. {Ref: *Genealogical Abstracts of Revolutionary War Pension Files*, by Virgil D. White (1990), Application S44132}

GEORGE DICKINSON

George Dickinson was born in Lincolnshire, England in 1758 and came to America when he was aged 10. He settled in Baltimore Co., MD and lived at Gunpowder Falls at the time of his enlistment in the Revolutionary War. In 1802 he moved to Washington Co., PA and in 1821 he moved to Tuscarawas Co., OH. He applied for a pension in Hamilton Co., OH on 11 Sep 1832, aged 74. {Ref: *Genealogical Abstracts of Revolutionary War Pension Files*, by Virgil D. White (1990), Application S4277}

JOSEPH DICKSON

Joseph Dickson was born on 17 or 23 Dec 1756 and enlisted in Baltimore, MD during the Revolutionary War. He married in Baltimore in June, 1783 (wife not named) and they moved to Ohio in 1817. He applied for a pension in Licking Co., OH on 11 Jul 1840, aged 83. At that time he had a wife nearly his age and they depended upon an only son (not named) for support. {Ref: *Genealogical Abstracts of Revolutionary War Pension Files*, by Virgil D. White (1990), Application R2944}

MOSES DILLON

On the 23rd day of the 6th month, 1813, **Moses Dillon** (sometimes spelled

Dillion) requested a certificate of removal from the Gunpowder Monthly Meeting, Baltimore Co., MD, for himself and his wife **Hannah Dillon** to Still Water Monthly Meeting in the State of Ohio. {Ref: Gunpowder Quaker Monthly Meeting Minutes}

On the 11th day of the 8th month, 1813, **Moses Dillon** requested a certificate of removal from the Baltimore Monthly Meeting, Western District, to the Still Water Monthly Meeting in Ohio for himself and his son **Isaac Dillon**. {Ref: Baltimore Quaker Monthly Meeting Minutes}

Moses Dillon, of Muskingum Co., OH, son of **Peter and Elizabeth Dillon** (both deceased), and **Martha Amoss**, of Harford Co., OH, daughter of **William and Susanna Amoss** (the latter deceased), married at Little Falls in Harford Co., MD on the 12th day of the 10th month, 1826. {Ref: Little Falls Monthly Meeting, Record of Marriage Certificates, 1818-1873, pp. 21-22}

WILLIAM J. DISNEY

William J. Disney was born on 17 Dec 1789 and enrolled at Annapolis, MD during the War of 1812. He served as a sergeant in the company of Lieut. **Francis Bealmear** for 29 days in July-August, 1813. **Richard J. Disney, Richard D. Disney**, and **Thomas Disney** served as privates in the same company. William married **Amelia Elliott** in Anne Arundel Co., MD on 26 Feb 1807 (by Rev. **Greenbury Pumphrey**, a Methodist minister). They subsequently moved to Ohio and William died in Clinton Township, Knox County, on 30 Mar 1842. **Gilman Bryant** appeared at that time and attested to a family record that *"William J. Disney departed this life the 30th day of March in the year of our Lord 1842, aged 62 years, 3 months and 13 days."* **William A.** Disney stated he was acquainted with **William J. Disney**, but no relationship was given. **Amelia Disney**, applied for bounty land (warrant 55-rej-23760) in Miller Township, Knox Co., OH, on 11 Feb 1856, aged 67. {Ref: *Maryland Militia, War of 1812, Volume 4, Anne Arundel & Calvert Counties*, by F. Edward Wright, pp. 15, 80}

ELIJAH DORMAN

Elijah Dorman, of Salisbury, Worcester Co., MD, married **Elizabeth Shockley** and moved to Sparta Township, Dearborn Co., IN circa 1820. Their son **John Dorman** married **Jane Truitt** (daughter of **Riley and Elizabeth Truitt** who had moved in 1817 from Worcester Co., MD to what is now the town of Sparta, IN). The children of **John and Jane Dorman** were **Frank R. Dorman, John S. Dorman, H. J. Dorman, Charles W. Dorman**, and **America A. Dorman**. {Ref: *History of Dearborn and Ohio Counties, Indiana* (1885), pp. 559, 690-691}

JOHN DORNECK

John Dorneck (sometimes spelled Dornick), of Cecil Co., MD, served as a private during the War of 1812 in the company of Capt. **James Gerry**, having volunteered at West Nottingham on or about 15 Aug 1814 and serving on active duty from 26 Aug to 27 Oct 1814. He subsequently moved to Ohio and applied for bounty land in Flushing Township, Belmont County, on 8 Mar 1852, aged 56. He applied again for bounty land (warrant 55-120-24945) on 9 Apr 1855, aged 60, and his claim was witnessed by **John Clevinger** and **William J. Chandler**, of Belmont Co., OH. {Ref: *Maryland Militia, War of 1812, Volume 3, Cecil & Harford Counties*, by F. Edward Wright, pp. 17, 46}

MARY DORSEY

Mary Dorsey moved from Baltimore, MD to Ohio (county not stated), with a certificate from the Methodist Episcopal Church, on 16 Aug 1832. {Ref: Class Lists, Baltimore City Station, Methodist Episcopal Church}

JOHN DOWNEY

John Downey was born in Hagerstown, MD on 12 Aug 1786 and married **Susannah Selwood** (b. 1791) on 7 Sep 1807. They moved to Washington Co., PA, then to Hamilton Co., OH, and in 1818 to Rising Sun, Dearborn Co., IN. Their son **Alexander C. Downey** was born in Ohio on 10 Sep 1817 and married **Sophia J. Tapley** on 19 Apr 1846. He became a judge and was dean of DePauw University. {Ref: *History of Dearborn and Ohio Counties, Indiana* (1885), pp. 694-695}

THOMAS DOWNEY

Thomas Downey was born in 1754 in Frederick Co., MD and served in the Pennsylvania Line during the Revolutionary War. He subsequently moved to Ohio and applied for a pension on 16 May 1818 in Pickaway Co., OH. On 5 Sep 1822 he lived in Henry Co., KY, aged 69 (no wife or children) and died on 15 Sep 1823. {Ref: *Genealogical Abstracts of Revolutionary War Pension Files*, by Virgil D. White (1990), Application S35895}

JOSEPH DRAKE

Joseph Drake was born circa 1748 in Somerset Co., NJ and lived within 6 miles of Hagerstown, MD at the time of his enlistment in the Revolutionary War. He served as second sergeant in the militia company of Capt. **James Walling** in Washington Co., MD in 1776-1777 and second lieutenant in the company of Capt. **James Patterson** on 21 Nov 1780. After the war Joseph moved to Juniata, PA and then went to Ohio. He applied for a pension in Warren County on 14 Jul 1836, aged 88 or 89. {Ref: *Genealogical Abstracts of Revolutionary War Pension Files*, by Virgil D. White (1990), Application S9387; *Archives of Maryland*, Volume 45, p. 220; *The Maryland Militia in the Revolutionary War*, by S. Eugene Clements & F. Edward Wright, p. 238}

DRIGGS FAMILY

Sarah Driggs removed from Baltimore, MD to Ohio (county not stated) in 1825. **Nathaniel Driggs** removed to Ohio (county not stated) on 8 May 1826. **Asa Driggs**, formerly of Baltimore, MD, wrote his will on 11 Nov 1818 on the Island of New Providence in the Bahama Islands (codicil dated 28 Jan 1819) and mentioned his siblings, viz., **Chloe Johnson** (wife of **Abijah Johnson**, of Baltimore, MD), **Hannah Barnes** (wife of **Oliver Barnes**, of Middleton, CT), and

66

Sarah Driggs, Nathaniel Driggs, Daniel Driggs, Joseph Driggs, Seth Driggs, and Elias Driggs (all of Baltimore, MD in 1819). His will was recorded in Baltimore circa 3 Aug 1829. {Ref: Class Lists, Baltimore City Station, Methodist Episcopal Church; Baltimore County, Maryland Will Book 13, pp. 319-324}

ISAAC DUKES

Isaac Dukes claimed that he served in the Maryland militia and in privateer service during the Revolutionary War. He may have been the Isaac Dukes, son of William Dukes, who was aged 16 when he was bound out (indentured) by the Worcester County Court on 10 Oct 1780 to learn the trade of a farmer; if so, he was born in 1764. Isaac Dukes married Elizabeth King (b. 12 Jul 1772) in Worcester Co., MD in April, 1793 and their children were as follows:

1. Davis Dukes (b. 18 Jan 1794)
2. Mary Dukes (b. -- May 1796)
3. James Dukes (b. 1798)
4. Isaac Dukes, Jr. (b. 1800)
5. Elizabeth Dukes (b. -- Jul 1802)
6. Katharine Dukes (b. 1806)
7. Spencer Dukes (b. 1808)
8. Samuel Dukes (b. 1811)

Isaac Dukes moved to Concord Township, Ross Co., OH in 1812 and applied for a pension on 17 Oct 1832. He died on 17 Apr 1835 in Clinton Co., IN and Elizabeth Dukes applied for a widow's pension on 11 Feb 1840, aged 68. {Ref: *Genealogical Abstracts of Revolutionary War Pension Files*, by Virgil D. White (1990), Application R3111; *Worcester County, Maryland, Orphans Court Proceedings, 1777-1800*, by David V. Heise, p. 20}

RICHARDSON DUNN

Richardson Dunn, of Cecil Co., MD, was drafted during the War of 1812 and served as a private in the company of Capt. Andrew Porter in 1814. He married Sarah Welch or Sarah Grayson either on 14 Sep 1808 in Elkton, MD or 16 Mar 1809 in Chester Co., PA (both names, dates and places were given, but no marriage license was found in Cecil Co., MD records). They later moved to Indiana where Richardson died in Floyd County on 7 Mar 1844. Sarah Dunn applied for bounty land on 1 Nov 1850, aged 60. John Welch and Harry Welch, of Floyd Co., IN, stated that Sarah and Richardson Dunn raised a large family of eight children *"who are adults now living."* On 1 May 1855, aged 66, Sarah Dunn applied again for bounty land (warrant 55-rej-170569) and stated that her husband served under Capt. Andy Porter and during the time he was home on furlough on account of sickness in the family his company was dispersed. {Ref: *Maryland Militia, War of 1812, Volume 3, Cecil & Harford Counties*, by F. Edward Wright, p. 46}

JOSHUA DURHAM

Joshua Durham, son of Samuel Durham (b. 1699, Durham, England, d. 1 Sep 1772, Harford Co., MD) and Eleanor Smissen (d. 12 Apr 1784, Harford Co.,

MD), was born on 1 Jan 1733 in Baltimore (now Harford) Co., MD and married **Sarah Thompson** (b. 7 Sep 1733, MD, daughter of **Andrew and Elizabeth Thompson**) on 10 Jan 1754 in Baltimore Co., MD. Their children were as follows:

1. **John Durham** (29 Jan 1755 - 1841)
2. **Elizabeth Durham** (9 Feb 1757 - 1842)
3. **Daniel Durham** (3 Jan 1760 - 1847)
4. **Benjamin Durham** (6 Mar 1762 - 1850)
5. **Alazanah or Aliceanna Durham** (20 Nov 1764 - 1847) married **Uriah Burdsal** (b. 6 Dec 1809, Hamilton Co., OH, d. 14 Feb 1904, Newtown, OH) and their children were as follows:
    5-1. **Aquila D. Burdsal** (1 Jan 1832 - 19 Mar 1837)
    5-2. **Aaron Burdsal** (4 Oct 1833 - 21 Jan 1854)
    5-3. **Elizabeth Burdsal** (17 Oct 1835 - 1903)
    5-4. **Leander G. Burdsal** (17 Nov 1837 - 1904)
    5-5. **Harriet Burdsal** (8 Dec 1839 - 24 Sep 1904)
    5-6. **John D. Burdsal** (16 Oct 1841 - 23 Apr 1843)
    5-7. **Charley H. Burdsal** (19 Sep 1843 - 8 Oct 1844)
    5-8. **Laura Burdsal** (17 Jul 1845 - 12 Sep 1906)
    5-9. **Riley G. Burdsal** (b. 25 Oct 1847)
    5-10. **Belle Burdsal** (1 Jul 1850 - 2 Apr 1908)
6. **Sarah Durham** (23 May 1767 - 29 Nov 1773)
7. **Clemency Durham** (5 Jun 1769 - 16 Jan 1801, OH)
8. **Prescilla Durham** (11 May 1771 - 9 Jul 1786, PA)
9. **Hannah Durham** (24 May 1773 - Dec 1795, PA)
10. **Martha Durham** (13 Mar 1777 - 1852, Butler Co., OH)
11. **Aquila Durham** (13 May 1779 - 30 Sep 1870, OH) married **Harriet Thompson** (b. 18 Apr 1785 on the Eastern Shore of Maryland, d. 30 Jan 1868 at Homestead, Hamilton Co., OH) on 24 Jun 1804 in Brown Co., OH; their children (all born in Hamilton County except John) were as follows:
    11-1. **John Durham** (17 Apr 1805 - 18 Jun 1873) married **Louise Webb** (1812-1874) in Hamilton Co., OH on 28 Dec 1829 and later divorced; married second to **Charlotte Ferrill** (1823, KY - 1868, IL) in Louisville, KY in 1841; their children were as follows:
        11-1-1. **Aquila Durham** (1842-1888, TN)
        11-1-2. **Leander Durham** (1848-1889, IN)
        11-1-3. **Harriet E. Durham** (1851-1856, KY)
        11-1-4. **Joseph D. Durham** (1855-1855, KY)
        11-1-5. **Joshua Durham** (1857-1857, KY)
    11-2. **Sarah B. Durham** (5 May 1807 - 21 Nov 1854)
    11-3. **Alazanah Durham** (24 Dec 1809 - 24 Feb 1903)
    11-4. **Hannah Durham** (8 Oct 1813 - 11 Aug 1884) married **Bennett Barrow** (1809-1890) in Hamilton Co., OH on 25 Jan 1835; their children were as follows:
        11-4-1. **Louisa Sydney Barrow** (b. 1836)
        11-4-2. **Harriet G. Barrow** (1838-1922)

11-4-3. **Mary J. Barrow** (b. 1841)

11-4-4. **Aquila D. Barrow** (1843-1921)

11-4-5. **America Barrow** (b. 1845)

11-4-6. **Thomas L. H. Barrow** (1849-1849)

11-5. **Harriet Durham** (22 Feb 1815 - 10 Aug 1902) married **Ferdinand Webb** (1807-1879) in Hamilton Co., OH on 28 Feb 1841; their children were as follows:

11-5-1. **Howard Webb** (1842-1858, OH)

11-5-2. **Anna Webb** (1844-1846, OH)

11-5-3. **Alvin C. Webb** (1847-1883, OH)

11-5-4. **Sarah Webb** (1850-1850, OH)

11-5-5. **Harriet Webb** (b. 1851, OH)

11-5-6. **Ferdinand Webb** (1854-1917, VA)

11-6. **Winfield S. Durham** (19 Jun 1817 - 15 Feb 1898) married first to **Narcissa Wilmington** (1821-1859) in Ohio on 4 Jul 1844 and second to **Ellen Williams** (b. 1841, KY) on 16 Nov 1859; his children were as follows:

11-6-1. **William Durham** (1845-1925, OH)

11-6-2. **Mary A. Durham** (1847-1885, NC)

11-6-3. **Eliza Durham** (1853-1926, OH)

11-6-4. **Alice I. Durham** (1856-1937, OH)

11-6-5. **Charles Durham** (1861-1917, NJ)

11-6-6. **Nellie Durham** (1865-1873, CA)

11-7. **Aquila Durham** (1 Jul 1820 - 7 Mar 1872) married **Sarah Thompson** (1820, OH - 1911) in Hamilton Co., OH on 24 Dec 1841; their children were as follows:

11-7-1. **Ellen Durham** (b. 1842)

11-7-2. **Hattie A. Durham** (1844-1912)

11-7-3. **Solon Durham** (b. 1846)

11-7-4. **Samuel Durham** (b. 1853)

11-7-5. **Manford Durham** (1857-1872)

11-7-6. **William B. Durham** (1862 - 1865)

11-8. **Leander Durham** (4 Apr 1823 - 21 Oct 1902) married **Eugenie Perdrizet** (b. 1831, Herancourt, France - d. 1871, Hamilton Co., OH) on 6 Feb 1851 in Clermont Co., OH; their children were as follows:

11-8-1. **Edward Durham** (1851-1916)

11-8-2. **Emma Durham** (b. 1855, m. **Mr. Webb**)

11-8-3. **James B. Durham** (b. 1857)

11-9. **Warren Durham** (23 Nov 1826 - 1 Feb 1897) married **Caroline Troy** (b. 1835, IN - 1873, OH) on 14 Oct 1850 in Clermont Co., OH

11-10. **Thompson Durham** (12 Jun 1829 - 20 Jul 1915) married **Mary Eliza Ellis** (b. 22 Aug 1831, St. Mary's Co., MD - d. 9 Mar 1917, OH) on 16 Jan 1851 in Hamilton Co., OH

Joshua Durham died in Hamilton Co., OH on 2 Sep 1829 and **Sarah Durham** died on 13 Oct 1800. {Ref: *Biography of the Durham Family* (author unknown; title page missing; a photocopy of this book is on file at the Historical

Society of Harford County); for early Durham family history see *Baltimore County Families, 1659-1759*, by Robert W. Barnes (1989), pp. 191-192}

JAMES DUNCAN

James Duncan moved from Maryland (county not stated) in 1815 to Sparta Township, Dearborn Co., IN and died there in 1864. {Ref: *History of Dearborn and Ohio Counties, Indiana* (1885), p. 559}

SAMUEL DYER

Samuel Dyer was born in what is now Montgomery Co., MD on 2 Jan 1751 and served in Maryland during the Revolutionary War. He married **Elizabeth Griffin** (b. 19 Oct 1759) on 10 Oct 1779 in Montgomery Co., MD. Their children were **Thomas Dyer, Sarah Dyer, George Swann Dyer, Mary "Polly" Dyer, Elizabeth "Betsy" Dyer, Nancy Dyer, Samuel Dyer, Jr., Edward Dyer, and William Dyer**. Samuel died in 1818 en route to Indiana and **Elizabeth Dyer** died in 1852 in Green Co., IN. {Ref: DAR Application 427325; *A Roster of Revolutionary Ancestors of the Indiana Daughters of the American Revolution* (1976), p. 100}

HENRY EDGELL

Henry Edgell was a farmer when drafted at Dick's Old Field in Caroline Co., MD to serve as a private in the 19th Regiment during the War of 1812. He was in the company of Capt. **Elijah Satterfield** from 15 Aug to 18 Aug 1813 and in the company of Capt. **Peter Willis** from 19 Aug to 1 Sep 1813. He stated that he had black *(sic)* eyes, black hair and a dark complexion. After his discharge he lived in Caroline Co., MD for about 12 years, then moved to Preble Co., OH for about 5 years, then to Elkhart Co., IN, near the town of Goshen, for about 12 years, then to Van Buren Township in Kosciusko Co., IN for 22 years, and then to Middletown in Logan Co., IL for 13 years. He had applied for bounty land in Kosciusko Co., IN on 17 May 1855, aged 66, and received 160 acres. He also applied for a pension (SC-23267) in Middletown, Logan Co., IL on 27 Apr 1878, aged 88. {Ref: *Maryland Militia, War of 1812, Volume 1, Eastern Shore*, by F. Edward Wright, pp. 81, 82, 110; *Index of War of 1812 Pension Files*, by Virgil D. White, p. 653}

THOMAS EDWARDS

Thomas Edwards was born in 1745 and served in Maryland during the Revolutionary War. He subsequently moved to Ohio and applied for a pension in Champaign County on 3 Jun 1818, aged 73, and indicated he had no family. {Ref: *Genealogical Abstracts of Revolutionary War Pension Files*, by Virgil D. White (1990), Application S42695}

JAMES EGAN

James Egan, of Cecil Co., MD, served in the War of 1812, having volunteered as a private under Capt. **George W. Lightner** at Battle Swamp in August, 1814. He later moved to Indiana and applied for bounty land (warrant 55-

160-19476) in Hendricks County on 17 Apr 1855, aged 69. Witnesses were **Cornelius Bantz** and **John Miller**, both of said county. {Ref: *Maryland Militia, War of 1812, Volume 3, Cecil & Harford Counties*, by F. Edward Wright, pp. 30, 46}

JOHN ELDER

John Elder enrolled in Anne Arundel Co., MD during the War of 1812, served on active duty as a private in the company of Capt. **Roderick Burgess** from 22 Jul to 19 Sep 1814 and was discharged at Baltimore in mid October. He later moved to Ohio and applied for bounty land in Perry County on 9 Nov 1850, aged 69. He applied again for bounty land (warrant 55-120-24951) on 12 Apr 1855, aged 75. Witnesses were **Josiah Defenbaugh** and **Jacob Thomas**. {Ref: *Maryland Militia, War of 1812, Volume 4, Anne Arundel & Calvert Counties*, by F. Edward Wright, pp. 42, 83}

L. G. ELDER

L. G. Elder (b. 1800) moved with his parents (names not given) from Maryland (county not stated) in 1808 to Hogan Township, Dearborn Co., IN. {Ref: *History of Dearborn and Ohio Counties, Indiana* (1885), p. 480}

WILLIAM ELKINS

William Elkins was born circa 1733 and enlisted on 8 Aug 1780 as a private at Frederick, MD during the Revolutionary War and marched to Annapolis under Capt. Beatty. After the war he moved to Ohio and applied for a pension in Jefferson County on 22 May 1818, aged 85. In 1820 he lived alone at Mount Pleasant, OH. {Ref: *Genealogical Abstracts of Revolutionary War Pension Files*, by Virgil D. White (1990), Application 42703; *Archives of Maryland*, Volume 18, p. 344}

SAMUEL ELLIOTT

Samuel Elliott (sometimes spelled Ellett) was born in Baltimore Co., MD on 31 Jan 1757 and served in the Revolutionary War as a private in the company of Capt. **William Webb** in Harford Co., MD on 14 Oct 1776. He was also a signer of the Association of Freemen in Deer Creek Upper Hundred in 1776. Samuel married **Catharine or Keziah Webb** in the spring of 1777. After the war they lived in Washington Co. and Allegheny Co., PA before moving to Trumbull Co., OH where **Catharine or Keziah Elliott** died in the spring of 1813. **Samuel Elliott** applied for a pension at Springfield, Portage Co., OH on 7 Jul 1834 and died on 14 Mar 1840 (one source stated 1841). A son, **John Elliott**, was aged 58 in 1853 and lived in Springfield, OH. {Ref: *Genealogical Abstracts of Revolutionary War Pension Files*, by Virgil D. White (1990), Application R3306; *Revolutionary Patriots of Harford County, Maryland, 1775-1783*, by Henry C. Peden, Jr. (1985), p. 73}

JOHN ELLIS

John Ellis served as a private in the company of Capt. **John Naylor** in the War of 1812 and enrolled at Bowen's Old Fields in Prince George's Co., MD around June, 1813. He subsequently moved to Indiana and applied for bounty land (warrant 50-rej-79444) in Bartholomew County on 19 Feb 1851, aged 65. {Ref: *Maryland Militia, War of 1812, Volume 6, Prince George's County*, by F. Edward Wright, p. 34}

SAMUEL ELLIS

Samuel Ellis was born on 22 Oct 1752 or 1754 in Frederick Co., MD and lived in Washington Co., MD at the time of his enlistment in the Revolutionary War. He served as a sergeant under the command of Col. **John Stevenson** who built Fort McIntosh at the mouth of the Tuscarawas. **Samuel Ellis** was also listed as an Associator in Frederick Co., MD in December, 1775. He married **Mary Fry** (b. 17 Apr 1760, VA, d. 1837, OH) and subsequently moved to Ohio. He applied for a pension in Brown County on 10 Jan 1834 and died on 3 Apr 1848. No family was mentioned in his application, but he had the following children:
1. **James Ellis**
2. **Noah Ellis**
3. **Abraham Ellis** (b. 12 Nov 1791) m. **Elizabeth Ellis**
4. **Samuel Ellis, Jr.** (b. 17 Mar 1795) m. **Sarah Ellis**
5. **Matilda Ellis**
6. **Mary Ellis**
7. **Christina Ellis**
8. **India Ann Ellis**
9. **Nancy Ellis**
10. **Rebecca Ellis**

{Ref: *Genealogical Abstracts of Revolutionary War Pension Files*, by Virgil D. White (1990), Application S8400; DAR Applications 506598 and 603632; *Index of Patriots, Revolutionary War Heroes and Their Families, Cincinnati Chapter DAR, 1893-1981*, by Jeraldyne Beets Clipson and Katherine Brewer Brinkdopke (1983), p. 103; "Journal of the Committee of Observation of the Middle District of Frederick County, September 12, 1775 - October 24, 1776," *Maryland Historical Magazine*, Volume XI, p. 166}

THOMAS ELSEY

Thomas Elsey was born on 16 May 1760 in Maryland and moved with his father (not named) to Fauquier Co., VA. He then moved to Augusta Co., VA where he lived at the time of his enlistment in the Revolutionary War. His brother **Edward Elsey** also served in the Virginia Troops and was at the Seige of Yorktown in 1781. He had other brothers, but no names were given. **Thomas Elsey** moved to Ohio and lived in Violet Township in Fairfield County in 1829. He applied for a pension in Walnut Township in Pickaway County on 10 Aug 1832. **Patrick Elsey** lived in Pickerington in Fairfield County in 1832, but no relationship was given. {Ref: *Genealogical Abstracts of Revolutionary War Pension Files*, by Virgil D. White (1990), Application S8404}

72

THOMAS ELWELL

Thomas Elwell (sometimes spelled Ellwell) served as a corporal in the 3rd and 4th Virginia Lines during the Revolutionary War. He married **Elizabeth** ---- in Frederick Co., MD, near the Baltimore County line (which is now part of Carroll County), in December, 1786 between Christmas and New Year's Day. Their children were as follows:

1. **Hannah Elwell** (b. 30 Jul 1787 and married **Nathaniel Middleton**)
2. **David Elwell** (b. 15 May 1789)
3. **Susannah Elwell** (b. 23 Jun 1791)
4. **Jonathan Elwell** (b. 20 Mar 1793)
5. **Thomas Elwell, Jr.** (b. 11 Apr 1797)
6. **Mary Elwell** (b. 15 Apr 1801)
7. **Sary Elwell** (b. 18 Oct 1803)
8. **Elizabeth Elwell** (b. 15 Dec 1806)

Thomas Ewell lived in Ohio and applied for a pension in Knox County on 4 Apr 1818. He died on 21 May 1825 and **Elizabeth Elwell** applied for a widow's pension in Knox County on 6 Aug 1844, aged 80. Their daughter **Hannah Middleton**, of Liberty Township, Fairfield Co., OH, made an affidavit on 22 Jan 1852 that her mother was deceased. {Ref: *Genealogical Abstracts of Revolutionary War Pension Files*, by Virgil D. White (1990), Application W7096; *Historical Register of Virginians in the Revolution, 1775-1783*, by John H. Gwathmey (1938), pp. 254-255}

ISAIAH ELY

On the 6th day of the 11th month, 1820, at a meeting held at Deer Creek Monthly Meeting in Harford Co., MD, it was announced that word had been received from the Concord Monthly Meeting (in Belmont Co., OH) that **Isaiah Ely** had accomplished his marriage with **Elizabeth Kennard**, a first cousin. He was subsequently disowned *"for outgoing in marriage"* on the 1st day of the 1st month, 1821. {Ref: Deer Creek Quaker Monthly Meeting Minutes}

SAMUEL EMBREE

Samuel Embree requested a certificate of removal from the Baltimore Monthly Meeting, Western District, to the Short Creek Monthly Meeting in Ohio on the 8th day of the 1st month, 1812, for himself, his wife **Hannah Embree**, and their six minor children, **Lydia Embree, Joseph Embree, Phebe Embree, John Embree, Jesse Embree** and **Israel Embree**, having already moved there. **Jesse Embree** requested a certificate to Waynesville Monthly Meeting in Ohio on the 10th day of the 12th month, 1813. {Ref: Baltimore Quaker Monthly Meeting Minutes}

JOHN EMMITT

John Emmitt (sometimes spelled Emmett) was born on 22 Oct 1759 near Elkton, Cecil Co., MD and lived there at the time of his enlistment in the

Revolutionary War. He enrolled as a private in the company of Capt. **Walter Alexander** on 25 Jul 1776. **David Emmitt** served in the same company in 1776 and **Abram Emmitt** took the Oath of Allegiance in 1778. After the war John moved to Pennsylvania, then to Virginia, then to Ohio, then to Illinois, then to Indiana, and then back to Ohio. He had been a minister of the Methodist Episcopal Church for many years and he had also represented Pickaway Co., OH in the State Legislature. John applied for a pension in Scioto Township, Ross Co., OH on 21 Mar 1833 and one of his sons (names not given) lived in Indiana. In 1839 he moved to White Co., IL to live with his daughter (name not given) and in September, 1844 he moved back to Ohio to live with another daughter (name not given). He died in Licking Co., OH in 1847. The first wife of **John Emmitt** was **Margery ----** and his second wife was **Margaret B. ----**, whom he married in 1808. His children were as follows:

1. **Mary Emmitt**
2. **Anna Emmitt**
3. **Rebecca Emmitt**
4. **Abraham Emmitt**
5. **Daniel Decatur Emmitt**
6. **Lafayette Emmitt**
7. **William Yates Emmitt**
8. **John Emmitt, Jr.**
9. **James Emmitt**
10. **Margaret Emmitt**
11. **Margaret B. Emmitt**

Margaret B. Emmitt applied for a widow's pension in Jefferson Co., IA on 25 May 1855, aged 90, and stated she had married John on 7 or 8 Jun 1808 and they had one living child (name not given), aged 42. {Ref: *Genealogical Abstracts of Revolutionary War Pension Files*, by Virgil D. White (1990), Application W8692; DAR Application 430911; *A Roster of Revolutionary Ancestors of the Indiana Daughters of the American Revolution* (1976), p. 108; *Revolutionary Patriots of Cecil County, Maryland, 1775-1783*, by Henry C. Peden, Jr. (1991), p. 32}

ISAAC ENOCH

Isaac Enoch and **Nancy Rollins**, of Maryland (county not stated), married in Indiana (county not stated) on 19 Aug 1819. {Ref: *Maryland Revolutionary Records*, by Harry Wright Newman (1938), p. 113}

SIMON ESSIG

Simon Essig was born in Hagerstown, MD on 27 Dec 1754 and served as a private in Northampton Co., PA in the militia company of Capt. **Frederick Klinhautz** during the Revolutionary War. In 1781 he married **Juliana Schnarin** (b. 5 Apr 1761) and later moved to Ohio. Their children were as follows:

1. **Polly Essig** (b. 1782) married **George Wike**
2. **Elizabeth Essig** (b. 1784) married **John Becher**
3. **John Essig** (22 Sep 1786 - 3 Nov 1857) married **Susan Holtz** (26 Aug 1789 - 7 Sep 1878) in 1808

4. **Adam Essig** (b. 1788) married **Catherine Lichenwalter**
5. **Jacob Essig** (b. 1791) married **Elizabeth Weaver**
6. **George Essig** (b. 1794) married **Catherine Schollenberger**
7. **Sally Essig** (b. 1797) married **John Trump**
8. **Julia Essig** (b. 1797) married **Jacob Troxel**
9. **Samuel Essig** (b. 1801) married **Salome Rank**
10. **William Essig** (b. 1804) married **Anna M. Haul**
11. **Catherine Essig** (b. 1804) married **Peter Pontius**
12. **Rebecca Essig** (b. 1806) married **Jacob Pontius**

Juliana Essig died on 30 Aug 1844 and **Simon Essig** died on 18 Mar 1852 in Stark Co., OH. {Ref: DAR Application 469394; *A Roster of Revolutionary Ancestors of the Indiana Daughters of the American Revolution* (1976), p. 109}

EDWARD EVANS

Edward Evans, of Cecil Co., MD, served in the War of 1812 as a sergeant in the company of Capt. **Thomas Courtney**. He later moved to Indiana and applied for bounty land (warrant 50-rej-38602) in Decatur County on 2 Nov 1850, aged 63. {Ref: *Maryland Militia, War of 1812, Volume 3, Cecil & Harford Counties*, by F. Edward Wright, p. 47}

WALTER EVANS

Walter Evans was born on 25 Jul 1762 and served in Maryland during the Revolutionary War. He was enlisted by Capt. Lynn on 15 Aug 1781 for 3 years as a private in the 4th MD Line. By March, 1782 he was a corporal, but had not been heard of since the March muster. He subsequently moved to Ohio and applied for a pension in Shelby County on 4 Apr 1836. He died on 22 Aug 1838 and his widow **Nancy Evans** died in January, 1846. The only surviving children in 1854 were **Philip Evans** (of Shelby Co., OH), **Nancy Wilson** and **Jeremiah Evans** (residences not indicated). **John Evans** witnessed Philip's affidavit, but his relationship was not given. {Ref: *Genealogical Abstracts of Revolutionary War Pension Files*, by Virgil D. White (1990), Application R3395; *Archives of Maryland*, Volume 18, pp. 402, 458}

HORACE FAIRALL

Horace Fairall was born in 1794 in Prince George's Co., MD and served as a private during the War of 1812. At enlistment he was aged 18, stood 5 ft. 8 in. tall, with dark hair, blue eyes and fair complexion. He enrolled in Prince George's County in April, 1812 and was discharged at Annapolis in the fall of 1814. He resided in Maryland until 1816 and then moved to Muskingum Co., OH. He applied for a pension (SC-34519) at Frazeysburg, OH on 7 May 1880, aged 85. His wife **Dorathea Fairall**, aged 52, witnessed his application and stated her husband often told of his mother and sisters crying for him when he went to leave for the war. His nephew **Levi Fairall**, aged 43, son of a brother of **Horace Fairall**, also witnessed the application and remembered his father (name not given) often told him of Horace going to the War of 1812. {Ref: *Maryland Militia, War of 1812, Volume 6,*

Prince George's County, by F. Edward Wright, p. 35}

NATHANIEL FARMER

Nathaniel Farmer was born circa 1757 and served in Maryland during the Revolutionary War as a sergeant in the 3rd MD Line from 1777 until March, 1779. He subsequently moved to Indiana and applied for a pension in Fayette County on 9 Oct 1827, aged 70. His wife was aged 61 and they had children, all away from home, but no names were given. {Ref: *Genealogical Abstracts of Revolutionary War Pension Files*, by Virgil D. White (1990), Application S35917; *Archives of Maryland*, Volume 18, p. 109}

EDWARD ANDREW FARQUHAR

Edward Andrew Farquhar, a minor, requested a certificate of removal on the 7th day of the 12th month, 1821, from the Baltimore Monthly Meeting, Western District, to the Cannel Monthly Meeting in Ohio, having already removed there. {Ref: Baltimore Quaker Monthly Meeting Minutes}

MALEN FARQUHAR

Mahlon Farquhar, son of **Allen Farquhar** and **Phebe Hibberd**, was born on the 27th day of the 6th month, 1778. **Malen Farquhar** requested a certificate of removal from the Baltimore Monthly Meeting, Western District, to the Centre Monthly Meeting in Ohio on the 9th day of the 12th month, 1808, having already moved there. {Re: Pipe Creek and Baltimore Quaker Monthly Meeting Minutes}

CHRISTIAN FAST

Christian Fast, son of **Nicholas Fast**, was born on 22 Jun 1762 in Frederick Co., MD and when he was 10 years old his parents moved to Monongahela Co., VA. He enlisted there during the Revolutionary War and served in the company of Capt. **Joseph Meeks** in 1778. He also served as a substitute for his brother **Jacob Fast**. (For a narrative about his capture by the Indians on the falls of the Ohio River, see *History of Knox County, Ohio*, by N. N. Hill, Jr. (1881), p. 189) Christian later moved to Fayette Co., PA and enlisted there in 1781. He married **Ann Barbara or Anna Barbary Mason** (b. 9 Sep 1767 or 1769) on 1 Aug 1783 and their children were as follows:

1. **Martin Fast** (12 Jun 1784 - 13 Jun 1838) married **Catharine Blosser** (1791-1876)
2. **Nicholas Fast** (b. 11 Jun 1786)
3. **Jacob Fast** (b. 13 Mar 1788 and lived in Richland Co., OH in 1843)
4. **Christian Fast** (15 Jan 1790 - 1 Sep 1792)
5. **Ann Catrine Margret Fast** (b. 27 Jul 1792)
6. **William Fast** (b. 24 Mar 1794)
7. **Christian Fast, Jr.** (b. 6 Oct 1795)
8. **David Fast** (b. 1 Aug 1797)
9. **Francis Fast** (b. 19 Jun 1799)
10. **Barbara Fast** (b. 12 Feb 1801)

11. **Nancy Fast** (7 Nov 1802 - 19 Sep 1804)
12. **Elizabeth Fast** (b. 29 Aug 1804)
13. **George Fast** (b. 4 Jun 1807)
14. **John Fast** (b. 10 Jul 1809)
15. **Christeany Fast** (b. 13 May 1811)

In 1816 **Christian Fast** moved to Orange Township in Richland Co., OH and applied for a pension on 23 Oct 1832. He died on 25 Jun 1841. **Ann Barbara Fast** applied for a widow's pension on 6 Nov 1843. She died on 19 Aug 1855. Other persons named Fast were mentioned in her application as follows:

1. **Jeremiah Fast** (b. 18 Dec 1807, son of **Ann C. Margret Fast**)
2. **John Fast** (b. 16 Oct 1814, son of **Christian Fast, Jr.**)
3. **Martin Fast** (b. 17 Feb 1816)
4. **David Fast** (b. 22 Sep 1818)
5. **Isaac Fast** (b. 19 Mar 1820)
6. **Levina Fast** (b. 22 Apr 1822)
7. **George Fast** (b. 13 Mar 1824)
8. **Clemmer Fast** (b. 24 Mar 1826)
9. **Christian Fast** (b. 12 Oct 1828)
10. **Ann Elizabeth Fast** (b. 24 Jun 1836)

Martin Mason, brother of the widow **Ann Barbara (Mason) Fast**, lived in Richland Co., OH in 1845 and **George Fast** was her guardian in Ashland Co., OH on 21 Apr 1855. {Ref: *Genealogical Abstracts of Revolutionary War Pension Files*, by Virgil D. White (1990), Application W4195; *Historical Register of Virginians in the Revolution, 1775-1783*, by John H. Gwathmey (1938), p. 266; DAR Application 407664; *A Roster of Revolutionary Ancestors of the Indiana Daughters of the American Revolution* (1976), p. 206}

JOHN FERRIS

John Ferris moved from the Federalsburg, MD area to Indiana by way of Wilmington, DE. He removed from the Northwest Fork Monthly Meeting in Caroline Co., MD to the Wilmington Monthly Meeting in Delaware circa 1809. He and his wife **Anna Ferris**, and their son **Joseph Ferris**, were given a certificate of removal at Wilmington which was received by the Milford Monthly Meeting in Wayne Co., IN on the 18th day of the 3rd month, 1829, along with a certificate for sons **Matthew Ferris** and **William Ferris**. Matthew later married **Elizabeth Morris**, daughter of **Aaron and Lydia Morris**, of Wayne Co., IN, at the Milford Meeting House (date not given). {Ref: "Migration of Caroline County Quakers to Indiana," by F. Edward Wright, *Maryland Genealogical Society Bulletin*, Volume 34, No. 3 (1993), p. 283}

PETER FINE

Peter Fine was born in 1750 in Morristown, NJ, moved to Frederick Co., MD when he was 21 years old, and lived there at the time of his enlistment in the Revolutionary War on 1 Jul 1776 as a private in the company of Capt. **Peter Mantz**. He participated in the Battle of Germantown on 4 Oct 1777 and was subsequently discharged. In 1825 he moved to Ohio and applied for a pension in Wayne Township, Knox Co., OH on 27 Sep 1832, aged 82. He stated that he *"had a record of his age on a blank leaf of his father's big Bible which he believes is now in his trunk, but he has been blind and unable to see for more than 14 years. Christopher Myers, William Myers, John Bates, Henry Rhodes, and others of his neighborhood can testify to his character for truth and veracity and good behavior."* On 2 Aug 1837 Peter made another application stating that his certificate had been lost some time between 4 Sep 1835 and 1 Mar 1836 at his residence in Wayne Township, Knox Co., OH, adding that he *"has no recollection of seeing (sic) it after the drawing of his pension on September 4, 1835."* {Ref: *Genealogical Abstracts of Revolutionary War Pension Files*, by Virgil D. White (1990), Application S2209; *Revolutionary Patriots of Frederick County, Maryland, 1775-1783*, by Henry C. Peden, Jr. (1995), pp. 124-125; *Maryland Pension Abstracts: Revolution, War of 1812, and Indian Wars*, by Lucy K. McGhee (1966), p. 26}

BASIL FISHER

Basil Fisher (sometimes spelled **Bazzel Fisher**) enrolled as a private in Anne Arundel Co., MD during the War of 1812 and served at Annapolis in the company of Capt. **Thomas Owings** in the 32nd Regiment from 13 to 26 May 1813. He also claimed he was drafted at New Lisbon, MD around 1 May 1814 and served under Capt. **George Barnes** in the 5th Regiment. He marched to Annapolis, where he was dismissed, and then was again called into service about 15 Aug 1814 and marched to Baltimore. He subsequently moved to Ohio and applied for bounty land (warrant 55-rej-146027) in Guernsey County on 17 Apr 1855, aged 59. Witnesses were **Matthew Doyle** and **Thompson Rose**. {Ref: *Maryland Militia, War of 1812, Volume 4, Anne Arundel & Calvert Counties*, by F. Edward Wright, pp. 41, 84}

JOHN FISHER

John Fisher was born in 1762 in Berks Co., PA, moved to Hagerstown, MD, and lived there at the time of his enlistment in the Revolutionary War. He served as a private in the Select Militia under Capt. **Adam Ott** and was enrolled for service in the Maryland Continental Line on 24 Aug 1781. He subsequently moved to Ohio and applied for a pension in Fairfield County on 5 Nov 1832, aged 70. {Ref: *Genealogical Abstracts of Revolutionary War Pension Files*, by Virgil D. White (1990), Application S2211; *Archives of Maryland*, Volume 18, p. 387; *The Maryland Militia in the Revolutionary War*, by S. Eugene Clements & F. Edward Wright, p. 238}

GEORGE FLECK

George Fleck (sometimes spelled Flick, Flack and Flake), born circa 1755, was enlisted in the Revolutionary War at Hagerstown, Washington Co., MD as a private by Lieut. **Christian Orndorff** on 20 Jul 1776, served under Capt. **John Reynolds** in the county militia in 1776-1777, and also served in the Pennsylvania Line. He was also recruited and passed by County Lieut. **Thomas Sprigg** on 22 Apr 1780. He subsequently moved to Ohio. He applied for a pension at Union Township in Washington County on 14 May 1818, aged 63. In 1821 his wife (name not given) was aged 58 and they had no minor children. {Ref: *Genealogical Abstracts of Revolutionary War Pension Files*, by Virgil D. White (1990), Application S42725; *Archives of Maryland*, Volume 18, pp. 50, 336; *The Maryland Militia in the Revolutionary War*, by S. Eugene Clements & F. Edward Wright, p. 240}

THOMAS FLEMING

Thomas Fleming (sometimes spelled Flemming), of Frederick Co., MD, was a first lieutenant in the 34th Militia Battalion on 15 May 1776 and later promoted to captain during the Revolutionary War. He participated in the battles of Brandywine and Germantown in 1777. Thomas married **Agnes Porter** "about the time of the war" and their children were as follows:

1. **Eleanor Fleming** (1782-1852) married **Mr. Corry** and had 5 children living in 1853, including **William Corry** and **Thomas H. Corry**

2. **Samuel Fleming** (1783-1845) had no living children

3. **Nancy Fleming** (died without issue before 1805)

4. **Alice Fleming** (1787-1809) died unmarried

5. **Mary Fleming** (b. 1788) was a widow in 1853; married Judge **Williamson Dunn** of Madison, IN

6. **Alexander P. Fleming** (b. 1790) lived in Springdale, Hamilton Co., OH in 1853

7. **Thomas Fleming** (1791-1841) died leaving 4 children who were living in 1853, but it was also stated that Thomas, son of Thomas, applied for his father's pension on 8 Feb 1853 in Iroquois Co., IL, aged 60 (there is an obvious error in this record)

8. **Arthur Fleming** (b. 1794) lived in Hamilton Co., OH in 1853

9. **David Fleming** (1796-1851) lived in Iroquois Co., IL and died leaving 2 children

10. **Harriet Fleming** (b. 1803) lived in Butler Co., OH in 1853

Thomas Fleming moved to Ohio in 1805 and settled near the line between Butler and Hamilton Counties. He died a widower at Fort Hambleton in Butler County on 15 Nov 1837, aged about 88. {Ref: *Genealogical Abstracts of Revolutionary War Pension Files*, by Virgil D. White (1990), Application R3607; *Baltimore Sun*, 14 Dec 1837; *Revolutionary Patriots of Frederick County, Maryland, 1775-1783*, by Henry C. Peden, Jr. (1995), pp. 129}

JOHN FLINT

John Flint was born on 6 Jul 1756 in Worcester Co., MD and lived there at the time of his enlistment in the Revolutionary War. He enlisted as a private in the militia company of Capt. **Ebenezer Handy** in the Snow Hill Battalion on 9 Apr 1776 and served in the militia company of Capt. **Robert Handy** in the Wicomico Battalion on 15 Jul 1780. John married **Elizabeth Johnson** and subsequently moved to Indiana where he applied for a pension on 13 Oct 1835 in Bath Township, Franklin County. He died on 13 Aug 1841. {Ref: *Genealogical Abstracts of Revolutionary War Pension Files*, by Virgil D. White (1990), Application R3614;

The Maryland Militia in the Revolutionary War, by S. Eugene Clements & F. Edward Wright, pp. 249, 254; *Revolutionary Patriots of Worcester & Somerset Counties, Maryland, 1775-1783*, by Henry C. Peden, Jr. (1999), p. 101}

JOSEPH R. FOARD

Joseph R. Foard, Esq., formerly of Baltimore, MD and lately of Zanesville, OH, died at Zanesville on 23 Sep 1834. {Ref: *Baltimore American*, 1 Oct 1834, abstracted by Lorrie A. E. Erdman}

AARON FORMAN

Aaron Forman lived in Pennsylvania at the time of the Revolutionary War and he served in the Pennsylvania and Maryland Lines during that war. In 1805 he moved to Ross Co., OH and 20 years later he moved to Delaware Co., OH, where he applied for a pension in April, 1834. {Ref: *Genealogical Abstracts of Revolutionary War Pension Files*, by Virgil D. White (1990), Application S8507}

ISAAC FRAMPTON

Isaac Frampton was born in Caroline Co., MD on the 28th day of the 7th month, 1782 and married **Deborah H. Dawson**, daughter of **Elisha Dawson**, circa 1810. She was born in Caroline Co., MD on the 22nd day of the 9th month, 1789. They were members of the Milford Monthly Meeting (Hicksite) as early as 1828 and lived in or near Milford, IN. Their children were as follows:

1. **William D. Dawson** (b. 26th day of 10th month, 1811, married **Sarah Bell**, daughter of **Lancelot and Mary Bell**, of Milton, IN, and probably moved to Madison Co., IN by 1860)

2. **Rhoda A. Dawson** (b. 3rd day of 6th month, 1814 and married on the 22nd day of the 12th month, 1831 to **George Morris**, son of **Aaron and Lydia Morris**, of Wayne Co., IN)

3. **Margaret Dawson** (married **Henry Puckett**)

Isaac Frampton died testate on the 28th day of the 11th month, 1847 in Milton, IN and **Deborah Frampton** died on the 11th day of the 1st month, 1856. {Ref: "Migration of Caroline County Quakers to Indiana," by F. Edward Wright, *Maryland Genealogical Society Bulletin*, Volume 34, No. 3 (1993), pp. 283-284, citing Wayne County, IN Will Book No. 3, p. 4}

HENRY FRANKS

Henry Franks was born on 29 Jun 1763 or 1764 west of Frederick, MD (now Washington Co.) and lived in German Township, Fayette Co., PA at the time of his enlistment in the Revolutionary War. In 1801 he moved to Columbiana Co., OH and 12 years later moved to Chippewa Township, Wayne Co., OH, where he applied for a pension on 3 Sep 1832. He died on 5 May 1836 and his widow **Christiana Franks** filed for a pension on 13 Jul 1839, aged 72. **Henry Franks** married **Christiana Mason** in April, 1786 (probably related to **Jacob Mason** who also lived in Wayne Co., OH in 1832) and their children were as follows:

1. **John Franks** (b. 14 Jan 1787) married **Polly Heckler** on 24 Feb 1814

2. **Michael Franks** (b. 4 Sep 1788) married **Martha Thompson** on 14 Jan 1813)

3. **Elizabeth Franks** (b. 12 Oct 1791) married **Samuel Higgins** on the first Tuesday in December, 1810

4. **Sarah Franks** (b. 9 Jan 1794) married **John Routzen** on 28 Feb 1816

5. **Henry Franks, Jr.** (b. 19 Apr 1796)

6. **Abraham Franks** (b. 9 Feb 1798) married **Lydia Blacker** on 19 May 1825

7. **Uriah Franks** (b. 21 Oct 1799) married **Elizabeth Walls** on 20 Jan 1823

8. **Abigail Franks** (b. 14 Feb 1802)

9. **Christiana Franks** (b. 15 Mar 1804)

10. **Catharine Franks** (b. 17 Aug 1806)

11. **Phebby Franks** (b. 1 Jun 1809)

{Ref: *Genealogical Abstracts of Revolutionary War Pension Files*, by Virgil D. White (1990), Application W4956}

JOHN FRESHOUR

John Freshour (sometimes spelled Froshour) was born on 13 May 1756 in Frederick Co., MD and lived in Berkeley Co., VA at the time of his enlistment in the Revolutionary War. **Adam Freshour** and **Jacob Freshour** also served during the war in Frederick Co., MD. **John Freshour** married **Margaret Funkhouser** (b. 3 Apr 1772) in Shenandoah Co., VA on 27 Sep 1791 and subsequently moved to Ohio. He applied for a pension on 12 Oct 1832 in Ross Co., OH and died on 13 Oct 1841. **Margaret Freshour** applied for a widow's pension on 22 Nov 1841 and she applied for a bounty land warrant on 15 May 1855, at which time **John Freshour, Jr.** and **James Knight** made affidavits in Ross Co., OH. {Ref: *Genealogical Abstracts of Revolutionary War Pension Files*, by Virgil D. White (1990), Application W7607; *Revolutionary Patriots of Frederick County, Maryland, 1775-1783*, by Henry C. Peden, Jr. (1995), pp. 137}

DAVID FULTON

David Fulton enrolled in Cecil Co., MD during the War of 1812 and served as a private in the company of Capt. **Cyrus Oldham** for 13 days in April-May, 1813 (records show that a **William Fulton** served with him). David stated that he served in the companies of Captains Garrett, Simpson, Jones, and Cazier; however, his name does not appear on those muster rolls. He subsequently moved to Ohio and applied for bounty land (warrant 12-160-10248) in Union County on 15 Mar 1855, aged 73. {Ref: *Maryland Militia, War of 1812, Volume 3, Cecil & Harford Counties*, by F. Edward Wright, pp. 11, 50}

WILLIAM GADD

William Gadd, son of **Absalom Gadd** and **Elizabeth Cullison**, was born on 30 Jun 1759 in Baltimore Co., MD, and lived in Bedford Co., PA at the time of his enlistment in the Revolutionary War. He served from April, 1779 to November, 1781 and he also served as a substitute for his father **Absalom Gadd**. William married **Nancy Drake** and subsequently moved to Ohio Co., VA and then to

Bealvill, Sunsbury Township, Monroe Co., OH. He applied for a pension on 23 Sep 1832, aged 73, and died on 14 Feb 1835. {Ref: *Genealogical Abstracts of Revolutionary War Pension Files*, by Virgil D. White (1990), Application S2231; *Baltimore County Families, 1659-1759*, by Robert W. Barnes (1989), p. 235, citing *Report of the Ohio Genealogical Society* (August, 1966), p. 3}

ELIHUE GALLOWAY

Elihue Galloway was born in Maryland (county not stated, possibly Baltimore County) in 1790 and moved to Kentucky (county not stated) where he married **Mary Elliott** (date not given). In 1817 they moved to Jennings Co., IN and he died there in June, 1863. In 1870 **Mary Galloway** moved to Dearborn Co., IN. Their children were as follows:

1. **William Galloway**
2. **Sarah A. Galloway**
3. **Samuel Galloway**
4. **Martha Galloway**
5. **John Galloway**
6. **Elisha Galloway**
7. **Joseph Galloway**
8. **Elijah Galloway**
9. **Ephraim Galloway**
10. **George W. Galloway** (see below)
11. **Robert Galloway**
12. **Harriet Galloway**

George W. Galloway, son of **Elihue and Mary Galloway**, was born on 20 Aug 1834 in Sparta Township, Jennings Co., IN and married **Rosealtha M. Myers** (b. 31 Dec 1851, Lawrenceburg, IN, daughter of **Benjamin H. Myers** and **Nancy A. Robinson**) on 23 May 1867. They lived in Jennings County until 1871 when they moved to Dearborn County. {Ref: *History of Dearborn and Ohio Counties, Indiana* (1885), p. 718}

LEWIS GATCH

Lewis Gatch was born in Baltimore, MD and moved to Ohio in 1809 where he married **Mariah Newton**, a native of Cape May, NJ. Their son **James D. Gatch** became a physician and married first to **Annie E. Cordry** in 1856 in Cincinnati, OH and second to **Fannie M. Lozier** in 1861 in Dearborn Co., IN. {Ref: *History of Dearborn and Ohio Counties, Indiana* (1885), p. 721}

PHILIP GATCH

Philip Gatch was born in Baltimore Co., MD on 2 Mar 1751 and rendered aid to the military in Virginia during the Revolutionary War. He married **Elizabeth Smith** on 14 Jan 1778 in Powhatan Co., VA and they subsequently moved to Ohio. She was born in Powhatan Co., VA on 29 Dec 1752 and died in Milford, OH on 12 Jul 1811. **Philip Gatch** was a son of **Conduce Gatch** and **Prescocia Burgan** of Baltimore Co., MD, and a grandson of **Godfrey Gatch** who came to America from

82

Prussia in 1727. Philip was one of the earliest American born Methodist preachers. He died on 28 Dec 1834 or 1835 in Milford, OH, and his children were as follows:

1. **Prescocia Gatch** (b. 16 Sep 1779) married first to **James Garland** and second to **David Osburn**
2. **Martha Gatch** (b. 11 Oct 1783) married **John Gest**
3. **Conduce Gatch** (b. 7 Feb 1783) married **Margaret McGrew**
4. **Elizabeth Gatch** (b. 7 Feb 1786) married **Aaron Matson**
5. **Ruth Gatch** (b. 25 Oct 1789) married **Michael Swing**
6. **Thomas Gatch** (b. 19 Apr 1791) married first to **Sarah Barber** and second to **Lucinda McCormick**
7. **Philip Gatch, Jr.** (b. 28 Aug 1793) married first to **Mary Dimmitt** and second to Mrs. **Susan Ulrey Terry**
8. **George Gatch** (b. 3 Feb 1796) married **Sarah Virginia Jones**

{Ref: DAR Application 589397; *Index of Patriots, Revolutionary War Heroes and Their Families, Cincinnati Chapter DAR, 1893-1981*, by Jeraldyne Beets Clipson and Katherine Brewer Brinkdopke (1983), p. 116; *Baltimore County Families, 1659-1759*, by Robert W. Barnes, pp. 246-247}

JACOB GATCHELL

Jacob Gatchell married **Elizabeth Dunbar** (daughter of **Andrew Dunbar** and **Mary Husband**) in Cecil Co., MD on 7 Apr 1789. Her father took the Oath of Allegiance in 1778 during the Revolutionary War and died intestate in 1802. Some of the Gatchells were defiant Quakers as **Elisha Gatchell, Elisha Gatchell, Jr. and Jeremiah Gatchell** took the Oath of Allegiance in 1778, which was contrary to their discipline to do so. Jacob subsequently moved to Ohio and the children of **Jacob and Elizabeth Gatchell** were mentioned in an 1840 land record in Cecil Co., MD as follows:

1. **Mary Gatchell** m. **Thomas Rogers** (Washington Co., OH)
2. **Hannah Gatchell** (of Guernsey Co., OH)
3. **Jacob Gatchell** (of Guernsey Co., OH)
4. **Nathan Gatchell** (of Guernsey Co., OH)
6. **Nancy Gatchell** m. **Noah Dillian** (Guernsey Co., OH)

{Ref: *Andrew and Mary (Husband) Dunbar of Octorara Hundred, Cecil County, Maryland*, by Judith Mitchell Plummer (1987), pp. 6-7, citing Cecil County Deed Book JS No. 38, pp. 35-39; *Revolutionary Patriots of Cecil County, Maryland*, by Henry C. Peden, Jr., p. 31}

PARKER GEE

Parker Gee was born in Maryland on 10 Jun 1753, lived in Pittsylvania Co., VA at the time of his enlistment in the Revolutionary War, and was married there (wife's name and date of marriage were not given). In 1818 they moved to Marion Co., KY and then to Butler Co., OH and finally settled in Henry Co., IN about 1834 or 1835. He applied for a pension in January, 1839, aged 86, and died in January, 1842. There were 3 surviving children, one of whom, **Job Gee**, made an affidavit in Hamilton Co., OH on 12 Apr 1851, but he lived in Kenton Co., KY. {Ref: *Genealogical Abstracts of Revolutionary War Pension Files*, by Virgil D. White (1990), Application R3964}

JOHN PRICE GILL

John Price Gill, son of **Edward Gill** and **Leah Price** (who were married in 1770 in Baltimore Co., MD) was a carpenter by trade. He married **Kirby Providence** on 29 Nov 1792 and had two sons, **Ezekiel C. Gill and Edward Gill**. Ezekiel married **Sarah Jones** and subsequently moved to Ohio. In 1850 he lived in Oxford Township in Guernsey County. **Mordecai Gill**, brother of John Price Gill, was a miller by trade. He married **Jane ----** and also lived in Guernsey Co., OH in 1850. {Ref: *Gill Family in Maryland*, by James D. Gill (1950), p. 5}

NICHOLAS GILL

Nicholas Gill, son of **Stephen Gill** and **Cassandra Cole** (who were married in 1772 in Baltimore Co., MD) married **Mary Ambrose** on 17 Feb 1807 and moved to Millersport, OH in 1818. Their children were as follows:

1. **Ambrose Gill** (19 Jul 1808 - 5 Jan 1849) married first to **Sarah Ketner** (d. 8 Mar 1841), second to **Susanna Kalb**, and his children were as follows:
   1-1. **Sylvanus Gill**
   1-2. **Stephen Gill**
   1-3. **Sarah Gill**
   1-4. **Mary E. Gill** (1 Jan 1844 - 9 Jan 1844)
   1-5. **Nicholas Gill** (1 Sep 1847 - 6 Sep 1847)
   1-6. **Tabitha Gill** (1 Dec 1848 - 9 Aug 1849)
   1-7. **William Carpenter Gill** married **Katherine Glick** of Grovesport, OH and their children were **George T. Gill, Charles Ambrose Gill, Joseph Gill, Nettie Gill and Lou Ella Gill**
2. **Didymus Gill** (20 Feb 1810 - 20 Apr 1883) married **Ann Ambrose** on 24 Jan 1843 in Ohio and settled in Maryland; their children were as follows:
   2-1. **William George Gill** (12 Jan 1844 - 25 Sep 1907)
   2-2. **John C. Gill** (11 Feb 1845 - 15 Aug 1918)
   2-3. **Thomas E. Gill** (30 Aug 1846 - 30 Jan 1911)
   2-4. **Mary E. Gill** (25 May 1848 - 8 Jan 1937)
   2-5. **Joshua N. Gill** (20 Dec 1850 - 4 Nov 1930)
   2-6. **R. Stephen Gill** (10 Apr 1854 - 18 Sep 1938)
   2-7. **Edward Gill** (died young)
   2-8. **Barbara Gill** (died young)
3. **Laurence Gill** (25 Apr 1812 - 14 Oct 1838)
4. **Elizabeth Gill** (8 Apr 1814 - 5 Sep 1815)
5. **Sarah Gill** (12 Apr 1816 - 20 Apr 1888)
6. **John Gill** (24 Oct 1818 - 10 Feb 1898)
7. **Ann O. Gill** (18 Jan 1821 - 21 Jan 1842)
8. **Nicholas Gill, Jr.** (6 Jul 1823 - 23 Apr 1893)
9. **Thomas Gill** (17 Jan 1826 - 21 Mar 1894)

10. **Edward Gill** (12 May 1828 - 10 Jul 1873)

11. **Tabitha Gill** (29 Aug 1831 - 13 Nov 1910)

12. **Mary E. Gill** (18 May 1836 - 21 Oct 1888)

{Ref: *Gill Family in Maryland*, by James D. Gill (1950), pp. 10-12}

WILLIAM GILMORE

William Gilmore (sometimes spelled Gilmor) was drafted on or about 1 Jul 1814 in Harford Co., MD during the War of 1812 and served on active duty as a private in the company of Capt. **John B. Bayles** from 27 Aug to 26 Sep 1814. He also served in the company of Capt. **John Smithson** from 12 Oct to 27 Oct 1814 and was discharged at Baltimore. He subsequently moved to Ohio and applied for bounty land in Jefferson County on 23 Dec 1850, aged 59. He applied again on 13 Mar 1855, aged 62 (warrant 55-120-48407) and his claim was witnessed by **John Vermillion** and **William C. Hayne**. {Ref: *Maryland Militia, War of 1812, Volume 3, Cecil & Harford Counties*, by F. Edward Wright, pp. 19, 28, 51}

GILBERT T. GIVAN

Robert Givan was born in Maryland on 12 Mar 1760 and married **Catherine Duncan** (b. 3 Sep 1763, MD) on 6 Jan 1781. Their children were as follows:

1. **Hetty Givan**
2. **Sallie Givan**
3. **Margaret Givan**
4. **Gilbert T. Givan** (see below)
5. **Elizabeth Givan**
6. **Matilda Givan**

Catherine Givan died on 13 Jul 1795 and **Robert Givan** married second to **Rosey Burton** on 28 Oct 1795. They had one child, **Nancy Givan**. **Rosey Givan** died on 5 May 1797 and Robert married third to **Ruth Robinson**. **Ruth Givan** died on 12 Apr 1817 and Robert married fourth to **Priscilla Cottingham** on 28 Jan 1818. In 1828 they started for Indiana and Robert died en route, about 90 miles from Baltimore, MD, on 26 Apr 1828. His wife continued on to Indiana, in company with **John Burbage** and family, and she died in Dearborn County on 8 Jan 1829.

Gilbert T. Givan, son of **Robert and Catherine Givan**, born in Worcester Co., MD 31 Jul 1789; married **Sarah C. Merrill** (b. 6 Sep 1795, dau. of **George and Charlotte Merrill**) in Accomack Co., VA on 2 Dec 1813. They lived in Worcester Co., MD until April, 1818 when they moved to Sparta Township, Dearborn Co., IN. **Sarah Givan** died 28 Jul 1861 and **Gilbert T. Givan** died 8 Feb 1862. Their children were as follows:

1. **Margaret M. Givan**
2. **Albert G. Givan**
3. **John W. Givan**
4. **Robert H. Givan**
5. **Elizabeth A. Givan**
6. **Maria J. Givan**

7. **George M. Givan** (see below)
8. **Sarah R. Givan**
9. **Adoniran J. Givan**
10. **Peter M. Givan**
11. **Alfred M. Givan**
12. **Alfred B. Givan**
13. **Sanford G. Givan**

George M. Givan, son of **Gilbert T. and Sarah C. Givan**, was born in Sparta Township, Dearborn Co., IN on 19 Jun 1827 and married **Ann E. Jaquith** (b. 25 Feb 1830) on 6 Jan 1848. Their children were **John F. Givan, Mary B. Givan, Sanford E. Givan, Harriet J. Givan, Sarah E. Givan, Eva A. Givan, Charles M. Givan, Ella J. Givan, Harry R. Givan, Irving P. Givan**, and **Cora A. Givan**.

{Ref: *History of Dearborn and Ohio Counties, Indiana* (1885), pp. 729-730; for more information on the early Givan-Givans-Gibbons families, see *Colonial Families of the Eastern Shore of Maryland, Volume 15*, by Ralph A. Riggin and F. Edward Wright (2003), pp. 74-93}

JOSHUA GIVAN

Joshua Givan was born in Worcester Co., MD on 2 Jul 1788 and married **Henrietta Davis** (b. 1795) in 1811. Their children were as follows:

1. **George Givan** (b. 1 Dec 1816, m. **Sabrina Jane Hall** on 16 Feb 1840)
2. **William L. H. Givan** (b. 22 Apr 1820) married **Jane M. Ferris** on 19 Oct 1843
3. **Martha Givan**
4. **Robert Givan**
5. **Mary Givan**
6. **Noah S. Givan** (b. 30 Sep 1833) married **Mary Martin** on 17 Oct 1866

In 1825 **Joshua Givan** moved to Dearborn Co., IN and died on 31 Jan 1874. **Henrietta Givan** died on 14 Jun 1876. {Ref: *History of Dearborn and Ohio Counties, Indiana* (1885), pp. 726-727}

JAMES W. GLADDEN

James W. Gladden, of Harford Co., MD, served as a private in the company of Capt. **James Rampley** during the War of 1812. **James Gladden** and **Jacob Gladden** both served in April, 1813. After the war James moved to Ohio and married **Eve Negley** in Butler County on 19 Aug 1823. He applied for bounty land (warrant 55-160-68788) in 1855 in Marion Co., IN, lived at Bridgeport in 1871, and died at Clermont circa 1883. {Ref: *Maryland Militia, War of 1812, Volume 3, Cecil & Harford Counties*, by F. Edward Wright, pp. 24, 34, 78}

JACOB GOMBER

The following notice appeared in the *Frederick-Town Herald* in Frederick, MD, on 8 Mar 1806: *"Whereas it appears that by letters received from Jacob*

Gomber, formerly of this county (now living on Wills Creek, State of Ohio) that he did, on or about 4 Oct 1805, inclose a bond in a letter directed to the subscriber, drawn in favor of said Gomber, and accepted by Abraham Shriver and Andrew Hedges, of this county, the amount being $600; said letter and bond have not come to the hands of the subscriber, James Robertson, Frederick Town." A similar notice appeared in *Bartgis's Republican Gazette* in Frederick, MD on 7 Mar 1806, but the name was listed as **Jacob Gombier**. {Ref: *Western Maryland Newspaper Abstracts, Volume 3, 1806-1810*, by F. Edward Wright, pp. 3, 99}

BENJAMIN GOSNELL

Benjamin Gosnell, son of **Peter Gosnell** (born in England and migrated to America, settling at Baltimore, MD circa 1750) was born on 15 Mar 1761 in Baltimore, MD (one source stated he was born on 4 Mar 1760 in Virginia) and lived in Bedford Co., VA at the time of his enlistment in the Revolutionary War. He participated in numerous battles and was present at the surrender of Lord Cornwallis at Yorktown in 1781. Benjamin married first to a **Miss Barlow** and they had five children: **Benjamin Gosnell, John Gosnell, Thomas B. Gosnell** (born 5 Feb 1798 in Virginia, married **Hetty Porter** in 1827; their son **Benjamin Gosnell** was born on 2 Mar 1828 in Rush Co., IN; Thomas was killed by lightning on 15 Jun 1829), **Edith Gosnell**, and **Patience Gosnell**. Benjamin married second to **Dorcas Fornash Porter**, a widow, on 1 Jan 1815 in Harrison Co., KY and they had five children: **George Gosnell, Washington Gosnell, Alexander Gosnell, Nancy Gosnell**, and **Delilah Gosnell**. Benjamin applied for a pension in Decatur Co., IN on 24 Oct 1832 and died on 28 Aug 1846. **Dorcas Gosnell** applied for a widow's pension on 10 Jan 1855, aged 74. {Ref: *Genealogical Abstracts of Revolutionary War Pension Files*, by Virgil D. White (1990), Application W11060; *History of Tipton County, Indiana*, by M. W. Pershing (1914), pp. 493-494}

WILLIAM GRAFTON

William Grafton, son of **Daniel Grafton**, was drafted on or about 28 Aug 1814 at Cooptown in Harford Co., MD and served as a private in the companies of Capt. **Corbin Grafton** and Capt. **James Rampley** during the War of 1812. He served for a term of about 30 days when he was taken sick with the measles and removed to the hospital in Baltimore near Hampstead Hill, where he remained about 10 days until the physicians declared him out of danger. He rejoined his company and continued in actual service for about 2 weeks and stated that he is not the **William Grafton** who is marked on the rolls of said company as having deserted. He stated that the other William was his cousin and the son of **Aquila Grafton**. William subsequently moved to Ohio and applied for a bounty land warrant in Columbiana County on 8 Sep 1851. He applied again on 13 Apr 1855, aged 69 (warrant 55-rej-281186) and his claim was witnessed by **Joshua S. Patterson** and **John --?--**, of Columbiana Co., OH. On 28 Aug 1857 **William Grafton** appeared again regarding his claim and stated he was aged 71, formerly of Harford Co., MD, now a resident of Columbiana Co., OH. On 8 Sep 1857 appeared Capt. **James Rampley**, a citizen of Harford Co., MD, and stated that he knows **William Grafton**, the applicant, and that he was on military duty at Baltimore, a good soldier, honorably discharged. Also appeared **George Lemmon** and **Elisha Meads** and stated that **William Grafton** was on military duty with them at Baltimore under Capt. **James Rampley**. On 18 Oct 1865 appeared **William Grafton**, aged 79, a resident of Wayne Township, Columbiana Co., OH, and acquaintances were **Thomas Hooey** and **Milo Pumphrey**, residents of Washington Township. {Ref: *Maryland Militia, War of 1812, Volume 3, Cecil & Harford Counties*, by F. Edward Wright, pp. 20, 52}

MICHAEL GRAHAM

Michael Graham requested a certificate of removal on the 8th day of the 1st month, 1807, from the Baltimore Monthly Meeting, Western District, to the Concord Monthly Meeting in Ohio for himself, his wife **Patience Graham**, and their three minor children, **Elizabeth Ann Graham, Deborah Graham and James Graham**. {Ref: Baltimore Quaker Monthly Meeting Minutes}

GEORGE GRAY

George Gray, of Prince George's Co., MD, served in the War of 1812 and subsequently moved to Ohio. On 26 Nov 1850 he applied for bounty land (warrant 55-160-29699) and stated he was called into the service in July, 1812 and served over 7 weeks. He served in the spring of 1813 and again in August, 1813, and also in the spring of 1814 and again in August, 1814. On 15 May 1855 he applied again for bounty land while residing at Newark Township, Licking Co., OH. On 12 May 1871, aged 81, he applied for a pension (SO-18958) in Licking Co., OH and stated his wife was **Sarah Mitchell** whom he married in Prince George's Co., MD in 1816; she died 30 years ago. During the War of 1812 he served in the Battle of Bladensburg and at the bombardment of Indian Head, MD. On 25 Jun 1873, aged 83, he applied again for a pension (SC-20940) at Jacksontown, OH and stated he was drafted in 1813. He gave a detailed account of his military activities during the war. On 16 Mar 1886 **Mary Gray**, widow of **George Gray**, of Jacksontown, Licking Co., OH, applied for a widow's pension (WC-34505, WO-44116) and stated George died on 12 Nov 1885. She had married him in Ohio in 1839 and her former name was **Mary Mentzer**. On 8 Jun 1886 **John Brunback**, aged 78, of Licking Co., OH, and **Nancy Padgett**, aged 81, of Franklin Co., OH, stated they were acquainted with **George and Mary Gray** who were married on 13 Jun 1839. **Mary Gray** had previously married **David Mentzer** who died on 19 Feb 1832 in Licking Co., OH, and **George Gray** had previously married **Sarah Mitchell** who died on 15 Nov 1834. **Nancy Padgett** stated she knew **George Gray** and **Sarah Mitchell** when they married on 10 Oct 1816 in Maryland and she came to Ohio with them in 1834. On 8 Jun 1886 **Mary Gray** stated **George Gray** died on 12 Nov 1885, aged 95 years, 7 months and 5 days. {Ref: *Maryland Militia, War of 1812, Volume 6, Prince George's County*, by F. Edward Wright, pp. 36-37}

JOSEPH GRAY

A certificate of removal was received at the Milford Monthly Meeting in

Wayne Co.. IN on the 15th day of the 11th month, 1832 from the Northwest Fork Monthly Meeting in Caroline Co., MD for **Joseph Gray**, his wife **Mary Gray**, and their children **William Gray, James Gray, Josephine Gray, and Mary Gray**. The Milford register, however, listed their children as **Elizabeth Gray, William Gray, James Gray, Joseph Gray, Mary Gray, and Lydia Ann Gray** (the latter child died on the 31st day of the 3rd month, 1843). Another certificate was also received at that time for **Peter Gray** and **Elizabeth Ann Gray**. {Ref: "Migration of Caroline County Quakers to Indiana," by F. Edward Wright, *Maryland Genealogical Society Bulletin*, Volume 34, No. 3 (1993), p. 284}

ELIZABETH GRAYLESS

Elizabeth Grayless (sometimes spelled Greyless) requested a certificate of removal from the Northwest Fork Monthly Meeting in Caroline Co., MD to the Milford Monthly Meeting in Wayne Co., IN on the 3rd day of the 12th month, 1828, and it was received at that meeting on the 17th day of the 12th month, 1828. Her death is recorded at the Milford (Hicksite) Meeting in the 8th month of 1839. {Ref: "Migration of Caroline County Quakers to Indiana," by F. Edward Wright, *Maryland Genealogical Society Bulletin*, Volume 34, No. 3 (1993), p. 284}

WESLEY GRAYSON

Wesley Grayson and **Rebecca Norman**, of Maryland (county not stated), married in Ohio (county not stated) after 1800. {Ref: *Maryland Revolutionary Records*, by Harry Wright Newman (1938), p. 114}

LEWIS GREEN

Lewis H. Green, of Barresville, OH, married **Mary N. Dorsey** on 14 Aug 1832. {Ref: *Baltimore American*, 17 Aug 1832, abstracted by Lorrie A. E. Erdman}

RICHARD GREEN

Richard Green, of Montgomery Co., MD, wrote his will on 23 May 1815 (probated 17 Sep 1818) and devised to his son **Allen Green**, of Cincinnati, OH, his dwelling plantation of 257¼ acres called *Peasant Farms* on condition that his son made it his permanent residence within one year. Richard also mentioned his daughters **Elizabeth Griffith, Mary Israel, Anna Dorsey, Amelia Dorsey** and **Ruth Darby**. He named his son Allen as his executor, but if he was unable to serve then the executor would be his friend and neighbor **Thomas Davis**. {Ref: *Abstract of Wills, Montgomery County, Maryland, 1776-1825*, by Mary G. Malloy, Jane C. Sween and Janet D. Manuel, pp. 57-58}

PHILIP GREENWOOD

Philip Greenwood was born in Frederick Co., MD on 28 Nov 1755 and was probably the son of **Philip Greenwood**, blacksmith, who wrote his will on 7 Oct 1779 and died by 4 Feb 1780 (date of probate). He lived in Frederick County at the time of his enlistment in the Revolutionary War. Philip was an Associator in December, 1775 and a private in the Middle District Militia in the company of

Capt. **Valentine Creager** in 1776. He also took the Oath of Allegiance in 1778 and subsequently moved to Pennsylvania (county not stated). He was married *"west of the mountains"* to **Sarah** ---- in the fall of 1788. They later moved to Indiana and he applied for a pension in Monroe County on 10 Oct 1832, aged 77. **Philip Greenwood** died on 5 Sep 1842 and **Sarah Greenwood** applied for a widow's pension in Owen Co., IN on 2 Dec 1843, aged 79. {Ref: *Genealogical Abstracts of Revolutionary War Pension Files*, by Virgil D. White (1990), Application R4289; *Archives of Maryland*, Volume 18, p. 72; *Maryland Historical Magazine*, Volume XI, p. 167; *Western Maryland Genealogy*, Volume 5, No. 4 (1989), p. 165}

REUBEN GRIFFITH

Reuben Griffith requested a certificate of removal on the 27th day of the 1st month, 1808, from the Gunpowder Monthly Meeting in Baltimore Co., MD, for himself, his wife **Elizabeth Griffith**, and their five minor children, **Ann Moore Griffith, Rebecca Griffith, Elizabeth Griffith, Mary Griffith and Keturah Griffith**, to the Salem Monthly Meeting in Columbiana Co., OH. {Ref: Gunpowder Quaker Monthly Meeting Minutes}

HUGH GUNION

Hugh Gunion was born in County Down, Ireland on 2 Apr 1755 and lived in Lancaster Co., PA at the time of his enlistment in the Revolutionary War. In 1783 he moved to Maryland, in 1800 he moved to Washington Co., PA, and in 1806 he moved to Jefferson Co., OH, where he applied for a pension on 28 May 1834, aged 78. {Ref: *Genealogical Abstracts of Revolutionary War Pension Files*, by Virgil D. White (1990), Application R4388}

ELISHA GUYTON

Elisha Guyton, son of **John and Frances Guyton**, was born in Harford Co., MD on 20 Jul 1796 and married **Catherine Shultz** (b. 26 Jan 1791, daughter of **George Shultz** and **Elizabeth Shoemaker**) on or about 21 Dec 1812 (date of license). Her father was born in Germany on 16 Mar 1752, her mother was born on 19 Dec 1762, and they lived at Harper's Ferry, VA which may have been where Elisha met Catherine. **George and Elizabeth Shultz** moved to Harrison Co., OH where he died on 6 Oct 1827 and she died on 4 Feb 1833. They are buried in Zion Cemetery near Germana, OH. In 1813 **Elisha Guyton** allegedly served in the War of 1812, but no proof of service has been found in Maryland records. After the war he began selling his land in the "My Lady's Manor" area of Harford and Baltimore Cos., MD. In 1825 he moved his family to Deersville in Franklin Township, Harrison Co., OH. The children of **Elisha and Catherine Guyton** were as follows:

1. **John Guyton** (23 Oct 1813, MD - 27 May 1881, OH) married **Amanda Fitzgerald** on 24 May 1838; their children were as follows:

1-1. **Ellen Ann Guyton** (married **Jacob Hughes**)

1-2. **Mary Elizabeth Guyton** (married first to **John Adair** and second to **Erastus Booth**)

1-3. **Adeline Amanda Guyton** (married **John Tedrick** or **John M.**

Teterick)

    1-4. **William Fitzgerald Guyton** (30 May 1840 - 30 Mar 1930) married **Mary Helen Smith** in McMinnsville, OR

    1-5. **Margaret Catherine Guyton** (1854-1888), unmarried

    1-6. **Thomas Elisha Guyton** (b. 8 Aug 1844) married **Florence Booth**

    2. **Benjamin Guyton** (7 Jun 1820, MD - 3 Apr 1896, OH) married **Eleanor Fitzgerald** on 20 Oct 1845

    3. **Augustus Guyton** (b. 23 Sep 1825, OH, d. before 1868; pre-deceased his father)

    4. **Elisha S. Guyton** (b. May 1828, OH, d. 22 Oct 1888) married when in his forties (name of wife not given)

    5. **Catherine Guyton** (married **W. T. Crabtree**)

    6. **Mary Guyton** (married **Mr. Crabtree**)

    7. **Elizabeth Guyton** (married **Adam Hotz** on 20 Oct 1843)

Elisha Guyton died testate in 1868. **Abraham Guyton** had also settled in Ohio, possibly as early as 1813. {Ref: *Guytons Galore*, by Helen Guyton Rees (1986), pp, 36-37, 44-51; *Harford County, Maryland Marriage Licenses, 1777-1865*, by Jon Harlan Livezey and Helene Maynard Davis (1993), p. 102}

RANDALL HALES

Randall Hales removed from Baltimore, MD to Ohio (county not given) on 4 May 1803. **Anna Hales**, of Baltimore, MD, *"removed out of town"* in 1803 and **Mary Hales** *"removed from town"* in March, 1804, but their destinations were not recorded. {Ref: Class Registers, Baltimore City Station, Methodist Episcopal Church}

THOMAS HALEY

Thomas Haley (sometimes spelled Healey and Hailey) was born circa 1752 and enlisted at Baltimore MD during the Revolutionary War on 17 Jul 1776. He was a private in the 4th MD Regiment from 11 Feb 1777 until discharged on 13 Feb 1780. He subsequently moved to Ohio and applied for a pension in Harrison Co., OH on 3 Sep 1819, aged 67. He then moved to Knox Co., OH on 19 Jun 1826 and at that time he stated he was aged 71, with wife **Cassander Haley**, aged 67, and four children, **Edward Haley, Thomas Haley, Jr., Anna Haley** and **Rachel Haley**. {Ref: *Genealogical Abstracts of Revolutionary War Pension Files*, by Virgil D. White (1990), Application S41625; *Revolutionary Patriots of Baltimore Town and Baltimore County, Maryland, 1775-1783*, by Henry C. Peden, Jr., p. 116; *Archives of Maryland*, Volume 18, p. 124}

HAMBLETON FAMILY

James Hambleton, of Baltimore Co., MD, son of **William and Mary Hambleton**, of Belmont Co., OH, and **Mary Brooks**, of Baltimore, MD, daughter of **Thomas and Mary Brooks**, late of Chester Co., PA (the father being deceased), married in Baltimore City on the 12th day of the 6th month, 1811 at the Baltimore Monthly Meeting, Western District. The witnesses included **Charles Hambleton,**

Benjamin Hambleton, Joseph Hambleton, and Rachel Hambleton.

James Hambleton requested a certificate of removal on the 11th day of the 1st month, 1815, from the Baltimore Monthly Meeting, Western District, to the Middleton Monthly Meeting in Ohio, for himself, his wife **Martha [Mary?] Hambleton** and their minor daughter **Mary Hambleton**. {Ref: Baltimore Quaker Monthly Meeting Minutes}

Charles Hambleton and **Benjamin Hambleton** requested a certificate of removal from the Baltimore Monthly Meeting, Western District, to the Middletown Monthly Meeting in Ohio on the 12th day of the 1st month, 1814, having already moved there. {Ref: Baltimore Quaker Monthly Meeting Minutes}

WILLIAM HAMILTON

William Hamilton requested a certificate of removal on the 12th day of the 2nd month, 1807, from the Baltimore Monthly Meeting, Western District, to the Short Creek Monthly Meeting in Ohio. {Ref: Baltimore Quaker Monthly Meeting Minutes}

GEORGE HAMMER

George Hammer was born near Philadelphia, PA on 4 May 1763 and lived in Frederick Co., MD at the time of his enlistment in the Revolutionary War. **Jacob Hammer** and **Tobias Hammer** also served as privates during the war. George subsequently moved to Putnam Co., IN where he applied for a pension on 25 Oct 1832 and died on 21 Jul 1834. {Ref: *Genealogical Abstracts of Revolutionary War Pension Files*, by Virgil D. White (1990), Application S41625; *Revolutionary Patriots of Frederick County, Maryland, 1775-1783*, by Henry C. Peden, Jr. (1995), pp. 158}

THOMAS HAMMOND

Thomas Hammond enlisted in the Revolutionary War in Prince George's Co., MD on 28 Apr 1781, aged 16, and served in the Maryland Continental Line. He married **Sarah Boyle** on 28 Jan 1793 in Montgomery Co., MD. They subsequently moved to Athens Co., OH where he applied for a pension on 10 Nov 1819, aged 57. In 1828 they lived in Crawford Co., IN and in 1831 they moved to Adams Co., IL. **Thomas Hammond** died in November, 1832 and **Sarah Hammond** applied for a widow's pension in Washington Co., OH on 27 Dec 1850, aged 76. She died on 20 Jul 1852, leaving children, but no names were given. {Ref: *Genealogical Abstracts of Revolutionary War Pension Files*, by Virgil D. White (1990), Application W4224; *Archives of Maryland*, Volume 18, p. 381}

JOHN HANCE

John Hance (sometimes referred to as **John Hance, Sr.**) enrolled in a company of volunteers in Anne Arundel Co., MD during the War of 1812 under Col. Taney around 1 May 1814 and also served on active duty as a private in the horse company of Capt. **John G. Mackall** in the 3rd Cavalry District on 9 and 10 Jun 1814 and for 9 days in July-August, 1814. He subsequently moved to Ohio and applied for bounty land in Belmont County on 18 Dec 1850, aged 58. He applied again for bounty land (warrant 55-rej-273544) in Stephenson Co., IL on 20 Apr 1857, aged 64. Witnesses were **Lorenz Lee** and **Joseph M. Bailey**. He also applied for a pension (SO-9947), but the date and place were not given. **Benjamin Hance** served in the Ohio Militia under Capt. **Charles Hilliard** during the War of 1812 and received a pension (SC-489), but his relationship to **John Hance** of Belmont Co., OH was not given. It should be noted that another **John Hance** also served in the War of 1812 and he resided in Calvert Co., MD in 1856, aged 59. {Ref: *Maryland Militia, War of 1812, Volume 4, Anne Arundel & Calvert Counties*, by F. Edward Wright, pp. 46, 90; *Index of War of 1812 Pension Files*, by Virgil D. White, p. 916}

HANDY HANDLEY

Handy Handley was born circa 1745 and lived in Dorchester Co., MD. He was head of household in Transquakin Hundred in 1776, aged between 30 and 40, with two males aged between 10 and 16, two males under age 10, one female aged between 30 and 40, and two females under age 10, plus 1 negro. In the Revolutionary War he was an ensign in the Transquakin Militia Company on 18 Oct 1777, a second lieutenant on 20 May 1778, and a first lieutenant on 1 Mar 1779. He subsequently moved to Sullivan Co., IN and applied for a pension on 5 May 1833 in Haddam Township. {Ref: *Genealogical Abstracts of Revolutionary War Pension Files*, by Virgil D. White (1990), Application S16401; 1776 Census of Dorchester County, MD}

LEONARD HARDACRE

Leonard Hardacre, of Prince George's Co., MD, was drafted in August, 1813 and served in the War of 1812. He subsequently moved to Ohio and applied for bounty land (warrant 55-rej-171108) in Green County on 13 Jun 1855, aged 58. **George Hardacre** was a witness. {Ref: *Maryland Militia, War of 1812, Volume 6, Prince George's County*, by F. Edward Wright, p. 37}

RICHARD HARDESTY

Richard Hardesty served as a private in Calvert Co., MD during the War of 1812 in the company of Capt. **Hillary Wilson** (other officers being Lieut. **John Chew** and Ensign **Thomas Reynolds**) in the 31st Regiment and was stationed at Plumb Point from 14 to 20 Apr 1813. He subsequently moved to Ohio and applied for bounty land (warrant 55-rej-282549) in Belmont County on 9 Oct 1857, aged about 75. Witnesses were **John Bradfield** and **Harrison Lowe**, of Barnesville, OH. {Ref: *Maryland Militia, War of 1812, Volume 4, Anne Arundel & Calvert Counties*, by F. Edward Wright, pp. 49, 92}

THOMAS HARDING

Thomas Harding was drafted during the War of 1812 at or near Carroll's Manor in Anne Arundel Co., MD around 1 Apr 1812. His company marched to Annapolis where they joined another regiment, the adjutant of which was a **Mr.**

Hughes and the major of that regiment was named Higgins. He was discharged at Annapolis, but was not paid for his service for another 6 months when he and the rest of the company were paid at **Richard Owens'** store. He was again drafted at the same place around 1 Aug 1812 and was an Orderly Sergeant in the company of Capt. **Thomas Owens** *(sic)*. He served as 3rd Sergeant under Capt. **Thomas Owings** in the 32nd Regiment and was stationed at Annapolis from 13 to 26 May 1813. His last drafting occurred at the same place under Capt. **John Thomas** and his company marched to Baltimore. It should be noted that **Barton Harding** (who was discharged on 21 Sep 1814, being 45 years old) and **Nicholas Harding** (who was furloughed on 23 Sep 1814) served in the same company in 1814, but their relationship was not given. **Thomas Harding** served on active duty from 24 Aug to 27 Sep 1814, but was noted as being absent without leave for 8 days on 3 Sep 1814. He married **Ruth Whips** and lived in Ohio when he applied for bounty land at Putnam in Muskingum County on 9 Dec 1850, aged 60. Thomas died in 1853 and **Ruth Harding** applied for bounty land (warrant 55-120-16225) on 19 Mar 1855, aged 63. Witnesses were **H. H. Sullivan** and **Caleb J. Sullivan**, of Putnam, OH. {Ref: *Maryland Militia, War of 1812, Volume 4, Anne Arundel & Calvert Counties*, by F. Edward Wright, pp. 41, 43, 92}

JOHN HARRISS

John Harriss removed from Baltimore, MD to Ohio (county not stated) in October, 1827. He was possibly related to **Ruth Harriss** (died in Baltimore in July, 1819), **Samuel Harriss** (removed from Baltimore in March, 1821), and **Harriet Harriss** (died in Baltimore in May, 1825). {Ref: Class Lists, Baltimore City Station, Methodist Episcopal Church}

MARY HARTSHORN

Mary Hartshorn requested a certificate of removal on the 7th day of the 1st month, 1817, from the Baltimore Monthly Meeting, Western District, to the Cincinnati Monthly Meeting in Ohio, she having already moved there with her husband (not named). {Ref: Baltimore Quaker Monthly Meeting Minutes}

PATIENCE HARTSHORN

Patience Hartshorn requested a certificate of removal on the 11th day of the 7th month, 1817, from the Baltimore Monthly Meeting, Western District, to the Cincinnati Monthly Meeting in Ohio, having already moved there. {Ref: Baltimore Quaker Monthly Meeting Minutes}

BENJAMIN HARWOOD

Benjamin Harwood moved from Baltimore, MD to Ohio (county not given) in 1818. {Ref: Class Registers, East Baltimore Station (Fell's Point), Methodist Episcopal Church}

REBECCA HATTON

Rebecca Hatton moved from Baltimore, MD to Ohio (county not stated) on 17 Oct 1825. {Ref: Class Lists, Baltimore City Station, Methodist Episcopal Church}

ANN HAWKINS

Ann Hawkins was received into the Methodist Episcopal Church in Baltimore City with a certificate from Harford Co., MD on 28 Apr 1826. **Ann Hawkins** moved from Baltimore to Ohio (county not stated) in 1828. {Ref: Class Lists, Baltimore City Station, Methodist Episcopal Church}

PHILIP HAWKINS

Philip Hawkins was born circa 1756, lived at Baltimore, MD during the Revolutionary War, and enlisted as a private in Capt. Smith's Company No. 8 on 26 Jan 1776. He subsequently moved to Ohio and applied for a pension in Guernsey County on 23 Mar 1832, aged 76. At that time he had two daughters aged 28 and 23 (names not given). {Ref: *Genealogical Abstracts of Revolutionary War Pension Files*, by Virgil D. White (1990), Application S41612; *Archives of Maryland*, Volume 18, p. 18}

THOMAS HAWKINS

Thomas Hawkins was born in 1758 in Charles Co., MD and lived in Loudoun Co., VA at the time of his enlistment in the Revolutionary War. After the war he moved to Monongalia Co., VA, then to Wood Co., VA for 20 years, and in 1805 he moved to Washington Co., OH where he applied for a pension on 29 Oct 1832. {Ref: *Genealogical Abstracts of Revolutionary War Pension Files*, by Virgil D. White (1990), Application S4310; *Historical Register of Virginians in the Revolution, 1775-1783*, by John H. Gwathmey (1938), p. 361}

JACOB HEFFNER

Jacob Heffner (sometimes spelled Hefner, Heifner and Heiffner) was born on 13 Sep 1752 (1757?) in Germany, married first to **Elizabeth Miller** and second to Mrs. **Elizabeth Priest**, and served in the Maryland Line during the Revolutionary War. He enlisted as a private in the Washington Co., MD militia company of Capt. **William Heyser** on 18 Aug 1776, served in the German Regiment of the Continental Line under Lt. Col. **Ludwick Weltner**, and was discharged at Fort Wyoming, PA on 12 Oct 1779. He subsequently moved to Ohio and applied for a pension in Richland County on 10 Feb 1819. In 1821 he had a wife aged 60 (name not given) and two sons **David Heffner** (aged 18) and **Felts Heffner** (aged 13) living with him. Jacob married again on 4 Nov 1824 or 4 Nov 1828 and died on 23 Nov 1848. **Elizabeth Heffner** applied for a widow's pension in Ashland Co., OH on 24 Feb 1853, aged 87 on 14 Oct 1852, but in 1857 she stated she was aged 96. She also stated that she and Jacob were married in 1828 and they had no children, but both she and Jacob had been married previously. Three of his sons were **David Heffner, Felts Heffner,** and **Valentine Heffner** (of

Ashland Co., OH in 1857), and Elizabeth's son **Hankey Priest** was aged 30 in 1857. {Ref: *Genealogical Abstracts of Revolutionary War Pension Files*, by Virgil D. White (1990), Application W2546; *Revolutionary Patriots of Washington County, Maryland, 1776-1783*, by Henry C. Peden, Jr., pp. 159-160}

WILLIAM HENDRICKSON

William Hendrickson was born on 3 Dec 1757 in Middletown, NJ and lived in Frederick, MD during the Revolutionary War. He enlisted as a private in the company of Capt. **Peter Mantz** on 1 Jul 1776 and marched from Frederick to Leonardtown, MD and then to Philadelphia, arriving on 23 Aug 1776. During the war he moved near Fort Cumberland, MD and lived there for 20 years. He then moved to Knox Co., OH for short time and then moved to Richland County where he applied for a pension on 7 Sep 1832, aged 75. {Ref: *Genealogical Abstracts of Revolutionary War Pension Files*, by Virgil D. White (1990), Application S2301; *Archives of Maryland*, Volume 18, p. 47}

JAMES HILL

James Hill was born in Ireland on 12 Aug 1764, immigrated to America with his father (name and date not given) and settled in Cecil Co., MD where he lived at the time of his enlistment in the Revolutionary War. He also took the Oath of Allegiance in 1778 and he may have been the **James Hill** who married **Ann Cavender** on or about 27 Sep 1791 (date of license). He subsequently moved to Ohio and applied for a pension in Fairfield County on 13 Nov 1834. {Ref: *Genealogical Abstracts of Revolutionary War Pension Files*, by Virgil D. White (1990), Application S9579; *Revolutionary Patriots of Cecil County, Maryland, 1775-1783*, by Henry C. Peden, Jr. (1991), p. 49}

WILLIAM HILL

William Hill and **Elizabeth Palmer**, of Maryland (county not stated), married in Ohio (county not stated) before 1831. {Ref: *Maryland Revolutionary Records*, by Harry Wright Newman (1938), p. 115}

BENJAMIN HINDS

Benjamin Hinds was born in Maryland (county not stated) and married **Elizabeth Hash** (of Pennsylvania) in Washington Co., PA (date not given). They moved to Ohio circa 1812 and settled near Seven Mile. After the War of 1812 they moved to Hamilton Co., OH and in 1825 he moved to Dearborn Co., IN, settling in Sparta Township, Section 14. Benjamin married a second time (wife's name not given) and altogether he fathered 13 children:
1. **Elizabeth Hinds**
2. **Ann Hinds**
3. **Mary Hinds**
4. **James Hinds**
5. **Sarah Hinds**
6. **John Hinds**

7. **Henry Hinds**
8. **Reizen Hinds** (b. 29 Jan 1818, OH) married 3 Dec 1837 in Sparta Township, IN to **Mary Heaton** (b. 29 Sep 1819, IN, daughter of **Eben Heaton** and **Sarah Streeter**)
9. **Emily Hinds**
10. **Jane Hinds**
11. ---- **Hinds** (died young)
12. ---- **Hinds** (died young)
13. ---- **Hinds** (died young)
{Ref: *History of Dearborn and Ohio Counties, Indiana* (1885), pp. 760-761}

JACOBUS HINDS

Jacobus Hinds (also known as **Jacob Hines**) was born in New Castle Co., DE on 28 Oct 1762 and lived in Kent Co., MD at the time of his enlistment in the Revolutionary War. He served as a private in the 9th Company, 13th Battalion, Kent County Militia. After the war he lived in Maryland, Virginia, Ohio, and then moved to Indiana where he applied for a pension in Parke County on 13 Nov 1832. {Ref: *Genealogical Abstracts of Revolutionary War Pension Files*, by Virgil D. White (1990), Application S16411; *Revolutionary Patriots of Kent & Queen Anne's Counties, Maryland*, by Henry C. Peden, Jr. (1995), p. 130}

ISAAC HITCHCOCK

Isaac Hitchcock, son of **Asel and Sarah Hitchcock**, was born on 4 Jan 1763 in Baltimore Co., MD and lived in Harford County at the time of his alleged service in the Revolutionary War (no proof of service has been found in Maryland records). **Isaac Hitchcock** was head of household in 1790 containing 3 inhabitants and in 1800 he lived in the 4th District of Harford County. **Asel Hitchcock** died testate by 3 Jan 1792 and in his will he mentioned his wife **Sarah Hitchcock** and son **Isaac Hitchcock**, among other children. Final distribution of the estate of **Sarah Hitchcock** was made in Harford County on 12 Mar 1822 to her children, viz., **Asael Hitchcock, William Hitchcock, Isaac Hitchcock, Mary Trulock and Ann Hicks**, and the children of her deceased sons **John Hitchcock** and **Josias Hitchcock**. Isaac lived in Maryland until 1821 or 1822, except for 17 months in Kentucky, and then moved to Muskingum Co., OH. In 1823 he moved to Perry Co., OH and applied for a pension on 18 Jun 1835. {Ref: *Genealogical Abstracts of Revolutionary War Pension Files*, by Virgil D. White (1990), Application R5054; Harford County Census Records; Harford County Will Book AJ No. 2, pp. 314-315; *Heirs and Legatees of Harford County, Maryland, 1802-1846*, by Henry C. Peden, Jr. (1988), p. 27}

NICHOLAS HITCHCOCK

Nicholas Hitchcock, of Harford Co., MD, served as a private during the War of 1812 under Capt. **James Rampley** from 28 Aug to 26 Sep 1814. He married first to **Ellen Clark** (date and place not given) and second to **Rachel Taylor** on 17 Dec 1819 in Perry Co., OH. He applied for bounty land in 1850 and 1855 (warrants 50-

40-23013 and 55-160-68323) in Perry Co., OH. **Nicholas Hitchcock** died on 24 Sep 1864 in Putnam Co., OH. **Rachel Hitchcock** lived at Dupont, Putnam Co., OH in 1878 and died there circa 1887. {Ref: *Maryland Militia, War of 1812, Volume 3, Cecil & Harford Counties*, by F. Edward Wright, pp. 31, 79}

JACOB HITE

Jacob Hite was born in Frederick Co., MD on 14 Feb 1761, served as a private in Frederick Co., VA for 7 years during the Revolutionary War and was at the surrender of Yorktown in 1781. He married **Catherine Shiner** (b. 1769, Potomac River, MD, d. 27 Oct 1844, Rush Co., IN) in Frederick Co., VA on 4 Apr 1785 or 1786. Their children were as follows:

1. **John Hite** (nothing further)
2. **George Hite** (War of 1812 soldier)
3. **William Hite** (b. 27 Mar 1791) married **Sarah Baxter** and acquired 700 acres of land in 1829 in Rush Co., IN
4. **Polly Hite** married **Archibald Crowdy**
5. **Alexander Hite** (b. 30 Nov 1805) married **Mary Ann Lowery**

Jacob Hite died on 27 Oct 1839 in Richland Township, Rush Co., IN. {Ref: DAR Application 330697; *A Roster of Revolutionary Ancestors of the Indiana Daughters of the American Revolution* (1976), p. 303}

JOSEPH HOBSON

Joseph Hobson, of Jefferson Co., OH, son of **Joseph and Ann Hobson**, of the same place, married at Bush Creek Meeting House on 18 Mar 1813 to **Rebeckah Talbott**, daughter of **John and Mary Talbott** (the father being deceased), of Frederick Co., MD. {Ref: "Pipe Creek Friends Monthly Meeting Records," *Western Maryland Genealogy*, Volume 1, No. 2 (1985), p. 70}

SAMUEL HODGKINS

Samuel Hodgkins was born in Carlisle, PA on 6 Jun 1757, moved with his father (name not given) to Rock Run on the Susquehanna River in Baltimore (now Harford) Co., MD, and lived in Harford County at the time of his enlistment in the Revolutionary War. He served as a private in the militia company of Capt. **Bennett Bussey** on 25 Jul 1776 and also served as a militia substitute in 1781. After the war Samuel and his first wife (name not given) moved to Pittsburgh, PA, then to Lexington, KY, and then to Brown Co., OH. He married second to **Lydia Wright** on 9 Mar 1831 in Brown County. He applied for a pension on 20 Apr 1841 and died on 13 Oct 1844. **Lydia Hodgkins** applied for a widow's pension on 27 Sep 1855, aged 66, and stated that she and Samuel had a daughter **Hannah Hodgkins** who was born on 16 Jun 1832 and still living in 1852. Samuel also had a daughter **Elizabeth Hodgkins** by his first wife and she was born on 13 Jul 1784, married **Aaron Berget**, and lived in Indiana in 1843. **Samuel Berget** (relationship not given) was in Brown Co., OH in 1855. {Ref: *Genealogical Abstracts of Revolutionary War Pension Files*, by Virgil D. White (1990), Application R5092; *Revolutionary Patriots of Harford County, Maryland, 1775-1783*, by Henry C.

98

Peden, Jr., p. 113; *Maryland Revolutionary Records*, by Harry Wright Newman (1938), p. 116}

JOHN HOGG

Martha Ann Hogg, second daughter of **John Hogg**, Esq., married **Edwin S. Mopps**, of Urbana, OH, on 12 Jul 1832. **Sarah Jane Hogg** married **Elias Brown** on 11 Jul 1833. **John W. Hogg** married **Martha Chambers** on 28 Jan 1836. {Ref: *Baltimore American*, 14 Jul 1832 and 13 Jul 1833 and 30 Jan 1836, abstracted by Lorrie A. E. Erdman}

JOSEPH HOLLINGSWORTH

Joseph Hollingsworth requested a certificate of removal on the 11th day of the 12th month, 1818, from the Baltimore Monthly Meeting, Western District, to the Little Miami Monthly Meeting in Ohio. {Ref: Baltimore Quaker Monthly Meeting Minutes}

LEVI HOLLOWAY

Levi Holloway was born on 9 Apr 1735 in Worcester Co., MD and lived there at the time of his enlistment in the Revolutionary War. He served as a private in militia company of Capt. **Josiah Dale** in 1779-1780. In 1813 he moved to Ohio and in the fall of 1838 he moved to Hamilton Co., IN where he applied for a pension on 1 Jun 1839, aged 104. {Ref: *Genealogical Abstracts of Revolutionary War Pension Files*, by Virgil D. White (1990), Application S32332; *The Maryland Militia in the Revolutionary War*, by S. Eugene Clements & F. Edward Wright, p. 254}

GEORGE HOLMAN

George Holman was born in Maryland (county not stated) on 11 Feb 1762 and when young he moved with his father (name not given) to Pennsylvania. His mother having died when he was a child, he was placed under the care of his father's brother **Henry Holman**. George moved with his uncle to Kentucky along with **Edward Holman**, brother of Henry, and another member of the family, **Richard Rue**, who was a year or two older than George, and settled near Louisville. George Holman and Richard Rue were later captured by Indians and remained captive for 3½ years. In 1804 they obtained land near Richmond, IN and moved there the following year. **George Holman** married (wife's name not given) and their children were as follows:
1. **Joseph Holman**
2. **William Holman**
3. **John Holman**
4. **Benjamin Holman**
5. **Joel Holman**
6. **Patsey Holman**
7. **Rebecca Holman**
8. **Sarah Holman**

9. **Greenup Holman**
10. **Jesse Holman**
11. **Catharine Holman**
12. **Isaac Holman**

{Ref: "Persons Who Migrated to Wayne County, Indiana From the Eastern Shore of Maryland," by F. Edward Wright, *Maryland Genealogical Society Bulletin*, Volume 34, No. 4 (1993), p. 466}

WILLIAM HORNEY

William Horney served as a private in the Talbot Co., MD militia, 2nd Volunteer Co., 4th Battalion, 1777-1778. He also enlisted in the 5th MD Regiment on 12 May 1778 and was still in service in November, 1780. In November, 1810, the Treasurer of Maryland was directed *"to pay annually to William Horney, of Talbot County, an old revolutionary soldier, a sum of money, quarterly payments, equal to half pay of a soldier during the war aforesaid, as a further remuneration to said William Horney for the services rendered his country, and as a relief from the indigence and misery which attend his decrepitude and old age."* He may have been the **William Horney** who was born in Maryland circa 1750-1751, married **Hannah Chipman**, served as a private in the Revolutionary War, and died in Ohio in 1829. {Ref: *Archives of Maryland*, Volume 18, p. 213; *Maryland Records: Colonial, Revolutionary, County and Church from Original Sources*, by Gaius M. Brumbaugh, Volume 2, p. 356; *The Maryland Militia in the Revolutionary War*, by S. Eugene Clements & F. Edward Wright, p. 225; *DAR Patriot Index, Centennial Edition*, p. 1485}

JOHN HOUGH

John Hough, son of **Paul Haugh** of Frederick Co., MD, was born in 1776, married **Hannah R. Miller**, daughter of ---- **Miller** and **Barbara Ott** (1750-1824), and moved to Ashland Co., OH in 1823. **Hannah Hough** died on 19 Oct 1858 and John died in 1862. {Ref: "John Ott of Frederick County" by J. Harold and Virginia Miller, *Western Maryland Genealogy*, Volume 2, No. 4 (1986), p. 148}

SAMUEL HOWELL

Samuel Howell lived in Frederick Co., MD at the time of his enlistment in the Revolutionary War and after his discharge he moved to Ohio. In 1798 he moved to Clermont Co., OH and applied for a pension on 9 Nov 1832. By 17 Jun 1840 he moved to live with a son (name not given) in Owen Co., KY. {Ref: *Genealogical Abstracts of Revolutionary War Pension Files*, by Virgil D. White (1990), Application S30496}

GIDEON HUGHES

On the 22nd day of the 10th month, 1806, at the Gunpowder Monthly Meeting in Baltimore Co., MD, **Gideon Hughes** (sometimes spelled Hugh, Hues, Huse and Hews) and **Rebecca Dillon** declared their intention to marry, parents consent being obtained, pending the young woman's clearness from all others. On the 26th day of the 11th month, 1806, the minutes stated that they were *"cleared to marry with parents consent obtained and nothing appearing to obstruct they going to settle a considerable distance the winter approaching."* On the 24th day of the 12th month, 1806, it was reported that they had been married in an orderly manner. **Gideon Hughes** requested a certificate of removal on the 8th day of the 1st month, 1807 to the Middleton Monthly Meeting in Ohio. **Rebecca Hughes** also requested a certificate of removal on the 25th day of the 2nd month, 1807. {Ref: Gunpowder Quaker Monthly Meeting Minutes}

ANN HULL

Ann Hull requested a certificate of removal on the 11th day of the 6th month, 1819, from the Baltimore Monthly Meeting, Western District, to the Still Water Monthly Meeting in Ohio, having already moved there. {Ref: Baltimore Quaker Monthly Meeting Minutes}

JOHN C. HULL

John C. Hull served as a private in Cecil Co., MD during the War of 1812 in the company of Capt. **John Brown** for 7 days in April-May, 1813 and in the company of Capt. **John Sample** in 1814. He subsequently moved to Ohio where he applied for bounty land (warrant 55-160-9198) in Union County on 19 Mar 1855, aged 65, stating, in part: *"I volunteered to leave the fortifications at Elk Landing to carry a supply of ammunition to French Towne, but the place was burned before the party could reach the breast work. The party was nearly cut off by the British, escaping capture by their knowledge of the nearest route to the fortifications of Elk Landing. They reached Elk Landing in time to beat off the enemy and save about 30 sail of bay craft that laid up there for protection. The British were computed at 200 strong, in 10 barges, armed with swivels in their bows ... I was in a second skirmish with the British boats in the following year at the same place, also under the same captain. In August, 1814 I was again called out by Capt. Sample in common with the whole brigade to repel an expected invasion near Baltimore. I remained at Baltimore until ordered to Cecil County by Col. Veazey to send out the delinquent members of my regiment to join his command ... I was employed by the government for several years, sending thirty-two and forty-two pounders (long guns) from Principio Furnace by direction from Col. John Rodgers for the frigate built at Philadelphia under his direction. I succeeded in getting them all to Philadelphia before the Principio works were destroyed by the British. I was later employed by Samuel T. Anderson, Naval Storekeeper of Philadelphia or New York, to superintend the transportation of heavy cannon from Elk Landing to Christiana for use of Sacketts Harbour. At that time I was acting partner of the firms of A. Scott & Company. I was from this time until peace was proclaimed, engaged in forwarding powder from Reni Dupont's powder works on the Brandywine to the city of New York ..."* **David Fulton** was acquainted with **John C. Hull**, stating he had known him for 45 years and had served in the same regiment. **William T. Fulton** stated he had known him for 28 years. John C. Hull further stated *"If any further proof of my identity is necessary the record of the State* *of Maryland will show that I was commissioned as a cornet in Capt. William Hollingsworth's Troop of Horse in Cecil County, Maryland (then only 18 years of age) and afterwards first lieutenant of artillery in Capt. John Evans' Company of Light Artillery, both these companies were attached to the first brigade then under the command of Brig. Gen. Hezekiah Foard, an officer of the revolution, gave me many a lesson in broadsword exercise at my father's house ... I was postmaster at Elkton in 1817 and 1818, successor to Joshua Richardson, and Adam Whann was my successor, I having removed from the town."* On 1 Oct 1859 appeared **William Giles**, age 61, who said he was acquainted with **John C. Hull** for 50 years; also stated he was living in Elkton during the War of 1812 and John was a resident there at that time. Giles was too young to engage in active service, but was employed by Hull as a wagoner. In that capacity he was engaged nearly all one winter in hauling thirty-two and forty-two pounders, long guns, from Principio Furnace to Christiana Bridge, New Castle Co., DE. He was later employed by Hull as wagoner to haul large quantities from Dupont's Powder Mills on the Brandywine to New York, which took about 6 weeks. On 24 Oct 1871 appeared **John C. Hull**, nearly age 87, a resident of Taylor Township, Union Co., OH, applied for a pension (SO-25563) and stated his wife's name was **Jane Thomson** (still living) when he married her at New Castle Co., DE on 1 Mar 1814. He received his discharge from Col. Veazey, but cannot find it, stating *"In a fire at Cumberland, MD I had a trunk full of old documents burned. I suppose my discharge was in that fire."* Hull stated he was engaged in the transportation of forty-two pounders from Elk Landing to Christiana, said to be for the steam(?) floating battery at New York. *"When the British fleet came into the Chesapeake Bay, about 20 sail of bay craft (sloops and schooners) came up to Elk Landing, a breastwork was thrown up, one long nine pounder gun and 4 six pounder canonades were mounted. When peace was announced I was on my way to New York with three wagon loads of powder. At Brunswick, NJ I was met by an order to deliver the powder at Perth Amboy ... I was in the employ, either in the ranks, agent for the army or navy, during the whole war."* **John C. Hull** gave his post office address as Boke's Creek, Union Co., OH in 1871. {Ref: *Maryland Militia, War of 1812, Volume 3, Cecil & Harford Counties*, by F. Edward Wright, pp. 14, 16, 54-55; *Index of War of 1812 Pension Files*, by Virgil D. White, p. 1047}

JAMES HUNT

James Hunt was born in March, 1764 and served in the Maryland Line during the Revolutionary War. He subsequently moved to Ohio and applied for a pension in Clark Co., OH on 17 Oct 1831, aged 67; his wife (name not given) was aged 52. {Ref: *Genealogical Abstracts of Revolutionary War Pension Files*, by Virgil D. White (1990), Application S41663}

JOHN HUNTER

John Hunter, son of **John Hunter, Sr.**, was born at Hagerstown, MD on 27 Nov 1762 and lived in Rockingham Co., VA at the time of his enlistment in the Revolutionary War. He also served as a substitute for his father, after which he moved to East Tennessee for 10 years, then to Madison Co., KY for 12 years, then to Montgomery Co., KY for 4 years, and then in 1807 to Knox (now Gibson) Co., IN. He subsequently lived in Lawrence Co., IL and Wabash Co., IL where he applied for a pension on 3 Dec 1832. He stated that **Joseph Hunter**, of Jonesborough, East TN, had his father's family bible. **Isaac Hunter**, son of **John Hunter, Jr.**, lived in Wabash Co., IL in 1854. {Ref: *Genealogical Abstracts of Revolutionary War Pension Files*, by Virgil D. White (1990), Application R5404; *Historical Register of Virginians in the Revolution, 1775-1783*, by John H. Gwathmey (1938), p. 405}

GEORGE HUSSEY

George Hussey requested a certificate of removal on the 8th day of the 1st month, 1807, from the Baltimore Monthly Meeting, Western District, to the Middleton Monthly Meeting in Ohio, having already moved there. {Ref: Baltimore Quaker Monthly Meeting Minutes}

WILLIAM IGLEHART

William Iglehart enrolled in a company of light dragoons under Capt. **Richard Ridgely, Jr.** in Anne Arundel Co., MD on 3 Sep 1808 (a **Richard Iglehart** also enrolled). William served as a private in August, 1814 in the company of Capt. **Larkin Hammond** in Tilghman's Cavalry Troops during the War of 1812. He married **Jane Smith** in Anne Arundel Co. on 26 Dec 1802 (by **Rev. N. Lane**, Protestant clergyman). Marriage records indicate **William Iglehart** and **Anne Smith** obtained a license on 24 Dec 1802. William died in Baltimore on 10 Oct 1831 and Jane later moved to Hamilton Co., OH where she applied for bounty land (warrant 50-40-27143) on 14 Jan 1851, aged 69. Their son **Nicholas P. Iglehart** was aged 39. On 25 Jan 1851 **Anthony Smith**, of Anne Arundel Co., MD, stated he was acquainted with the military service of **William Iglehart** who was the husband of his sister **Jane Iglehart**. On 3 Jun 1873 **Nicholas P. Iglehart** stated his mother had died intestate at Cincinnati, OH on 19 Apr 1851, leaving the following children:

1. **Margaret A. Iglehart** married **Mr. Green** and was a widow by 1873
2. **John S. Iglehart** (died before 1873)
3. **Mary Ann Iglehart** married **Mr. Shays** and she was a widow by 1873
4. **Ellen P. Iglehart** married **Asa Vail**
5. **Nicholas P. Iglehart**

{Ref: *Maryland Militia, War of 1812, Volume 4, Anne Arundel & Calvert Counties*, by F. Edward Wright, pp. 6, 48, 98; *Anne Arundel County, Maryland Marriage Records, 1777-1877*, by John W. Powell, p. 60}

JOHN JACKSON

John Jackson moved from Maryland (county not stated) circa 1798 to what is now Miller Township in Ohio Co., IN. He married (wife's name not given) and had the following children:

1. **John Jackson, Jr.** married ---- in Kentucky and settled in Ohio Co., IN

circa 1798

2. **Ezekiel Jackson** married ---- and their daughter **Margaret Jackson** married in 1838 to **Virgil Dowden** (b. 1813, IN)

3. **Enoch Jackson**

4. **Susan Jackson** married **John Dawson**

5. **Sally Jackson** married **Charles Dawson**

John Jackson died in 1814 and his widow died in 1823, she having been accidentally drowned while crossing Tanner's Creek. {Ref: *History of Dearborn and Ohio Counties, Indiana* (1885), pp. 459, 693}

WILLIAM JACOBS

William Jacobs was born on 19 Jun 1755 in Frederick Co., MD and lived there at the time of his service in the Revolutionary War. He enlisted as a private in the flying camp under Capt. **Philip Meroney** on 5 Aug 1776 and was a private in the horse troops in 1781. After the war he moved to Frederick Co., VA, then to Hardy Co., VA, then to Hampshire Co., VA, and then to Morgan Co., OH. He applied for a pension on 3 Nov 1832 and died on 3 Jun 1836; his wife **Sarah Jacobs** had died about 1834. Their known children were as follows:

1. **Elizabeth Jacobs** (b. 1785) married **Paul Coffman** in 1810 in Hampshire Co., VA and lived in Perry Co., OH in 1851

2. **Catharine Jacobs** married **Mr. Sprage** and lived in Guernsey Co., OH in 1851

3. **William Jacobs, Jr.** (lived in Virginia in 1851)

John Coffman stated in 1851 that **William Jacobs** and wife Sarah lived with him at one time. {Ref: *Genealogical Abstracts of Revolutionary War Pension Files*, by Virgil D. White (1990), Application S2289; *Archives of Maryland*, Volume 18, p. 54; *The Maryland Militia in the Revolutionary War*, by S. Eugene Clements & F. Edward Wright, pp. 167, 168}

JOHN JAMES

John James was born in Frederick Co., MD and moved to Ohio Co., IN with his family in 1807. They settled first at Lawrenceburg, IN, then moved to Cincinnati, OH, then to Louisville, KY in 1812 due to Indian problems, and returned to Ohio in the fall of 1813. John founded the town of Rising Sun in Ohio Co., IN. His sons Col. **Pinkney James** and **Henry James** built the steamer *Dolphin* in 1835 and made daily trips between Rising Sun, IN and Cincinnati, OH for 3 years. In 1838 Pinkney built the steamer *Herald* and he built the steamer *Indiana* in 1839. John's son **Basil James** became a physician and died on 8 Aug 1877. {Ref: *History of Dearborn and Ohio Counties, Indiana* (1885), pp. 173-174, 447-448}

THOMAS JAMES

Thomas James was born in 1756 and served in Harford Co., MD during the Revolutionary War. **Thomas James and Thomas James, Jr.** both served in the militia in 1776, both signed the Association of Freemen in Bush River Upper Hundred in 1776, and both took the Oath of Allegiance in 1778. **Thomas James**

married **Mary Eagon** on or about 11 Nov 1780 (date of license). He subsequently moved to Indiana and applied for a pension in Rush County on 14 Nov 1832, aged 76. {Ref: *Genealogical Abstracts of Revolutionary War Pension Files*, by Virgil D. White (1990), Application S16423; *Revolutionary Patriots of Harford County, Maryland, 1775-1783*, by Henry C. Peden, Jr. (1985), pp. 122-123; *Harford County, Maryland Marriage Licenses, 1777-1865*, by Jon Harlan Livezey and Helene Maynard Davis (1993), p. 128}

ISAAC JENNINGS

Isaac Jennings, son of **Isaac Jennings** and **Sarah Dick**, was born in Cecil Co., MD in 1766. His siblings were **Thomas Jennings, James Jennings**, and **Deborah Jennings**. Isaac married in 1788 to **Elizabeth Campbell** (b. 1766, Ireland, daughter of **David Campbell** and **Elizabeth Thompson**) in Cecil Co., MD and shortly thereafter moved to Westmoreland Co., PA, the part that later became Indiana County. In 1820 they moved to Butler Co., OH and in 1825 they moved to Hamilton Co., OH; he died in 1828 and she died in 1829. Their children were as follows:

1. **David Jennings**
2. **Deborah Jennings**
3. **Sarah Jennings**
4. **Isaac Jennings**
5. **Elizabeth Jennings**
6. **Ann Jennings**
7. **James Jennings**
8. **Susan Jennings**
9. **Thomas Jennings** (see below)

Thomas Jennings, son of **Isaac and Elizabeth Jennings**, was born on 25 Oct 1807 in Indiana Co., PA and moved with his parents to Ohio in 1820. He taught the first free school in Cincinnati, OH in 1826 and afterwards engaged in dairy farming in 1830. He married **Emeline L. S. Jones** on 13 Aug 1833 and in 1835 they moved to Wilmington, Dearborn Co., IN. **Emeline Jennings** died in 1836 and Thomas married **Catherine Quarry**. He was the father of one child by his first wife and six children by his second wife, as follows:

1. **Thomas W. Jennings** (died young)
2. **Samuel G. Jennings**
3. **Rebecca A. Jennings**
4. **Thomas A. Jennings**
5. **Isaac Jennings** (died young)
6. **Sarah L. Jennings**
7. **Susan Jennings**

{Ref: *History of Dearborn and Ohio Counties, Indiana* (1885), pp. 781-782}

MARY JOHN

On the 28th day of the 8th month, 1806 **William John** produced a certificate for himself and his wife **Mary John** from the London Grove Monthly Meeting

(Chester Co., PA), as members of the Fawn Preparative Meeting (York Co., PA), to the Deer Creek Monthly Meeting in Harford Co., MD. On the 15th day of the 1st month, 1823 the Women's Meeting of the Deer Creek Monthly Meeting in Harford Co., MD produced a certificate of removal for **Mary John** to Carmel Monthly Meeting in Columbiana Co., OH. {Ref: Deer Creek Quaker Monthly Meeting Minutes}

BENJAMIN JOHNSON

Benjamin Johnson was born in Worcester Co., MD on 1 Feb 1778 and married **Sarah Dashiell** (b. 22 Aug 1777). In 1817 they moved to Sparta Township, Dearborn Co., IN and lived there until 1848 when they moved to Jackson, IA. It was said that Benjamin *"was true as steel to a friend and could be relied upon at all times."* He died on 30 Aug 1852 and **Sarah Johnson** died in 1854. Their children were as follows:

1. **William P. Johnson** (m. **Maria L. Olmsted**)
2. **Anna Johnson**
3. **Margaret Johnson**
4. **Samuel J. Johnson**
5. **Edward K. Johnson**
6. **Elizabeth Johnson**
7. **Benjamin Johnson, Jr.**
8. **John D. Johnson** (see below)

John D. Johnson, son of **Benjamin and Sarah Johnson**, was born in 1808 in Worcester Co., MD and married **Sarah Brumblay** (b. 29 Apr 1809, daughter of **John Brumblay** and **Elizabeth McGee**) in Dearborn Co., IN on 23 Oct 1828. **John and Elizabeth Brumblay** were natives of Worcester Co., MD; he was born on 15 Jan 1781 and she was born on 23 Sep 1787. They moved to Indiana in 1817; he died on 31 Jul 1853 and she died on 11 Oct 1854. They had the following children:

1. **Sarah Brumblay**
2. **Mary Brumblay**
3. **Elizabeth Brumblay**
4. **John Brumblay, Jr.**
5. **Anna Brumblay**
6. **David M. Brumblay**

John D. Johnson was elected to the Indiana Legislature in 1846 and 1848 and to the constitutional convention in 1850. He died in Sparta Township in January, 1878, and his wife **Sarah Johnson** died on 12 Mar 1881. They had the following children:

1. **Sarah E. Johnson** (died young)
2. **Margaret Johnson** (died young)
3. **Francis M. Johnson**
4. **John W. Johnson** (b. 31 May 1835) married **Henrietta Davis** (daughter of **Noah Davis** and **Sarah Montgomery**) on 2 Oct 1856
5. **Joseph S. Johnson**

106

6. **Benjamin F. Johnson**
7. **Mahala J. Johnson**
8. **Mary J. Johnson** (died young)
9. **Edward P. Johnson**
10. **Charles J. Johnson**
11. **William G. Johnson**
12. **Anna Johnson**

{Ref: *History of Dearborn and Ohio Counties, Indiana* (1885), pp. 559, 784-785}

CHRISTOPHER JOHNSON

Christopher Johnson, formerly of Baltimore, MD, died in Cincinnati, OH on 2 Sep 1835. {Ref: *Baltimore American*, 11 Sep 1835, abstracted by Lorrie A. E. Erdman}

WILLIAM JOHNSON

William Johnson was born circa 1758 and enlisted at Frederick, MD during the Revolutionary War. He subsequently moved to Ohio and applied for a pension in Fairfield Co., OH on 16 May 1818, aged 70. On 22 Apr 1820 William was aged 72 and had a wife (not named), aged 61, and they had 13 children, of whom 8 were still living (7 boys and 1 girl, names not given). In 1820 two sons were aged 19 and 17 and still living at home, plus a daughter aged about 25 and her daughter aged about 6. {Ref: *Genealogical Abstracts of Revolutionary War Pension Files*, by Virgil D. White (1990), Application S41704}

BENJAMIN JOHNSTON

Benjamin Johnston was born on 23 Nov 1756 in Kent Co., MD and lived there at the time of his enlistment in the Revolutionary War. He served as a private in the 1st Company, 27th Battalion, Kent County Militia. He lived in Maryland until he was 30 and then moved to Ohio (county not stated). He subsequently moved to Illinois and applied for a pension in Perry County on 30 Mar 1833, aged 77 on 23 Nov 1833. {Ref: *Genealogical Abstracts of Revolutionary War Pension Files*, by Virgil D. White (1990), Application R5602; *Revolutionary Patriots of Kent & Queen Anne's Counties, Maryland*, by Henry C. Peden, Jr. (1995), p. 145}

JAMES JOHNSTON

James Johnston, of Cecil Co., MD, served in the War of 1812 as a private in the company of Capt. **John Sample** in Elkton, MD. He later moved to Indiana and applied for bounty land in Hamilton County on 4 Nov 1850, aged 57. He applied again (warrant 55-120-67996) on 15 May 1855, aged 62. Acquaintances were **Peter Hoosier** and **Phillip Hoosier**, both of Hamilton Co., IN. **James Johnston** was still living there on 29 Mar 1845. {Ref: *Maryland Militia, War of 1812, Volume 3, Cecil & Harford Counties*, by F. Edward Wright, p. 56}

JACOB JONES

Jacob Jones served as a private for 20 days in August, 1813 in Capt. **Thomas Hood**'s Battalion in Anne Arundel Co., MD during the War of 1812. He also stated he was pressed into service at Annapolis around 16 Aug 1814 and was discharged at Baltimore on 16 Sep 1814. He subsequently moved to Ohio and applied for bounty land (warrant 55-rej-153389) in Meigs County on 18 May 1855, aged 78. Witnesses were **Levi Reeves** and **J. D. Stewart**. {Ref: *Maryland Militia, War of 1812, Volume 4, Anne Arundel & Calvert Counties*, by F. Edward Wright, pp. 33, 100}

NATHAN JONES

Nathan Jones was born in Frederick (now Montgomery) Co., MD on 3 Nov 1760 and served in the militia of Montgomery County during the Revolutionary War. There was another Nathan Jones who also served in the militia and died in Montgomery County in 1812. His wife was named Nancy. Nathan Jones, our subject, married **Anna Brittia Buxton** on 21 Jan 1800 and their children were as follows:

1. **Sarah Jones** (b. 7 Nov 1800), unmarried
2. **Cassandra Jones** (b. 3 May 1802), unmarried
3. **Charlotte Jones** (b. 30 Mar 1804) married **Mr. Weir**
4. **Ann Buxton Jones** (b. 13 May 1806) married **Daniel Kane**
5. **William Jones** (b. 6 Oct 1808) unmarried
6. **James Jones** (b. 2 Apr 1810) married **Martha Robertson**
7. **Jane Jones** (b. 7 May 1811) married **Mr. McDonald**
8. **Eliza Jones** (b. 4 Jun 1814) married **Philip Runyon**
9. **Rose Ann Jones** (b. 6 Nov 1816), unmarried

Nathan Jones moved his family to Richmond, Ohio and **Anna Jones** died in 1824. He died on 20 Aug 1856. {Ref: *Directory of Maryland State Society DAR, 1892-1965*, p. 430}

THOMAS JONES

Thomas Jones was born on 26 Jan 1756 in Frederick (now Washington) Co., MD and lived there at the time of his enlistment in the Revolutionary War. After the war he moved to Westmoreland Co., PA for 16 years, then to Mason Co., KY for 3 years, and then to Clermont Co., OH, where he applied for a pension on 5 Nov 1832. {Ref: *Genealogical Abstracts of Revolutionary War Pension Files*, by Virgil D. White (1990), Application S2655}

ISAAC JULIAN

The family name was originally St. Julian, but was shortened and anglicized to Julian. **Rene St. Julian**, native of Paris, fought under the Prince of Orange, afterward William III of England, at the Battle of the Boyne in Ireland in 1690. He came to America and settled on the Eastern Shore of Maryland soon thereafter. One of his sons, **Isaac Julian**, moved to Randolph Co., NC and his son, also named Isaac Julian, moved to Wayne Co., NC in 1815; later moved to Henry Co., IN where he died (date not given). **Isaac Julian**, third of the same name, remained in Wayne Co., IN. He was born on 4 Jun 1781 in Randolph Co., NC and taught school there and in Wayne Co., IN in 1808-1809. He married **Rebecca Hoover**, a Quaker, on 29 Mar 1809. {Ref: "Persons Who Migrated to Wayne County, Indiana From the Eastern Shore of Maryland," by F. Edward Wright, *Maryland Genealogical Society Bulletin*, Volume 34, No. 4 (1993), p. 466}

WILLIAM KEETS

William Keets volunteered to serve as a private in the War of 1812 for an indefinite period of time at Purnell's Township *(sic)* in Caroline Co., MD under Capt. Bell in the spring of 1813. He was a private, and then a corporal, in the company of Capt. **Joseph Talbott** from 11 May to 18 May 1813. He subsequently moved to Ohio and applied for bounty land (warrant number not given) in Washington County on 2 Mar 1852, aged 63. {Ref: *Maryland Militia, War of 1812, Volume 1, Eastern Shore*, by F. Edward Wright, pp. 80, 111}

JOHN KEEVER

John Keever lived in Maryland at the time of his enlistment in the Revolutionary War. He married **Mary Roby** on 2 Sep 1813 in Jefferson Co., OH and died on 23 Jan 1852. **Mary Keever** applied for a widow's pension in Washington Co., OH on 7 Jul 1857, aged 75, and also applied for a bounty land warrant on 5 Jun 1855. **William Keever** (relationship not stated) made an affidavit in Morgan Co., OH on 1 Sep 1856 and stated he knew **John Keever** and his wife Mary for 45 to 50 years and they had 5 children (names not given). John lived in Maryland, moved to Pennsylvania, then moved in 1801 to Jefferson Co., OH for 30 years, and then moved to Morgan Co., OH, where he died. {Ref: *Genealogical Abstracts of Revolutionary War Pension Files*, by Virgil D. White (1990), Application R5814; *Maryland Revolutionary Records*, by Harry Wright Newman (1938), p. 117}

JAMES KELBRETH

James Kelbreth moved from Baltimore, MD to Cincinnati, OH in 1831. {Ref: Class Lists, Baltimore City Station, Methodist Episcopal Church}

JOSHUA KELLEY

Joshua Kelley was born in Baltimore Co., MD in 1751 and lived there at the time of his enlistment in the Revolutionary War. **Joshua Kelley, of William,** was second lieutenant in the militia company of Capt. **Nicholas Kelley** on 7 Feb 1782. In 1793 Joshua moved to Huntington Co., PA and in 1797 he moved to Ross Co., OH for 2 years and 5 months, then to Kentucky (county not stated) for 7 or 8 years, and then to Owen Co., IN where he applied for a pension on 18 Oct 1833. He mentioned his brother **William Kelley** who served as a captain. **Moses Kelley**, of Owen Co., IN, made an affidavit on 18 Oct 1833 and stated that both he and **Joshua Kelley** were born in Baltimore Co., MD and they had enlisted together in that county. {Ref: *Genealogical Abstracts of Revolutionary War Pension Files*, by

Virgil D. White (1990), Application R21706; *Revolutionary Patriots of Baltimore Town and Baltimore County, Maryland, 1775-1783*, by Henry C. Peden, Jr. (1988), p. 149}

MOSES KELLEY

Moses Kelley was born in Baltimore Co., MD on 27 Feb 1752 and live there at the time of his enlistment in the Revolutionary War. He served in the militia with **Joshua Kelley**, *q.v.* About 40 years after the war Moses moved to Washington Co., TN for 3 years, then moved to Washington Co., VA for 9 years, then to Grant Co., KY, then to Indiana and lived in Dearborn, Ripley, Green, and Marion Counties for short periods of time, and then moved to Owen Co., IN where he lived for one week on 17 Oct 1833. He applied for a pension on that date and was aged 81 on 27 Feb 1833. **Joshua Kelley, Sr.** and **John Kelley** made affidavits at that time, but did not state their relationship. On 10 Apr 1835 **Moses Kelley** lived in Hamilton Co., OH. {Ref: *Genealogical Abstracts of Revolutionary War Pension Files*, by Virgil D. White (1990), Application S8786}

WILLIAM KELLEY

William Kelley was born in Virginia on 10 Jan 1760 and served in the Revolutionary War. After the war he lived in Virginia (county not stated) for several years and then moved to Maryland and lived in Dorchester and Somerset Counties for 11 years. He then moved to Kentucky (county not stated) and then to Indiana where he applied for a pension in Spencer County in November, 1834. He died on 18 Mar 1846 leaving no widow, but left children who in 1847 were **William J. Kelley** (aged 57, of Warwick, IN), **Jacob Kelley** and **Elizabeth Ruble** (both of Spencer Co., IN). {Ref: *Genealogical Abstracts of Revolutionary War Pension Files*, by Virgil D. White (1990), Application R5833}

KENNARD FAMILY

Thomas Kennard, son of **Levy and Ann Kennard**, of Fawn Township, York Co., PA, married **Elizabeth Medcalf**, daughter of **Moses and Susannah Medcalf**, of Deer Creek Monthly Meeting, Harford Co., MD, on the 1st day of the 12th month, 1813 at Deer Creek. On the 23rd day of the 6th month, 1814, and again on the 28th day of the 7th month, 1814, **Levi or Levy Kennard** requested a certificate of removal from Deer Creek Monthly Meeting for himself, his wife **Ann Kennard** and their minor son **Levi or Levy Kennard, Jr.**, to Short Creek Monthly Meeting in Ohio. **Thomas Kennard** also requested a certificate to the Short Creek Monthly Meeting for himself and his wife **Elizabeth Kennard**. On the 28th day of the 7th month, 1814, the Women's Meeting produced certificates for **Ann Kennard, Mary Kennard and Elizabeth Kennard** to Short Creek Monthly Meeting. {Ref: Deer Creek Quaker Monthly Meeting Minutes}

MARTIN KEPHART

Martin Kephart was born circa 1758, became a cooper by trade, and enlisted at Frederick, MD during the Revolutionary War. He served from the fall of 1775 until 1780 as a private in the 1st MD Regiment under Capt. **George Stricker**. He fought in the battles of Long Island, White Plains, Trenton, Princeton, Brandywine, Germantown, and Monmouth, and was discharged at Morristown, NJ (exact date not given). He subsequently moved to Ohio and applied for a pension in Stark County on 10 Jun 1818, aged 60. In 1821 he had wife nearly aged 60 and two daughters, the youngest aged 15 (no names were given). Martin died on 5 Jul 1832. {Ref: *Genealogical Abstracts of Revolutionary War Pension Files*, by Virgil D. White (1990), Application S41727; *Maryland Pension Abstracts: Revolution, War of 1812, and Indian Wars*, by Lucy K. McGhee (1966), p. 47}

BENJAMIN KERCHEVALL

Benjamin Kerchevall and **Margaret Montgomery**, of Maryland (county not stated), married in Indiana (county not stated) after 1800. {Ref: *Maryland Revolutionary Records*, by Harry Wright Newman (1938), p. 117}

WILLIAM KILGORE

William Kilgore served as a private in the 8th Cavalry District in Cecil Co., MD during the War of 1812 and subsequently moved to Ohio. He applied for bounty land in Fairfield County on 1 Apr 1851, aged 57, stating he served under Capt. **John R. Evans** and Capt. **William Hollingsworth** in the Regiment of Light Dragoons, commanded by Col. **Adam Whann**, from 23 Apr to 20 May 1813 and from 21 Aug to 18 Sep 1814. He applied again for bounty land (warrant 55-120-12974) on 13 Apr 1855, aged 76. Witnesses were **John Shaw** and **Robert P. Alford**, all of Fairfield County. {Ref: *Maryland Militia, War of 1812, Volume 3, Cecil & Harford Counties*, by F. Edward Wright, pp. 22, 57}

GEORGE KINKEAD

George Kinkead (sometimes spelled Kinkeid) served as a private in Cecil Co., MD during the War of 1812 in the company of Capt. **John Sample** in the 49th Regiment from 18 Apr to 18 May 1813. He subsequently moved to Ohio and applied for bounty land in Ashland County on 9 Nov 1850, aged 57. He stated he served in a regiment of Delaware Volunteers and was stationed at Fort Hollingsworth at the Head of Elk in Cecil Co., MD. He applied again for bounty land (warrant 55-120-83841) in Linn Co., IA on 6 Oct 1855, aged 61, and stated he had served in a regiment of artillery. His post office address was at Marion, IA. {Ref: *Maryland Militia, War of 1812, Volume 3, Cecil & Harford Counties*, by F. Edward Wright, pp. 13, 57}

GERRARD KING

Gerrard King was born in July, 1759 in Charles Co., MD and lived in Prince William Co., VA at the time of his enlistment in the Revolutionary War. After the war he lived in Maryland, then moved to Pennsylvania, and about 1796 moved to Ohio. He applied for a pension in Hamilton Co., OH on 17 Nov 1836 and died on 7 Jun 1840. **Kesiah C. King** applied for a widow's pension on 26 Apr 1852 and requested that her name be placed on the Cincinnati, OH pension rolls). {Ref:

Genealogical Abstracts of Revolutionary War Pension Files, by Virgil D. White (1990), Application W7984}

MARIA KING

Maria King was recorded as *"a member from the City"* when she was received into the Methodist Episcopal Church at Fell's Point in Baltimore, MD in 1828. She later removed to Cincinnati, OH on 9 Jan 1831. {Ref: Class Registers, East Baltimore Station (Fell's Point), Methodist Episcopal Church}

ELIZABETH KIRBY

Elizabeth Kirby moved from Baltimore, MD to Cincinnati, OH on 4 May 1830. {Ref: Class Registers, East Baltimore Station (Fell's Point), Methodist Episcopal Church}

JOHN KIRK

John Kirk was born circa 1755 and served in the Maryland troops during the Revolutionary War as a private in Capt. Henry Hardman's Company on 19 Jul 1776 in Frederick (now Washington) County. He later moved to Ohio and applied for a pension in Morgan Co., OH on 30 Mar 1821, aged 67. He stated his wife (name not given) was aged 78 and a granddaughter (name and age not given) lived with them. {Ref: *Genealogical Abstracts of Revolutionary War Pension Files*, by Virgil D. White (1990), Application R5989; *Archives of Maryland*, Volume 18, p. 51}

WILLIAM KITTLE

William Kittle enrolled as a private in the company of Capt. **Adam Barnes** in Anne Arundel Co., MD during the War of 1812. One time he stated he enrolled about 5 Sep 1812 and was discharged at Baltimore on 10 Dec 1812 and another time he stated he enrolled about 15 Aug 1812 and was discharged at Baltimore on 30 Oct 1812. Maryland military records show that William served under Capt. **Thomas Owings** in the 32nd Regiment at Annapolis from 13 to 26 May 1813 and also for 17 days in August, 1813 in Capt. **Thomas Hood**'s Battalion. He subsequently moved to Ohio and applied for bounty land (warrant 50-rej-114517) in Licking County on 22 Jul 1851, aged 67. He applied again for bounty land (warrant 55-160-86071) on 12 Jul 1855, aged 69 *(sic)*. **James Welsh** and **John Ramsower** stated they knew him at the time of said service. In a letter dated 3 Jul 1857 **William Kittle** stated he was first drafted at Poplar Spring in Anne Arundel Co., MD under the command of Capt. **Charles D. Warfield** and went with him to Annapolis and there placed under the command of Capt. **Thomas Owins** *(sic)*. He remained there for 8 or 10 days and was dismissed and sent home. He went again under the terms of a general call some 2 or 3 months after his dismissal from Capt. Owins and was placed under the command of Capt. Barnes. {Ref: *Maryland Militia, War of 1812, Volume 4, Anne Arundel & Calvert Counties*, by F. Edward Wright, pp. 34, 41, 101, 102}

JACOB KNIGHT

Jacob Knight was born circa 1750, enlisted on 19 May 1778 at Fredericktown, MD for the duration of the Revolutionary War, and served in the 2nd Maryland Regiment. He subsequently moved to Ohio and applied for a pension in Belmont Co., OH on 13 Aug 1819, age 68. In 1820 he stated he was aged 67 *(sic)* and his wife (name not given) was nearly 70. {Ref: *Genealogical Abstracts of Revolutionary War Pension Files*, by Virgil D. White (1990), Application S41733; *Archives of Maryland*, Volume 18, pp. 294, 323}

IGNATIUS KNOTT

Ignatius Knott was born on 17 Apr 1747 in St. Mary's Co., MD and when he was 21 years old he moved to Frederick (now Washington) Co., MD. He lived in Hagerstown at the time of his enlistment in the Revolutionary War and served as a private in the Washington Co., MD militia company of Capt. **James Smith** in 1776-1777. He also served with the Maryland troops who wintered at Valley Forge. In 1799 he moved to Clermont Co., OH and applied for a pension in November, 1832, aged 85. **Ignatius Knott** died on 15 Jul 1835 and his children were as follows:

1. **John Knott** married **Nancy Dumford** in 1805
2. **William Knott**
3. **Elizabeth Knott** married **Joseph Stouder**
4. **Susan Knott** married **Solomon Dumford**
5. **Hannah Knott** (b. 27 Sep 1790) married **Samuel Stouder** on 17 Jun 1813 and died in Clermont Co., OH on 19 Nov 1830

{Ref: *Genealogical Abstracts of Revolutionary War Pension Files*, by Virgil D. White (1990), Application S4481; *The Maryland Militia in the Revolutionary War*, by S. Eugene Clements & F. Edward Wright, p. 239; DAR Application 433359; *Index of Patriots, Revolutionary War Heroes and Their Families, Cincinnati Chapter DAR, 1893-1981*, by Jeraldyne Beets Clipson and Katherine Brewer Brinkdopke (1983), p. 163}

AMOS LACEY

Amos Lacey (sometimes spelled Lasy) stated in a letter, dated the 11th day of the 5th month, 1804, that he was *"a friend by birth and education, but through inattention in early life he deviated and married a woman of a different profession with the assistance of a hireling, for which he was justly disowned. He sincerely condemned his misconduct and requested reinstatement again in membership at Short Creek Monthly Meeting in Jefferson County, State of Ohio."* On the 26th day of the 1st month, 1805, the Gunpowder Monthly Meeting in Baltimore Co., MD approved his letter and forwarded a certificate to him in Ohio. {Ref: Gunpowder Quaker Monthly Meeting Minutes}

THOMAS LAMBERTSON

Thomas Lambertson moved from Maryland (county not stated) in 1817 to Sparta Township, Dearborn Co., IN and died there in 1865. {Ref: *History of Dearborn and Ohio Counties, Indiana* (1885), p. 559}

JAMES LARKINS

James Larkins was born circa 1756 and lived in Frederick Co., MD at the time of his enlistment in the Revolutionary War. **John Larkings** *(sic)* provided wheat for the use of the military on 31 May 1782. He married **Catharine Gerlinger** on 3 Jul 1783 in Lancaster, PA and later moved to Ohio. He applied for a pension in Harrison Co., OH on 4 Feb 1819, aged 63. In 1820 he was aged 62 *(sic)*, his wife **Catharine Larkins** was aged 60, and they had 3 children living at home: a son aged 21 on 17 Oct 1820, a son aged 18 on 5 Aug 1820, and daughter aged 14 (names not given). **Betsy Cook**, a daughter, aged 49, made an affidavit on 5 Jan 1856 in Wyandott Co., OH, stating her parents married on 3 Jul 1783 in Lancaster, PA, her father died on 12 Jul 1828 in Hamilton Co., OH, and her mother died on 27 Apr 1837 in Tuscarawas Co., OH. {Ref: *Genealogical Abstracts of Revolutionary War Pension Files*, by Virgil D. White (1990), Application R6167; *An Inventory of Maryland State Papers, Volume I, 1775-1789*, by Edward C. Papenfuse, *et al.* (1977), p. 517, citing Accession No. MdHR 6636-42-35/17}

GEORGE LASHLEY

George Lashley was born in Prince George's Co., MD in 1738 and lived there at the time of his enlistment in the Revolutionary War. About 6 years after the war he moved to Frederick Co., MD and in 1790 he moved to Mason Co., KY. In 1812 he moved to Daviess Co., IN and applied for a pension on 20 Mar 1834. {Ref: *Genealogical Abstracts of Revolutionary War Pension Files*, by Virgil D. White (1990), Application S31814}

WILLIAM LAWRENCE

William Lawrence and **Rachel Roberts** (widow), of Maryland (county not stated), married in Guernsey Co., OH on 29 Jul 1828. {Ref: *Maryland Revolutionary Records*, by Harry Wright Newman (1938), p. 117}

EDMOND R. LEACH

Edmond R. Leach (sometimes spelled Leech) served as a private in Major **Thomas Hood**'s Battalion for 20 days in July-August 1813 in Anne Arundel Co., MD during the War of 1812. He served in the company of Capt. **Adam Barnes** in the 32nd Regiment from 23 Aug to 27 Sep 1814 and was discharged at Baltimore. He subsequently moved to Ohio and applied for bounty land at Clay Township in Jackson County. He applied again for bounty land (warrant 55-120-10813) on 22 Mar 1855, aged 74. Witnesses were **Isaac Price** and **Adam Winpough**. {Ref: *Maryland Militia, War of 1812, Volume 4, Anne Arundel & Calvert Counties*, by F. Edward Wright, pp. 34, 42, 102}

JOSHUA LEACH

Joshua Leach was born in Maryland on 10 May 1756 and lived in Calvert Co., MD at the time of his enlistment in the Revolutionary War. He married **Priscilla Wilkinson** on 6 Jan 1783 or 6 Jan 1789 (both dates were given) in Calvert

114

County and later moved to Ohio. He applied for a pension in Butler County on 19 Oct 1832 and died on 6 Jun 1845. **Priscilla Leach** applied for a widow's pension on 30 Nov 1849, aged 85. **Robert B. Wilkinson**, a Justice of the Peace in Calvert Co., MD, was mentioned in 1849, but no relationship was given. {Ref: *Genealogical Abstracts of Revolutionary War Pension Files*, by Virgil D. White (1990), Application W1786}

THOMAS LEATHERBURY

Thomas Leatherbury, Jr., son of **Thomas Leatherbury** and **Lydia Dudley**, was born circa 1785 in Maryland, probably Queen Anne's Co., possibly Somerset Co., on the Eastern Shore. He married on 21 May 1812 to **Mary Forwood** (b. 28 Mar 1790, daughter of **Jacob Forwood** and **Martha Warner** who were members of the Quaker Meeting at Forest Hill, MD). **Thomas Leatherbury** served as a private during the War of 1812 in the company of Capt. **Nicholas Burke**, 6th Regiment, Baltimore City, from 19 Aug to 18 Nov 1814. After the war he and Mary moved to Switzerland Co., IN. Their children were as follows:

1. **Elizabeth Leatherbury** (b. circa 1814)
2. **Caroline Leatherbury** (b. circa 1816)
3. **Martha Leatherbury** (11 Apr 1818 - 4 Aug 1872) married **Thomas Lawton** on 16 Mar 1851
4. **Eli Leatherbury** (b. circa 1820)
5. **John T. Leatherbury** (b. circa 1823) married **Mary Ann Johnson**
6. **Jacob Forwood Leatherbury** (b. circa 1825 - 23 Aug 1889) married **Elizabeth Barchley**
7. **Parthenia Leatherbury**
8. **Mary Leatherbury**

Thomas Leatherbury died on 15 Oct 1831 and **Mary Leatherbury** died after 1855 in Switzerland Co., IN. {Ref: Information compiled in 1982 by Mr. & Mrs. B. C. Lawton, of Green Valley, AZ; *Maryland Militia, War of 1812, Volume 2, Baltimore*, by F. Edward Wright, p. 10}

CHARLES G. LEE

Charles G. Lee and **Maria Hutcheson**, of Maryland (county not stated), married in Indiana (county not stated) after 1800. {Ref: *Maryland Revolutionary Records*, by Harry Wright Newman (1938), p. 117}

ELIZABETH LEEDS

Elizabeth Leeds, youngest daughter of Capt. **Lodowick Leeds**, formerly of Baltimore, MD, married **William Marshall** in Hagerstown, MD on 1 Dec 1831. **George Leeds** married **Henrietta Stapleton**, of Hamilton, OH, in 1836 (exact date not given in newspaper) in Cincinnati, OH. {Ref: *Baltimore American*, 5 Dec 1831 and 9 Sep 1836, abstracted by Lorrie A. E. Erdman}

MARIA LETTER

Maria Letter moved from Baltimore, MD to Ohio (county not stated), with a certificate from the Methodist Episcopal Church, on 25 Apr 1831. {Ref: Class Lists, Baltimore City Station, Methodist Episcopal Church}

CHARLES LEVERTON

Charles Leverton, son of **Moses and Rachel Leverton**, of Caroline Co., MD, married **Lydia Gray**, daughter of **William and Elizabeth Gray**, of Caroline Co., MD, at the Marshy Creek Meeting in Caroline Co., MD (date not given). They moved to Milford, IN by the 15th day of the 11th month, 1832 at which time their certificate of removal from the Northwest Fork Monthly Meeting was received by the Milford Monthly Meeting in Wayne County. On the 25th day of the 11th month, 1833 **Charles Leverton** was reported for *"marrying contrary to the rules of discipline and guilty in a case of illegitimacy."* His children were as follows:

1. **Louisa Leverton** (b. 4th day of 10th month, 1833)
2. **Rachel Leverton** (b. 1st day of 3rd month, 1835)
3. **Thomas F. Leverton** (b. 4th day of 3rd month, 1837)
4. **John Edward Leverton** (b. 19th day of 11th month, 1839)
5. **Ann J. Leverton** (b. 2nd day of 2nd month, 1841)
6. **Lemuel Leverton** (b. 14th day of 4th month, 1843
7. **Willis Leverton** (b. 16th day of 10th month, 1844, d. 13th day of 3rd month, 1851)
8. **Arthur Leverton** (b. 31st day of 3rd month, 1846, d. 27th day of 3rd month, 1863)
9. **Oliver Leverton** (b. 25th day of 2nd month, 1849, died 19th day of 7th month, 1849)

Thomas Leverton, John Edward Leverton, Lemuel Leverton, Willis Leverton, and Arthur Leverton were received into membership of the Milford (Hicksite) Monthly Meeting (date not given). {Ref: "Migration of Caroline County Quakers to Indiana," by F. Edward Wright, *Maryland Genealogical Society Bulletin*, Volume 34, No. 3 (1993), p. 284}

ADAM LINN

Adam Linn enlisted in the Revolutionary War in Gettysburg, PA and married **Anna Hefley** on 17 Aug 1780 at Hagerstown, MD. They lived in Adams Co., PA and Washington Co., MD and Augusta Co., VA before moving to Guernsey Co., OH in 1811. Their children were as follows:

1. **John Linn** (b. 20 Nov 1784)
2. **Joseph Linn** (b. 18 Feb 1787)
3. **George Linn** (b. 2 Mar 1790)
4. **Samuel Linn** (b. 3 Sep 1793)
5. **Aaron Linn** (b. 10 Dec 1796)
6. **Andrew F. Linn** (b. 1805)

Adam Linn applied for a pension in Guernsey Co., OH on 19 Sep 1833, aged 83, and died on 17 Oct 1834. **Anna Linn** applied for a widow's pension on 19 Oct

1841, aged 80, stating she had lived in Guernsey Co., OH for 34 years and before that she had lived in Augusta Co., VA. **A. M. Linn** was mentioned in 1846 in Guernsey Co., OH, but no relationship was indicated. {Ref: *Genealogical Abstracts of Revolutionary War Pension Files*, by Virgil D. White (1990), Application W5023}

AQUILA LINTHICUM

Aquila Linthicum served as a private in the companies of Capt. **Benjamin Milliken** and Capt. **Richard H. Battee** in Anne Arundel Co., MD during the War of 1812. He subsequently moved to Ohio and applied for bounty land in Knox County on 3 Jan 1852, aged 65, stating he was drafted in Anne Arundel Co., MD around 12 Jan 1813. He applied again for bounty land (warrant 55-120-41203) at Liberty Township, Henry Co., OH, on 3 May 1855, aged 69. Witnesses were **George Cranford** and **John McWilliams**. On 9 May 1871 he applied for a pension (SO-15212) in Henry Co., OH, aged 85, and stated he married **Mary O'Rourke** at Annapolis on 12 May 1831, but was not now married, adding the following: *"I enrolled as a substitute for a drafted man in Capt. Battee's Co., 2nd Regiment. The regiment to which I belonged was assigned to the duty of guarding the city of Annapolis and that in said duty I served during the time that I was in the service of the United States as aforesaid, except that of a few days of said time when I was taken across the river Severn and employed in constructing earth works after which I was then returned to said city and there on the 12th of September 1813 was discharged."* Witnesses were **Larkin Linthicum** and **S. M. Hague**, of Henry Co., OH. In a letter dated 3 Mar 1873, **Aquila Linthicum** stated that he was a substitute for **Thomas Hall** around 18 May 1813, adding that *"Sgt. Joseph Lee, I well recollect, detailed and placed me on guard duty on the 4th of July in Annapolis ... some of my comrades that was in the company with me were William Williams, William Disney, Richard Butler, and James Elliot. On the 4th of July James Elliot was put under guard and I had to stand guard in his place and lost my dinner that was given to celebrate the day ..."* An undated letter from **Carrie Linthicum**, of Toledo, OH, stated **Aquila Linthicum** died on 10 Oct 1877. **Carrie Rachel Linthicum** was living on Monroe Street in Toledo, OH on 11 Mar 1879 and by 13 Nov 1882 she was living at 124 North Charles St., Baltimore, MD, at which time she wrote another letter, stating in part, *"My grandfather James O'Rourke gave my mother, his daughter, 160 acres of land what was given him from the Government for service in the war of 1776 revolution war. She never got it deed or papers to that affect are lost. I come to this state from Ohio to see about it. Fifty acres this state says is all that was awarded to him in Garrett County and that is on record that he sold it shortly after it was awarded to him. Whare did my mother get or how did my grandfather get deed to give to my mother is a mistery. Can you do anything for me in regard to it. My father Aquila Linthicum was in the War of 1812, died in 1877. Is there a pension that can be collected as he was an old soldier and I had to take care of him."* In a letter dated 26 Mar 1917 from Carrie R. Linthicum, aged 73, of 536 Virginia St., Toledo, OH, she requested part of her father's pension. In another letter from her, dated 18 Aug 1918, she stated in part, *"I was a teacher in* *the schools the time the law was passed in 1871 ... after his death, was house keeper and nurse ... took up dressmaking ... "* Maryland military records show that **Aquilla Linthicum** was a private in Capt. **Benjamin Milliken's** Company in the 2nd Regiment foe 21 days in April, 1813 and **John Linthicum, Jonathan Linthicum,** and **Thomas O'Rourke** served with him. He also served in Capt. **Richard H. Battee's** Company in Watkins' Regiment, at Annapolis, from 8 Jun to 8 Sep 1813. Maryland marriage records also show that **Aquila Linthicum** and **Mary O'Rouke** *(sic)* obtained a license in Anne Arundel County on 2 May 1831. {Ref: *Maryland Militia, War of 1812, Volume 4, Anne Arundel & Calvert Counties,* by F. Edward Wright, pp. 15, 41, 103, 104; *Index of War of 1812 Pension Files,* by Virgil D. White, p. 1185; *Anne Arundel County, Maryland Marriage Records, 1777-1877,* by John W. Powell, p. 72}

HANNAH LINTON

Hannah Linton requested a certificate of removal from the Baltimore Monthly Meeting, Western District, to the Plymouth Monthly Meeting in Ohio on the 8th day of the 3rd month, 1809, for herself, her husband (not named) and their four minor children, **Elizabeth Linton, Esther Linton, William Linton** and **Samuel Miller,** having already moved there. {Ref: Baltimore Quaker Monthly Meeting Minutes}

FRANCES LITTELL (LITTLE)

Frances Littell was recorded as *"a member from Harford Circuit"* (i.e., Harford Co., MD) when she was received into the Methodist Episcopal Church in Baltimore City on 12 Feb 1827. **Frances Little** removed to Ohio (county not stated) on 24 Apr 1827. {Ref: Class Lists, Baltimore City Station, Methodist Episcopal Church}

JOSEPH LONG

Joseph Long was born on 24 Oct 1761 and served in Maryland during the Revolutionary War. He married **Elizabeth ----** (b. 23 Feb 1761) in Frederick Co., MD on 26 Oct 1784 and their children were as follows:
1. **John Long** (b. 24 Jul 1785) married **Sarah ----**
2. **Jacob Long** (b. 31 Mar 1788) married **Catherine ----**
3. **Elizabeth Long** (b. 3 Sep 1790) married **John Mallincott**
4. **Sarah Long** (b. 12 Feb 1793) married **Robert Alstott**
5. **Margrett Long** (b. 12 Sep 1795) married **John Alstott**
6. **Susannah Long** (b. 24 Jul 1798) married first to **Epapheras Phelps** and second to **Mr. Housh**
7. **Nancy Long** (b. 21 May 1801) married **John Perry**
8. **Anna Long** (b. 1804) married first to **John Umbarger** and second to **Mr. Lewis**
9. **Mary Long** married **James Brown**

Joseph Long died on 9 Jul 1827 and **Elizabeth Long** subsequently applied for a widow's pension in Washington Co., IN on 27 Sep 1843. {Ref: DAR

Application 496639; *A Roster of Revolutionary Ancestors of the Indiana Daughters of the American Revolution* (1976), p. 205; *Genealogical Abstracts of Revolutionary War Pension Files*, by Virgil D. White (1990), Application W10201}

J. M. LOPEZ

J. M. Lopez, for many years the prompter (director of performances) in the theaters of Philadelphia, PA and Baltimore, MD, died in Cincinnati, OH on 3 May 1833. {Ref: *Baltimore American*, 22 May 1833, abstracted by Lorrie A. E. Erdman}

HENRY LORAH (LOAR)

Henry Lorah (Loar) was a private in the Baltimore Mechanical Militia Company on 4 Nov 1775, a corporal in Capt. Cox's Militia Company on 19 Dec 1776, took the Oath of Allegiance in 1778, and was a private in Capt. McClellan's Militia Company on 4 Sep 1780. **Henry Loar** applied for a pension in Hamilton Co., OH on 8 Jun 1818. He also applied for bounty land (warrant 1393-100-23) on 21 Apr 1827 in Hamilton County and mentioned his brother **John Loar**. In 1828 his nephew **Daniel Isgrig** lived in Ripley Co., IN and **Michael Isgrig, Sr.**, aged 73, lived in Hamilton Co., OH in 1827. {Ref: *Genealogical Abstracts of Revolutionary War Pension Files*, by Virgil D. White (1990), Application S41779; *Revolutionary Patriots of Baltimore Town and Baltimore County, 1775-1783*, by Henry C. Peden, Jr., p. 164}

CHARLES LOWNES

Charles Lownes requested a certificate of removal on the 13th day of the 7th month, 1814, from the Baltimore Monthly Meeting, Western District, to the Short Creek Monthly Meeting in Ohio, having already removed there. {Ref: Baltimore Quaker Monthly Meeting Minutes}

HIRAM LOY

Hiram Loy and **Nancy Denune**, of Maryland (county not stated), married in Ohio (county not stated) after 1825. {Ref: *Maryland Revolutionary Records*, by Harry Wright Newman (1938), p. 118}

JOHN LUCAS

John Lucas was born in Frederick Co., MD on 7 Sep 1760 and lived in Fayette Co., PA at the time of his enlistment in the Revolutionary War. After the war he moved to Kentucky for 12 years and in 1798 moved to Ohio. He applied for a pension in Butler Co., OH on 30 Jun 1832. {Ref: *Genealogical Abstracts of Revolutionary War Pension Files*, by Virgil D. White (1990), Application S4584}

WILLIAM LUCAS

William Lucas was born in Prince George's Co., MD on 7 Jul 1730 and served as a private in Westmoreland Co., PA in the company of Capt. **William**

Butler from 5 Jan 1776 to 25 Nov 1776 during the Revolutionary War. One record states he married **Sarah Higgens** on 18 Dec 1759 in Prince George's Co., MD and another record states he married **Armintha Jane Diehl** circa 16 Nov 1761. Additional research will be necessary before drawing any further conclusions. The children of William Lucas were **John Lucas, Jesse Lucas, William Lucas, Richard Lucas, Samuel Lucas, Cassandra Lucas, James Lucas, Thomas Lucas, Charles Lucas, and Basil Lucas**, and possibly **Jane Lucas**. William died in Liberty Township, Highland Co., OH in October, 1810. {Ref: DAR Applications 576596 and 608873; *A Roster of Revolutionary Ancestors of the Indiana Daughters of the American Revolution* (1976), p. 208}

JOSEPH LUSBY

Joseph Lusby, of Prince George's Co., MD, was drafted in the militia on 10 Apr 1813 and served under Capt. **William Minor** in the Virginia Militia and under Capt. **Samuel Coe** in the Maryland Militia during the War of 1812. He was discharged in Prince George's Co., MD on 24 Apr 1813, enrolled again on 17 Jun 1813, and was discharged at Washington, DC on 20 Aug 1813. He subsequently moved to Ohio and applied for bounty land (warrant 55-160-10095) in Logan County on 28 Nov 1850, aged 57. {Ref: *Maryland Militia, War of 1812, Volume 6, Prince George's County*, by F. Edward Wright, p. 42}

JACOB LUTHER

Jacob Luther was born circa 1757 and enlisted at Frederick, MD during the Revolutionary War. He married **Sarah ----** in 1791 and in 1829 they moved to Clay Co., IN. Jacob applied for a pension in Bowling Green, OH on 30 Oct 1832 and his wife **Sarah Luther** died in 1833. He died in September, 1836, and a daughter **Barbary Kendall** lived in Clay County in 1852. {Ref: *Genealogical Abstracts of Revolutionary War Pension Files*, by Virgil D. White (1990), Application R6533}

JAMES LYON

James Lyon, merchant of Ohio, married **Jane Clowdsley** on 11 Sep 1834. {Ref: *Baltimore American*, 13 Sep 1834, abstracted by Lorrie A. E. Erdman}

CHARLES MAGIN

Charles Magin served in the Maryland Line during the Revolutionary War and subsequently moved to Ohio. He applied for a pension in Adams Co., OH on 2 May 1818 and in 1820 he was aged 75 or 76 and had a wife **Sarah Magin** aged 64 or 65. {Ref: *Genealogical Abstracts of Revolutionary War Pension Files*, by Virgil D. White (1990), Application S41812}

JOHN MALOTT

John Malott was born in Frederick (now Washington) Co., MD in 1758 and lived in Washington County at the time of his enlistment in the Revolutionary War. In the year of St. Clair's Defeat [1792] he moved to Mason Co., KY for 4 years and then moved to Clermont Co., OH. He applied for a pension in November, 1832 and

Elizabeth Malott applied for a widow's pension in Brown Co., OH on 1 Nov 1838. She stated they were married in 1784 and John had died in February, 1838. **Dory Malott** was also mentioned in Brown County in 1838, but no relationship was given. {Ref: *Genealogical Abstracts of Revolutionary War Pension Files*, by Virgil D. White (1990), Application W3839}

THEODORE MALOTT

Theodore or **Dory Malott** was born on 7 Dec 1755 in Frederick (now Washington) Co., MD and lived there at the time of his enlistment in the Revolutionary War. In 1805 he moved to Ohio and applied for a pension in Clermont County in November, 1832. {Ref: *Genealogical Abstracts of Revolutionary War Pension Files*, by Virgil D. White (1990), Application S2737}

THOMAS MALOTT

Thomas Malott (sometimes spelled Melott and Molett) was born on 15 Apr 1753 in Frederick Co., MD and lived in Washington Co., MD at the time of his enlistment in the Revolutionary War. He served as second sergeant in the company of Capt. **James Smith** in 1776 and took the Oath of Allegiance in 1778. In the year of St. Clair's Defeat [1792] he moved to Kentucky and in 1812 he moved to Adams Co., OH where he applied for a pension on 11 Aug 1832. **John Malott**, of Clermont Co., OH, made an affidavit on 6 Aug 1832, aged 75. No relationship was given to Thomas, but **John Malott or Molett** took the Oath of Allegiance in Washington Co., MD in 1778. {Ref: *Genealogical Abstracts of Revolutionary War Pension Files*, by Virgil D. White (1990), Application S5059; *Revolutionary Patriots of Washington County, Maryland, 1776-1783*, by Henry C. Peden, Jr. (1998), p. 238}

JOHN MANLEY

John Manley (sometimes spelled Manly) lived in Cecil Co., MD at the time of his enlistment in the Revolutionary War. He was a private in Lee's Partizan Corps on 7 Apr 1778, was promoted to sergeant by December, 1780, and was granted leave "until called for" on 17 Jun 1783. **Thomas Manly** enrolled in the same corps on 7 Apr 1778. **John Manly** married **Mary Connolly** on or about 26 Mar 1788 (date of license) and **John Manley** married **Susanna Cox** on 15 Apr 1790 in Cecil County (license dated 13 Apr 1790). He subsequently moved to Fairfield Co., OH where he died on 13 or 14 Feb 1814. **Susanna Manley** applied for a widow's pension on 20 May 1844, aged 74 years and 6 months, and lived in Walnut Township, Fairfield Co., OH. {Ref: *Genealogical Abstracts of Revolutionary War Pension Files*, by Virgil D. White (1990), Application W5339; Cecil County, Maryland Marriage Licenses; *Revolutionary Patriots of Cecil County, Maryland, 1775-1783*, by Henry C. Peden, Jr. (1991), p. 69}

JESSE MANLY

Jesse Manly was born in 1751 in Cecil Co., MD and lived in Harford Co., MD at the time of his enlistment in the Revolutionary War. He was a private in

Militia Company No. 4 under Capt. **Aquila Hall** on 9 Sep 1775. After the war he lived in Frederick Co., VA for 20 years and then moved to Muskingum Co., OH where he applied for a pension on 28 May 1838. His sister **Elizabeth Hill**, of Fairfield Co., OH, made an affidavit on 24 May 1838, aged over 80 years. {Ref: *Genealogical Abstracts of Revolutionary War Pension Files*, by Virgil D. White (1990), Application R6866; *History of Harford County, Maryland*, by Walter W. Preston (1901), p. 109}

SAMUEL MANSFIELD

Samuel Mansfield enlisted at Elk Ridge, MD during the Revolutionary War and married **Charity Boyles** (b. 7 Jul 1755) at Hardwick, Sussex Co., NJ on 7 Apr 1778 at her father's house. They subsequently moved to Ohio and Samuel died on 15 Sep 1819 or 1820. **Charity Mansfield** applied for a widow's pension in Athens Co., OH on 1 Dec 1838. Their only child mentioned was **Martin Mansfield** (b. 25 Dec 1779) who married **Margaret ----** (b. 13 Jul 1788) and had a daughter **Esther Mansfield** (b. 9 Dec 1804). In 1838 Martin lived in Athens Co., OH and Charity's brother **Peter Boyles** lived in Goshen, Elkhart Co., IN, aged 60. {Ref: *Genealogical Abstracts of Revolutionary War Pension Files*, by Virgil D. White (1990), Application W4275}

THOMAS MANSFIELD

Thomas Mansfield was born on 14 Feb 1750 in Queen Anne's Co., MD and lived there at the time of his enlistment in the Revolutionary War. He also took the Oath of Allegiance in 1778. Thomas married **Anna Wilkinson** on 1 Oct 1795 at the home of **George Plummer** at Easton in Talbot Co., MD and in 1815 or 1816 they moved to the western country. He died on 11 or 19 Jan 1837 in Athens Co., OH and **Anna Mansfield** applied for a widow's pension at Trimble in Athens County on 5 Aug 1850. Their third child and oldest son **Thomas W. Mansfield** was aged 53 in 1850. {Ref: *Genealogical Abstracts of Revolutionary War Pension Files*, by Virgil D. White (1990), Application W7404; *Revolutionary Patriots of Kent & Queen Anne's Counties, Maryland*, by Henry C. Peden, Jr. (1995), p. 168}

JOSEPH MARK

Joseph Mark was born in 1752 in Frederick Co., MD and enlisted as a private in the 4th Battalion, Lancaster Co., PA militia on 28 Oct 1775. He married first to **Julia ----** in 1775 and second to **Catherine Plaugher or Plougher** (date not given). His children were as follows:

1. **Peter Mark** (b. 18 Feb 1776) married **Mary Legore**
2. **Mary Mark** married **Joseph Pratzman**
3. **John Mark** (b. 10 Aug 1781) married first to **Christina ----** and second to **Polly Loofburrow**
4. **Jacob Mark**
5. **Henry Mark**
6. **Elizabeth Mark**
7. **George Mark** married **Polly Free**

8. **Susan Mark** (b. 17 Aug 1784) married **George Sever**

9. **Samuel Mark** (b. 14 Aug 1793) married **Elizabeth Hare**

10. **Jonathan Mark** (b. 27 Dec 1795) married **Susannah Plaugher or Plougher**

Joseph Mark died in 1820 in Fayette Co., OH. {Ref: DAR Application 383052; *A Roster of Revolutionary Ancestors of the Indiana Daughters of the American Revolution* (1976), p. 404}

WILLIAM MARRIOTT

William Marriott married **Edith Waters** in Prince George's Co., MD on 29 Apr 1804 (by **Rev. Scott**, an Episcopal minister) and he served as a captain in Anne Arundel Co., MD during the War of 1812. He volunteered in 1813 and was stationed at Beard's Old House on the Severn River from 19 to 21 Jul 1814. He subsequently moved to Ohio and drew a pension (Old War File WF-12418) for several years before his death in Knox County on 18 Jul 1843. **Edith Marriott** applied for bounty land at Claibourn Township, Union Co., OH, on 1 Feb 1851, aged 66, and stated that **William Marriott** had commanded a company under General Winder in Maryland. **Joseph Penn** stated that he has been acquainted with the Marriotts for the last 58 years. On 15 May 1852 **John B. Lucas** and **John Wood** appeared at the Howard Co., MD courthouse and stated that **William Marriott, of Thomas**, of Anne Arundel Co., MD, was the captain of their company in the War of 1812. On 5 Mar 1853 **John Hood** stated that he served under Capt. Marriott until transferred to Capt. Bellmear's Company (no dates were given). On 9 Apr 1855 **Edith Marriott**, aged 70, applied for bounty land (warrant 55-rej-84059) in Union Co., OH. Witnesses were **William Hamilton** and **Greenberry Babbs**, of Union County. {Ref: *Maryland Militia, War of 1812, Volume 4, Anne Arundel & Calvert Counties*, by F. Edward Wright, pp. 22, 106; *Index of War of 1812 Pension Files*, by Virgil D. White, p. 1257}

JOHN MARSH

John Marsh was born in Northumberland Co., VA on 30 Oct 1756 and moved to Stafford Co., VA where he enlisted during the Revolutionary War. In the fall of 1777 he returned to Northumberland Co. and enlisted there. In May, 1780 he moved to Baltimore, MD and also enlisted there. In 1815 he moved to Belmont Co., OH where he applied for a pension on 10 Mar 1835, aged 78. {Ref: *Genealogical Abstracts of Revolutionary War Pension Files*, by Virgil D. White (1990), Application R6922}

JONATHAN MARSH

On the 22nd day of the 5th month, 1806, the Women's Meeting of the Gunpowder Monthly Meeting in Baltimore Co., MD reported that **Jonathan Marsh** and **Levinia Naylor** had been married in an orderly manner. On the 8th day of the 8th month, 1810, **Jonathan Marsh** requested a certificate of removal from the Baltimore Monthly Meeting, Western District, for himself, his wife **Leviney Marsh**, and their two minor children, **Margaret Marsh** and **Mary Marsh**, to the

Plymouth Monthly Meeting in Ohio, having already moved there. {Ref: Baltimore and Gunpowder Quaker Monthly Meeting Minutes}

WILLIAM MARSH

On the 8th day of the 6th month, 1808, **William Marsh** requested a certificate of removal from the Baltimore Monthly Meeting, Western District, to the Gunpowder Monthly Meeting, Baltimore Co., MD, for himself, his wife **Ann Marsh**, and their four minor children, **John Marsh, Margarett Marsh, William Marsh and Susanna Morthlin Marsh**. On the 28th day of the 3rd month, 1810, **William Marsh** requested a certificate of removal from the Gunpowder Monthly Meeting for himself, his wife **Ann Marsh** and their four minor children, **John Marsh, Margaret Marsh, William Marsh and Susanna Morthland Marsh**, to the Plymouth Monthly Meeting in the State of Ohio. {Ref: Baltimore and Gunpowder Quaker Monthly Meeting Minutes}

ROBERT MARTIN

Robert Martin (sometimes spelled Martain) was born in January, 1755 and served in Maryland during the Revolutionary War. He married **Nancy Phebus** in March, 1780 at Princess Anne, Somerset Co., MD, and they later moved to Bullitt Co., KY by 1810. They subsequently moved to Pickaway Co., OH where Robert applied for a pension on 18 May 1818. He died on 13 or 30 Nov 1836 in Ohio and **Nancy Martin** applied for a pension in Fountain Co., IN on 25 Apr 1845, aged 85, and her brother (name not given) lived there in 1846. Their children were as follows:

1. **George Martin** (died in infancy)
2. **Elizabeth Martin** (died before 1845)
3. **Luther Martin** (living in 1845)
4. **Ann Martin** married **Mr. Cory**
5. **Dorothy Martin** married **Mr. Cory**
6. **Cassia Martin** married **Mr. Grant**
7. **John P. Martin** (b. circa 1794)

Nancy Martin died on 19 Sep 1845 at the home of her son John (aged 51) in Fountain Co., IN, and left children **John P. Martin, Luther Martin, Ann Cory, Dorothy Cory**, and **Cassia Grant**. In 1846 **Jeremiah Cory** (relationship not stated) lived in Indiana. {Ref: *Genealogical Abstracts of Revolutionary War Pension Files*, by Virgil D. White (1990), Application W9535; *Revolutionary Patriots of Worcester & Somerset Counties, Maryland, 1775-1783*, by Henry C. Peden, Jr. (1999), pp. 189-190}

SAMUEL MARTIN

Samuel Martin moved from Baltimore, MD to Cincinnati, OH on 24 Aug 1828. {Ref: Class Lists, Baltimore City Station, Methodist Episcopal Church}

ISAAC AND MOSES MARTS

Isaac Marts and **Moses Marts** (twin brothers) married **Lavina McCormick** and **Tabitha McCormick** (twin sisters) near Connersville, IN on 27 May 1834. {Ref: *Baltimore American*, 21 Jan 1835, abstracted by Lorrie A. E. Erdman}

MATHIAS MASTEN

Mathias Masten was born on 8 Mar 1765 in Maryland (county not stated) and served as a private during the last 6 months of the Revolutionary War. He was present at the surrender of Yorktown in 1781. He married **Sarah Stanely** (b. 7 Jun 1775) in Stokes (now Forysth) Co., NC on 9 Dec 1794 and their children were as follows:

1. **Darius Masten** (b. 25 Sep 1795) married **Polly Fair**
2. **Mary Masten** (b. 8 Mar 1797) married **Coleman Jenkins**
3. **John Masten** (b. 2 Apr 1799) married **Sarah Cosner**
4. **Hezekiah Masten** (b. 6 May 1801)
5. **Sarah Masten** (b. 28 Nov 1803) married **Joseph Bodenhammer**
6. **Mathias Masten, Jr.** (b. 11 Oct 1809)
7. **Charlotte Masten** (b. 25 Oct 1812) married **Morgan Johnson**
8. **David Masten** (31 Mar 1816 - 20 Apr 1885) married first to ---- (not known) and second to **Elizabeth Appa(bel?)** *(sic)* in December, 1862 (she was born on 8 May 1849 *(sic)* and died on 24 Aug 1909)

Mathias Masten died in Coatesville, IN on 9 Nov 1856 and **Sarah Masten** died on 18 Dec 1862. {Ref: DAR Application 194224; *A Roster of Revolutionary Ancestors of the Indiana Daughters of the American Revolution* (1976), p. 411}

EZEKIEL MASTERS

Ezekiel Masters, of Prince George's Co., MD, served in the War of 1812 and later moved to Ohio. On 15 Oct 1850, aged 65, he applied for bounty land in Jackson Co., OH and stated he was pressed into service with his one horse and cart at Bladensburg, MD in August, 1813 for carrying baggage and was retained until the end of November, 1813. On 21 Mar 1855, aged 70, he applied again. On 28 Mar 1871, aged 87, he applied for a pension (SO-5791, SC-7736) and stated he married **Mary Stiffler** on 20 May 1856 in Jackson Co., OH. On 20 May 1878 **Mary Masters**, aged 80, widow of **Ezekiel Masters**, applied for a widow's pension (WO-12729) and stated they both had been previously married. He died in Jackson County on 9 Jun 1874. **George Masters**, aged 64 and **James B. Johnson**, aged 55, of Jackson Co., OH, stated they were acquainted with **Mary Masters** and Ezekiel died from cancer on his face, having been sick from 19 Aug 1878 to the date of his death. **J. B. Johnson**, M.D., stated that he practiced medicine at a point called Four Mile in Jackson Co., OH in the immediate neighborhood of the late **Ezekiel Masters** who died about 9 Jun 1874. He also said he was acquainted with the widow **Mary Masters** and he also knew Ezekiel's first wife **Sarah Masters** who is dead. Reference was made to the marriage license of **Ezekiel Masters** and **Mary Stiffler** dated 27 May 1856 and they were married on that same day by **James B.**

Johnson. It was also noted that **Mary Masters** died on 26 Oct 1878. {Ref: *Maryland Militia, War of 1812, Volume 6, Prince George's County*, by F. Edward Wright, p. 43}

MARY MATTHEWS
On the 25th day of the 10th month, 1809, a certificate of removal was produced by the Gunpowder Monthly Meeting for **Mary Matthews, Sr.** to Plymouth Monthly Meeting in the State of Ohio. {Ref: Gunpowder Quaker Monthly Meeting Minutes}

OLIVER MATTHEWS
Oliver Matthews, son of **William Matthews**, requested a certificate of removal on the 27th day of the 11th month, 1805, from the Gunpowder Monthly Meeting in Baltimore Co., MD, for himself, his wife **Phebe Matthews** and their three minor children, **Joel Matthews, William Matthews and Ann Matthews**, to Miami Monthly Meeting in the State of Ohio. {Ref: Gunpowder Quaker Monthly Meeting Minutes}

JOHN MAXWELL
John Maxwell was born circa 1741 and served in the Maryland and Pennsylvania Lines during the Revolutionary War. He later moved to Stark Co., OH and applied for a pension on 15 Jan 1820, aged 79. He had no family living with him at the time, and he died on 15 Dec 1826. {Ref: *Genealogical Abstracts of Revolutionary War Pension Files*, by Virgil D. White (1990), Application S41817}

WILLIAM McCLAIN
William McClain was born circa 1734 and served in Maryland during the Revolutionary War. He subsequently moved to Ohio and applied for a pension in Monroe County on 3 Jun 1818, aged 84. In 1820 he had a wife **Betsy McClain**, aged 52, and daughters **Martha McClain**, aged 19, **Rachel McClain**, aged 16, **Betsy McClain**, aged 14, **Hannah McClain**, aged 11, and **Matilda McClain**, aged 10; also, a child of his daughter **Rachel McClain** named **Martha McClain** lived with him. {Ref: *Genealogical Abstracts of Revolutionary War Pension Files*, by Virgil D. White (1990), Application S41838}

CARY McCLELLAND
Cary McClelland was born in Ireland on 15 Mar 1750 (1753?) and lived in Harford Co., MD at the time of his enlistment in the Revolutionary War. He also claimed service in the Pennsylvania Line, stating he enlisted in 1776 in the regiment of Col. **Walter Stewart** and served in the battles of Brandywine, Germantown and Princeton. After the war he moved to Greene Co., PA where he lived for about 50 years and then moved to Ohio. He applied for a pension in Knox County on 31 May 1834. In 1850 his children were mentioned, but no names were given. Cary died in Ross Co., OH on 8 Mar 1846 and was buried in the Bell Cemetery at Utica. He married first to **Miss McVay**, second to **Henrietta Myers** (died in 1829), and his

children were as follows:
1. **Margaret McClelland** (b. 1781)
2. **Cary McClelland, Jr.** (b. 6 Oct 1783) married **Mary Wathen** (2 Oct 1785 - 8 May 1853)
3. **Elizabeth McClelland** (b. 1784, d. in Emporia, KS, but is buried in the Bell Cemetery in Knox Co., OH) married **Benjamin Bell** (17 Feb 1782 - 19 Oct 1851, son of **James Bell** and **Mary Knox**) about 1804; their children were as follows:
    3-1. **Cary Bell** (22 Aug 1805 - 11 Mar 1826)
    3-2. **Jacob Bell** (1807 - 15 Oct 1874) married **Rachel Letts** (1811 - 6 Feb 1876)
    3-3. **Mary Bell** married **S. W. Hanger**
    3-4. **Henrietta Bell** married **Daniel Paul, Jr.**
    3-5. **Nancy Bell** married **David M. Elliott**
    3-6. **Amy Bell** married **Dr. D. W. McCann)**
    3-7. **Eunice Bell** married **Harrison Elliott**
    3-8. **James Bell** (15 Apr 1818 - 9 Apr 1879) married first to **Rowena Robinson** and second to **Phoebe J. Wright**
    3-9. **Belinda Bell** (1819 - 17 Jul 1875) married **Rev. Isaiah Jones**
    3-10. **Benjamin Bell, Jr.** married **Eliza Gearhart**
4. **John McClelland** (1786-1840) married **Nancy Montgomery** (died 5 May 1862, daughter of **Michael Montgomery** and **Nancy Evans**); their children were as follows:
    4-1. **Ellen McClelland** (b. 1818) married **Samuel Fulton** in 1838)
    4-2. **Marinda McClelland** married **Abner Ross**
    4-3. **Nancy McClelland** (1 Feb 1823 - 18 Sep 1873) married **Henry Grimes**)
    4-4. **Cary McClelland** married **Mary ----**
    4-5. **Michael M. McClelland** (b. 22 Dec 1824) married **Elizabeth Mettler**
    4-6. **Hannah McClelland** married **John Keys**
5. **William McClelland** (nothing further)
6. **---- McClelland** (nothing further)
7. **Jane McClelland** (nothing further)
8. **Nancy McClelland** married **William Buckingham** (son of **John Buckingham** and **Mary Bell**)
9. **Asa McClelland** married first to **Catherine Brown** and second to **Eliza McClelland**; their children were as follows:
    9-1. **Nancy McClelland** married **Mr. McFann**
    9-2. **Elizabeth McClelland** married **Mr. Porter**
    9-3. **Mary McClelland**
    9-4. **Mariah McClelland** married **Levi Rinehart**
    9-5. **Dawson McClelland** married **Sarah Hughes**
    9-6. **Asa McClelland, Jr.**
{Ref: *Genealogical Abstracts of Revolutionary War Pension Files*, by Virgil D.

White (1990), Application S9006; *The Tenmile Country and Its Pioneer Families*, by Howard L. Leckey (1950), pp. 468-469}

AQUILA McCOMAS

Aquila McComas, son of **James McComas** and **Anne Amos**, was born before 1778 in Harford Co., MD and died in November, 1848 in Monroe Co., OH; buried in Weeks Cemetery. He married **Sarah Montgomery** (25 Aug 1790 - 10 Jun or Jul 1885) on 8 Dec 1807 and their children were as follows:

1. **James McComas** (5 Oct 1808 - 2 Aug 1815)
2. **Elizabeth Ann McComas** (b. 15 Mar 1811, d. 1 Apr 1898; married **James McComas** (3 Jun 1809 - 29 Jan 1889, Monroe Co., OH), son of **Amos McComas** and **Isabella Glenn**. Their son **William Glenn McComas** (b. 28 Feb 1835, OH - died 22 Jun 1918, OH) married **Agnes Ann Finney** and is buried in Beallsville Cemetery.
3. **Orpah Ellen McComas** (b. 14 Apr 1816 in Harford Co., MD, d. 25 Jul 1897 at St. Clairsville, Belmont Co., OH) married on 19 Apr 1832 to **Joshua Amos** (b. 1805, York Co., PA - died 1867, Belmont Co., OH), son of **Benjamin Amos** (b. 30 Apr 1774 in Maryland and died on 10 Oct 1869 in Ohio; wife **Catherine Wiley** (1774-1854); their children were as follows:
    3-1. **James Oliver Amos** (b. 30 Mar 1833, Monroe Co., OH and died on 7 Dec 1918 at Sidney, OH) married **Nancy J. Craig** on 9 Sep 1856
    3-2. **William Thomas Amos** (b. 8 Feb 1836, d. 25 Mar 1859, Monroe Co., OH)
    3-3. **Sarah Catherine "Kate" Amos** (b. 23 Feb 1838) married **James Ferguson** on 11 Nov 1869, Belmont Co., OH
    3-4. **Elizabeth Jane Amos** (b. 13 Jul 1842, d. 1905, Monroe Co., OH) married **Wesley Prewitt**
    3-5. **Aquila McComas Amos** (b. 27 Mar 1843) married first to **Elsie R. ----** and second to **Sarah Jane Carl**
    3-6. **Benjamin Franklin Amos** (b. 8 Aug 1846) married **Mary W. Mitchell**
    3-7. **Anna Morice Amos** (b. 18 Feb 1852)
    3-8. **Eldridge Gerry Amos** (b. 6 May 1862, d. 20 Oct 1956) married **Blanche Grove**
4. **Augustus McComas** (b. circa 1820, OH) married **Delilah ----** and lived in Monroe Co., OH; their children born between 1843 and 1860 were as follows:
    4-1. **James McComas**
    4-2. **Sarah J. McComas**
    4-3. **John W. McComas**
    4-4. **Aquilla McComas**
    4-5. **Franklin McComas**
    4-6. **Augustus McComas, Jr.**
    4-7. **John McComas**
5. **Sarah Jane McComas** (b. 18 May 1822)
6. **Amanda McComas** (b. 20 Nov 1824)

128

7. Sarah A. McComas (19 Jul 1831 - 11 Sep 1835)
{Ref: McComas family information compiled by Gertrude J. Stephens, of Spanish Fort, AL, and published in her 1992 book titled *Children of Mt. Soma*, pp. 487-496}

JOHN McCORMICK

John McCormick was born in Kent Co., MD on 22 Sep 1750 and lived in Washington Co., MD at the time of his enlistment in the Revolutionary War. He later moved to Franklin Co., PA and also enlisted there. He subsequently moved to Ohio and filed for a pension in Richland County on 20 Feb 1834. {Ref: *Genealogical Abstracts of Revolutionary War Pension Files*, by Virgil D. White (1990), Application R6651}

ANN McCOY

Ann McCoy moved from Baltimore, MD to Cincinnati, OH in April, 1831. {Ref: Class Lists, Baltimore City Station, Methodist Episcopal Church}

PATRICK McCRISTAL

Patrick McCristal (sometimes spelled McCristel and McChristal) served in Annapolis and Baltimore during the War of 1812. He was a private in the company of Capt. **Charles Pumphrey** in the 22nd Regiment in Anne Arundel Co., MD, stationed at Fort Madison and at the Bodkin Point for 9 days between 13 Apr and 5 May 1813 and at Sandy Point from 16 to 24 Aug 1813. He also served in that company at Fort Madison for 11 days in September, 1814, but was *"fined by court martial to forfeit 10 days' pay."* He claimed to have volunteered in a company of Irish Greens commanded by Capt. McConkey in the 25th Regiment at Baltimore around 12 Sep 1814, but he was referring to Capt. **James McConkey** of the 27th Regiment. Maryland military records show that **Patrick McCristal** (misspelled as McCustal) joined Capt. McConkey's company on 11 Sep 1814 and was discharged on 20 Sep 1814. He apparently participated in the Battle of Fort McHenry. He subsequently moved to Ohio and applied for bounty land (warrant 50-rej-84463) in Perry County on 13 Mar 1851, aged 66. {Ref: *Maryland Militia, War of 1812, Volume 4, Anne Arundel & Calvert Counties*, pp. 33, 37, 105, and *Volume 2, Baltimore*, p. 19, by F. Edward Wright; *The British Invasion of Baltimore, 1812-1815*, by William M. Marine, pp. 363, 364}

WALTER McDANIEL

Walter McDaniel, brother of **William McDaniel**, *q.v.*, was born in Anne Arundel Co., MD in 1747 and lived in Prince George's Co., MD at the time of his enlistment in the Revolutionary War in 1776. After the war he moved to Virginia and then to Brown Co., OH where he applied for a pension on 30 Apr 1833. {Ref: *Genealogical Abstracts of Revolutionary War Pension Files*, by Virgil D. White (1990), Application S18505; *Revolutionary Patriots of Prince George's County, Maryland, 1775-1783*, by Henry C. Peden, Jr. (1997), pp. 210-211}

WALTER McDANIEL

Walter McDaniel, of Prince George's Co., MD, was drafted into the War of 1812 in early August, 1814 and was discharged a few days later at Nottingham, MD. On 22 Aug 1814 he was drafted again and was discharged about 11 Sep 1814 at Fort Washington, MD. He later moved to Ohio and settled in Fairfield County. On 13 Jan 1853, aged 59, he applied for bounty land (warrant 50-rej-158664) at Lancaster, OH. {Ref: *Maryland Militia, War of 1812, Volume 6, Prince George's County*, by F. Edward Wright, p. 43}

WILLIAM McDANIEL

William McDaniel, brother of **Walter McDaniel**, *q.v.*, lived in Calvert Co., MD at the time of his enlistment in the Revolutionary War. He was enlisted by Lt. **Frederick Skinner** on 23 Aug 1776 and served as a private in the company of Capt. **Frisby Freeland** on 1778. He also took the Oath of Allegiance in 1778, as did **Edward McDaniel**. William subsequently moved to Ohio and applied for a pension in Clinton County on 22 Oct 1835, aged 81. He died on 24 Dec 1836. {Ref: *Genealogical Abstracts of Revolutionary War Pension Files*, by Virgil D. White (1990), Application R6683; *Revolutionary Patriots of Calvert & St. Mary's Counties, Maryland, 1775-1783*, by Henry C. Peden, Jr. (1996), p. 188; *Archives of Maryland*, Volume 18, p. 33}

JAMES McDERMUT

James McDermut was born in Maryland in 1758 and lived in Northampton Co., PA at the time of his enlistment in the Revolutionary War. After the war he moved to Mercer Co., PA and in 1818 moved to Richland Co., OH. He applied for a pension on 15 Oct 1833 and applied for bounty land (warrant 55-160-26082) on 29 Mar 1855. **Mark McDermut** (relationship not stated) was a witness. {Ref: *Genealogical Abstracts of Revolutionary War Pension Files*, by Virgil D. White (1990), Application S9014}

HUGH McDONOUGH

Hugh McDonough was born in Dublin, Ireland on 4 Jul 1752 and came to America when he was 14 years old. He settled in Cecil Co., MD and then moved to Chester Co., PA before the Revolutionary War began. He enlisted there during the war and in 1780 moved to Washington Co., PA. A few years later he moved to Jefferson Co., OH and then to Harrison Co., OH. Hugh applied for a pension on 14 Sep 1832. His heirs were mentioned in 1850, but no names were given. {Ref: *Genealogical Abstracts of Revolutionary War Pension Files*, by Virgil D. White (1990), Application S2794}

JOSEPH McDOUGAL

Joseph McDougal (sometimes spelled McDugal) was born in Northern Ireland in 1753 and came to America in 1772. He lived in Cecil Co., MD at the time of his enlistment in the Revolutionary War, having enrolled as a private in the

130

militia on 1 Oct 1778. He also took the Oath of Allegiance in 1778. Around 18 years later he moved to the forks of the Shenandoah River in Virginia and 9 years later he moved to Morgantown, VA. Seven years later he moved to Scioto Co., OH where he applied for a pension on 28 Nov 1834, aged 81. {Ref: *Genealogical Abstracts of Revolutionary War Pension Files*, by Virgil D. White (1990), Application R6693; *Revolutionary Patriots of Cecil County, Maryland, 1775-1783*, by Henry C. Peden, Jr. (1991), p. 75}

JOHN McDOWELL

John McDowell was born in Cecil Co., MD in 1748 and married **Martha Johnstone** circa 1776 at New London Crossroads, PA. They later moved to Virginia (county not stated). Their children were as follows:

1. **Alexander McDowell** (married **Mary Shelton**)
2. **John McDowell, Jr.** (married **Catherine Wells**)
3. **Anna McDowell** (married first to **William R. Dickinson** and second to **George Woods**)
4. **Maria Antoinette McDowell** (married **Humphrey H. Leavitt**)

John McDowell served as a captain in Virginia during the Revolutionary War and later moved to Ohio. He died on 1 Jan 1825 in Steubenville, OH. {Ref: DAR Application 305990; *Index of Patriots, Revolutionary War Heroes and Their Families, Cincinnati Chapter DAR, 1893-1981*, by Jeraldyne Beets Clipson and Katherine Brewer Brinkdopke (1983), p. 176}

ANDREW McGREW

Andrew McGrew (sometimes spelled McGrue and Megrue) was born in Baltimore, MD on 14 Mar 1760 and served as a private in Pennsylvania during the Revolutionary War. He married **Hannah Rust** (1762-1822) and moved to Milford, OH where he died on 5 Aug 1821. Their children were as follows:

1. **Charles McGrew** married **Nancy Lloyd**
2. **Paul McGrew** married **Nancy Newton**
3. **Jonathan McGrew** married **Ruth Crawford**
4. **Andrew McGrew, Jr.** married **Ann McClelland**
5. **William McGrew** married **Rachel Newton**
6. **Joseph McGrew**
7. **Margaret McGrew** married **Conduce Gatch**
8. **Anna McGrew** married **John Gest**
9. **Isaac McGrew** (unmarried)

{Ref: DAR Application 270948; *Index of Patriots, Revolutionary War Heroes and Their Families, Cincinnati Chapter DAR, 1893-1981*, by Jeraldyne Beets Clipson and Katherine Brewer Brinkdopke (1983), citing *History of Clermont County, Ohio*, by Rockey, p. 464}

JAMES McKAY

James McKay was born in Prince George's Co., MD circa 1752 and lived in Frederick Co., MD at the time of his enlistment in the Revolutionary War. **William**

McKay, a probable relative, also served as a private in Frederick Co., MD in 1776. James subsequently moved to Clermont Co., OH where he applied for a pension on 6 Aug 1832, aged 80, and died on 2 Aug 1833. {Ref: *Genealogical Abstracts of Revolutionary War Pension Files*, by Virgil D. White (1990), Application S16199; *Revolutionary Patriots of Frederick County, Maryland, 1775-1783*, by Henry C. Peden, Jr. (1995), p. 247}

BENJAMIN McKINSEY

Benjamin McKinsey, of Cecil Co., MD, served as a private in the War of 1812, at which time he was 5 ft. 5 in. tall, with brown hair, blue eyes, and a florid complexion. In 1852 **Elizabeth McKinsey**, aged 54, applied for bounty land (warrant 50-40-72240) in Ohio. Her temporary address was Cincinnati, OH, and she had lived a short period in St. Louis, MO. She stated that she married **Benjamin McKinsey, Jr.** on 1 May 1817 at Elkton, MD, by Rev. **John Sharpley**, a Methodist Episcopal minister, and her former name was **Elizabeth Purnell** [Note: Cecil Co., MD records indicate a marriage license was issued to **Benjamin McKinzie** and **Elizabeth Purnell** on 1 May 1817]. Her brothers were **James S. Purnell** and **G. Purnell**. She also stated that **Benjamin McKinsey** died on 24 May 1844 in Elkton, MD. On 23 Apr 1855, aged 58, **Elizabeth McKinsey** lived in Hamilton Co., OH and acquaintances were **A. U. Plattenburg** and **E. A. Plattenburg**. A letter in the file written by **Mrs. J. V. Maloney (Mildred Pratt Maloney)**, 624 N. Wilton St., West Philadelphia, PA, dated 12 Feb 1937, stated she was the great granddaughter of **Benjamin McKinsey** and both of her great grandparents were buried in Elkton, MD. {Ref: *Maryland Militia, War of 1812, Volume 3, Cecil & Harford Counties*, by F. Edward Wright, p. 59; *Cecil County, Maryland Marriage Licenses, 1777-1840*, compiled by DAR, p. 38}

McKINZEY (McKENZIE) FAMILY

Bennett McKenzie (sometimes spelled McKensey, McKenzie, McKinsey and McKinzey) made inquiry from Ross Co., OH to the U. S. War Department on 15 Jan 1793 and stated his father **Joshua McKenzie** was born in Baltimore, MD and he enlisted with his brother **Moses McKenzie** during the Revolutionary War. On 31 Jul 1856 **A. B. McKenzie** made inquiry from Bourneville, OH as to the service of **Jesse McKenzie** who was a brother of **Moses McKenzie** and **Joshua McKenzie**, Revolutionary War soldiers. He stated that Jesse's wife **Catharine McKenzie** drew a pension, which has been confirmed by her application. **Jesse McKinzey** enlisted at Frederick, MD during the Revolutionary and married **Catharine ----** on 22 Jan 1784 in Allegany Co., MD. Their children were as follows:

1. **John McKinzey** (b. 9 Dec 1788)
2. **Bennett McKinzey** (b. 5 Jan 1791)
3. **Elenor McKinzey** (b. 10 Apr 1793)

Jesse McKinzey lived near Cumberland, MD from 1791 to 1793 and then moved to Knox Co., OH. He applied for a pension on 8 Jul 1818, aged 55, and died on 3 Nov 1818 at Vincennes, IN. **Catharine McKinzey** applied for a widow's pension in Ross Co., OH on 15 Oct 1838, and bounty land (warrant 11513-100-15), and in 1848 she lived in Cincinnati, OH. Her son **Bennett McKinzey** and her daughter **Elenor McKinzey** died before 1838 and her son **John McKinzey** served as an officer in the War of 1812, went to South America after the war, and was never heard from again. In 1839 **John McKenzie**, of Ross Co., OH, stated that he had known **Jesse McKinzey** and his wife since 1792 or 1793. In 1848 **Enoch Cockrell** made an affidavit at Cincinnati, OH and stated that **Jesse McKinzey** had two brothers **Joshua McKinzey** and **Moses McKinzey** who served in the Revolutionary War. In 1856 two of his grandchildren, **Mariah L. Walter** and **Abner Cockeral**, were mentioned as living. **Bennett McKenzie**, of Ross Co., OH, stated that he was a son of **Joshua McKenzie**. In 1856 **A. B. McKenzie** (relationship not given) lived in Brownsville, OH. {Ref: *Genealogical Abstracts of Revolutionary War Pension Files*, by Virgil D. White (1990), Application W7432}

JOHN McKNIGHT

John McKnight served in Maryland during the Revolutionary War and subsequently moved to Ohio. He applied for a pension in Warren County on 25 Apr 1818, but lived in Clermont County. In 1823 he had a wife named **Rachel McKnight**, aged about 40, and John stated he was aged 65, but in 1831 he gave his age as 75. {Ref: *Genealogical Abstracts of Revolutionary War Pension Files*, by Virgil D. White (1990), Application S41860}

WILLIAM McMEEKEN

The following notice appeared in the *Frederick-Town Herald* in Frederick, MD on 2 Jun 1810: *"Subscribers have purchased from Rev. Patrick Davidson several lots laid off of said Davidson's farm near Emmittsburg; since then we have found on the records in Frederick County a mortgage on said farm for 900 pounds, unto William McMeeken now of State of Ohio; until release of mortgage is obtained in hands of Dr. Robert L. Annan, we forewarn persons from taking assignment on bonds used in payment."* [followed by the names of the 8 subscribers]. {Ref: *Western Maryland Newspaper Abstracts, Volume 3, 1806-1810*, by F. Edward Wright, pp. 36-37}

DANIEL McMILLEN

Daniel McMillen was born in Ireland in 1757 and lived in Cecil Co., MD at the time of his enlistment in the Revolutionary War. By 1806 he was in Kentucky and married **Jane Sconce** in Cumberland County on 17 Jan 1811. They moved in 1818 to Jefferson Co., IN and in 1821 their children were as follows:
1. **Julia Ann McMillen** (b. 1815)
2. **Franklin McMillen** (b. 1817)
3. **Stephen McMillen** (b. 1819)
4. **Margaret McMillen** (b. 1820)

John W. McMillen was a Magistrate in Monroe Co., KY in 1821, but no relationship was given to **Daniel McMillen** who applied for a pension in Ripley Co., IN on 20 Aug 1832 and died on 15 or 16 Aug 1838 or 1839 (all dates were given in application). **John C. Sconce**, brother of Jane (Sconce) McMillen, lived in Cumberland Co., KY in 1852, aged 63. **Jane McMillen** applied for a widow's pension in Dearborn Co., IN on 30 May 1853, aged 68, and died on 23 Mar 1855. {Ref: *Genealogical Abstracts of Revolutionary War Pension Files*, by Virgil D. White (1990), Application S6800}

DANIEL JAMES McMULLEN

Daniel James McMullen was born in County Antrim, Ireland in May, 1760, and came to America in the spring of 1774. He landed at New Castle, DE and then went to Chester Co., PA where he lived at the time of his enlistment in the Revolutionary War. After the war he lived in Delaware and Maryland until 1819 when he moved to Ohio. He applied for a pension in Ross Co., OH on 4 Jun 1833. {Ref: *Genealogical Abstracts of Revolutionary War Pension Files*, by Virgil D. White (1990), Application S9007}

THOMAS McQUEEN

Thomas McQueen, probably a son of **Thomas McQueen** and grandson of **Dugal McQueen**, of Scotland and Baltimore Co., MD, was born in Baltimore County in 1761 and lived near the Mingo Bottoms on the Ohio River in Virginia (Ohio County) at the time of his enlistment in the Revolutionary War. He later moved to Indiana and applied for a pension in Bartholomew County on 12 Sep 1832, stating that his brother **Joshua McQueen**, of Kentucky, knew about his service. Thomas died in 1838 leaving a widow and 11 children (no names were given) and his widow died in 1839. A son-in-law **Moses Tomer**, of Randolph Co., MO, stated in July, 1851 that **Thomas McQueen** had married about 1801, but he did not give the name of his wife. {Ref: *Genealogical Abstracts of Revolutionary War Pension Files*, by Virgil D. White (1990), Application S33080; *Historical Register of Virginians in the Revolution, 1775-1783*, by John H. Gwathmey (1938), p. 538; *Baltimore County Families, 1659-1759*, by Robert W. Barnes (1989), pp. 440-441}

MOSES MEDCALF

On the 23rd day of the 6th month, 1814, and again on the 25th day of the 8th month, 1814, **Moses Medcalf** (sometimes spelled Midkelf) requested a certificate of removal from Deer Creek Monthly Meeting in Harford Co., MD, for himself, his wife **Susannah Medcalf** and their eight minor children, **Abraham Medcalf, Mary Medcalf, Rebeckah or Rebecca Medcalf, Jesse or Jessy Medcalf, Joseph Medcalf, Rachel Medcalf, Moses Medcalf, Jr., and David Medcalf**, to Short Creek Monthly Meeting in Ohio. Earlier, in 1813, their daughter **Elizabeth Medcalf** married **Thomas Kennard**, *q.v.* {Ref: Deer Creek Quaker Monthly Meeting Minutes}

WILLIAM MEDLEY

William Medley or **William Glover Medley** was born circa 1763 and lived in Montgomery Co., MD at the time of his enlistment in the Revolutionary War. He stated that he had entered the service under the name of **William Glover**, but no explanation was given. He subsequently moved to Ohio and applied for a pension in Washington County on 24 Jun 1834, aged 71. Although his application was rejected, Maryland military records indicate that men by both names served in the war. **William Glover** was recruited in 1780 as a private to serve in the Continental Army. **William Medley** was a private in the Montgomery Co., MD militia on 15 Jul 1780. **William Medley**, born in Maryland, about 17 years of age, 5 feet 2 or 3 inches tall, smooth faced, light colored hair, and well made, was recruited by **Philip Casey** and **David O'Neale** on 26 Mar 1781 in Montgomery Co., MD. {Ref: *Genealogical Abstracts of Revolutionary War Pension Files*, by Virgil D. White (1990), Application R7089; *Archives of Maryland*, Volume 18, p. 341; *Maryland Genealogical Society Bulletin*, Volume 33, No. 1, p. 155; Maryland State Archives Microfilm M3218}

ANDREW METER

Andrew Meter, of Stark Co., OH, married **Eliza Haslett**, youngest daughter of Major **James Haslett**, on 24 Jan 1833. {Ref: *Baltimore American*, 26 Jan 1833, abstracted by Lorrie A. E. Erdman}

ISAAC METTLER

Isaac Mettler (b. 1774) and family moved from Maryland (county not stated) and settled on the east bank of the Whitewater in Harrison Township, Dearborn Co., OH in 1813. They were accompanied by the Andres family. Isaac had four brothers (names not given) who served in the Revolutionary War and *"he, himself, attended the funeral of President Washington at Trenton, NJ, on which occasion he was one of the strewers of flowers."* {Ref: *History of Dearborn and Ohio Counties, Indiana* (1885), p. 526}

JACOB MIKESELL

Jacob Mikesell was born in Frederick Co., MD on 2 Nov 1756 and lived there at the time of his enlistment in the Revolutionary War. He served as a sergeant in the company of Capt. **Jacob Snowdenberger** in 1776. **George Mikesell, John Mikesell, Martin Mikesell, and Michael Mikesell** also served in the militia and **Andrew Mikesell** took the Oath of Allegiance in 1778. **Jacob Mikesell** married **Mary Valentine** (1759-1846) in 1779 and subsequently moved to Clark Co., IN. He applied for a pension in Jefferson County on 7 Sep 1832. A son, **Peter Mikesell** (1782-1860) died in Preble Co., OH. {Ref: *Genealogical Abstracts of Revolutionary War Pension Files*, by Virgil D. White (1990), Application S16202; Maryland Society, Sons of the American Revolution, Application No. 1998; *Revolutionary Patriots of Frederick County, Maryland, 1775-1783*, by Henry C. Peden, Jr. (1995), p. 254}

JOHN MILES

John Miles was born in Anne Arundel Co., MD on 28 Mar 1755 and lived there at the time of his enlistment in the Revolutionary War. He was enrolled by

Capt. **Edward Tillard** on 10 Jul 1776 and he was 5 ft. 9 in. tall. After the war he moved to Pennsylvania and then to Knox Co., OH. He applied for a pension in Licking Co., OH on 29 Oct 1832. {Ref: *Genealogical Abstracts of Revolutionary War Pension Files*, by Virgil D. White (1990), Application S2827; *Archives of Maryland*, Volume 18, p. 39}

GEORGE MILLER

George Miller was born in 1764 in Hagerstown, MD and lived in Washington Co., PA at the time of his enlistment in the Revolutionary War. He subsequently moved to Ohio and applied for a pension on 29 Sep 1832. {Ref: *Genealogical Abstracts of Revolutionary War Pension Files*, by Virgil D. White (1990), Application R7190}

GEORGE MILLER

George Miller was born in February, 1760 in Frederick (now Washington) Co., MD, about 6 or 8 miles south of Hagerstown. When he was 5 years old he moved with his father (name not given) to Buffalo Creek in western Pennsylvania (now Washington Co., PA) and enlisted there in the Revolutionary War. In 1785 George moved to Ohio Co., VA and served in the military in 1787 and 1791. He moved to Jefferson Co., OH in 1792 and then to Guernsey Co., OH, the part that later became Monroe County. He applied for a pension in 1834. {Ref: *Genealogical Abstracts of Revolutionary War Pension Files*, by Virgil D. White (1990), Application R7191}

JOHN MILLER

On the 26th day of the 6th month, 1806, **John Miller, Jr.** produced a certificate from the New Garden Monthly Meeting (Chester Co., PA) to the Deer Creek Monthly Meeting in Harford Co., MD, for himself, his wife **Edith Miller**, and their two minor children, **Lidia Miller** and **Rachel Miller**. On the 28th day of the 12th month, 1809, **John Miller** requested a certificate for himself, his wife **Edith Miller**, and their three minor children, **Lydia Miller, Rachel Miller** and **William John Miller**, to Baltimore Monthly Meeting, Western District. On the 8th day of the 11th month, 1810, **John Miller** requested a certificate of removal from the Baltimore Monthly Meeting, Eastern District, to the Short Creek Monthly Meeting in Ohio, for himself, his wife **Edith Miller**, and their three minor children, **Lydia Miller, Rachel Miller** and **William Miller**. {Ref: Deer Creek Quaker and Baltimore Quaker Monthly Meeting Minutes}

JOSIAS MILLER

Josias Miller was born in 1757 and served in the Maryland Line during the Revolutionary War. He applied for a pension in the District of Columbia on 16 Apr 1818, but was a resident of Franklin Co., Ohio. He was aged 63 on 8 Apr 1820 and lived in Ohio at the time, but had no family living with him. {Ref: *Genealogical Abstracts of Revolutionary War Pension Files*, by Virgil D. White (1990), Application S40160}

THOMAS MILLER

Thomas Miller, son of **Samuel Miller**, was born in 1760 in Cecil Co., MD and served in the Virginia Line during the Revolutionary War. He married **Ann or Nancy Ball**, daughter of **James and Susan Ball**, on 7 Aug 1784 in Chesterfield Co., VA. Thomas subsequently moved to Ohio and applied for a pension in Franklin County on 2 May 1818, aged 58. He died in Chillicothe, Ross Co., OH, on 16 or 17 Jul 1821 and **Ann Miller** applied for a widow's pension in Pittsylvania Co., VA on 22 Oct 1838, aged 71 or 72. A son **Samuel T. Miller** was mentioned, as were Thomas' sisters **Agness Williams** and **Deborah Miller**. Thomas' brother **John M. Miller** lived near Farmington, Cecil Co., MD in 1838. {Ref: *Genealogical Abstracts of Revolutionary War Pension Files*, by Virgil D. White (1990), Application W7454; *Historical Register of Virginians in the Revolution, 1775-1783*, by John H. Gwathmey (1938), p. 550}

THOMAS MILLER

Thomas Miller was born in 1782 and was drafted during the War of 1812 in Caroline Co., MD in August, 1813 for a period of 6 months. He served as a private in the company of Capt. **Peter Willis** from 15 Aug to 30 Aug 1813. He subsequently moved to Ohio and applied for bounty land (warrant number not given) in Fairfield County on 29 Oct 1850, aged 68, and received 120 acres. {Ref: *Maryland Militia, War of 1812, Volume 1, Eastern Shore*, by F. Edward Wright, pp. 82, 112}

ELIJAH MILLS

Elijah Mills was born in Frederick Co., MD on 5 Sep 1757 and lived in Washington Co., MD at the time of his enlistment in the Revolutionary War. On 22 Jan 1777 **Elijah Mills, Jacob Mills, and Michael Mills** were among those who were ordered by the Committee of Observation "to march with some company to the reinforcement of his Excellency General Washington or appear before the Committee and state his reason for not marching." They apparently marched since they never appeared in the proceedings to the contrary. Elijah later moved to the Monongahela Valley in Pennsylvania and in 1790 he moved to Ohio. He applied for a pension in Butler Co., OH on 30 Jul 1832 and mentioned **Joseph Mills** and **Daniel Mills**, but no relationship was indicated. {Ref: *Genealogical Abstracts of Revolutionary War Pension Files*, by Virgil D. White (1990), Application S2825; "Proceedings of the Committee of Observation for Elizabeth Town District," *Maryland Historical Magazine*, Volume 12 (1917) and Volume 13 (1918), p. 48}

JOHN MONDY

John Mondy (sometimes spelled Monday) was born in 1757 in Frederick Co., MD and enlisted in the Revolutionary War as a private in the militia company of Capt. **John Bennet** in Washington Co., MD in 1776-1777. **Balser Mondy** was a sergeant in the same company. John married **Rosannah Huffman** at Williamsport, Washington Co., MD, in February, 1790 (another source stated 16 Mar 1788) and moved to Bedford Co., PA. In the winter of 1819 they moved to Wayne Co., OH and in 1824 to Richland Co., OH. He died on 4 Feb 1849 in Ashland Co., OH and **Rosannah Mondy** applied for a widow's pension on 27 Jan 1852. {Ref: *Genealogical Abstracts of Revolutionary War Pension Files*, by Virgil D. White (1990), Application R7296; *The Maryland Militia in the Revolutionary War*, by S. Eugene Clements & F. Edward Wright, p. 246; *Revolutionary Patriots of Washington County, Maryland, 1776-1783*, by Henry C. Peden, Jr. (1995), p. 249}

ALEXANDER MONTGOMERY

Alexander Montgomery was born on 21 Dec 1742 and enlisted at Baltimore, MD during the Revolutionary War. He subsequently moved to Indiana and applied for a pension in Jefferson County on 22 Jun 1818, aged 77. He then moved to Scott Co., IN by 30 Oct 1820 and gave his age as 77 on 21 Dec 1819 and his wife **Mary Montgomery** was aged 72 in 1819. She died (date not given), he married **Lydia Cox** on 27 Apr 1827, and died on 9 Jan 1837. **Lydia Montgomery** applied for a widow's pension in Johnson Co., IA on 23 Mar 1853, aged 67. {Ref: *Genealogical Abstracts of Revolutionary War Pension Files*, by Virgil D. White (1990), Application W566}

ISAAC MONTGOMERY

Isaac Montgomery was born in 1770 at Comber in County Down, Ireland and immigrated to the United States before 1798 (exact date not known). He married **Ruth Hargrove** (daughter of **Richard Hargrove** and **Rachel Armstrong**) on or about 1 Oct 1798 (date of license) in Harford Co., MD and their children were as follows:

1. **John Montgomery** (b. 6 Jul 1799, MD)
2. **William Montgomery** (b. 1 Dec 1800, MD)
3. **Isaac Montgomery, Jr.** (b. 16 Feb 1802, MD)
4. **Richard Montgomery** (b. 25 Mar 1804, PA)
5. **Thomas Montgomery** (b. 15 Jun 1808, PA)
6. **Polly Montgomery** (b. 6 Dec 1809, PA)
7. **George Montgomery** (b. 1814, PA)

Isaac Montgomery moved to East Bethlehem, PA by 1804. He purchased land in Wayne Co., OH in 1820 and died in 1840. **Ruth Montgomery** died in 1850. {Ref: Information compiled by Keith A. Montgomery, of Spokane, WA and London, England; 1800 Census of Harford Co., MD; *Harford County, Maryland Marriage Licenses, 1777-1865*, by Jon Harlan Livezey and Helene Maynard Davis (1993), p. 176}

WILLIAM MOODY

William Moody, druggist, of Baltimore, MD, died on 13 Aug 1834, aged 60, after a few days illness. His daughter, **Louisa Brooks Moody**, married in Sringfield, Clarke Co., OH, to **William B. Culbertson**, Esq., of Zanesville, OH, on 30 Jun 1835. **William M. Moody, Jr.** married **Sophia McComas** on 30 Aug 1835. **Rev. Granville Moody** married **Elizabeth A. Harris**, of Springfield, Clarke Co.,

138

OH, on 29 Jan 1836. {Ref: *Baltimore American*, 16 Aug 1834 and 13 Jul 1835 and 1 Sep 1835 and 4 Feb 1836, abstracted by Lorrie A. E. Erdman}

ADAM MOORE

Adam Moore, of Maryland (county not stated), married **Judith Smith** and moved to Sparta Township, Dearborn Co., IN, in 1818. He was one of the founders of Moore's Hill College & Methodist Church. Their son **John C. Moore** was born in Maryland on 8 Feb 1810 and married **Indiana R. Dowden** (daughter of **Samuel Dowden** and **Sophia McCracken**, of Virginia). {Ref: *History of Dearborn and Ohio Counties, Indiana* (1885), p. 845}

ASA MOORE

Asa Moore was born circa 1764 and lived in Prince George's Co., MD at the time of his enlistment in the Revolutionary War. He married **Elizabeth Thomas** on 7 Mar 1790 and subsequently moved to Hardin Co., KY by 1830. In 1831 he mentioned a daughter aged 32 and her child aged 2, but no names were given. He applied for a pension in Edgar Co., IL on 27 Sep 1832, aged 68, and died in Posey Co., IN on 20 Sep 1834. In 1839 a daughter **Lucy Moore**, aged 40, and Asa's sister-in-law Mrs. **Elenor Peck or Peek**, aged 68, lived in Hardin Co., KY. In 1840 his sister-in-law **Ann Wilson Selby**, aged 74, and her husband **Richard Selby**, aged 69, lived in Washington Co., KY. **John Moore** was also a Justice of the Peace, but no relationship was given. **Elizabeth Moore** applied for a widow's pension in Hardin Co., KY on 18 Oct 1839 and she was still there in 1848. {Ref: *Genealogical Abstracts of Revolutionary War Pension Files*, by Virgil D. White (1990), Application W3030; *Archives of Maryland*, Volume 18, pp. 475, 507}

GEORGE MOORE

George Moore, Jr., son of **George and Phoebe Moore**, was born on 14 Oct 1749 in Frederick Co., MD and enlisted four times during the Revolutionary War: once at Old Town or Skipton on the north branch of the Potomac River in the Washington County militia company of Capt. **Griffith Johnson** in 1776-1777, once in New York, once in Washington Co., MD as a substitute for his brother-in-law **Obadiah Forshay**, and lastly as a substitute for his brother **William Moore**. After the war he moved to Mason Co., KY in 1793, then to Champaign Co., OH in 1806, to Logan Co., OH in 1826, and to Jasper Co., IN in 1842 with his son **William Moore**. On 22 Jun 1848 **George Morrison** applied for a pension and died on 18 Jul 1848. He had married **Nancy or Ann Ball** on 24 Oct 1780 and allegedly had 21 children, but the only ones mentioned were as follows:
1. **William Moore**
2. **George Moore III**
3. **John Moore**
4. **Mahala Moore** married **Mr. Woodfield**
5. **Nancy Moore** married **Mr. Dowden**
6. **Phoebe Moore**
7. **Mary Moore** married **Mr. Standage**

The widow **Nancy Moore** died on 26 Feb 1854. {Ref: *Genealogical Abstracts of Revolutionary War Pension Files*, by Virgil D. White (1990), Application S33116; *The Maryland Militia in the Revolutionary War*, by S. Eugene Clements & F. Edward Wright, p. 243; *Revolutionary Patriots of Frederick County, Maryland, 1775-1783*, by Henry C. Peden, Jr. (1995), pp. 251-252}

CORNELIUS MORRIS

Cornelius Morris was born circa 1758 and enlisted in Montgomery Co., MD in February, 1780 during the Revolutionary War. He served as a private in the company of Capt. **Lloyd Beall** and participated in the battles of Camden, Guilford Court House, and the Seige of 96. He was discharged in June, 1783 and subsequently moved to Ohio where he applied for a pension in Clark County on 13 May 1818, aged about 60. In 1820 **Cornelius (Neel) Morris** had a wife **Sarah Morris**, aged 53, and the following children:

1. **Jane Morris** (b. 1799)
2. **Cornelius Morris, Jr.** (b. 1802)
3. **Harriet Morris** (b. 1805)
4. **Elizabeth Morris** (b. 1808)

According to one source, the following Bible record of **Daniel Morris alias Morrison**, of Frederick Co., MD, was submitted in support of the pension claim of **Cornelius Morris** (as well as pension application R7416 filed by **Anna Morrison** in 1851), but the relationship of Daniel and Anna to Cornelius was not indicated:

Marriages:
Daniel Morrison m. **Anna or Anny** ---- 27 Jul 1786
John H. Shields m. **Eve Ann Benshoof** 29 May 1849
Births:
Daniel Morrison, b. 18 Jan 1756
Anny Morrison, b. 18 Jan 1765
Mordecai Morrison, b. 27 Nov 1788
John Morrison, b. 27 May 1791
Daniel Morrison, b. 18 Jul 1793
Alexander Morrison, b. 3 Feb 1796
Margaret Morrison, b. 1 Jun 1798
William Morrison, b. 5 Dec 1800
Nancy Morrison, b. 17 Jul 1804
Daniel Morrison, b. 23 Sep 1808
John Henry Shields, b. 9 Aug 1823
Andrew Jackson Shields, b. 7 Feb 1829
William Van Buren Shields, b. 1 Nov 1832
Deaths:
John Morrison, d. 19 Mar 1765
Nancy Morrison, d. 6 Oct 1804
Margaret Morrison, d. 8 Mar 1805
Daniel Morrison, d. 30 Nov 1806 in 14th year
Daniel Morrison, d. 11 Oct 1821 in 14th year

140

Mordecai Morrison, d. Mon. 23 Aug 1847, 2 a.m.,
aged 58 years, 8 months and 27 days
Margaret Morrison, d. 10 Dec 1847, 2 a.m.,
aged 49 years, 6 months and 9 days
Daniel Morrison, d. 23 Feb 1850,
aged 95 years, 6 months and 1 day

{Ref: *Genealogical Abstracts of Revolutionary War Pension Files*, by Virgil D. White (1990), Application S40175; "Revolutionary War Pension of Cornelius (Neel) Morris," abstracted by Mary K. Meyer, *Maryland Genealogical Society Bulletin*, Volume 35, No. 1 (1994), p. 56}

WILLIAM MORRIS

William Morris was born on 4 Aug 1744 in Worcester Co., MD and lived there at the time of his enlistment in the Revolutionary War. He took the Oath of Allegiance in 1778 and served as a private in militia company of Capt. **Elisha Purnell**, Sinepuxent Battalion, in 1779-1780. In 1816 he moved to Highland Co., OH and applied for a pension on 28 Oct 1832. {Ref: *Genealogical Abstracts of Revolutionary War Pension Files*, by Virgil D. White (1990), Application S9040; *The Maryland Militia in the Revolutionary War*, by S. Eugene Clements & F. Edward Wright, p. 253; *Revolutionary Patriots of Worcester & Somerset Counties, Maryland, 1775-1783*, by Henry C. Peden, Jr. (1999), p. 208}

SAMUEL MUMMEY

Samuel Mummey moved from Baltimore, MD to Ohio (county not stated) on 16 Mar 1826. He was probably related to **Jacob Mummey** who married **Maria C. Working** at the Methodist Episcopal Church in Baltimore on 13 Oct 1817. {Ref: Marriage Register and Class Lists, Baltimore City Station, Methodist Episcopal Church}

DARBY MURPHY

Darby Murphy was born circa 1740 in Baltimore Co., MD and was enlisted by **John Eager Howard** at Baltimore on 17 Jul 1776. **Thomas Murphy** enlisted at the same time (relationship not known). Darby married by 1766 (wife's name not known) and subsequently moved to Belmont Co., OH where he died after 1830. Their children were as follows:
1. **Benjamin Murphy** (b. 1766) married **Eleanor ----**
2. **James Murphy** (b. 1769) married **Henrietta Selby**

{Ref: DAR Application 639797; *Index of Patriots, Revolutionary War Heroes and Their Families, Cincinnati Chapter DAR, 1893-1981*, by Jeraldyne Beets Clipson and Katherine Brewer Brinkdopke (1983), p. 193; *Archives of Maryland*, Volume 18, p. 53; *Revolutionary Patriots of Baltimore Town and Baltimore County, Maryland, 1775-1783*, by Henry C. Peden, Jr. (1988), p. 191}

CHRISTOPHER MYERS

Christopher Myers was born in 1759 in Frederick Co., MD and lived there at the time of his enlistment in the Revolutionary War. He was an Associator in December, 1775, was commissioned a second lieutenant in the Linganore Battalion on 13 Oct 1777, and took the Oath of Allegiance in 1778. He appears to have also served in the Southern Army of the United States in 1781. After the war he lived in Frederick County and then moved near Winchester, VA before moving to Muskingum Co., OH. He applied for a pension on 27 Sep 1832 in Wayne Township, Knox Co., OH. {Ref: *Genealogical Abstracts of Revolutionary War Pension Files*, by Virgil D. White (1990), Application S2890; *Revolutionary Patriots of Frederick County, Maryland, 1775-1783*, by Henry C. Peden, Jr. (1995), pp. 265-266}

JACOB NAGLE

Jacob Nagle was born in Reading, PA on 15 Sep 1741 and lived there at the time of his enlistment in Revolutionary War, serving both in the Pennsylvania troops and in privateer service in Maryland. He followed the sea for 44 years and returned to Baltimore, MD in 1824. He then moved to Washington Co., MD and two years later moved to Canton, OH. He applied for a pension on 22 Apr 1833 in Stark Co., OH. {Ref: *Genealogical Abstracts of Revolutionary War Pension Files*, by Virgil D. White (1990), Application S16492}

JOHN NAYLOR

On the 25th day of the 10th month, 1809, a certificate of removal was requested from the Gunpowder Monthly Meeting, Baltimore Co., MD, by **John Naylor** to Plymouth Monthly Meeting in the State of Ohio. On the 26th day of the 2nd month, 1811, **John Naylor** requested a certificate of removal from the Gunpowder Monthly Meeting for himself, his wife **Mary Naylor** and minor son **Abraham Naylor**, to the Plymouth Monthly Meeting in the State of Ohio. {Ref: Gunpowder Quaker Monthly Meeting Minutes}

MARGARET NAYLOR

On the 8th day of the 4th month, 1813, a certificate of removal was requested for **Margaret Naylor**, a minor, of the Baltimore Monthly Meeting, Eastern District, to the Plymouth Monthly Meeting in Ohio. On the 13th day of the 5th month, 1813, **Margaret Naylor**, a minor daughter of **James Naylor**, requested a certificate from the Baltimore Monthly Meeting, Eastern District, to the Plymouth Monthly Meeting in Ohio, having removed there with her father. {Ref: Baltimore Quaker Monthly Meeting Minutes}

SAMUEL NAYLOR

Samuel Naylor requested a certificate of removal on the 25th day of the 7th month, 1810, from the Gunpowder Monthly Meeting in Baltimore Co., MD, for himself, his wife **Rebecca Naylor** and their six minor children, **Ann Naylor, John Naylor, Joseph Naylor, Charles Naylor, Mary Naylor and Rebecca Naylor**, to

142

the Plymouth Monthly Meeting in the State of Ohio. It was also reported that **William Naylor** had removed and settled within the limits of Plymouth Monthly Meeting and had been married *"contrary to the good order of Friends."* {Ref: Gunpowder Quaker Monthly Meeting Minutes}

JOHN NICHOLSON

John Nicholson requested a certificate of removal on the 10th day of the 8th month, 1814, from the Baltimore Monthly Meeting, Western District, to the Plymouth Monthly Meeting in Ohio, for himself, his wife **Alice Nicholson** and their three minor children, **William L. Nicholson, Eliza Nicholson** and **Charles L. Nicholson**, they having already removed there. {Ref: Baltimore Quaker Monthly Meeting Minutes}

JONATHAN NOBLE

Jonathan Noble was born near Salisbury in Wicomico Co., MD in 1807 and moved to Cincinnati, OH in 1832 where he worked as a carpenter and house builder. He soon after moved to Dearborn Co., IN and married **Elizabeth Dashiell** in March, 1833. She was born near Salisbury, MD in 1812. They moved to Cincinnati, OH until 1834 when they returned to Indiana and lived near Moore's Hill. A short time later they moved back to Cincinnati, then moved to Wilmington, IN, and in 1843 returned to Cincinnati. **Elizabeth Noble** died in 1843 and Jonathan returned in 1844 to Aurora, IN. He married **Isabelle Hiatt** in 1844 and in 1849 they moved to Petersburg, KY where he remained until 1851. He then returned to Dearborn Co., IN and died in March, 1857. His son **John H. Noble** was born at Cheviot, Hamilton Co., OH on 29 Mar 1834 and lived at Sparta Township, Dearborn Co., IN where he worked as a carpenter. {Ref: *History of Dearborn and Ohio Counties, Indiana* (1885), p. 856}

LEVIN NOBLE

Levin Noble was a private in Caroline Co., MD by 13 Aug 1777 and served during the Revolutionary War in the militia company of Capt. **Joseph Douglas** in the 14th Battalion. He also rendered patriotic service by providing wheat for the use of the military in August, 1781, as verified by **Giles Hick 3rd**, Commissary for Caroline County. **Levin Noble** married first to **Ann Ward** by license dated 31 Dec 1779 and second to **Mary White Ward** by license dated 30 Mar 1789. He died before 6 Aug 1805 in Ohio. In an 1816 land commission record, filed by his son **William Noble**, it stated that **Levin Noble** died intestate and seized of land tracts called *Mt. Andrew* and *Nabb's Ceasant* and *Double Purchase*. He left a widow (name not given, but still living in 1816) and the following children:
1. **Nancy Noble** married **William Williams**
2. **Tamsey Noble** married **Thomas Hurt**
3. **Charity Noble**
4. **Levin Noble, Jr.**
5. **Caleb Noble**
6. **Nathan Noble**

7. **Summers Noble**
8. **William Noble**

All of the above children were in Ross Co., OH by 1816, at which time **William Noble** filed a land commission petition. He also noted that *"William Noble, an uncle, occupies the farm."* {Ref: *Revolutionary Patriots of Caroline County, Maryland, 1775-1783*, by Henry C. Peden, Jr., p. 120; *Republican Star*, 6 Apr 1819; *Heirs and Legatees of Caroline County*, by Irma Harper, p. 32; Original 1782 Commissary Accounts at the Maryland State Archives, Accession No. MdHR 6636-42-7/9; *Marriage Licenses of Caroline County, Maryland, 1774-1815*, by Henry Downes Cranor (1904), pp. 11, 19}

AQUILA NORRIS

Aquila Norris was born circa 1750 in Baltimore Co., MD and took the Oath of Allegiance in 1778 in Harford Co., MD. He married **Priscilla Temperance Norris** circa 1775 and died in Brown Co., OH on 6 Feb 1812. Their children were as follows:

1. **Elizabeth Norris** married **James Norris**
2. **Martha Norris** married **Whitfield Hyatt**
3. **William Norris**
4. **Temperance Norris** married **William Miller**
5. **Elijah Norris** (b. 21 Apr 1785) married **Elizabeth Bush**
6. **James Norris** married **Nancy Gates**
7. **Aquila Norris, Jr.** (b. 4 Jan 1787) married **Sarah Sargent**
8. **Nathan Norris** married **Mary Walton**
9. **Naomi Norris** (twin)
10. **Ruth Norris** (twin)
11. **Priscilla Norris** (b. 1792) married **Benjamin Norris**

{Ref: *Index of Patriots, Revolutionary War Heroes and Their Families, Cincinnati Chapter DAR, 1893-1981*, by Jeraldyne Beets Clipson and Katherine Brewer Brinkdopke (1983), p. 286; *Revolutionary Patriots of Harford County, Maryland, 1775-1783*, by Henry C. Peden, Jr. (1985), p. 167}

ARNOLD NORRIS

Arnold Norris was born in St. Mary's Co., MD on 25 Jun 1761 and lived there at the time of his enlistment in the Revolutionary War. He later moved to Virginia, married **Elizabeth Paine** on 10 Apr 1795 (both were of Berkeley County) and then moved to Ohio. He applied for a pension on 10 Oct 1832 in Ross Co., OH and died on 3 Aug 1836. **Elizabeth Norris** applied for a widow's pension on 14 Aug 1852, aged 76. {Ref: *Genealogical Abstracts of Revolutionary War Pension Files*, by Virgil D. White (1990), Application W3710}

ISAAC NORRIS

Isaac Norris, of Harford Co., MD, served in the War of 1812 as a corporal in the company of Capt. **George W. Bradford** in Abingdon, MD from 28 Aug to 2 Sep 1814. He then served 23 days in the company of Capt. **Thomas R. Buchanan**

and his march to Baltimore began from Patterson's Fields. After the war he moved to Ohio and applied for bounty land (warrant 50-rej-91743) in Steubenville on 29 Mar 1851, aged 55. {Ref: *Maryland Militia, War of 1812, Volume 3, Cecil & Harford Counties*, by F. Edward Wright, pp. 18, 30, 61}

JOHN NORRIS

John Norris, of Harford Co., MD, served in the War of 1812 as a private in the companies of Capt. **Joshua Amos** and Capt. **James Rampley** from 28 Aug to 26 Sep 1814 and was discharged at Hanson's Fishery in Baltimore. After the war he moved to Ohio and applied for bounty land in Fairfield County on 25 Mar 1851, aged 70. He applied again (warrant 55-160-50154) on 10 Nov 1855, aged 75. {Ref: *Maryland Militia, War of 1812, Volume 3, Cecil & Harford Counties*, by F. Edward Wright, pp. 30, 61}

RICHARD NORRIS

Richard Norris was born in Baltimore (now Harford) Co., MD in 1760 and enlisted in the North Carolina Line at Wilkes County in the Revolutionary War. He returned to Maryland after the war and later moved to Kentucky. In 1817 he moved to Ohio and applied for a pension in Brown County on 27 Oct 1835, aged 75, indicating that **Bazel Norris** and **Nathan Norris** knew of his service. **Abraham F. Ellis**, who had lived in Ohio since 1797, stated **Richard Norris** died in 1837 or 1838 and his wife died about 1822. In 1855 **Aquilla Norris**, of Brown County (relationship not indicated), stated that Richard had died about the middle of March, 1837, his wife **Elizabeth Norris** had died in 1822, and their children were as follows:

1. **Gabriel Norris**
2. **Gilbert Norris**
3. **Hannah Norris**
4. **Elizabeth Norris** married **Robinson Morford** and died in 1827 or 1828, leaving one child **Elizabeth Morford**
5. **Gibson Norris**
6. **Ellen Norris**

All of the above children except Elizabeth were still living in 1855. {Ref: *Genealogical Abstracts of Revolutionary War Pension Files*, by Virgil D. White (1990), Application R7704}

WILLIAM NORRIS

William Norris, of Belmont Co., OH, wrote his will on 15 Oct 1807 (probated 10 Aug 1812 and recorded in Montgomery Co., MD) and named his wife **Mary Norris** and children **Otho Norris, Sarah Martin, Mary Ann Norris, Luther Norris, Benjamin Norris, William Norris, Ann Mariah Norris** and **Eliza Norris**. {Ref: *Abstract of Wills, Montgomery County, Maryland, 1776-1825*, by Mary G. Malloy, Jane C. Sween and Janet D. Manuel, p. 100}

145

WILLIAM OARD

William Oard (sometimes spelled Ord) was born in Charles Co., MD on 22 Sep 1754 and lived in St. Mary's Co., MD when he enlisted as a private in the militia in the Revolutionary War in 1777. **Jesse Ord** also served in the county militia and **Jesse Oard** died intestate by October, 1789. During the war William moved to Virginia and after the war he moved to Ohio (county not stated) and then to Indiana. He applied for a pension in Parke County on 11 May 1833 and died on 15 Sep 1833. {Ref: *Genealogical Abstracts of Revolutionary War Pension Files*, by Virgil D. White (1990), Application S16496; *The Maryland Militia in the Revolutionary War*, by S. Eugene Clements & F. Edward Wright, p. 213; St. Mary's County Orphans Court Proceedings, 1777-1801, pp. 146, 171}

CHARLES ORME

Charles Orme served in Maryland during the Revolutionary War and subsequently moved to Kentucky. He applied for a pension in Lewis County on 20 Jul 1818, aged 56, and by 1830 he had moved to Marion Co., IN where he died on 18 Aug 1840. {Ref: *Genealogical Abstracts of Revolutionary War Pension Files*, by Virgil D. White (1990), Application S35543}

STEPHEN OWENS

Stephen Owens served as a private in the 6th MD Regiment during the Revolutionary War and was in the company of Capt. Henry Dobson by October, 1780. **Stephen Owens** married **Elizabeth Harwood** on or about 18 Sep 1785 (date of license) in Cecil Co., MD and **Stephen Owen** *(sic)* married **Mary Ann Gaunce** on 1 Nov 1804 (license dated 31 Oct 1804) in Cecil Co., MD (one source stated he married **Nancy or Ann Gaunce**). They later moved to Ohio and he applied for a pension in Muskingum County on 9 Aug 1828. **Stephen Owens** died on 8 Jun 1837 in Perry Co., OH and **Nancy Owens** applied for a widow's pension on 26 Aug 1853, aged 70. She also applied for bounty land (warrant 55-60-200) on 26 Mar 1855, aged 70. {Ref: *Genealogical Abstracts of Revolutionary War Pension Files*, by Virgil D. White (1990), Application W8281; Cecil County, Maryland Marriage Licenses; *Revolutionary Patriots of Cecil County, Maryland, 1775-1783*, by Henry C. Peden, Jr. (1991), p. 85}

WILLIAM PACK

William Pack, son of **Thomas and Elizabeth Pack**, was born in Frederick Co., MD on 16 Oct 1758 and lived there at the time of his enlistment in the Revolutionary War on 5 Aug 1776. He served as a private in the Maryland Line and fought in the battles of Ten Mile Stone, White Plains, and Germantown. **William Pack** married **Phoebe O'Neale** (b. 16 Jun 1760), daughter of **John and Margaret O'Neale**, in Montgomery Co., MD on 11 Apr 1782. Their children were as follows:
1. **Mary Pack** (b. 18 Aug 1783)
2. **John O'Neale Pack** (b. 10 Nov 1785)
3. **Enos Pack** (b. 12 Jan 1788)
4. **Ann Pack** (b. 30 May 1790) married **Mr. Martin**

146

5. **Elizabeth Pack** married **Mr. Enyart**

6. **Rachel Pack** (7 Feb 1797 - 30 Mar 1880) married **David Allen** on 11 Dec 1814

William Pack moved to Hamilton Co., OH in 1804 and applied for a pension on 17 Sep 1832. He died on 23 Sep 1838 and **Phoebe Pack** applied for a widow's pension on 5 Aug 1839. She was still living in 1842. {Ref: *Archives of Maryland*, Volume 18, p. 44; *Genealogical Abstracts of Revolutionary War Pension Files*, by Virgil D. White (1990), Application R7852; DAR Application 70132; *Index of Patriots, Revolutionary War Heroes and Their Families, Cincinnati Chapter DAR, 1893-1981*, by Jeraldyne Beets Clipson and Katherine Brewer Brinkdopke (1983), p. 201; *Revolutionary Patriots of Frederick County, Maryland, 1775-1783*, by Henry C. Peden, Jr. (1995), pp. 279-280}

WILLIAM PAINE

William Paine was born in England on 17 Dec 1736 and immigrated to Maryland in 1763. He served in the Maryland Line during the Revolutionary War and subsequently moved to Ohio. William applied for a pension in Belmont Co., OH on 20 Jul 1818, aged 81 on 17 Dec 1817. He had a wife (name not given), aged about 60, and they had 11 grown children (no names given). {Ref: *Genealogical Abstracts of Revolutionary War Pension Files*, by Virgil D. White (1990), Application S40240}

RICHARD PALMER

Richard Palmer requested a certificate of removal from the Baltimore Monthly Meeting, Western District, to the West Branch Monthly Meeting in Ohio on the 13th day of the 6th month, 1810. {Ref: Baltimore Quaker Monthly Meeting Minutes}

THOMAS PARKINSON

Thomas Parkinson was born in 1762 or 1763 in Frederick Co., MD and lived there at the time of his enlistment in the Revolutionary War. He served as a substitute in the militia, marched to Annapolis, and served from May to 10 Dec 1781. He married **Elizabeth Stif** on the 1st Tuesday in 1784 or on 27 Dec 1785 (both dates were given, but no marriage license is recorded in Frederick County). After the war they moved from Frederick Co., MD to Pennsylvania for 3 years and then moved to Allegany Co., MD. They had several children, but only mentioned their son **John S. Parkinson** (living in Ohio in 1846) and their 5th child **Polly Parkinson** (b. 17 Feb 1793 in Allegany Co. MD). About 25 years later (circa 1810) Thomas moved to Ohio and applied for a pension in Harrison County on 11 Sep 1832. He died on 19 Oct 1832 and **Elizabeth Parkinson** applied for a widow's pension on 1 May 1843, aged 85. {Ref: *Genealogical Abstracts of Revolutionary War Pension Files*, by Virgil D. White (1990), Application W5475; *Revolutionary Patriots of Frederick County, Maryland, 1775-1783*, by Henry C. Peden, Jr. (1995), p. 281}

NICHOLAS PARRISH

Nicholas Parrish was drafted at Baltimore, MD during the War of 1812 and first served under Capt. **John Leach** for 3 months and then served under Capt. Marshall after returning from Bladensburg (no dates were given). He and **Jacob Parrish** (relationship not stated) served as privates in the company of Capt. **Isaac Raven** in the 2nd Regiment from 27 Jul to 1 Dec 1814. Nicholas was discharged at Baltimore and subsequently moved to Ohio where he applied for bounty land (warrant 55-80-34425) in Fairfield County in 1855. In 1856 **Nicholas Parrish**, aged 66, resided at Millersport, OH. Witnesses were **Asa Clark** and **James Sheriff**, of Baltimore, OH *(sic)*. {Ref: *Maryland Militia, War of 1812, Volume 4, Anne Arundel & Calvert Counties*, pp. 84, 112, 113, and *Volume 2, Baltimore*, p. 84, by F. Edward Wright}

GANER PARSONS

On the 5th day of the 4th month, 1819, the Deer Creek Monthly Meeting (Orthodox), Harford Co., MD, produced a certificate of removal for **Ganer Parsons** and her husband (not named) to the Smithfield Monthly Meeting in Jefferson Co., OH. {Ref: Deer Creek Quaker Monthly Meeting Minutes}

NEAL PEACOCK

Neal Peacock enlisted in the Revolutionary War at Frederick, MD and subsequently moved to Ohio where he applied for a pension on 1 May 1818. On 31 Jul 1820 he gave his age as 67 years, 11 months and 1 day and his residence was Cadiz, OH. He had a wife (name and age not given), a daughter aged 16 and a son aged 13 (names not given). **Neale Peacock**, formerly of Washington Co., MD, died near Cadiz, Harrison Co., OH, on 17 Aug 1827, and was for many years a soldier of the Maryland Line. He fought with the gallant Col. **John Eager Howard** at the battles of Eutaw and Cowpens. He also served under Gen. **Nathaniel Green** and *"other illustrious chiefs."* {Ref: *Marriages and Deaths from the Newspapers of Allegany and Washington Counties, Maryland, 1820-1830*, by F. Edward Wright, p. 95; {Ref: *Genealogical Abstracts of Revolutionary War Pension Files*, by Virgil D. White (1990), Application S40247}

THOMAS PEARCE

Thomas Pearce was born in Frederick Co., MD and served as a private in the militia during the Revolutionary War. He married first to **Mary Barnes** on 1 Jan 1780 and second to **Elizabeth Collins** in 1799. The children by his first wife were as follows:
1. **Joseph Pearce** (b. 18 Sep 1780) married **Elizabeth Hubbard**
2. **Louis Pearce** (b. 11 Jan 1782), unmarried
3. **Elizabeth Pearce** (b. 14 Jan 1783) married first to **Bruce Worley** and second to **J. Frizelle**
4. **Thomas Pearce** (b. 24 Aug 1785) married first to **Nancy Ross** and second to **Phoebe George**
5. **James Pearce** (b. 3 Jan 1787) married **Elizabeth Byram**

6. **John Pearce** (b. 3 Sep 1788) married **Elizabeth Steward**

7. **Jane Pearce** (b. 15 Apr 1790) married **Jacob Beedle**

8. **Jesse Pearce** (b. 27 Aug 1792) married **Nancy Williams**

9. **Mary Pearce** (b. 16 Oct 1794) married **Robert Bay**

10. **Andrew Pearce** (b. 17 Dec 1796) married first to **Malinda Lewis** and second to **E. Cobb**

Thomas Pearce had ten children by his first wife (as noted above) and seven children by his second wife (names were not given). He died at Urbana, OH on 15 Jun 1826. {Ref: *Directory of Maryland State Society DAR, 1892-1965*, p. 430}

WILLIAM PELL

William Pell was born in Kent Co., MD on 1 Jan 1760 and lived in Hampshire Co., VA at the time of his enlistment in the Revolutionary War. In 1790 he moved to Kentucky and in 1819 he moved to Harrison Co., IN. He returned to Kentucky in 1831 and in March, 1833 he returned to Indiana and applied for a pension in Harrison County on 2 Apr 1833. He died on 17 Jan 1839, leaving a widow (no name was given). {Ref: *Genealogical Abstracts of Revolutionary War Pension Files*, by Virgil D. White (1990), Application S16503; *Historical Register of Virginians in the Revolution, 1775-1783*, by John H. Gwathmey (1938), p. 614}

BENJAMIN PENN

Benjamin Penn was born in 1740 in Maryland (county not stated) and married **Mary Sargent** (b. 1755) in 1774. He enlisted on 27 Aug 1776 and served as a private under Col. **J. Carvil Hall** during the Revolutionary War. The children of **Benjamin and Mary Penn** were as follows:

1. **Joseph Penn** (b. 16 Nov 1774, d. unmarried)

2. **Benjamin Penn, Jr.** (b. 16 Apr 1776) married **Ann Phillips**

3. **Eleanor Penn** (b. 10 Dec 1777) married **Richard Tucker**

4. **Nancy Ann Penn** (b. 12 Apr 1779) married **George Richards**

5. **Elizabeth Penn** (b. 5 Sep 1780) married **Bartin Molen**

6. **Rachel Penn** (b. 12 Mar 1782) married **Robert Lanham**

7. **Rebecca Penn** (b. 17 May 1783) married **Benjamin Thrasher**

8. **Mary Penn** (b. 17 May 1785) married **John Richards**

9. **Nackey Penn** (b. 2 Sep 1787) married **Joshua Pigman**

10. **Rhoda Penn** (b. 5 Aug 1789) married **Nathaniel Hines**

11. **Elijah Taylor Penn** (27 Dec 1792 - 1877) married **Philomena Walraven** in 1815

12. **Sophia Penn** (b. 8 Jan 1795) married **James Prather**

Mary Penn died in 1817 and **Benjamin Penn** died on 13 Aug 1834 in Clermont Co., OH. {Ref: DAR Applications 163276 and 206438; *Index of Patriots, Revolutionary War Heroes and Their Families, Cincinnati Chapter DAR, 1893-1981*, by Jeraldyne Beets Clipson and Katherine Brewer Brinkdopke (1983), p. 205; *Archives of Maryland*, Volume 18, p. 41; *A Roster of Revolutionary Ancestors of the Indiana Daughters of the American Revolution* (1976), p. 503}

JOSEPH PERSONETT

Joseph Personett was born circa 1780 in Maryland (county not stated) and moved to Hamilton Co., OH circa 1821-1822. He later settled near Williamsburg, IN and died there in 1864, aged 84. His wife **Susannah** ---- was born in Virginia. The children of **Joseph and Susannah Personett** were as follows:

1. **Lavina Personett** married **William Case**
2. **Rolla Personett** married **Thamer Livingston**
3. **John Personett** married **Jane Clingon**
4. **William Personett** married **Julia Ann Fulton**
5. **Joseph H. Personett** married **Therissa Jane Murray**
6. **Lorenzo D. Personett** married **Ann E. Ogborn**

{Ref: "Persons Who Migrated to Wayne County, Indiana From the Eastern Shore of Maryland," by F. Edward Wright, *Maryland Genealogical Society Bulletin*, Volume 34, No. 4 (1993), p. 466}

GEORGE PHEBUS

George Phebus (sometimes spelled Phoebus) was born in Somerset Co., MD on 12 Jul 1762 and lived there at the time of his enlistment in the Revolutionary War. **George Phebus, Jr.** was a private in Monie Company, Princess Anne Battalion, under Capt. **Thomas Irving** in 1780. On 30 Jul 1781 **Levin Miles** recruited **George Phebus** from Somerset County to serve in the Continental Army until 10 Dec 1781. In 1786 George moved to Virginia for 9 years, then moved to Kentucky for 4 years, and then to Pickaway Co., OH where he applied for a pension on 10 Aug 1832. **Samuel Phebus** (relationship not stated) also lived there. {Ref: *Genealogical Abstracts of Revolutionary War Pension Files*, by Virgil D. White (1990), Application S3683; *Archives of Maryland*, Volume 48, p. 11; "Draftees from Somerset County in June, July and August, 1781, Reported by George Dashiell," Maryland State Archives, Accession No. MdHR 6663-31; *Revolutionary Patriots of Worcester & Somerset Counties, Maryland, 1775-1783*, by Henry C. Peden, Jr. (1999), p. 225}

WILLIAM PHILIPS

William Philips was born on 17 Jul 1766 in York Co., PA and lived in Frederick Co., MD at the time of his enlistment in the Revolutionary War. He enlisted on 1 May 1778 and served as a private in the 2nd MD Regiment. After the war he moved to Washington Co., PA and in 1812 he moved to Columbiana Co., OH where he applied for a pension on 9 May 1836. He indicated that **Samuel Philips** knew him, but no relationship was given. {Ref: *Genealogical Abstracts of Revolutionary War Pension Files*, by Virgil D. White (1990), Application R8213; *Revolutionary Patriots of Frederick County, Maryland, 1775-1783*, by Henry C. Peden, Jr. (1995), p. 285}

HUGH PIERCE

Hugh Peirce (sometimes spelled Pierse and Pearce) was born in Kent Co., MD circa 1757 and lived there at the time of his enlistment on 23 Aug 1781 by Lt.

W. **Bordley** in the Revolutionary War. He subsequently moved to Ohio and applied for a pension at Wheeling Township in Belmont County on 12 Mar 1833, aged 76. The enlistment certificates and discharge papers for **Hugh Pearce** and **John Pearce** in 1781 are at the Maryland State Archives in Annapolis, MD. {Ref: *Genealogical Abstracts of Revolutionary War Pension Files*, by Virgil D. White (1990), Application S3690; *Revolutionary Patriots of Kent & Queen Anne's Counties, Maryland*, by Henry C. Peden, Jr. (1995), p. 198; *An Inventory of Maryland State Papers, Volume I, 1775-1789*, by Edward C. Papenfuse, *et al.* (1977), p. 349, citing Accession Nos. MdHR 6636-53-119/1 and MdHR 6636-53-120/1}

BENJAMIN PLUMMER

Benjamin Plummer, of Prince George's Co., MD, served as a sergeant in the War of 1812 and subsequently moved to Ohio. On 20 Sep 1852, in Guernsey Co., OH, **Alfred Ewell** appeared and declared that **Francis William Plummer**, aged 16 on 13 Mar 1848, and **Ann Eliza Plummer**, aged 12 on 5 Dec 1848, were the only minor children of **Benjamin Plummer** who died in November, 1837, *"and hath no widow surviving him."* In a letter written around 24 Sep 1852 by **Alfred Ewell**, regarding the service of **Benjamin Plummer** in Queen Ann Company, Prince George's Co., MD, he stated he expected to sell his own land warrant, *"but cannot get more than $36."* On 30 May 1856 **Mariah A. Davis**, late **Mariah A. Plummer**, aged 45, of Cambridge, Guernsey Co., OH, appeared and stated that she was the widow of **Benjamin Plummer** who served in the War of 1812 from 27 Apr to 15 May 1813. They were married in Maryland by Rev. **Jesse E. Weems**, a Methodist Episcopal minister, on 4 Sep 1827 and her former name was **Mariah A. Ewell**. She married **Manloff Davis** at said Cambridge, OH, and during the time of said marriage relation some time in the winter of 1852 application was made by **J. J. Grimes**, guardian of **Ann Eliza Plummer** and **Frances W. Plummer** for bounty land (warrant 50-120-84520). On 30 May 1856 **John R. Plummer**, of Guernsey Co., OH, son of **Benjamin Plummer** and step-son of **Mariah A. Davis**, stated he was present at the marriage ceremony of his father and step-mother. **James J. Grimes** was appointed guardian for **Ann E. Plummer**, aged 12 on 5 Dec 1848, and for **Francis W. Plummer**, aged 16 on 13 Mar 1848. {Ref: *Maryland Militia, War of 1812, Volume 6, Prince George's County*, by F. Edward Wright, p. 61}

JOSEPH P. PLUMMER

Joseph P. Plummer, of Anne Arundel Co., MD, son of **John and Johannah Plummer** (the father being deceased), and **Susanna Husband**, daughter of **Joseph and Mary Husband**, of Harford Co., MD (the father being deceased), were married in Baltimore City on the 10th day of the 3rd month, 1806. **Joseph P. Plummer** requested a certificate of removal on the 11th day of the 3rd month, 1812 to the Baltimore Monthly Meeting, Eastern District, for himself, his wife **Susannah Plummer**, and their three minor children, **John Plummer, Mary Plummer** and **Johannah Plummer**. On the 9th day of the 12th month, 1813 **Sarah Cresson Plummer**, daughter of **Joseph P. and Susanna Plummer**, was born in Baltimore City. On the 4th day of the 9th month, 1817 a certificate of removal was requested for **Thomas Plummer, Mary Mifflin Plummer** and **Joanna Plummer**, minor children of **Joseph P. Plummer**, who were placed at school within the limits of Nine Partners Monthly Meeting in the State of New York. At the Baltimore Monthly Meeting, Western District, on the 5th day of the 5th month, 1820, a certificate of removal was requested for **John T. Plummer, Mary M. Plummer** and **Sarah C. Plummer** (all minors) who had moved to Cincinnati Monthly Meeting in Ohio to reside with their father **Joseph P. Plummer**. {Ref: Baltimore Quaker Monthly Meeting Minutes and Marriage Records}

THOMAS PLUMMER
On the 10th day of the 7th month, 1806, the Baltimore Monthly Meeting, Western District, recorded the following with respect to **Thomas and Phoebe Plummer**: *"Our ancient friend Thomas Plummer and Phoebe Plummer his wife, being about to remove within the limits of Concord Monthly Meeting in Ohio, requested a certificate of removal. We certify they are of orderly life and conversation and, considering the infirmities of advanced age, they have been frequent attenders of our religious meetings."* **Eleanor Plummer** also requested a certificate to the same meeting. {Ref: Baltimore Quaker Monthly Meeting Minutes}

CASPAR POTTORF
Casper Pottorf (sometimes spelled Pottorff and Potterf) was born in Lancaster Co., PA on 19 Dec 1759 and at the age of 9 he moved to Frederick Co., MD. He served in Maryland and Virginia as a private during the Revolutionary War and married **Susanna Ridenour** (b. 1768) in Frederick Co., MD in 1784. They moved to Rockbridge Co., VA and then to Preble Co., Ohio. Their children were as follows:
1. **Jacob Pottorf** (b. 1784) married **Christiana Brown**
2. **Susanna Pottorf** (b. 26 Mar 1787) **married Mr. Neff**
3. **John Pottorf** (b. 8 Nov 1788) married **Elizabeth ----**
4. **Elizabeth Pottorf** (b. 10 Feb 1790) married **Mr. Fudge**
5. **Joseph Pottorf** (b. 25 Sep 1792) married **Elizabeth Kestling**
6. **Polly Pottorf** (b. 11 Jun 1795) married **Mr. Kessler**
7. **Nancy Pottorf** (b. 2 Jul 1797) married **Mr. Albaugh**
8. **Samuel Pottorf** (b. 1798) married **Mary Leathers**
9. **Sarah Pottorf** (b. 12 Apr 1799) married **Mr. Ozias**
10. **Anna Pottorf** (b. 19 Mar 1801) married **Mr. Douglas**
11. **David Pottorf** (b. 14 Sep 1802) married **Anna Garber**
12. **Rosanna Pottorf** (b. 3 Dec 1805) married **Jonathan Ridenour**
13. **Jefferson Pottorf** (b. circa 1807) married **Susanna Shideler**
14. **James Pottorf** (b. circa 1810, probably died young)

Susanna Pottorf died on 7 Nov 1831 and **Casper Pottorf** married **Nancy Longnecker** on 6 Aug 1832. They had the following children:
15. **Casper T. Pottorf** (b. 27 Jun 1833)
16. **James S. Pottorf** (b. 25 Sep 1834)
17. **Nancy Jane Pottorf** (b. 22 Jul 1836) married **John Butler**

Casper Pottorf applied for a pension in Preble Co., OH and died on 4 Oct 1836. **Nancy Pottorf** later married **William Arrasmith** on 1 Dec 1850. On 2 Jun 1855 she applied for bounty land (warrant 55-160-49468) and indicated that **James Pottorf** and **Nancy Jane Pottorf** were Casper's only surviving minor children. **Nancy Arrasmith** applied for a widow's pension on 1 Sep 1856, aged 56. {Ref: *Genealogical Abstracts of Revolutionary War Pension Files*, by Virgil D. White (1990), Application S17024; DAR Application 93767; *Index of Patriots, Revolutionary War Heroes and Their Families, Cincinnati Chapter DAR, 1893-1981*, by Jeraldyne Beets Clipson and Katherine Brewer Brinkdopke (1983), p. 212; *Maryland Revolutionary Records*, by Harry Wright Newman (1938), p. 121}

SAMUEL POULTNEY

Samuel Poultney, of Frederick Co., MD, born 18 Jan 1780, son of **Anthony Poultney** (1752-1805) and **Susanna Plummer** (1752-1812), married at Bush Creek Meeting House on 1 Oct 1812 to **Elizabeth Wright**, daughter of **Joel Wright** and **Elizabeth Farquhar**, of Warren Co., OH. {Ref: "Pipe Creek Friends Monthly Meeting Records," *Western Maryland Genealogy*, Volume 1, No. 3 (1985), p. 124}

WILLIAM H. POWELL

William H. Powell was born in Maryland (county not stated) in December, 1806, moved to Ohio with his parents (names not given), and then moved to what is now Switzerland Co., IN where he grew to manhood. He married **Lucinda North**, daughter of **Levi North**, on 24 Sep 1835 and they had the following children:
1. **Rosanna Powell**
2. **John H. Powell**
3. **George W. Powell** (married **Cynthia A. Lostutter**)
4. **Mary E. Powell**
5. **Marcus L. Powell** (married **Mary A. Dibble**)
6. **William J. Powell**
7. **Sarah J. Powell** (died young)

{Ref: *History of Dearborn and Ohio Counties, Indiana* (1885), p. 876}

THOMAS PRATHER

Thomas Prather was born in Prince George's Co., MD on 26 Mar 1756 and lived at Mulberry Fields, NC (county not given) at the time of his enlistment in the Revolutionary War. After the war he moved to Henry Co., VA and in October, 1789 he moved to Kentucky. In 1805 he moved to Fleming Co., KY and in 1817 he moved to Jackson Co., IN. In 1828 **Sally Wilson** stated that she had lived with his family for 17 years and about 1802 she moved away from them. A son **Bazil Prather** was still living in November, 1841. {Ref: *Genealogical Abstracts of Revolutionary War Pension Files*, by Virgil D. White (1990), Application S17030}

ISAAC PRICE

Isaac Price requested a certificate of removal on the 13th day of the 3rd month, 1806, from the Baltimore Monthly Meeting, Western District, to the Short Creek Monthly Meeting in Ohio for himself, his wife **Hannah Price**, and their four minor children, **Elizabeth Price, William Price, Frances Price, and Israel Price**, having already moved there. {Ref: Baltimore Quaker Monthly Meeting Minutes}

JOHN H. PRICE

John H. Price requested a certificate of removal on the 6th day of the 3rd month, 1818, from the Baltimore Monthly Meeting, Western District, to the Smithfield Monthly Meeting in Ohio, having already moved there. {Ref: Baltimore Quaker Monthly Meeting Minutes}

NATHANIEL PRICE

Nathaniel Price served in Maryland during the Revolutionary War and subsequently moved to Knox Co., OH where he applied for a pension on 25 Jul 1818, aged 67 (69?). On 29 Aug 1820 he stated he was aged 71 and had no family living with him. {Ref: *Genealogical Abstracts of Revolutionary War Pension Files*, by Virgil D. White (1990), Application S40298}

STEPHEN R. PRICE

Stephen R. Price served in Maryland during the Revolutionary War and was in Rockbridge Co., VA by March, 1806 at which time he signed a power of attorney. He subsequently moved to Ohio and applied for a pension in Franklin County on 1 Aug 1828. {Ref: *Genealogical Abstracts of Revolutionary War Pension Files*, by Virgil D. White (1990), Application S46467}

WARRICK PRICE

Warrick Price requested a certificate of removal from the Baltimore Monthly Meeting, Eastern District, to the Plymouth Monthly Meeting in Ohio on the 10th day of the 10th month, 1811, for himself, his wife **Susanna Price**, and their four minor children, **William Price, Ann Price, Isaac Price** and **Susanna Miller**. Their son **Isaac Price** was born on the 18th day of the 10th month, 1802 and another child, **Warrick Price, Jr.**, was born on the 27th day of the 10th month, 1807 and died on the 7th day of the 8th month, 1808. {Ref: Baltimore Quaker Monthly Meeting Minutes and Birth Records}

JAMES PRITCHARD

James Pritchard was born in Frederick Co., MD on 1 Nov 1763 and allegedly enlisted as a private on 15 May 1778 and served in the 2nd Maryland Line; however, if such was the case, he was only 14½ years old at the time. Yet, there was a James Pritchard who enlisted in Maryland on that date, but the records indicated he was subsequently reported as dead (no date was given) and it appeared that he was from Dorchester County, not Frederick County. Therefore, additional research will be necessary before drawing any further conclusions. The **James**

Pritchard born on 1 Nov 1763, married first to **Tabitha White** and second to **Mrs. Radinger**, and died in Chillicothe, OH on 6 Feb 1813. His daughter **Kezia Pritchard** married **Louis Kinney** and died in 1852. {Ref: DAR Application 44622; *Index of Patriots, Revolutionary War Heroes and Their Families, Cincinnati Chapter DAR, 1893-1981*, by Jeraldyne Beets Clipson and Katherine Brewer Brinkdopke (1983), p. 213; *Archives of Maryland*, Volume 18, pp. 151, 293}

JESSE PRY

Jesse Pry was born in Anne Arundel Co., MD on 27 Aug 1761 and lived in Washington Co., MD at the time of his enlistment in the Revolutionary War. He lived in Hagerstown, MD until 1810, then moved to the Green River in Kentucky, and in 1816 he moved to Spencer Co., IN. He applied for a pension on 12 Apr 1847, aged 86. {Ref: *Genealogical Abstracts of Revolutionary War Pension Files*, by Virgil D. White (1990), Application S46467; *Maryland Revolutionary Records*, by Harry Wright Newman (1938), p. 43}

GEORGE H. PUNTENNEY

George H. Puntenney, son of **Joseph and Sarah Puntenney**, was born in Baltimore (now Harford) Co., MD on 10 Apr 1759 (one source incorrectly suggested he was born circa 1767) and lived in Harford County at the time of his enlistment in the Revolutionary War. He was also a signer of the Association of Freemen in Harford Lower Hundred in 1776. During the war he moved to Westmoreland Co., PA, the part which later became Allegheny County, and enlisted there. He also lived with his father in western Maryland and also enlisted there. George later moved to Bourbon Co., KY and five years afterwards he moved to Adams County in the Northwest Territory, which part later became Ohio. He applied for a pension on 16 Jul 1852 and lived near Rome, OH when he was age 94. George married (wife's name not given) and had 10 children, 64 grandchildren and 37 great-grandchildren, most of whom lived in Adams Co., OH (see below). {Ref: *Genealogical Abstracts of Revolutionary War Pension Files*, by Virgil D. White (1990), Application R8522; *Baltimore County Families, 1659-1759*, by Robert W. Barnes (1989), p. 526; *Revolutionary Patriots of Harford County, Maryland, 1775-1783*, by Henry C. Peden, Jr. (1985), p. 184}

George Hollingsworth Puntenney was born in Baltimore Co., MD and married **Margaret Hamilton** (c1765-1841) at Fort Pitt, Allegheny Co., PA on 1 Jan 1789. They lived in Bourbon Co., KY between 1793 and 1799 and subsequently moved to Ohio. He died in Green Township, Adams Co., OH on 30 Jan 1853. The children of **George and Margaret Puntenney** were as follows:

1. **Sarah Puntenney** (9 Feb 1790, PA - 18 Aug 1849, OH) married **William Russell** on 2 Jul 1807 in Adams Co., OH

2. **William Hamilton Puntenney** (9 Aug 1792, PA - 6 Aug 1870, IN) married **Lydia Pixley** on 3 Mar 1814 in Adams Co., OH and died in Fayette Co., IN

3. **Mary Puntenney** (6 Oct 1794, KY - 7 Sep 1877, OH)

4. **Joseph Puntenney** (16 Jul 1796, KY - 1 Aug 1893, IN) married **Martha Russell** on 3 Jan 1822 in Adams Co., OH and died in Rush Co., IN

5. **George Hollingsworth Puntenney, Jr.** (15 Jun 1798, KY - 21 Jun 1849, OH) married **Rhoda Truitt** on 7 Aug 1823 in Adams Co., OH

6. **James Puntenney** (1 Sep 1800, OH - 7 May 1890, OH) married **Martha Waite** on 10 Apr 1823

7. **John Puntenney** (30 Jul 1804, OH - 13 Mar 1865, OH) married **Aramintah Wright** on 12 Apr 1827

8. **Ann Puntenney** (b. 30 Jun 1806, OH) married **Stephen Beach** on 12 Oct 1826

{Ref: Puntenney family information compiled by Joseph Mack Ralls, of Albuquerque, NM, in 1997 and published, in part, in *More Marylanders to Kentucky, 1778-1828*, by Henry C. Peden, Jr., pp. 133-134}

JAMES PUNTENNEY

James Puntenney, son of **Joseph and Sarah Puntenney**, was born circa 1774 in Harford Co., MD, married **Achsah Wood** on 18 Oct 1798 in Baltimore Co., MD (his name was listed as **James Pontenay** in the marriage license book), and died in Wells Township, Jefferson Co., OH (no date given). They had three children who all lived in Brooke Co., VA:

1. **John Puntenney** (married **Charlotte Clayton** in 1826)
2. **James Puntenney** (married **Mary** ---- and died in 1888)
3. **Elizabeth Puntenney** (married **William Clayton** in 1830)

{Ref: Puntenney family information compiled by Joseph Mack Ralls, of Albuquerque, NM, in 1997 and published, in part, in *More Marylanders to Kentucky, 1778-1828*, by Henry C. Peden, Jr., p. 135}

NELSON PUNTENNEY

Nelson Puntenney, son of **Joseph and Sarah Puntenney**, was born circa 1770 in Baltimore Co., MD and married **Jane McDowell** circa 1790. They moved to Logan Co., KY, then to Franklin Co., OH and then to Wabash Township, Parke Co., IN. **Jane Puntenney** died in 1833 and **Nelson Puntenney** died on 1 Feb 1843 in Mecca, IN. Their children were as follows:

1. **George Hollingsworth Puntenney** (b. circa 1791, KY - d. circa 1795, age 14)
2. **Aquilla Puntenney** (3 Mar 1793 - 15 Dec 1878) married first to **Eliza Kirby** and second to **Ellen Headley**, and died in Parke Co., IN
3. **Joseph Puntenney** (b. c1797, KY - 24 Jan 1852, Parke Co., IN)
4. **Sarah Puntenney** (married **Abram Williams** in 1821 in Franklin Co., OH)
5. **Nelson Hollingsworth Puntenney** (31 Oct 1806 - 16 May 1848) married **Fanny Mapes** in 1834 in Franklin Co., OH and died in Parke Co., IN
6. **Matilda Puntenney** (married **George Shick** in 1829 in Franklin Co., OH)
7. **Prisilia Puntenney** (married **Mr. Hoaglin**)
8. **Pamelia Puntenney**
9. **James Guffy Puntenney**

{Ref: *Baltimore County Marriage Licenses, 1777-1798*, by Dawn Beitler Smith, p.

151; Puntenney family information compiled by Joseph Mack Ralls, of Albuquerque, NM, in 1997 and published, in part, in *More Marylanders to Kentucky, 1778-1828*, by Henry C. Peden, Jr., p. 134}

SAMUEL PUNTENNEY

Samuel Puntenney, son of **Joseph and Sarah Puntenney**, was born circa 1771-1772 in Baltimore Co., MD, married **Nancy McDowell** (c1780-1833), lived in Logan Co., KY by 1795, and probably died in Franklin Co., OH. Their children were as follows:
1. **Joseph Puntenney** (married **Eliza Cook**)
2. **Lucinda Puntenney** (married **William B. Cook**)
3. **Reason Gamble Puntenney** (married **Julia Ann Cook**)
4. **McDowell Puntenney**
5. **Eliza Puntenney** (married **Fielden Kelly**)

{Ref: Puntenney family information compiled by Joseph Mack Ralls, of Albuquerque, NM, in 1997 and published, in part, in *More Marylanders to Kentucky, 1778-1828*, by Henry C. Peden, Jr., p. 134}

JOSEPH PUTERBAUGH

Joseph Puterbaugh was born in 1761 in Hunterdon Co., NJ and lived in Frederick Co., MD at the time of his enlistment in the Revolutionary War. After the war he lived in Pennsylvania before moving to Ohio where he applied for a pension in Perry County on 10 Jun 1850. He was still living in 1852. {Ref: *Genealogical Abstracts of Revolutionary War Pension Files*, by Virgil D. White (1990), Application R8143}

JOHN RAINSBURG

John Rainsburg was born circa 1759 and lived in Frederick Co., MD at the time of his enlistment in the Revolutionary War. He subsequently moved to Ohio and applied for a pension in Carroll County on 19 Aug 1834, aged 75. On 9 Oct 1861 **George Reinsberger** made an inquiry from Eldora, Hardin Co., IA to the U. S. War Department. It should also be noted that there was a Ramsberg family in Frederick Co., MD whose male members served in the Revolutionary War. including John Ramsburg. The surname was sometimes spelled Ramsberg, Remsburg, Ramsburgh, Ransberg, Rannesperger, and Reimensperger. Additional research will be necessary before drawing any further conclusions. {Ref: *Genealogical Abstracts of Revolutionary War Pension Files*, by Virgil D. White (1990), Application S7351; *Revolutionary Patriots of Frederick County, Maryland, 1775-1783*, by Henry C. Peden, Jr. (1995), pp. 295-296}

ALLEN RAMSEY

Allen Ramsey was born in Baltimore (now Harford) Co., MD on 12 Jun 1764 and moved with his mother (name not given) to Washington Co., MD where he enlisted in the Revolutionary War and served in the Pennsylvania Line. In 1784 he moved to what is now Vincennes, IN and in 1792 he was taken prisoner by the

157

Pottawatmie Indians and was later released. In 1819 he moved to Illinois and applied for a pension in Wabash County on 3 Dec 1833. {Ref: *Genealogical Abstracts of Revolutionary War Pension Files*, by Virgil D. White (1990), Application S32467}

WILLIAM RANDALL

William Randall was born circa 1738 in Kent Co., MD and served as a wagoner during the Revolutionary War. He married **Hannah Briscoe** and their children were as follows:
1. **Sarah Randall** (married **William Frazier**)
2. **William Randall, Jr.** (married **Rebecca Frazier**)
3. **Isaac Randall** (married **Phoebe Misner**)
4. **John Randall** (b. 1 Apr 1794) married **Rebecca Smyth**
5. **Bethiah Randall** (b. 1795) married **George Frazier**

William Randall moved his family to Ohio and he died in Trumbull County on 21 Nov 1815. {Ref: *Directory of Maryland State Society DAR, 1892-1965*, p. 596}

BENJAMIN F. RANEY

Benjamin F. Raney and **Maria Beckett**, of Maryland (county not stated), married in Ohio (county not stated) before 1830. {Ref: *Maryland Revolutionary Records*, by Harry Wright Newman (1938), p. 121}

DANIEL RANKIN

Daniel Rankin (sometimes spelled Rankins) was born circa 1754 and served in Maryland during the Revolutionary War. **Daniel Rankins** enlisted on 3 Feb 1776 at Annapolis, MD and **Daniel Rankin** enlisted in the 1st MD Regiment on 10 Dec 1776 and was discharged on 27 Dec 1779. He subsequently moved to Virginia and married **Ellender or Eleanor Tongues** on or after 29 Mar 1792 (date of bond signed by him and **Milburn Coe**) in Loudoun County. They later moved to Ohio and he applied for a pension in Brown County on 22 Apr 1818. In 1824 he was aged 70 and living with him were these children:
1. **James Rankin** (b. 1806, aged 18 in 1824)
2. **Nancy Rankin** (b. 1808, aged 16 in 1824)
3. **John Rankin** (b. 1809, aged 15 in 1824)

Daniel Rankin died on 30 Apr 1833. **Eleanor Rankin** married **George Washburn** in September, 1834 and he died on 9 Mar 1850. **Levina Ayers** made an affidavit in Montgomery Co., OH in 1850, but no relationship was given. **Eleanor Washburn** applied for a widow's pension in Montgomery Co., IN on 9 Sep 1851, aged 81. {Ref: *Genealogical Abstracts of Revolutionary War Pension Files*, by Virgil D. White (1990), Application W9877; *Archives of Maryland*, Volume 18, pp. 8, 154}

158

GEORGE RAY

George Ray was born in Kent Co., DE in 1761 and lived there at the time of his enlistment in the Revolutionary War. After the war he moved to Baltimore, MD and subsequently moved to Ohio where he applied for a pension in Jefferson County on 5 Apr 1841. {Ref: *Genealogical Abstracts of Revolutionary War Pension Files*, by Virgil D. White (1990), Application R8610}

JONATHAN RAY

Jonathan Ray was born in March, 1759 in Frederick Co., MD and served in Maryland during the Revolutionary War. He lived at Hagerstown, Washington Co., MD at the time of his enlistment and moved to Huntington Co., PA after the war. Four years later he moved to Ohio and in 1823 he moved to Indiana where he applied for a pension in Marion County on 29 Mar 1833. He indicated that a cousin, **Samuel Davis**, of Ohio, had his birth record. {Ref: *Genealogical Abstracts of Revolutionary War Pension Files*, by Virgil D. White (1990), Application S16513}

CHARLES REED

Charles Reed was born in Cumberland Co., NJ on 12 Nov 1760 and lived at Salem, NJ at the time of his enlistment in the Revolutionary War. After the war he moved to Dorchester Co., MD and lived there until 1829 when he moved to Richland Co., OH. In 1838 he moved to Illinois and applied for a pension in Lawrence County on 23 Apr 1841. He mentioned his wife (name not given), who was about his age, and a **Rev. Joseph H. Reed** made an affidavit, but no relationship was given. {Ref: *Genealogical Abstracts of Revolutionary War Pension Files*, by Virgil D. White (1990), Application R8652}

JOHN REED

John Reed was born in Baltimore Co., MD on 1 May 1758 and lived there at the time of his enlistment in the Revolutionary War. He also took the Oath of Allegiance in 1778. John subsequently moved to Ohio and applied for a pension in Darke County on 6 Nov 1832. He married **Mariam or Marion Ashley** on 30 Nov 1833 and died on 27 Aug 1844 or 9 Sep 1845 (both dates were given). **Mariam or Marion Reed** applied for a widow's pension in Howard Co., IN on 2 Oct 1855, aged 80. {Ref: *Genealogical Abstracts of Revolutionary War Pension Files*, by Virgil D. White (1990), Application R8667; *Maryland Revolutionary Records*, by Harry Wright Newman (1938), p. 121; *Revolutionary Patriots of Baltimore Town and Baltimore County, Maryland, 1775-1783*, by Henry C. Peden, Jr. (1988), p. 222}

JOSIAS REEVES

Josias Reeves, Sr. was born in Charles Co., MD in October, 1760 and served in the Revolutionary War as a private in the 3rd MD Regiment in 1779. After the war he moved to Culpeper Co., VA and from there he moved to Ohio in 1824. He died in Pickaway County in 1841, aged 81. {Ref: *Baltimore Sun*, 9 Oct 1841;

Archives of Maryland, Volume 18, p. 288}

JOHN REILLEY

John Reilley (sometimes spelled Reilly and Riley) was born in Cecil Co., MD on 9 Dec 1751 and served in the 8th Pennsylvania Regiment during the Revolutionary War. He married **Elizabeth McCullock** (b. 3 Jun 1764) on 23 Mar 1784 and subsequently moved to Indiana. Their son **Robert Reilley** (b. 21 Jan 1785) married **Hester Stevens**. **Elizabeth Reilley** died in Rush Co., IN on 5 Sep 1840 and **John Reilley** died on 22 Dec 1845. {Ref: DAR Application 516149; *Index of Patriots, Revolutionary War Heroes and Their Families, Cincinnati Chapter DAR, 1893-1981*, by Jeraldyne Beets Clipson and Katherine Brewer Brinkdopke (1983), p. 218}

ROBERT REYNOLDS

Robert Reynolds served in Maryland during the Revolutionary War and later moved to Ohio. Although a resident of Jefferson Co., OH, he applied for a pension in Brooke Co., VA on 28 Jul 1834. {Ref: *Genealogical Abstracts of Revolutionary War Pension Files*, by Virgil D. White (1990), Application S40321}

PETER RHUFF (ROAFF)

Peter Rhuff (Roaff) was born circa 1761 and enlisted at Frederick, MD during the Revolutionary War. He later moved to Ohio and applied for a pension in Montgomery County on 25 Jul 1821, aged 60. His wife **Margaret Rhuff**, was aged 65 in 1820, and a **Matthias Rhuff** made an affidavit on 16 Jun 1822 in Ohio, but no relationship was given. {Ref: *Genealogical Abstracts of Revolutionary War Pension Files*, by Virgil D. White (1990), Application S40352}

GABRIEL RICHARDS

Gabriel Richards, of Prince George's Co., MD. served as a private in the War of 1812. He volunteered at Bocker's Ship Station in June, 1813 and volunteered again at White's Landing on Patuxent River in June, 1814. He was discharged while on furlough and was never called out again. He later moved to Ohio and applied for bounty land (warrant 55-rej-116148) in Clermont County on 3 Apr 1855, aged 65. {Ref: *Maryland Militia, War of 1812, Volume 6, Prince George's County*, by F. Edward Wright, p. 46}

SAMUEL RICHARDSON

Samuel Richardson served as a private during the Revolutionary War, having enlisted at Hagerstown, MD. He was enrolled by Capt. **Henry Hardman** and passed on 19 Jul 1776 in Frederick (now Washington) Co., MD. He was also recruited and passed by County Lieut. **Thomas Sprigg** on 22 Apr 1780. He subsequently moved to Ohio where he applied for a pension in Warren County on 26 Jun 1818, aged 65. In 1820 Samuel indicated he had not had any family with him for 25 years. On 20 Aug 1831 his brother and sole heir **William T. Richardson** assigned his rights to bounty land (warrant 1764-100) to **Joseph Writson** in

Highland Co., OH. {Ref: *Genealogical Abstracts of Revolutionary War Pension Files*, by Virgil D. White (1990), Application S40346; *Archives of Maryland*, Volume 18, pp. 51, 336}

EDWARD RICKETTS

Edward Ricketts was born on 19 Apr 1758 at Antietam, south of Hagerstown, MD, and moved with his father (not named) to Huntington Co., PA, where he lived at the time of his enlistment in the Revolutionary War. Around 1800 he moved to Fairfield Co., OH and applied for a pension on 30 Oct 1832. He mentioned his brother **Thomas Ricketts** had served with him during the war and his brother **Reson Ricketts** lived in Fairfield County in 1832. Edward's heirs were mentioned in 1853, but only a son Col. **John Ricketts**, of Fairfield County, was named. {Ref: *Genealogical Abstracts of Revolutionary War Pension Files*, by Virgil D. White (1990), Application R8796}

NATHAN RICKETTS

Nathan Ricketts was born on 26 Aug 1759 or 1760 at Antietam, MD and lived in Pennsylvania *"between the Juniata's"* at the time of his enlistment in the Revolutionary War. Around 1795 he moved to Kentucky and in 1804 he moved to Indiana, settling in Dearborn County. He applied for a pension in Switzerland Co., IN on 17 Sep 1832 and mentioned Capt. **Edward Ricketts** and Capt. **Thomas Ricketts**, but no relationship was given. In 1832 **Robert Ricketts**, of Switzerland Co., IN, stated he had served with **Nathan Ricketts** during the Revolutionary War. {Ref: *Genealogical Abstracts of Revolutionary War Pension Files*, by Virgil D. White (1990), Application S32480}

ROBERT RICKETTS

Robert Ricketts was born on 15 Jan 1765 near Hagerstown, MD and lived in Cumberland Co., PA at the time of his enlistment in the Revolutionary War. About 10 years after the war he moved to Kentucky for about 15 years and then moved to Indiana. He applied for a pension in Dearborn County on 18 Sep 1832 and his brother **Nathan Ricketts** made an affidavit in Switzerland Co., IN. Robert died on 14 Feb 1853, leaving a wife and 11 children (no names were given). His widow died on 20 Feb 1853. {Ref: *Genealogical Abstracts of Revolutionary War Pension Files*, by Virgil D. White (1990), Application S17047}

JONATHAN RIDGEWAY

Jonathan Ridgeway, of Prince George's Co., MD, served in the War of 1812. He enrolled about June, 1813 and was discharged at Bladensburg, MD on 30 or 31 Aug 1814. He later moved to Ohio and applied for bounty land in Tuscarawas County on 20 Dec 1850, aged 64, and again on 7 May 1855, aged 69 (warrant 55-160-2433). {Ref: *Maryland Militia, War of 1812, Volume 6, Prince George's County*, by F. Edward Wright, p. 46}

WILLIAM RIGBY

William Rigby was born on 11 Jun 1753 and enlisted in Calvert Co., MD during the Revolutionary War. He subsequently moved to Fairfield Co., OH and married on 25 Feb 1817 to **Airy "Ara" Williamson** (neé **Airy Lemon**, born 1 Feb 1782, daughter of **William and Margaret Lemon**, and widow of **David Williamson** to whom Ara had married on 12 Dec 1804 in Fairfield County; he died on 4 Sep 1811). William applied for a pension on 18 Oct 1819, and applied again on 28 Jun 1820, aged 67. In 1820 he had a wife **Ara Rigby**, aged 37 or 38, one son **William Lemon Rigby**, aged 2, and five step-daughters **Sarah Williamson**, aged 13, **Elizabeth Williamson**, aged 11, **Olive Williamson**, aged 10, **Mary Williamson**, aged 8, and **Mercy Williamson**, aged about 7. **William Rigby** died on 20 Mar 1830 and Ara Rigby applied for a widow's pension on 16 Aug 1853, aged 71. **William L. Rigby**, son of William, made an affidavit in Fairfield Co., OH on 16 Aug 1853 and stated that his half-brother **James Rigby** had put the family data in a bible in 1830. **Ara Rigby** also applied for a bounty land warrant (55-160-5438) on 9 Apr 1855. {Ref: *Genealogical Abstracts of Revolutionary War Pension Files*, by Virgil D. White (1990), Application W2248; *Maryland Revolutionary Records*, by Harry Wright Newman (1938), p. 121}

NICHOLAS RILEY

Nicholas Riley was born circa 1778 in Maryland (county not stated) and moved to Wellsburg, VA circa 1800. He moved to Coshocton Co., OH in 1803 and was the second person to settle on Owl Creek in Butler Township. He died on 15 Dec 1866. {Ref: *History of Knox County, Ohio*, by N. N. Hill, Jr. (1881), p. 433}

AZEL ROBERTS

Azel or Hazel Roberts and **Rachel Gassaway**, of Maryland (county not stated), married in Ohio (county not stated) before 1828. {Ref: *Maryland Revolutionary Records*, by Harry Wright Newman (1938), p. 121}

JOHN ROBINSON

John Robinson was born circa 1751 and served in Maryland during the Revolutionary War. He later moved to Ohio and applied for a pension in Harrison County on 21 May 1818, aged about 67. He died on 11 Jun 1819. {Ref: *Genealogical Abstracts of Revolutionary War Pension Files*, by Virgil D. White (1990), Application S40355}

ANDREW ROCK

Andrew Rock was born circa 1762 about 12 miles east of Baltimore, MD and lived there at the time of his enlistment in the Revolutionary War. After the war he lived at Cumberland on the Potomac River and then moved to Morgantown, VA (now WV) where he was married (name of wife not given). About 10 or 12 years later they moved to Lawrenceburg, IN for 8 years and then lived in Hancock, Shelby and Hamilton Counties, all in Indiana. He applied for a pension in Hamilton Co., IN on 14 Nov 1850, aged 88. {Ref: *Genealogical Abstracts of Revolutionary*

War Pension Files, by Virgil D. White (1990), Application R8920}

WILLIAM ROCK

William Rock was born on 10 Jan 1760 in Baltimore Co., MD and lived there at the time of his enlistment in the Revolutionary War. He was a private in the 4th MD Regiment on 26 Apr 1778 and served to at least 1 Nov 1778. **Edward Rock, John Rock and Oliver Rock** also served in the same regiment. About 12 years after the war William moved to the District of Columbia for 4 years, then to Pittsburgh, PA, then to Cincinnati, OH for a few years, and then to Lawrenceburg, IN. In 1820 he moved to Madison Co., IL and in 1835 he moved to Jersey Co., IL where he applied for a pension on 6 Mar 1852. {Ref: *Genealogical Abstracts of Revolutionary War Pension Files*, by Virgil D. White (1990), Application R8921; *Archives of Maryland*, Volume 18, p. 157}

SELAH ROLLINS

Selah Rollins and **Isabella Fuller**, of Maryland (county not stated), married in Indiana (county not stated) on 12 Aug 1831. {Ref: *Maryland Revolutionary Records*, by Harry Wright Newman (1938), p. 122}

MARTIN ROOSS

Martin Rooss (sometimes spelled Roos and Rose), probable son of **Gottlieb Rose** of Frederick Co., MD, was born on 26 Oct 1760 and married **Rebecca Thukston or Thickston** on 27 Dec 1786 in Jefferson Co., KY. In 182 they moved to Knox Co., IN and Martin died testate in 1828. {Ref: "Gottlieb Rose of Frederick County" by Christine Rose, *Western Maryland Genealogy*, Volume 3, No. 3 (1987), p. 130}

REUBEN ROSS

Reuben Ross was born circa 1758 in Maryland and enlisted at Bush in Harford Co., MD during the Revolutionary War. He was a private in the militia company of Capt. **William Bradford** on 13 Sep 1775 and was probably the **Reuben Rose** who signed the Association of Freemen in Harford Hundred in 1776. **Reuben Ross** was a rifleman at the Battle of Fort Washington on 16 Nov 1776, served in the 4th MD Regiment, 1776-1777, and was hospitalized in September-October, 1777. He married **Henrietta Biven** and after the war they moved to Ohio where he applied for a pension in Hamilton County on 9 Jun 1818. In 1819 his brother **Ignatius Ross** made an affidavit at Cincinnati, OH. In 1820 Reuben was aged 65 and mentioned 3 children, but he did not give their names. {Ref: *Genealogical Abstracts of Revolutionary War Pension Files*, by Virgil D. White (1990), Application S40361; *Revolutionary Patriots of Harford County, Maryland, 1775-1783*, by Henry C. Peden, Jr. (1985), p. 194; "Men of 76," by Ella Rowe and Joseph Carroll Hopkins, *Maryland Genealogical Society Bulletin*, Volume 25, No. 3 (1984), p. 325}

163

HARRIET O. RUFFIN

Harriet Olive Ruffin, youngest daughter of **William Ruffin**, of Cincinnati, OH, married **David T. Monsarrat** in Cincinnati on 29 May 1834. {Ref: *Baltimore American*, 7 Jun 1834, abstracted by Lorrie A. E. Erdman}

JESSE RUSSELL

Jesse Russell, of New Market, Frederick Co., MD, born 5 Mar 1810, son of **Thomas Russell** (1768-1811) and **Sarah Roberts**, married at Bush Creek Meeting House on 19 Jun 1834 to **Elizabeth Coale**, daughter of **William Coale** and **Anna Talbott**, of Harford Co., MD, and moved to Cincinnati, OH. {Ref: "Pipe Creek Friends Monthly Meeting Records," *Western Maryland Genealogy*, Volume 1, No. 3 (1985), pp. 125-126}

PETER RUTLEDGE

Peter Rutledge was born in Baltimore Co., MD on 16 Feb 1760 and lived there at the time of his enlistment in the Revolutionary War. After the war he moved to Kentucky and in 1808 he moved to Indiana. Peter married first to **Miriam Sanford(?)** who died in Kentucky and married second to **Ruth Robinson** in June, 1816 in Harrison Co., KY. The children of Peter Rutledge were as follows:

1. **Abraham W. Rutledge** (c1786, MD - 1840, Vermilion Co., IL) married **Mary Huffman** on 15 Aug 1805 in Harrison Co., KY

2. **Isaac Rutledge** (1788, MD - 30 May 1878, Grant Co., KY) married **Margaret Wright** on 15 Nov 1819 in Harrison Co., KY

3. **Jacob Rutledge** (5 Feb 1793, MD - 31 Mar 1839, Ripley Co., IN) married **Mary Robinson** on 2 Nov 1818 in Harrison Co., KY

4. **Mary Rutledge** married **William Young** on 24 Sep 1811 in Harrison Co., KY

5. **Nancy Rutledge** married **Newgent Matthews** on 3 Nov 1814 in Harrison Co., KY

6. **Miriam Rutledge** (1799, KY - 6 Dec 1838, Vermilion Co., IL) married **John Shaver or Shafer** on 24 Jun 1819 in Harrison Co., KY

7. **Ruth Rutledge** (16 Mar 1800, KY - 9 Jun 1860, Vermilion Co., IL) married first to **Samuel McCullough** on 4 Oct 1819 in Harrison Co., KY, second to **John Martin** (date not given correctly), third to **William McMillan** on 10 Oct 1844, and fourth to **John Shaver or Shafer** on 5 Sep 1848

8. **Elizabeth Rutledge** married **William Wright** on 17 Mar 1829 in Vermilion Co., IL

9. **Sarah (Matilda) Rutledge** (b. 1818, Tennessee)

10. **America Ann Rutledge** (b. 1820, IN, twin) married **Madison Grashaw** on 16 Oct 1840 in Ripley Co., IN

11. **Benjamin Rutledge** (b. 1820, IN, twin - d. 19 Oct 1872, a cripple, Ripley Co., IN; buried beside mother)

12. **Eliza Rutledge** (b. 1823, IN) married **Samuel Roberts** on 21 Oct 1851 in Ripley Co., IN

Peter Rutledge applied for a pension on 13 May 1834 in Ripley Co., IN and

164

died on 29 May 1844. **Ruth Rutledge** applied for a widow's pension on 12 Jan 1854, aged 72, and mentioned children **Sarah Rutledge, Eliza Rutledge**, and twins **America Rutledge** and **Benjamin Rutledge**. Ruth died on 17 Nov 1872. {Ref: *Genealogical Abstracts of Revolutionary War Pension Files*, by Virgil D. White (1990), Application R9115; *My Rutledge Family From Early Maryland to 1990*, by Rachel Demaree Clemons (1990), Chapter III, p. 7}

JAMES RYAN

James Ryan served in Maryland (county not stated) during the Revolutionary War, subsequently moved to Ohio, and died prior to 1824. **Nancy Goodlin** made an affidavit on 17 Jul 1824 in Jefferson Co., OH, stating she had been the wife of **James Ryan** and that **William Ryan** was his son. William received bounty land in April, 1825. {Ref: Genealogical Abstracts of Bounty Land Warrant 1120-100-15}

ALEXANDER SANDS

Alexander Sands was born on 16 Jan 1760 in Baltimore Co., MD and lived there at the time of his enlistment in the Revolutionary War. After the war he lived in Frederick Co. MD and Anne Arundel Co., MD and then moved to Ohio. He applied for a pension in Monroe County on 28 Sep 1835. {Ref: *Genealogical Abstracts of Revolutionary War Pension Files*, by Virgil D. White (1990), Application R9191}

JAMES SARGENT

James Sargent, Jr. (sometimes spelled Sergeant), son of **James Sargent** (b. 1717 in Snow Hill, England, married **Eleanor Taylor**, and died 1794 in Frederick Co., MD), was born in Maryland on 25 Jan 1747 and married **Philena Pigman** (b. 25 Jan 1747 in New Jersey) in 1773. Their children were as follows:

1. **Mary Ann Sargent** (b. 1771) married first to **John Garret Prather** on 3 Nov 1791 and second to **William Fee**, and died in 1817 in Chillicothe, OH
2. **James Sargent** (unmarried)
3. **Silas Sargent** married **Kezia ----**
4. **Eleanor or Nelly Sargent** married **John Journey**
5. **Anna Sargent** (b. 1786) married **Edward Sargent**
6. **Sarah Sargent** married **Samuel Walraven**

Elijah Sergeant, James Seargent, Jr., James Seargent, Sr., John Sergeant, Richard Sergeant, Richard Sergeant, Jr., Snowden Sergeant, and William Sergeant were Associators in Frederick Co., MD in December, 1775 and they also took the Oath of Allegiance in 1778. **James Sergeant, Jr.** subsequently moved to Clermont Co., OH where his wife **Philena Sargent** died in 1822 and he died on 13 Dec 1826. {Ref: DAR Applications 553909 and 614510; *Index of Patriots, Revolutionary War Heroes and Their Families, Cincinnati Chapter DAR, 1893-1981*, by Jeraldyne Beets Clipson and Katherine Brewer Brinkdopke (1983), p. 227; *Revolutionary Patriots of Frederick County, Maryland, 1775-1783*, by Henry C. Peden, Jr. (1995), p. 319}

DAVID SAUNDERS

David Saunders requested a certificate of removal on the 11th day of the 7th month, 1817, from the Baltimore Monthly Meeting, Western District, to the Cincinnati Monthly Meeting in Ohio, having already moved there. {Ref: Baltimore Quaker Monthly Meeting Minutes}

BENJAMIN SCOTT

Benjamin Scott served in Maryland during the Revolutionary War and married second to **Lotty** ---- on 27 Sep 1800 in Worcester Co., MD, his first wife (name not given) having died several years previously. They subsequently moved to Ohio and he died in Hamilton County on 15 Jul 1832. **Lotty Scott** then married **George Crestmore or Cristmore** on 26 Mar 1836 and he was run over by a mail stage coach on the road from Sharonville to Cincinnati, OH (date not given). **Lotty Crestmore or Cristmore** then married **Isaac Furgeson or Ferguson** on 21 Jan 1838 and he died about 1840. **Lotty Furgeson or Ferguson** applied for a widow's pension in Hamilton Co., OH on 27 May 1859, aged 84. She stated that **Benjamin Scott** had four brothers (names not given) who died by 1859 and he was 77 or 78 when he died in 1832, having no children. [It should be noted that published Maryland marriage records indicate that **Benjamin Scott** obtained a license on 23 Sep 1800 to marry **Sally Anderson**, so perhaps Lotty was mistakenly transcribed as Sally.] {Ref: *Genealogical Abstracts of Revolutionary War Pension Files*, by Virgil D. White (1990), Application W25601; *Maryland Revolutionary Records*, by Harry Wright Newman (1938), p. 112} *Worcester County Marriage Licenses, 1795-1865*, by Mary Beth and Vanessa Long (1990), p. 9; *Revolutionary Patriots of Worcester & Somerset Counties, Maryland, 1775-1783*, by Henry C. Peden, Jr. (1999), pp. 260-261}

ISAAC SCOTT

Isaac Scott was born 12 Jun 1756 at Chestertown, Kent Co., MD and lived in Cecil Co., MD at the time of his enlistment in the Revolutionary War, serving under his brother Capt. **John Scott**. He also took the Oath of Allegiance in 1778. In 1801 Isaac moved to Ohio and settled in Trumbull Co. He applied for a pension on 2 Oct 1832 and died on 3 Oct 1833, leaving children (no names were given). In 1853 the only surviving child was **Matthew Scott** who lived in Howland Township, Trumbull Co., OH. {Ref: *Genealogical Abstracts of Revolutionary War Pension Files*, by Virgil D. White (1990), Application S17666; *Revolutionary Patriots of Cecil County, Maryland, 1775-1783*, by Henry C. Peden, Jr. (1991), p. 102}

JAMES SCOTT

James Scott, of Cecil Co., MD, served in the War of 1812 as a private in the company of Capt. **James Gerry** from 22 Apr to 15 May 1813. After the war he moved to Indiana and applied for bounty land in Morgan County on 11 Nov 1851, aged 61. He applied again (warrant 55-120-89522) on 26 Nov 1855, aged 64, in Vigo Co., IN. James was still living on 6 Dec 1871, aged 80, in Sandford, IN. {Ref:

166

Maryland Militia, War of 1812, Volume 3, Cecil & Harford Counties, by F. Edward Wright, pp. 10, 61}

ANDREW F. SEDERBORG

Andrew F. Sederborg, native of Baltimore, MD, died in Cincinnati, OH on 28 May 1833, aged 22. {Ref: *Baltimore American*, 8 Jun 1833, abstracted by Lorrie A. E. Erdman}

ELIJAH SERJEANT

Elijah Serjeant was born circa 1758 and lived at Frederick, MD at the time of his enlistment in the Revolutionary War. He later moved to Berkeley Co., VA and enlisted there. He subsequently moved to Ohio and applied for a pension in Clermont County on 9 Aug 1832, aged 74. {Ref: *Genealogical Abstracts of Revolutionary War Pension Files*, by Virgil D. White (1990), Application S16245}

ELIJAH SEWARD

Elijah Seward was born in Queen Anne's Co., MD and married **Starling Bright** (date not given). They moved to Tuscarawas Co., OH before 1819 and then in 1825 to Rising Sun, Dearborn Co., IN. Their children were as follows:

1. **Samuel Seward**
2. **Stephen Seward** (see below)
3. **Matilda Seward** (married **Mr. Noble**)
4. **Elizabeth Seward** (married **Mr. Blake**)

Stephen Seward, son of **Elijah and Starling Seward**, was born in Ohio in 1819 and married in 1846 to **Elizabeth Dickinson** (daughter of **Thomas Dickinson** and **Elizabeth Mason**, natives of England who married in 1819 in Elizabethtown, OH). Their children were as follows:

1. **Jennie Seward** (married **J. Dalrymple**)
2. **Matilda Seward**
3. **Stephen Seward, Jr.**
4. **Sherman Seward**
5. **Rea Seward**
6. ---- **Seward** (son, died young)
7. ---- **Seward** (son, died young)
8. ---- **Seward** (son, died young)

{Ref: *History of Dearborn and Ohio Counties, Indiana* (1885), pp. 901-902}

ANDREW SHAFER

Andrew Shafer was born circa 1759 and enlisted at Hagerstown, MD during the Revolutionary War. He subsequently moved to Ohio, applied for a pension in Highland County on 22 Jan 1820, aged 61, and applied again on 27 Jul 1832. One of his heirs in 1856 was **Adam Shafer**, of Highland Co., OH. {Ref: *Genealogical Abstracts of Revolutionary War Pension Files*, by Virgil D. White (1990), Application S4820}

JOHN SHAW

John Shaw served in Maryland during the Revolutionary and later moved to Ohio where he applied for a pension in Delaware County on 15 May 1818. {Ref: *Genealogical Abstracts of Revolutionary War Pension Files*, by Virgil D. White (1990), Application S40401}

FREDERICK SHAWN

Frederick Shawn was born on 12 Aug 1760 in Kent Co., MD and lived there at the time of his enlistment in the Revolutionary War. About 13 years after the war he moved to Washington Co., MD and four years later he moved to Berkeley Co., VA. About 15 years later he moved to Fairfield Co., OH and five years later he moved to Wayne Co., OH. About 13 years later he moved to Richland Co., OH and two years later he moved to Wood Co., OH. He applied for a pension on 3 Oct 1833 in Seneca Co., OH, but he lived in Perry Township, Wood Co., OH at the time. {Ref: *Genealogical Abstracts of Revolutionary War Pension Files*, by Virgil D. White (1990), Application S7509}

ABRAHAM SHEELER

Abraham Sheeler was born circa 1770 in Pennsylvania, married **Mary Miller**, of Frederick Co., MD, daughter of ---- **Miller** and **Barbara Ott** (1750-1824), and moved to Ashland Co., OH. **Abraham Sheeler** died in Vermillion Township on 10 Feb 1851 and **Mary Sheeler** died later. {Ref: "John Ott of Frederick County" by J. Harold and Virginia Miller, *Western Maryland Genealogy*, Volume 2, No. 4 (1986), p. 148}

THOMAS SHERWOOD

Thomas Sherwood requested a certificate of removal from the Baltimore Monthly Meeting, Eastern District, to the Miami Monthly Meeting in Ohio on the 11th day of the 2nd month, 1808, having already moved there. {Ref: Baltimore Quaker Monthly Meeting Minutes}

JOHN SHLIFE

John Shlife was born circa 1757 and enlisted at Baltimore, MD during the Revolutionary War. He joined the Baltimore Mechanical Company of Militia on 4 Nov 1775 and was a private in Capt. Graybill's German Regiment on 12 Jul 1776. He subsequently moved to Ohio and applied for a pension in Fairfield County on 15 May 1819, aged 62. In 1820 he had living with him 2 daughters aged 30 and 23 and a grandson aged 17 who had been entirely helpless since infancy. He also had 6 other children living elsewhere (no names were given). {Ref: *Genealogical Abstracts of Revolutionary War Pension Files*, by Virgil D. White (1990), Application S40417; *Archives of Maryland*, Volume 18, p. 265 and Volume 12, p. 32}

HENRY SHIPLEY

Henry Shipley was raised in Anne Arundel Co., MD, about 18 miles from Baltimore, and lived there at the time of his enlistment in the Revolutionary War. He was enrolled by Capt. Thomas Watkins for service to the State of Maryland on 21 Oct 1776. He also took the Oath of Allegiance in 1778. One record incorrectly stated that he married **Ruth Howard** in August, 1782 at Baltimore, but their marriage license was not obtained until 11 Sep 1782. They later moved to Fayette Co., PA where he died on 11 Feb 1828. Their children were as follows:

1. **Adam Shipley** (b. 10 Jun 1782 *sic*)
2. **Aaron Shipley** (b. 24 Dec? 1784 *sic*)
3. **Henry Shipley, Jr.** (b. 24 Mar 1789)
4. **Ruth Shipley** (b. 30 Mar 1791)
5. **Mary Shipley** (b. 24 -?- 1793 *sic*)
6. **Rachel Shipley** (b. 13 Oct 1795)
7. **Benedict Shipley** (b. 26 Sep 1797 and lived in Knox Co., OH by 1838)
8. **Betsey Shipley** (b. 24 Sep 1799)
9. **Nansey Shipley** (b. 16 Jun 1802)
10. **Amanmaseene Shipley** (b. 15 Jul 1806)

Ruth Shipley later moved to Ohio where she applied for a widow's pension in Knox County on 1 Oct 1838, aged 73; however, in December, 1843 she gave her age as 76 "last Christmas" and when she applied for bounty land (warrant 55-160-38579) in 1855 she gave her age as 91. **Mary Ann Hobbs**, sister of **Henry Shipley**, made an affidavit in Knox Co., OH in 1839, aged 72 or 73. His brother **Adam Shipley** lived in Allegheny Co., PA. {Ref: *Genealogical Abstracts of Revolutionary War Pension Files*, by Virgil D. White (1990), Application W6046; *Baltimore County Marriage Licenses, 1777-1798*, by Dawn Beitler Smith, p. 170; *Revolutionary Patriots of Anne Arundel County, Maryland, 1775-1783*, by Henry C. Peden, Jr. (1992), p. 182}

THOMAS SIMPSON

Thomas Simpson served in Maryland (county not stated) during the Revolutionary War. He may have been either the **Thompson Simpson, Sr.** who was enrolled in the Flying Camp on 16 Jul 1776, aged 25, who was 6 ft. tall and a native of Charles Co., MD, or the **Thomas Simpson** who was a private in the 1st MD Regiment on 28 May 1777, was promoted to corporal on 1 Aug 1777, and discharged on 5 Jan 1780. He subsequently moved to Ohio and applied for a pension in Muskingum County on 5 Nov 1819. In 1821 he was aged 65 with a wife **Mary Simpson**, aged 55, and daughter **Catharine Simpson**, aged 14. {Ref: *Genealogical Abstracts of Revolutionary War Pension Files*, by Virgil D. White (1990), Application S40436; *Archives of Maryland*, Volume 18, pp. 36, 160; *Revolutionary Patriots of Charles County, Maryland, 1775-1783*, by Henry C. Peden, Jr. (1997), p. 268}

169

JAMES SIMS

James Sims, of Cecil Co., MD, served in the War of 1812 as a private in the company of Capt. **James Gerry** in 1813 and then enrolled at age 18 in the company of Capt. **Andrew Porter** until June, 1813 when *"I was drafted into the regular service. After the war began Captain Porter's company of which I was a member, did guard duty along the Chesapeake Bay until June, 1813 when I was drafted aforesaid. After my time was out as a drafted man I was kept as a teamster at least ten days during which time I hauled the Regimental baggage from Port Deposit to Elkton, Maryland when I was discharged some time during the summer of 1813 ... I removed to Ohio in the fall of 1813 with my parents and immediately joined a company of cavalry under command of Capt. William St. Clair and Capt. Hoover and remained in said company which was ordered to the frontier in the spring of 1814, which order was countermanded after we were ready to start .. During my service under Captain Porter I was at Haverdegrass [i.e., Havre de Grace in Harford Co., MD] where the British ships burned that place or part of it ..."* **James Sims** applied for bounty land (warrant 55-rej-333539) at Martinsburg in Knox County on 24 Jun 1878, aged 85. {Ref: *Maryland Militia, War of 1812, Volume 3, Cecil & Harford Counties*, by F. Edward Wright, pp. 11, 66}

JOHN SHOEMAKER

John Shoemaker was born in Hunterdon Co., NJ on 1 Jan 1745 and lived there at the time of his enlistment in the Revolutionary War. After the war he moved to Maryland for 10 years, then moved to Pennsylvania for 5 years, and then to Ohio for 11 years (counties not indicated). In 1824 he moved to Indiana and applied for a pension in Dearborn County on 2 Apr 1834. {Ref: *Genealogical Abstracts of Revolutionary War Pension Files*, by Virgil D. White (1990), Application S32515}

JOHN SHRINER

John Shriner was born in Bucks Co., PA on 21 Feb 1753 and lived there at the time of his enlistment in the Revolutionary War, but his parents (not named) lived in Frederick Co., MD. He also enlisted there for his third and fourth tours of duty. In 1821 he moved to Wayne Co., OH and applied for a pension on 29 May 1834. **Barbary Shriner** applied for a widow's pension in Morrow Co., OH on 3 Oct 1853, but no dates of marriage or death for **John Shriner** (sometimes spelled Shiner and Shinner) were given. {Ref: *Genealogical Abstracts of Revolutionary War Pension Files*, by Virgil D. White (1990), Application R9632}

WILLIAM SIMMONS

William Simmons enlisted during the Revolutionary War at Chestertown, Kent Co., MD. **William Simmons, Jr.** served as a private in the 4th Company, 27th Battalion, Kent County Militia, 1775/1778, and **William Simmons** took the Oath of Allegiance in 1778. He later moved to Baltimore where he applied for a pension on 27 Apr 1818, aged 54; however, on 28 Aug 1820 he gave his age as 61. On 10 Nov 1826 he moved to Stark Co., OH. {Ref: *Genealogical Abstracts of*

170

Revolutionary War Pension Files, by Virgil D. White (1990), Application S40434; *Revolutionary Patriots of Kent & Queen Anne's Counties, Maryland*, by Henry C. Peden, Jr. (1995), p. 238}

DANIEL SIPES

Daniel Sipes (sometimes spelled Sipe) was born before 1760 in Lancaster Co., PA and lived in Frederick Co., MD at the time of his enlistment in the Revolutionary War. Initially he was a non-enroller who was fined by the Committee of Observation in April, 1776, but he apparently enrolled because the fine was remitted in June, 1776. After the war he lived in Maryland, North Carolina and Indiana. He applied for a pension in Harrison Co., IN on 1 Oct 1832, aged 71. **Paul Sipes**, of Harrison Co., IN, was aged 61 in 1832, but no relationship was given. **Daniel Sipes** died on 14 Feb 1834. {Ref: *Genealogical Abstracts of Revolutionary War Pension Files*, by Virgil D. White (1990), Application S17092; *Revolutionary Patriots of Frederick County, Maryland, 1775-1783*, by Henry C. Peden, Jr. (1995), p. 334}

P. SKELTON

Mrs. P. Skelton, formerly of Annapolis, MD, but the for last 30 years a resident of Cincinnati, OH, died in Cincinnati on 3 Nov 1832, aged 66. {Ref: *Baltimore American*, 13 Jun 1832, abstracted by Lorrie A. E. Erdman}

JAMES SLADE

James Slade, son of **William Slade** (b. circa 1790, MD or KY, married **Malvina Clements** on 14 Apr 1808, and d. 13 Feb 1863, Harrison Co., KY) and grandson of **Ezekiel Slade, Jr.** and **Mary Hodgskin** (of *Verdant Valley* on "My Lady's Manor" in Baltimore (now Harford) Co., MD), was born on 4 Feb 1810, Harrison Co., KY, married **Eleanor Orr** (b. 12 Jul 1808, Woodford Co., KY, daughter of **James Orr** and **Catherine Williams**) on 27 Sep 1830 in Harrison Co., KY, and died on 13 Dec 1870 in Harrison Co., KY. **Eleanor Slade** died on 28 Dec 1878 in Clay Co., IN. {Ref: Slade family information compiled by the late John H. Pearce, Jr., of Butler, MD, and published in 1997 in *More Marylanders to Kentucky, 1778-1828*, by Henry C. Peden, Jr., p. 158, and corrected above, in part}

JOHN SLADE

John Slade, son of **Ezekiel Slade, Jr.** and **Mary Hodgskin**, of *Verdant Valley* on "My Lady's Manor" in Baltimore Co., MD, was born on 1 Apr 1795 in Kentucky and died on 13 Dec 1871 at Alton in Clermont Co., OH. He married four times: (1) **Elizabeth Crosley** (25 Sep 1789 - 10 Mar 1830) in Clermont Co., OH on 23 May 1816; (2) **Sarah Gruwell** (28 Jun 1790, DE - 5 Mar 1852, OH) on 20 Jul 1830; (3) Mrs. **Eleanor Waterman**(?) on 19 May 1853 in Brown Co., OH; and, (4) **Joanna McCann** on 16 Jul 1865 in Clermont Co., OH. **John Slade** had seven children by his first wife, one child by his second wife, and none by his last two wives, as follows:

1. **William Crosley Slade** (18 Apr 1817, Levina, OH - 4 Sep 1876, Nichols Station, IA) married **Elizabeth Temple Dunn** (b. 1818, KY) on 24 Jan 1836 at

Cincinnati, OH

    2. **Ezekiel Slade** (4 Apr 1819, Georgetown, Brown Co., OH - 5 Mar 1900, Clermont Co., OH) married **Susanna Monday** (7 Mar 1823, OH - 18 Aug 1897, Batavia, OH) on 26 Dec 1840 at Clermont Co., OH

    3. **James Slade** (6 Jun 1822, Clermont Co., OH - died in Kansas, date not given) married **Eleanor Jane Manker** on 26 Mar 1842 in Clermont Co., OH

    4. **Powell Slade** (17 Jan 1825, Brown Co., OH - 23 Dec 1914, Abington, Wayne Co., IN) married **Hannah Huntington** (19 Jul 1828, OH - 6 Jun 1920, IN) on 3 Dec 1846 in Clermont Co., OH

    5. **John Strange Slade** (11 Nov 1828, Clermont Co., OH - 15 Aug 1876, Concord, OH) married first to **Mary Malvina Willis** (17 Nov 1830 - 28 Jul 1860) on 24 Aug 1851 in Clermont Co., OH, and married second to **Sarah Ann Catherine Smith** (c1827 - 16 Feb 1888) on 20 Jun 1861

    6. **Wayland Slade** (11 Nov 1828, Clermont Co., OH - 28 Apr 1853, OH; buried in Greenbrier Cemetery, Clermont Co., OH)

    7. **Mary A. Slade** (c1830, Clermont Co., OH - 1 Mar 1833; buried in Greenbrier Cemetery, Clermont Co., OH)

    8. **Charles Slade** (8 Apr 1832, Clermont Co., OH - 13 Jan 1902, North Henderson, IL; buried in Fuller Cemetery, North Henderson, IL)

{Ref: Slade family information compiled by the late John H. Pearce, Jr., of Butler, MD, published in 1997 in *More Marylanders to Kentucky, 1778-1828*, by Henry C. Peden, Jr., pp. 158-159, and corrected above, in part}

LEMUEL W. SLADE

    Lemuel W. Slade, son of **Ezekiel Slade, Jr.**, of Baltimore Co., MD, and his second wife **Sarah ----**, was born on 3 Sep 1800 in Clark Co., KY and died on 28 Dec 1886 in Clermont Co., OH. He married first to **Nancy ----** and second to **Ann Williams** (1802, KY - 1881, OH). They are buried in Union Cemetery at Batavia, Clermont Co., OH. All of his children were by his second wife. The eldest was born in Clark Co., KY and the others in Clermont Co., OH.

    1. **John W. Slade** (b. 2 Aug 1826, KY - died at New Hartford, IL, date not given) married **Malinda C. Hayes** on 1 Sep 1849

    2. **Mary A. Slade** (b. Clermont Co., OH, date not given - d. 27 Mar 1870 at Clermont Co., OH) married **Strange Hunt** on 7 Mar 1838; buried in Goshen Cemetery

    3. **Sarah Ann Slade** married **Hiram McClure** on 7 Mar 1842 in Clermont Co., OH

    4. **George Washington Slade** (b. 1833, OH - d. OH, date not given) married **Mary A. Turner** on 8 Feb 1858

    5. **Charlotte Slade** (b. 1840, OH) married **Lewis Nash** on 8 Aug 1863

    6. **Alice Slade** (b. 1841, OH - d. 1907) married **Thomas J. Lewis** on 22 Jul 1863

    7. **James Slade**

    8. **Isaac Newton Slade**

    9. **Lemuel Alexander Slade**

172

{Ref: Slade family information compiled by the late John H. Pearce, Jr., of Butler, MD, and published in 1997 in *More Marylanders to Kentucky, 1778-1828*, by Henry C. Peden, Jr., pp. 158-159, and corrected above, in part}

SAMUEL SLADE

Samuel Slade, son of **Ezekiel Slade, Jr.** and **Mary Hodgskin**, of *Verdant Valley* on "My Lady's Manor" in Baltimore Co., MD, was born in 1796 in Kentucky, married **Lydia Jennings** on 9 Feb 1815 in Clermont Co., OH, and died in 1825. {Ref: Slade family information compiled in 1997 by the late John H. Pearce, Jr., of Butler, MD}

JOHN SLUTS

John Sluts served in Maryland during the Revolutionary War, probably in Baltimore County (extant militia rolls do not list his name, but this is where he took the Oath of Allegiance in 1778). He married **Catharine Welsh** (b. 8 May 1774) in Frederick Co., MD on 22 Jun 1790. They moved to Ohio in 1806 and John died in Jefferson County on 10 Oct 1833. **Catharine Sluts** applied for a widow's pension on 23 Jul 1856, stating they had many children, of which 11 were still living (no names were given). {Ref: *Genealogical Abstracts of Revolutionary War Pension Files*, by Virgil D. White (1990), Application R9667; *Revolutionary Patriots of Baltimore Town and Baltimore County, Maryland, 1775-1783*, by Henry C. Peden, Jr. (1988), p. 247}

WILLIAM SLYE

William Slye (sometimes spelled Sly) was born circa 1758 and served in Maryland during the Revolutionary War. He enlisted in the 7th MD Regiment as a private on 30 Apr 1778, was promoted to corporal by July, 1780, participated in the Battle of Camden on 16 Aug 1780, and was discharged on 30 Apr or 1 May 1781 (both date were given). He later moved to Ohio and applied for a pension in Clermont County on 28 Aug 1834, aged 76. His five surviving children (names not given) received his final payment and were paid to 27 Jan 1838. {Ref: *Genealogical Abstracts of Revolutionary War Pension Files*, by Virgil D. White (1990), Application S1479; *Archives of Maryland*, Volume 18, pp. 249, 555}

JOSEPH SMITH

Joseph Smith was born in Cecil Co., MD on 14 Feb 1753 and lived there at the time of his enlistment in the Revolutionary War. He also took the Oath of Allegiance in 1778. After the war Joseph lived part of the time in Cecil County and for 2 years he lived 5 miles above Pittsburgh, PA before moving to Ohio. He applied for a pension in Belmont County on 9 Aug 1832. {Ref: *Genealogical Abstracts of Revolutionary War Pension Files*, by Virgil D. White (1990), Application S4861; *Revolutionary Patriots of Cecil County, Maryland, 1775-1783*, by Henry C. Peden, Jr. (1991), p. 105}

MICHAEL SMITH

Michael Smith was born circa 1758 and enlisted at Frederick, MD on 20 May 1778 and served as a private in the Revolutionary War. He married **Rebecca Ludwig** in 1784 at Middletown, MD and applied for a pension in Baltimore Co., MD on 13 Apr 1818, aged about 62, at which time he stated he had no family. **Michael Smith** died in 1821 and **Rebecca Smith** applied for a widow's pension in Fairfield Co., OH on 8 Apr 1859, aged 97, stating she had lived with **Michael Smith** until about 1794 when she returned to her mother. They had a daughter **Katharine Smith**, born in 1791 or 1792, who later married **George or John George Kuhns** and lived in Waynesboro, PA before moving to Pleasantville in Fairfield Co., OH. **Rebecca Smith** moved from Frederick Co., MD to Ohio in 1819 and lived part of the time with her daughter **Katharine Kuhns**. She referred to her brother **George Ludwig** as having married a sister of her husband Michael Smith and George died many years ago in Lafayette, IN. Rebecca had several sisters by the last name of Arnold who were children of her mothers's second husband (name not given), of which one married **Thomas McNamee** who had also moved from Maryland to Ohio. Rebecca's nephew **Jacob Ludwick** *(sic)* made an affidavit in Frederick Co., MD on 26 Apr 1859, aged 69, and stated that his father was **Jacob Ludwick** and his mother was **Peggy Kline**, and his grandfather Kline was the stepfather of his uncle **Michael Smith** the Revolutionary War soldier. He also stated that Michael Smith was the half-brother of his mother **Peggy (Kline) Ludwick** and Michael's widow **Rebecca Smith** lived in Washington Co., MD, having moved from there to Ohio with a **John Huffman**. On 7 Apr 1859 **Katharine Kuhns**, aged 67, daughter of Michael Smith, made an affidavit at Pleasantville, OH, stating her uncle **George Ludwig** married her father's half-sister **Peggy Kline** who died many years ago. She also stated that her uncle George Ludwig died in 1855 and her mother's sister **Nancy Ludwig** married **Thomas McNamee** and both had died many years prior to 1859. **Katharine (Smith) Kuhns** stated she was born at Baltimore, MD, married **George Kuhns** in 1822, moved to Waynesburg, PA, then to Washington Co., MD for 5 years, and then moved to Ohio. **George McNamee** made an affidavit in Fairfield Co., OH on 8 Apr 1859, aged 68, stating he was the oldest son of **Thomas and Nancy McNamee** and his sister **Polly NcNamee** married **Daniel Baker** in 1815. **Polly Baker** made an affidavit on 8 Apr 1859, referred to her grandmother Arnold as being formerly Ludwig, and Michael Smith's widow Rebecca had lived with her (Polly's) grandmother Arnold because of Michael's drinking habits. {Ref: *Genealogical Abstracts of Revolutionary War Pension Files*, by Virgil D. White (1990), Application W4339; *Revolutionary Patriots of Frederick County, Maryland, 1775-1783*, by Henry C. Peden, Jr. (1995), pp. 341-342}

NATHAN SMITH

Nathan Smith was born on 8 Oct 1754 in Baltimore Co., MD and enrolled in Harford County on 25 Jul 1776 during the Revolutionary War. He married **Ann J. Chew** in Cecil Co., MD on or about 3 Jul 1784 (date of license) and they later moved to Kentucky. In 1823 bounty land (warrant 1069-300-16) was granted to

Nathan's heirs, viz., **William C. Smith, Benjamin C. Smith, Francis D. Smith, Cassandra Foulke** (wife of **Thomas D. Foulke**), **Nathan C. Smith, Ann M. Smith, Kozciouski Smith**, and **Pulaski Smith** (these children applied on 12 Mar 1823 in Hamilton Co., OH and referred to their father as late of Boone Co., KY). Nathan's granddaughter **Ann Eliza (Foulke) Barbour**, wife of **Oliver P. Barbour**, made an affidavit in Hamilton Co., OH on 18 Sep 1854, aged 35. and stated her mother and father, **Thomas D. Foulke** and **Cassandra Smith**, were both dead; her mother died in Boone Co., KY on 9 Sep 1825 and her father died there in November, 1837. Ann was the only heir of her parents and she stated her grandfather **Nathan Smith** died on 21 Sep 1821. She also stated her uncles **Kosciouski C. Smith** and **Francis D. Smith** were both dead and Francis left four children (names not given). She further stated her grandmother **Ann J. Smith** died in Boone Co., KY on 1 Oct 1838 and Nathan's son **Francis D. Smith** died on 25 May 1840 at Lafayette, Tippecanoe Co., IN, leaving these children in 1854: **S. C. Smith**, aged 24, **Amanda F. Smith**, aged 28, **Louisa Smith**, aged 19, and **Pulaski K. Smith**, aged 21 (and they made an affidavit on 21 Oct 1854 in Hamilton Co., OH, witnessed by **William P. Smith**). These children had moved from Lafayette, IN to Cincinnati, OH about 1845.

Nathan's brother **Winston Smith** was of Boone Co., KY in 1822 and was formerly of Harford Co., MD. In 1822 **John Smith** of Jefferson Co., KY (relationship not given) stated he knew **Nathan Smith** during the Revolutionary War. In 1840 **Thomas Smith** and **Nathan Smith** of Boone Co., KY (relationship not given) testified they had known **Nathan Smith** for a long time. **Pulaski Smith**, son of Nathan, was living in Boone Co., KY on 6 Jul 1840 when he inquired about a pension for his mother and his father's other heirs. {Ref: *Genealogical Abstracts of Revolutionary War Pension Files*, by Virgil D. White (1990), Application W8730; *History of Harford County*, by Walter W. Preston (1901), p. 128; *Archives of Maryland*, Volume 18, p. 60}

PETER SMITH

Peter Smith was born in Maryland (county not stated) and acquired land in Kentucky (county not stated) circa 1805, but did not move there until 1820, and subsequently moved to Wayne Co., IN. He married (wife's name not given) and they had the following children:
1. **Nicholas Smith** (married **Rebecca Hunt**)
2. **Mary Smith** (married **David Railsback**)
3. **Barbara Smith** (married **Christopher C. Beeler**)
4. **John P. Smith** (married **Mary Sedgwick**)
5. **George H. Smith** (married **Clarissa Lewis**)
6. **James Smith** (married **Mary H. Hunt**)
7. **Irvin Smith** (lived in Madison Co., IN)
8. **Joseph W. Smith** (never married)
9. **Margaret Smith** (married **Nelson Crow**)

{Ref: *History of Wayne County, Indiana*, by Andrew W. Young (1872), p. 150}

PHILIP D. SMYTH

Philip D. Smyth was born on 26 Apr 1759 at Hagerstown, MD and served in Maryland during the Revolutionary War. He subsequently moved to Indiana where he applied for a pension in Switzerland County on 10 Oct 1825. He moved to Cincinnati, OH on 10 Mar 1828. {Ref: *Genealogical Abstracts of Revolutionary War Pension Files*, by Virgil D. White (1990), Application S40466}

JOHN SNOOK

The following notice appeared in *Bartgis's Republican Gazette* in Frederick, MD on 20 Feb 1807: *"John Yondiss forewarns persons from taking assignment on bonds given to John Snook, now living in Ohio."* {Ref: *Western Maryland Newspaper Abstracts, Volume 3, 1806-1810*, by F. Edward Wright, p. 101}

GEORGE SNYDER

George Snyder was born on 19 Mar 1754 and lived in Frederick Co., MD at the time of his enlistment in the Revolutionary War. He may have been the **George Schneider** who was an Associator in December, 1775 and took the Oath of Allegiance in 1778. In 1782 he had two brothers then living (no names were given). After the war George lived in Baltimore, MD for 22 years and then moved to Montgomery Co., OH. He applied for a pension in Dayton, OH on 11 Sep 1832. {Ref: *Genealogical Abstracts of Revolutionary War Pension Files*, by Virgil D. White (1990), Application S6135; *Revolutionary Patriots of Frederick County, Maryland, 1775-1783*, by Henry C. Peden, Jr. (1995), p. 316}

PETER SNYDER

Peter Snyder was born in 1759 and lived in Washington Co., MD at the time of his enlistment in the Revolutionary War. In 1803 or 1804 he moved to Bedford Co., PA for 3 or 4 years, then to Washington Co., PA for 15 or 20 years, and then moved to Richland Co., OH. He applied for a pension on 31 Oct 1832, aged 73, and died on 22 Aug 1842. {Ref: *Genealogical Abstracts of Revolutionary War Pension Files*, by Virgil D. White (1990), Application S3947}

PHILIP SOLLADAY

Philip Solladay lived at Sharpsburg in Washington Co., MD at the time of his enlistment in the Revolutionary War and married **Christena or Anna Christena Fleck** about 1779. They later moved to Ohio and Philip died on 1 Apr 1813 in Scioto County. **Christena Solladay** applied for a widow's pension on 16 Dec 1847 and **George Solladay** was their only surviving child in 1852. {Ref: *Genealogical Abstracts of Revolutionary War Pension Files*, by Virgil D. White (1990), Application R9929}

ISAAC SOLLERS

Isaac Sollers (sometimes spelled Sollars) married **Elizabeth Blackmore**, daughter of **Samuel Blackmore** who died in Frederick Co., MD in 1773. Isaac also lived in Youhogania Co., VA and Washington Co., PA by 1781 where he was a captain in the militia during the Revolutionary War. The children of **Isaac and Elizabeth Sollers** are tentatively placed as follows:

1. **Ruth Sollers** (married **Matthew Perkins** circa 1782)
2. **Nancy Ann Sollers** (b. circa 1772 and married **Labon Record** on 6 Oct 1789? in Mason Co., KY)
3. **Mary "Polly" Saunders** (b. 1775 and married **Alexander Buchanan** on 30 May 1796 in Mason Co., KY)
4. **Eleanor Sollers** (b. circa 1783, Allegheny Co., PA)
5. **Samuel Sollers** (b. 12 Jan 1784 in St. Clair, Allegheny Co., PA, married **Elizabeth Train** on 20 Sep 1803 in Dormont, PA, and d. 23 Nov 1842 in Greenfield, Fayette Co., OH)
6. **Isaac Sollers, Jr.** (married **Patty ----**, of Concordia Parish, LA, and d. in Ohio in March, 1830)

{Ref: Sollers family information compiled by Elise Greenup Jourdan, of Knoxville, TN, and published in her 1994 book titled *Early Families of Southern Maryland, Volume 3*, pp. 267-268}

SOULE FAMILY

Jane Soule moved from Baltimore, MD to the State of Ohio (county not stated) in 1828. **Maria Soule** and **Sarah Soule** also moved to Ohio (county not stated) in 1829. {Ref: Class Lists, Baltimore City Station, Methodist Episcopal Church}

WILLIAM SOUTH

William South, of Middlesex Co., NJ, served in New Jersey during the Revolutionary War and married **Hannah ----** (b. 22 Aug 1765 in Frederick Co., MD) in 1780 or 1782 in Washington Co., MD. They lived near Hagerstown, MD for 10 years and then moved to Kentucky for 5 or 6 years. Around 1806 they moved to Clermont Co., OH and William died there on 27 Jun 1811 or 13 Jun 1812 (both dates were given). **Hannah South** subsequently filed for a widow's pension and died on 6 Oct 1843. In 1840 **James South**, of Clermont Co., OH, made an affidavit that he was William's brother and he had served under him during the war. Their known children were as follows:

1. **Peter South** (lived near Dayton, OH in 1852 and died in Indiana before 1856)
2. **Benjamin South** (alive in 1843 but deceased by 1856)
3. **Sarah South** married **Perry Garland** and died before 1856
4. **John South** (died before 1856)
5. **Zedekiah South** (died before 1856)
6. **---- South** (unnamed child)
7. **William South, Jr.** (the 7th child, born 27 Feb 1797, lived in Clermont Co., OH in 1856)
8. **Mary South** married **Charles Waits** and lived in Clermont Co., OH in 1856

{Ref: *Genealogical Abstracts of Revolutionary War Pension Files*, by Virgil D. White (1990), Application W4077}

WILLIAM SPRY

William Spry was born in Queen Anne's Co., MD on 1 Jan 1756. He lived there at the time of his enlistment as a private in July, 1776 during the Revolutionary War and he also took the Oath of Allegiance in 1778. William subsequently moved to Ohio and applied for a pension in Knox County on 29 Sep 1832. He died on 10 Jun 1836 and his wife **Ruth Spry** (who was his second wife; name of first wife was not given) died in October, 1845. Ruth had no living children at her death, but William's children were as follows:

1. **Samuel Spry**, the oldest child, born 25 Dec 1787, lived in Knox Co., OH on 18 May 1846

2. **Mary Spry** married **Mr. Downs**

3. **Nathan Spry** (nothing further)

4. **Elizabeth Spry** married **Mr. Herrington**, died several years after her father and left not less than 7 children (no names were given)

5. **Perry Spry** died before his father and left 6 children, all living in 1846 (no names were given)

6. **Catharine Spry** married **Mr. Bixby**, died several years before her father, and left 4 children, all living in 1846 (no names were given)

Thomas Spry, brother of **William Spry**, also served as a private in Queen Anne's Co., MD in 1776 and made an affidavit in Knox Co., OH on 13 Aug 1832, He verified that William was born in Queen Anne's Co., MD and had served in the Revolutionary War. {Ref: *Genealogical Abstracts of Revolutionary War Pension Files*, by Virgil D. White (1990), Application S4878; *Revolutionary Patriots of Kent & Queen Anne's Counties, Maryland*, by Henry C. Peden, Jr. (1995), p. 247}

RICHARD SPYERS

Richard Spyers (sometimes spelled Spires) was born circa 1753 and served in Maryland during the Revolutionary War as a private in the 3rd Company, 3rd Regiment, 1781-1782. He married **Rebecca Gentle** (b. 25 Mar 1771 in what is now Montgomery Co., MD) between 1786 and 1789 in Prince George's Co., MD. Their children were as follows:

1. **William Spyers** (lived in Brown Co., OH in 1852)

2. **Elizabeth Spyers** (b. 19 Jul 1790) married **Samuel A. Butt** (b. 30 Mar 1790) on 13 Feb 1811 and lived in Brown Co., OH in 1852; their children were as follows:

    2-1. **Aaron Butt** (b. 24 Dec 1811)
    2-2. **Samuel A. Butt, Jr.** (b. 28 Aug 1814)
    2-3. **Elizabeth Butt** (b. 17 Apr 1816)
    2-4. **Nancy Butt** (b. 28 May 1818)
    2-5. **Abram S. Butt** (b. 3 Nov 1820)
    2-6. **John B. Butt** (b. 24 Nov 1822)
    2-7. **Mary Ann Butt** (b. 25 Nov 1824)

2-8. **Sarah Jane Butt** (b. 28 Mar 1826)

2-9. **Rebecca Butt** (b. 20 Mar 1828)

2-10. **Pitcherd Butt** (b. 27 Feb 1831)

2-11. **Alexander Butt** (b. and died 28 May 1833)

3. **Nancy Spyers** (b. -- Dec 1795) married **Henry Young**

4. **John Spyers** (b. 1804)

5. **Dorcus Spyers** (b. 1806) married **Mr. Colvin**

6. **Henry Spyers** (b. 1808)

7. **Jane Miller Spyers** (b. 4 Feb 1811)

8. **Richard Spyers, Jr.** married ----; son, **Martin Spyers**

Richard Spyers applied for a pension in Brown Co., OH on 18 May 1818, aged 65, and died on 19 Mar 1838. **Rebecca Spyers** applied for a widow's pension on 14 Oct 1840. **Herrington Eubank**, of Brown Co., OH, aged 68 in 1852, stated he had known **Richard Spyers** and his family since 1792. {Ref: *Genealogical Abstracts of Revolutionary War Pension Files*, by Virgil D. White (1990), Application W6145; *Archives of Maryland*, Volume 18, pp. 394, 453}

PETER STANTON

Certificates of removal were received at the Milford Monthly Meeting in Wayne Co., IN from the Northwest Fork Monthly Meeting in Caroline Co., MD on the 25th day of the 8th month, 1827 for **Peter Stanton**, his wife **Celia Stanton**, and their sons **Isaac W. Stanton and James B. Stanton**. Peter was born on the 30th day of the 8th month, 1794 and Celia was born on the 28th day of the 1st month, 1803. They joined the Hicksite branch of Quakers and were listed in Washington Township, Wayne Co., IN, in the 1830 census. Their children were as follows:

1. **Isaac W. Stanton** (b. 25th day of 3rd month, 1823)

2. **James B. Stanton** (b. 1st day of 10th month, 1826)

3. **Edward Stanton** (b. 6th day of 6th month, 1828

4. **Mary E. Stanton** (b. 24th day of 4th month, 1830)

5. **Ann M. Stanton** (b. 2nd day of 9th month, 1832)

6. **Lucrecia Stanton** (date of birth not given)

Peter Stanton was disowned on the 20th day of the 12th month, 1832 for *"conducting himself unbecomingly toward a young woman and not denying the charge."* On the 18th day of the 5th month, 1843, **Celia Stanton** and children **Isaac Stanton, James Stanton, Mary Stanton, and Lucrecia Stanton**, were granted a certificate of removal to the Fall Creek Monthly Meeting. {Ref: "Migration of Caroline County Quakers to Indiana," by F. Edward Wright, *Maryland Genealogical Society Bulletin*, Volume 34, No. 3 (1993), pp. 284-285}

STEWART STERRIT

Stewart Sterrit, son of **James Sterrit**, was born in 1761 at Londonderry, Ireland and lived in Frederick Co., MD at the time of his enlistment in the Revolutionary War. He married after the war (name of wife not given) and later moved near Winchester, VA for 6 years, then to Kentucky (county not named), then to the Apolusa Country *(sic)*, then to New Orleans, LA, then to Hardin Co., KY for 25 years, and then to Harrison Co., IN. He applied for a pension on 10 Feb 1834 and died in Vigo Co., IN on 28 Aug 1839, leaving a widow **Rebecca Sterrit**. His brother **James Sterrit** lived in Virginia in 1834 (county not named). {Ref: *Genealogical Abstracts of Revolutionary War Pension Files*, by Virgil D. White (1990), Application S31991}

WILLIAM STERRIT

William Sterrit was born in Maryland, probably Frederick County, and served in the Revolutionary War, first as a lieutenant on 3 Jan 1776 (was taken prisoner at Long Island on 27 Aug 1776, later exchanged), then as a captain in 1776 and a major in 1777, and resigned his commission on 16 Dec 1777. He married **Mary Creighton** and died in Columbus, OH (date not given). Their daughter **Jane Eliza Sterret** married **Robert Wallace**. {Ref: DAR Application 9271; *Index of Patriots, Revolutionary War Heroes and Their Families, Cincinnati Chapter DAR, 1893-1981*, by Jeraldyne Beets Clipson and Katherine Brewer Brinkdopke (1983), p. 244; *Archives of Maryland*, Volume 18, pp. 9, 160}

WILLIAM L. STEWART

William L. Stewart, formerly of Baltimore, MD, died in Cincinnati, OH on 6 Sep 1834, aged 39. {Ref: *Baltimore American*, 25 Sep 1834, abstracted by Lorrie A. E. Erdman}

SYLVESTER STONE

Sylvester Stone and **Lucy Beckett**, of Maryland (county not stated), married in Ohio (county not stated) on 11 Dec 1817. {Ref: *Maryland Revolutionary Records*, by Harry Wright Newman (1938), p. 124}

PHILIP STONER

Philip Stoner was born in Frederick Co., MD on 16 Aug 1763 and when one year old he moved with his father (not named) to Bedford Co., PA. Philip lived there at the time of his enlistment in the Revolutionary War and by 1791 he lived in York Co., PA. He married **Sarah Ringer** (b. 18 Apr 1766 in Pennsylvania) on 11 Aug 1791. They lived in York County for 6 years and then returned to Bedford Co., PA. In 1802 they moved to Clermont Co., OH for 1½ years, then moved to Warren Co., OH for 4 years, then moved to Montgomery Co., OH, returned to Clermont County, then moved to Hamilton Co., OH, and then returned to Clermont County in 1829. Philip applied for a pension on 9 Nov 1832 and died on 14 Sep 1837. **Sarah Stoner** applied for a widow's pension on 29 Dec 1838 and died in 1852. Their children were mentioned, but none were named except for **Joseph Stoner** who was their second child. **Andrew Stoner** (b. 23 Dec 1793) may have also been a son, but his relationship was not indicated. **Anna Smith**, aged 42 in 1839, of Clermont Co., OH, stated she was raised by Philip and Sarah Stoner, and **Frederick Ringer** and **Joseph Ringer** were also mentioned, but no relationship was given. {Ref: *Genealogical Abstracts of Revolutionary War Pension Files*, by

Virgil D. White (1990), Application W4804}

JACOB STORTS
Jacob Storts and **Polly Notestine**, of Maryland (county not stated), married in Ohio (county not stated) on 17 Oct 1839. {Ref: *Maryland Revolutionary Records*, by Harry Wright Newman (1938), p. 124}

JOHN STRUTHERS
John Struthers was born in Cecil Co., MD on 11 Feb 1759. His father (name not given) was a Scotchman and in 1773 they moved to Washington Co., PA, where John served in the Revolutionary War. He married (name of wife not given) and later moved to Ohio where he applied for a pension in Coitsville, Trumbull County, on 26 Mar 1841. He died on 31 Dec 1845, leaving no widow, but these children:
1. **Ann Struthers** (married **Mr. McBride**)
2. **Mary Struthers** (married **William D. Hirst**)
3. **John Struthers, Jr.**
4. **Ebenezer Struthers**
5. **Thomas Struthers**
6. **Matilda Struthers** (married **A. M. Galbraith**; she was aged 45 in 1855 and lived at Coitsville, OH)

{Ref: *Genealogical Abstracts of Revolutionary War Pension Files*, by Virgil D. White (1990), Application R18262}

STUTSON FAMILY
Genett Stutson was noted in Methodist Episcopal Church records in Baltimore, MD as *"removed with certificate"* on 31 May 1828, but no destination was given; he subsequently returned to Baltimore (date not given). **Jennet Stutson** (misspelled as **Jannet Shutson**) married **Sidney Swamstedt** (also spelled Swormstedt) on 18 Aug 1829. **Amelia Stutson** and **James Stutson** were received in Baltimore as *"members from Montgomery"* on 30 Nov 1829. **Sidney Stutson** died in Baltimore in January, 1831. **Bethiah Stutson** and **Gennett Stutson** moved from Baltimore to Ohio (county not stated) on 31 Jan 1832. **James Stutson** was also shown as *"removed with certificate"* in 1832, but his destination was not recorded. Methodist Church records also indicate **Jernet Stutson** and **Bethia Worn** were married on 2 Oct 1831, but the marriage license gave their names as **Jennet Stutson** and **Bethia Wonn**. {Ref: Class Lists and Marriage Register, Baltimore City Station, Methodist Episcopal Church; Baltimore City Marriage Licenses}

DANIEL SULLIVAN
Daniel Sullivan was born in October, 1740 and lived in Maryland during the Revolutionary War. He married **Sarah** ---- at Bladensburg, MD about 6 to 8 weeks before he enlisted in 1776 or 1777. They subsequently moved to Indiana where he applied for a pension in Clark County on 13 Jul 1818. In 1820 he gave his age as 80 (in October, 1820) and stated he had no family but himself; however, **Sarah Sullivan** applied for a widow's pension in Bartholomew Co., IN on 17 Jul 1843,

aged 105, at which time she was living with **Jacob Lain** (relationship not given). She died on 5 Sep 1845 at the home of a **Mr. Mounts** (relationship not given). In 1844 **Abraham Miller**, of Jeffersonville, IN, stated that he was aged 57 on 9 Apr 1844 and that he knew **Daniel and Sarah Sullivan** had 4 children, of which 3 were then deceased, viz., **John Sullivan, Daniel Sullivan, Jr.**, and a daughter who married a **Mr. Clark**. The only surviving child in 1844 was **Mary Miller** who lived in Clark and Jefferson Cos., IN (she was still living in 1851). In 1854 her son **Ephraim G. Miller** lived in Jeffersonville, IN. **Daniel Sullivan**, the soldier, died in the fall of 1820 or 1821 at the home of **Abraham Miller** in Clark Co., IN. {Ref: *Genealogical Abstracts of Revolutionary War Pension Files*, by Virgil D. White (1990), Application W25169}

MARIA SUMWALT

Maria Sumwalt moved from Baltimore, MD to Ohio (county not given) in August, 1823. She was probably related to **Jacob Sumwalt, Jemima Sumwalt** and **Dorcas Sumwalt** who moved from Baltimore City in 1814, but their destinations were not recorded. {Ref: Class Registers, East Baltimore Station (Fell's Point), Methodist Episcopal Church}

WILLIAM SWAIN

William Swain, of Prince George's Co., MD, served as a private in the War of 1812. He volunteered around 23 Jul 1814 and was discharged in December, 1814. He later moved to Ohio and applied for bounty land (warrant 55-160-78375) in Monroe County on 23 Nov 1850, aged 73. In 1856 **Samuel Swain**, aged 17, with his next friend **Jesse L. Bevan**, residents of Noble Co., OH, declared that he with **Zachariah Swain**, aged 21, **Adaline Swain**, aged 16, and **Jeremiah Swain**, aged 12, were the [minor] heirs of **William Swain**, their father, who died in Franklin Township, Monroe Co., OH on 25 Jun 1852. He stated that there is no surviving widow and that the surviving children over the age of 21 were **Thomas Swain**, aged 52, **James Swain**, aged 48, **William Swain, Jr.**, aged 46, **Henry Swain**, aged 30, **Mary Picker**, aged 28, **Otha Swain**, aged 26, and **John Swain**, aged 23. {Ref: *Maryland Militia, War of 1812, Volume 6, Prince George's County*, by F. Edward Wright, p. 50}

RICHARD SWIFT

Richard Swift, of southern Cecil Co., MD, was drafted in the War of 1812 as a private in the Elkton Company of Capt. **John Sample** about 1 May 1813. He proceeded to Baltimore and remained about one month. He later volunteered in the company of Capt. **William Mackey** about 15 Aug 1814 and proceeded to Baltimore where he remained about 3 weeks. After the war he moved to Ohio and applied for bounty land (warrant 55-120-290136) in Medina County on 4 May 1858, aged 71. {Ref: *Maryland Militia, War of 1812, Volume 3, Cecil & Harford Counties*, by F. Edward Wright, pp. 12, 67}

SOLOMON SWIGGETT

A certificate of removal was requested from the Northwest Fork Monthly Meeting in Caroline Co., MD, on the 16th day of the 8th month, 1826, to the White Water Monthly Meeting in Wayne Co., IN, for **Solomon Swiggett**, his wife **Euphemia Swiggett**, and their daughter **Jane Swiggett**. Solomon and Euphemia joined the Hicksite branch of Quakers and were disowned by the Orthodox branch of the Milford Monthly Meeting on the 27th day of the 9th month, 1828. Jane was disowned on the 28th day of the 5th month, 1842. **Solomon Swiggett** died on the 31st day of the 5th month, 1864 and **Euphemia Swiggett** died on the 16th day of the 8th month, 1873. {Ref: "Migration of Caroline County Quakers to Indiana," by F. Edward Wright, *Maryland Genealogical Society Bulletin*, Volume 34, No. 3 (1993), pp. 279-280}

JAMES TALBOTT

James Talbott was born in Anne Arundel Co., MD on 15 Feb 1758 and served in the Revolutionary War. He subsequently moved to Ohio and married **Nancy Harland** on 8 Jan 1817 in Steubenville. James died on 9 Mar 1855 at Smithfield in Jefferson Co., OH and **Nancy Talbott** applied for a widow's pension on 26 Jun 1860, aged 72, stating they had raised 18 children (no names were given). {Ref: *Genealogical Abstracts of Revolutionary War Pension Files*, by Virgil D. White (1990), Application R18337}

RICHARD TALBOTT

Richard Talbott, Jr., son of **Richard Talbott** and **Ruth Dorsey**, of Anne Arundel Co., MD, was born on 25 Dec 1753 and served in the Revolutionary War. He was commissioned an ensign on 1 Jun 1776, became a lieutenant on 15 Apr 1777, participated in the battles of White Plains, Brandywine, and Germantown, and resigned his commission on 17 Mar 1778. He married first to **Achsah Wells** (1760-1789) on 20 Aug 1778 in Baltimore and second to **Temperance Wells** (1769-1830) on 20 Jan 1790 in Washington Co., PA. All of his children were as follows:

1. **Absalom Talbott** (1779-1816) married **Elizabeth Mehollin or Mulholland**

2. **Elizabeth Talbott** (b. 1780) married **Jesse Birch**

3. **Benjamin Talbott** (1782-1845) married first to **Ann (Nancy) Fouts** and second to **Sarah Gibbs**

4. **Charles Talbott** (1784-c1791)

5. **Nancy Talbott** (b. 1786) married **John Lawhead**

6. **Temperance Talbott** (b. 1787) married **Nathan Bradfield**

7. **Ruth Talbott** (1789-1881) married **Alexander McGee**

8. **Charles Wells Talbott** (28 Sep 1791 - 1874) married **Eliza Smith McMunn**

9. **Providence Talbott** (18 Nov 1792 - 24 Jun 1850), unmarried

10. **Richard Talbott III** (27 Jan 1794 - 19 Feb 1848) married first to **Dorinda Wells**, second to **Dorcas McIntyre** and third to **Anne Agnew**

183

11. **Michal Talbott** (13 Jan 1796 - 16 Aug 1871) married **Benjamin James**
12. **Achsah Talbott** (30 May 1798 - 1845) married **Bemont Hubbard**
13. **John Dorsey Talbott** (16 Jul 1800 - 1851) married **Mary Sheets**
14. **Ethelinda Talbott** (21 Sep 1802 - 21 Apr 1873) married first to **Albert or Henry Jolly** and second to **Bemont Hubbard**
15. **Ephraim Talbott** (5 Sep 1804 - 22 Mar 1873), unmarried
16. **Basil Dorsey Talbott** (b. 20 Oct 1806), unmarried
17. **Joshua Owen Talbott** (b. 30 Jul 1809) married **Adeline Williamson**
18. **Wells Talbott** (25 Aug 1811 - 17 Oct 1871) married first to **Betsy Cline** and second to **Barbara Ann Meek**

Richard Talbott moved to Ohio and applied for a pension in Washington County on 15 Jun 1818, aged 66 *(sic)*. He died in Monroe Co., OH on 22 Dec 1821. {Ref: *Genealogical Abstracts of Revolutionary War Pension Files*, by Virgil D. White (1990), Application S40552; DAR Application 509664; *Index of Patriots, Revolutionary War Heroes and Their Families, Cincinnati Chapter DAR, 1893-1981*, by Jeraldyne Beets Clipson and Katherine Brewer Brinkdopke (1983), p. 251; Research by Peter E. Broadbent, Jr., Esq., of Richmond, VA, citing "The Big Wells Family" by William A. Wells in *Wells Chronicles* (1989, p. 158, and 1990, pp. 212-213); also see Ida Shirk's *Descendants of Richard and Elizabeth (Ewen) Talbott* (1927)}

RICHARD TAYLOR

Richard Taylor was born circa 1756 and lived in Cecil Co., MD at the time of his enlistment in the Revolutionary War. He also took the Oath of Allegiance in 1778. Richard married **Ann ----** on 29 Dec 1793 in Hampshire Co., VA and they subsequently moved to Ohio. He applied for a pension in Preble County on 21 Sep 1832, aged 76, and died on 29 Aug 1838. **Ann Taylor** applied for a widow's pension on 12 Sep 1840, aged 66. Their son **James Taylor** made an affidavit on 22 Jun 1844 in Preble Co., OH. {Ref: *Genealogical Abstracts of Revolutionary War Pension Files*, by Virgil D. White (1990), Application W4598; *Revolutionary Patriots of Cecil County, Maryland, 1775-1783*, by Henry C. Peden, Jr. (1991), p. 111}

THOMAS THARP

Thomas Tharp was a farmer when he was drafted at Denton, MD about 1 Mar 1813 to serve in the War of 1812 for a period of 6 months. He stated he was about age 22 at the time and 5 ft. 9½ in. tall, with black hair, hazel eyes and dark complexion. He was first sergeant in the company of Capt. **Joseph Talbott** from 15 Aug to 30 Aug 1813. He also served as a substitute in Caroline County on two occasions in the militia in 1814, once for **Joseph Smith** and once for **Matthew Saulsbury**. Following his discharge he lived in Denton, MD for about 2 years, then moved to New Castle Co., DE for 1 year, and then to Chester Co., PA for about 14 years. **Thomas Tharp** married **Elizabeth Withers** in October, 1818 in Chester Co., PA and they moved to Muskingum Co., OH for about 6 years, then to Delaware Co., OH for about 22 years, then to Jay Co., IN for about 6 years, then to Decatur

Co., IA for about 12 years, and then to Reno Co., KS for about 2 years. He applied for bounty land in Morrow Co., OH on 28 Oct 1850, aged 61. He also applied for a pension on 28 Apr 1871, aged 84 *(sic)*, at which time he lived 6 miles northeast of Leon, Decatur Co., IA. He applied again for a pension (SC-24389) on 19 Oct 1878, aged 87, in Troy Township, Reno Co., KS (post office address: Riverton, KS). A letter from the postmaster on 30 Jul 1878 stated that **Thomas Tharp** lived with his son (name not given) about a mile from the Riverton post office, and he had been unable to work for the previous 10 years. {Ref: *Maryland Militia, War of 1812, Volume 1, Eastern Shore*, by F. Edward Wright, pp. 81, 93, 114-115; *Index of War of 1812 Pension Files*, by Virgil D. White, p. 1699}

BENJAMIN THOMAS

Benjamin Thomas requested a certificate of removal on the 6th day of the 8th month, 1818, from the Baltimore Monthly Meeting, Eastern District, to the Plainfield Monthly Meeting in Ohio. {Ref: Baltimore Quaker Monthly Meeting Minutes}

DANIEL THOMAS

Daniel Thomas (b. 1776, DE, d. 9 Aug 1846, IN) married **Sarah Amos** (b. 12 Dec 1781, daughter of **Nicholas Day Amos** and **Christiana Ditto**, of Harford Co., MD) in Bourbon Co., KY on 3 Apr 1801. She died in Rush Co., IN on 24 Dec 1844 and Daniel married second to **Mary McConnaughey** on 12 Sep 1845. The children of **Daniel and Sarah Thomas** were as follows:

1. **Elias Bird Thomas** (b. 18 Jan 1803, married first possibly to **Sarah G. Harwood**, second to **Henrietta (Endicott) Moore**, third to **Mahala Neale** in Rush Co., IN, and died 1 Oct 1891. The children of Elias Thomas were as follows:

1-1. **Sarah Thomas** (25 Sep 1835, IN - 20 Jul 1923, Rush Co., IN) married **Sanford Moore**

1-2. **Henry Parker Thomas** (b. circa 1838, IN) married first to **Elizabeth Francis** and second to **Harriet Kerr**

1-3. **Ransom A. Thomas** (11 Aug 1847, IN - 8 Jun 1861) married **Miss Carson**

1-4. **Melinda Thomas** (b. circa 1848)

1-5. **Anna Rebecca Thomas** (b. circa 1850) married **John B. Casey**

1-6. **Mary N. Thomas** (b. circa 1853) married **Oren E. Smith**

1-7. **Eli Bird Thomas** (5 Oct 1855, IN - 16 Dec 1936, TX) married first to **Elizabeth Angeline King** and second to **Martha J. Bycourt**

1-8. **Sylvester H. Thomas**

1-9. **Miriam Sarah Thomas**

1-10. **Eva Thomas**

1-11. **Martha Thomas**

2. **William Thomas** (20 Apr 1804 - 12 Mar 1900, Rush Co., IN) married first to **Margaret Hannah** and second to **Sarah (Houston) Green**. The children of William Thomas were as follows:

2-1. **Wesley Thomas** (circa 1827 - 21 Jul 1854)

2-2. **Daniel Thomas**

2-3. **Sarah Ann Thomas**

2-4. **Martha Jane Thomas**

2-5. **Joseph M. Thomas**

2-6. **Mary Frances Thomas**

2-7. **William M. Thomas**

3. **John Thomas** (1805 - 1879, Darke Co., OH) married **Abigail Carter** (b. 1814, NJ, d. 1887, Rush Co., IN); their children were as follows:

3-1. **Samuel C. Thomas** (5 Mar 1832, Hamilton Co., OH - 7 Apr 1914, Rush Co., IN) married **Emily Clements** on 14 Oct 1858

3-2. **Rebecca Thomas**

3-3. **Martha Thomas**

3-4. **Joseph Thomas**

3-5. **Daniel Thomas**

3-6. **Clement Thomas**

3-7. **John Thomas, Jr.**

4. **Amos Thomas** (23 Nov 1806 - 3 Apr 1887, Rush Co., IN) married **Lucinda Bowles** on 26 Mar 1833; their children, all born in Rush Co., IN, were as follows:

4-1. **William Thomas** (b. circa 1835)

4-2. **Robert Thomas** (26 Feb 1837 - 25 May 1874)

4-3. **Eliza J. Thomas** (30 Mar 1839 - 2 Jul 1862)

4-4. **Sarah M. Thomas** (b. circa 1841)

4-5. **Harriet Thomas** (1842 - 26 Oct 1847)

4-6. **Franklin Thomas** (b. circa 1844)

4-7. **Ann M. Thomas** (5 Dec 1845 - 13 Jan 1865)

4-8. **James M. Thomas** (b. circa 1849)

4-9. **Amos Thomas, Jr.** (7 Apr 1851 - 7 Oct 1852)

4-10. **Amanda Thomas** (28 Dec 1853 - ? Oct 1862)

4-11. **Oliver A. Thomas** (5 Nov 1857 - 15 Mar 1877)

4-12. **Lola Thomas** (20 Jan 1861 - 30 Jul 1862)

5. **Jesse Thomas** (6 Apr 1806, Bourbon Co., KY - 26 Feb 1883, Boone Co., IN) married **Cynthiana Tompkins** (25 Dec 1811 - 3 Jun 1893) in Rush Co., IN on 31 Oct 1833; their children, all born in Rush Co., IN, were as follows:

5-1. **James S. Thomas**

5-2. **Sarah Thomas**

5-3. **Nathan Thomas**

5-4. **Laura Thomas** married **Samuel B. Sweeney**

5-5. **Daniel Thomas**

5-6. **Wesley Thomas**

6. **Elijah Thomas** (b. circa 1811) married **Mary Tompkins** on 22 Apr 1831 and settled in Decatur Co., IN; their children were as follows:

6-1. **Priscilla Thomas**

6-2. **Susan Thomas**

6-3. **John Thomas**

6-4. **Oscar Thomas**
6-5. **Francis M. Thomas**
6-6. **William S. Thomas**
6-7. **Zenith Thomas**
6-8. **Alice Thomas**
6-9. **Cynthia Thomas**
6-10. **Rebecca A. Thomas**
7. **Priscilla Thomas** (b. 18 Oct 1815) married **Milton Ballinger** (b. 7 Jul 1811, Bourbon Co., KY) in Rush Co., IN on 2 Oct 1834 and in 1842 they moved to Kirklin Township, Clinton Co., IN; their children were as follows:
    7-1. **Manerow Ballinger**
    7-2. **Rebecca Ballinger**
    7-3. **Sarah Ballinger**
    7-4. **William Ballinger**
8. **Rebecca Thomas** (circa 1820 - 11 Sep 1854) married **William S. Wyatt** (died 23 Aug 1843) in Rush Co., IN on 8 Dec 1836; their children were as follows:
    8-1. **John L. Wyatt**
    8-2. **Oliver M. Wyatt**
{Ref: *Children of Mt. Soma*, by Gertrude J. Stephens, pp. 302-308}

JAMES B. THOMAS

James B. Thomas was born in Hagerstown, MD in 1777 and moved to Kentucky in 1799. He practiced law with his brother **Richard Symmes Thomas** in Bracken County. When the county of Dearborn, IN was organized on 7 Mar 1803 he moved there and practiced law at Lawrenceburg. He was elected to the Territorial Legislature on 3 Jan 1805 and was appointed Judge of the Illinois Territory. He served as a U. S. Senator for 10 years and died at Mt. Vernon, OH in 1853. {Ref: *History of Dearborn and Ohio Counties, Indiana* (1885), p. 149}

RACHEL THOMAS

Rachel Thomas moved from Baltimore, MD to Cincinnati, OH in February, 1833. {Ref: Class Lists, Baltimore City Station, Methodist Episcopal Church}

ANN THOMPSON

Ann Thompson moved from Baltimore, MD to Ohio (county not stated), with a certificate from the Methodist Episcopal Church, on 10 Apr 1831. She may have been related to **Ann Thompson** who died on 16 Nov 1826 and **Mary Thompson** who died on 9 Aug 1827, all of whom were members of the Methodist Episcopal Church in Baltimore. {Ref: Church Register and Class Lists, Baltimore City Station, Methodist Episcopal Church}

JAMES THOMPSON

James Thompson was born in Dorchester Co., MD on 6 Jun 1759 and lived there at the time of his enlistment in the Revolutionary War. He lived in Maryland for some time after the war and then moved to Kentucky (county not named) and then to Indiana. He applied for a pension in Vigo County on 8 May 1833 and moved to Galena Co., IL on 24 Jul 1835 to live with a son (name not given). In 1837 **James Thompson** made an affidavit in Stephenson Co., IL, having moved there to be with his wife's relatives (no names were given). {Ref: *Genealogical Abstracts of Revolutionary War Pension Files*, by Virgil D. White (1990), Application S32553}

MARY TIMANUS

Mary Timanus moved from Baltimore, MD to Ohio (county not stated), with a certificate from the Methodist Episcopal Church, on 12 Jun 1828. She was probably related to **Martha Timanus** who died in Baltimore in 1810, **John Timanus** who married **Elizabeth Wall** on 19 Oct 1815, and **Jacob Timanus** who married **Margaret McGrath** on 13 Dec 1827. {Ref: Church Register and Class Lists, Baltimore City Station, Methodist Episcopal Church}

LUKE TIPTON

Luke Tipton was born on 14 May 1760 in Baltimore Co., MD and lived in Bedford Co., PA at the time of his enlistment in the Revolutionary War. After the war he lived in Maryland and Virginia, moved to Holmes Co., OH, and married **Tersa or Teresa Cole** after 1805. He applied for a pension on 8 Oct 1832 and by 1846 he had moved to Henry Co., VA with a son and daughter and their families (no names were given). In 1853 he was living in Weakley Co., TN where he applied for bounty land warrant (55-160-26150) in 1855. He mentioned his brother **Meshac Tipton**. Luke died on 8 Oct 1855. {Ref: *Genealogical Abstracts of Revolutionary War Pension Files*, by Virgil D. White (1990), Application S3812; *Maryland Revolutionary Records*, by Harry Wright Newman (1938), p. 124}

LUKE TIPTON

Rebeckah Tipton and **Luke Tipton** (a minor) requested a certificate of removal on the 28th day of the 8th month, 1802 from Gunpowder Monthly Meeting in Baltimore Co., MD to Deer Creek Monthly Meeting in Harford Co., MD. On the 27th day of the 3rd month, 1811, **Luke Tipton** (sometimes spelled Tipten) requested a certificate of removal from Gunpowder Monthly Meeting to Deer Creek Monthly Meeting. On the 7th day of the 6th month, 1819, at a meeting held at Fawn Grove, PA, **Luke Tipton** and wife (not named) requested their five minor children, **David Tipton, Mary Tipton, Esther or Hester Tipton, Rachel Tipton and Abijah Tipton**, be received into membership from Deer Creek Monthly Meeting (Orthodox) in Harford Co., MD. On the 12th day of the 12th month, 1822, **Luke Tipton** requested a certificate for himself and his wife **Priscilla Tipton** and their eight minor children, **David Tipton, Mary Tipton, Esther or Hester Tipton, Rachel Tipton, Abijah Tipton, Elihu Tipton, John Tipton and Hannah Tipton**, to Smithfield Monthly Meeting in Ohio. A certificate of removal was requested again on the 16th day of the 1st month, 1823. {Ref: Gunpowder and Deer Creek Quaker Monthly Meeting Minutes}

THOMAS TIPTON

Thomas Tipton was born circa 1738 in Baltimore Co., MD and lived in Fairfax Co., VA at the time of his enlistment in the Revolutionary War. After the war he move to Kentucky and lived in various parts of that state, including Montgomery County. He later moved to Ohio and lived in various parts of that state, including Champaign County where he applied for a pension on 9 Mar 1838, aged nearly 100. Thomas had a wife and 3 children (names not given) during the war. Also mentioned were **William Tipton, Sr.** (a resident of Washington Co., KY in 1835 and a Revolutionary War veteran) and nephew Hon. **John Tipton** (U. S. Senator in 1838). {Ref: *Genealogical Abstracts of Revolutionary War Pension Files*, by Virgil D. White (1990), Application S16274}

AQUILLA TOLAND

Aquilla Toland, of Harford Co., MD, was drafted in the War of 1812 at Cook's Tavern and served as a private in the company of Capt. **James Rampley** around 28 Aug 1814. He was in actual service for two months except for what time he was sick with the measles and taken to the hospital which was about the time of the attack on Baltimore. Maryland military records indicate he was a corporal when discharged at Baltimore on 27 Oct 1814. After the war he moved to London, OH and applied for bounty land (warrant 55-160-13029) in Medina County on 23 Jan 1854, aged 60. **James Rampley, George Lemon** and **Elisha Meads** appeared on 27 May 1854 and verified his service. {Ref: *Maryland Militia, War of 1812, Volume 3, Cecil & Harford Counties*, by F. Edward Wright, pp. 16, 31, 69}

CHRISTOPHER TOMER

Christopher Tomer (sometimes spelled Tomar) was born circa 1751 and lived with his father (name not given) in Baltimore, MD at the time of his enlistment in the Revolutionary War. He subsequently moved to Ohio and applied for a pension in Ross County on 29 Mar 1834, aged 83. His daughter **Mary Wilt** signed a power of attorney on 23 Jul 1851 and stated that the other surviving children of her father were **John Tomer, Nancy N--?--**, and **Eliza Davis**. {Ref: *Genealogical Abstracts of Revolutionary War Pension Files*, by Virgil D. White (1990), Application R10637}

ELIZABETH TOWNSEND

Elizabeth Townsend requested a certificate of removal from the Baltimore Monthly Meeting, Eastern District, to the Concord Monthly Meeting in Ohio on the 13th day of the 8th month, 1807, having already moved there with her husband (not named). {Re: Baltimore Quaker Monthly Meeting Minutes}

THOMAS TOWNSEND

Thomas Townsend requested a certificate of removal from the Baltimore Monthly Meeting, Western District, to the Concord Monthly Meeting in Ohio on the 11th day of the 5th month, 1808. {Re: Baltimore Quaker Monthly Meeting Minutes}

THOMAS TREADWAY

Thomas Treadway, son of **Daniel Treadway** (1724-1810) and **Sarah Norris** (b. 1727), of Baltimore Co., MD, married circa 1770 to **Christiana Saunders** (c1750-c1815, daughter of **Edward and Christiana Saunders**). Thomas took the Oath of Allegiance in 1778 in Harford Co., MD during the Revolutionary War. After the death of his wife he moved west with some family members in 1816 and died in Hamilton Co., OH in 1819. The children of **Thomas and Christiana Treadway** were as follows:

1. **Daniel Treadway** (b. 3 Apr 1774) married **Hannah Magness** and died in Kentucky

2. **Sarah Treadway** (b. 26 Nov 1776) married **Bailey Warren** on 7 Feb 1800 and died in Menard Co., IL

3. **Charity Treadway** (b. 5 Dec 1778, died young)

4. **Elizabeth Treadway** (b. 7 Sep 1780 - d. February, 1838, Harford Co., MD) married **Martin Taylor Gilbert** (1771-1837) on 2 Apr 1805

5. **Thomas Treadway, Jr.** (b. 8 Nov 1782 - d. 6 Sep 1837) married **Sarah Ann Gilbert** on 9 Jan 1806

6. **Edward Treadway** (b. 15 Dec 1784, MD - d. 23 Jan 1859, Cass Co., IL) married **Elizabeth Anderson** (1789-1831) on 20 Mar 1810

7. **Mary Treadway** (b. 6 Mar 1786, Harford Co., MD - d. July, 1849, Beardstown, Cass Co., IL) married **Benjamin Warren** on 21 Sep 1807 in Harford Co., MD. He died in December, 1845 in Mason Co., IL. Their children were as follows:

    7-1. **Levi Warren** (b. 2 Apr 1807, MD)

    7-2. **Evan Warren** (b. 24 Dec 1811, MD or OH - d. 6 May 1841, Schuyler Co., IL

    7-3. **Amos T. Warren** (b. 6 Feb 1816, MD or OH)

    7-4. **James Madison Warren** (b. 13 Nov 1818, OH) married on 22 Jul 1814 in Mason Co., IL (wife's name not given)

    7-5. **Benjamin Warren, Jr.** (b. 6 Apr 1822, OH) married on 11 Apr 1844 in Mason Co., IL (wife's name not given)

    7-6. **Wrightson Jackson Warren** (b. 26 Jul 1824, OH)

    7-7. **Elizabeth Warren** (b. 30 Oct 1826) married on 30 Oct 1843 in Mason Co., IL (husband's name not given)

8. **Aquila Treadway** (b. 8 Apr 1787 - d. 1844) married **Nancy Anderson** on 21 Dec 1809 and died in Cass Co., IL

9. **Ann Treadway** (b. 17 May 1789, MD - d. Morgan Co., IN) married first to **James Anderson** on 6 Jan 1815 and second to **Henry Woolen** on 27 Jun 1818

10. **John Norris Treadway** (b. 26 Feb 1795 - d. 11 Mar 1884, Beardstown, Cass Co., IL) married **Rebecca McKean** on 29 Dec 1822 in Hamilton Co., OH

{Ref: Treadway information compiled by Henry C. Peden, Jr., of Bel Air, MD, Robert W. Barnes, of Perry Hall, MD, and Doris M. Warren of Dayton, OH; *Edward Treadway (1784-1859) and His Descendants*, by Oswell Garland Treadway, pp. 5-6; St. John's Protestant Episcopal Parish Register}

CRISPIN TREDWAY

Crispin Tredway (sometimes spelled Treadway), brother of **Thomas Treadway**, *q.v.*, was born on 5 Nov 1767 in Baltimore Co., MD and married on 13 Oct 1794 to **Elizabeth Peteet** (sometimes spelled Poteet, Potee, and Puttee) who was born on 2 Feb 1777. They moved to Coshocton Co., OH in September, 1817 and settled at Zeno in Jackson Township. Crispin died there on 20 May 1866. The children of **Crispin and Elizabeth Tredway** were as follows:

1. **John Tredway** (b. 6 Nov 1796, MD - d. 1817, MD)

2. **Thomas Tredway** (18 Aug 1799, MD - 13 May 1881, OH) married first to **Olive Severns**, of Monongahelia Co., VA, on 4 Mar 1823 and she died on 1 Sep 1840; married second to **Mary Clark**, of Washington Co., PA (27 Jul 1809 - 31 Jul 1868). Thomas fathered eight children by his first wife and three by his second wife, as follows:

2-1. **Mahala Tredway** (b. 18 Mar 1825) married first to **Aaron C. Morgan** on 18 Dec 1846 and he died on 9 Aug 1847; married second to **James Greer** on 13 Apr 1848 and he died on 20 Jun 1880 near Greersville, Knox Co., OH

2-2. **Elizabeth Tredway** (b. 28 May 1826) married **William Orr** and lived and died in Coshocton Co., OH (date not given)

2-3. **Mary Tredway** (b. 27 Jun 1828)

2-4. **Resin Hammond Tredway** (b. 2 Sep 1832, near Warsaw, OH; was a Civil War soldier; d. 14 Apr 1920 near Coshocton, OH) married on 19 Sep 1866 to **Mary Elizabeth Welling** (b. 22 Feb 1838) of West Bedford or Carlisle, Bedford Township, Coshocton Co., OH

2-5. **Crispen Tredway** (b. 9 Aug 1834) married on 9 Oct 1856 to **Melvina James** (17 Jul 1840 - 27 May 1876) in Coshocton Co., OH

2-6. **Joseph Tredway** (b. 23 Jul 1836, d. 12 Mar 1915)

2-7. **John Tredway** (b. 9 Dec 1838)

2-8. **James H. Tredway** (b. 27 Jul 1840)

2-9. **Garret S. Tredway** (b. 8 Oct 1844)

2-10. **Thomas Franklin Tredway** (b. 30 Jun 1848)

2-11. **William H. Tredway** (b. 20 Aug 1851)

3. **Elizabeth Tredway** (b. circa 1803 in Harford Co., MD and moved with her parents to Coshocton Co., OH in September, 1817)

4. **Hannah Tredway** (b. 22 Feb 1805) married **William Severns** (b. 4 Jan 1800, son of **Joseph and Mary Severns**, of Cumberland Co., VA) on 27 Nov 1823 in Coshocton Co., OH. **Hannah Severns** died on 9 Nov 1859 and **William Severns** died on 17 Feb 1887. Their children were as follows:

4-1. **Malona Severns** (b. 15 Oct 1824) married **Alexander Barrett** and lived in Fulton Co., IN

4-2. **Leonard Severns** (b. 26 Aug 1826) married **Mary Cullison** and lived in Lawrence Co., IL

4-3. **James Severns** (b. 12 Nov 1828) married **Maria Bahaw** and lived in Fulton Co., IN

4-4. **Elizabeth Severns** (b. 7 Sep 1830) married **Joseph Cullison** and died in 1878; he died in 1877 in Lawrence Co., IL

4-5. **Mary Severns** (b. 24 Oct 1832) married **George Thompson** in March, 1872 and lived in Coshocton Co., OH

4-6. **Joseph Severns** (7 Aug 1834 - 19 Mar 1835)

4-7. **Robert Severns** (5 Jun 1836 - 2 Aug 1836)

4-8. **Sarah Severns** (b. 29 Nov 1837) married **Martin V. Coplin** and lived in Fulton Co., IN

4-9. **Samuel Severns** (b. 8 Mar 1840, OH, d. 6 Sep 1877, Livingston, MO)

4-10. **Christine Severns** (b. 14 Jul 1842) married **Aaron Drake** in 1873 and lived in Coshocton Co., OH

4-11. **Ransom L. Severns** (b. 1 Jan 1847) married **Hannah Clark** on 29 Mar 1876 and lived in Coshocton Co., OH

4-12. **Almeda Severns** (b. 5 Jan 1850) married **Seth McClain** on 25 Dec 1877 and lived in Kosciusko Co., IN

5. **Mary Tredway** (b. 28 Dec 1809) married **Owen Marshall** (19 Apr 1804 - 15 Feb 1896) and **Mary Marshall** died on 13 Aug 1893. Their children were as follows:

5-1. **Thomas Marshall** (25 Jul 1836 - 1917)

5-2. **Crispen Marshall** (28 Dec 1837 - 1917)

5-3. **Owen Marshall** (b. 22 Jul 1839)

5-4. **Elizabeth Marshall** (b. 4 Apr 1841)

5-5. **Nancy Marshall** (28 Oct 1842 - 1928)

5-6. **Malona Marshall** (9 May 1844 - 1927)

5-7. **Irwin Marshall** (b. circa 1846)

5-8. **Allen Marshall** (1848-1924)

6. **Corbin Tredway** married **Mary Fry** on 10 Sep 1832 in Ohio and their children were as follows:

6-1. **Abraham F. Tredway** (b. 21 Sep 1833)

6-2. **Crispen Tredway** (b. 6 Dec 1834)

6-3. **Thomas B. Tredway** (b. 5 Jul 1836)

6-4. **Calvin S. Tredway** (b. 9 Oct 1837)

6-5. **Elijah L. Tredway** (b. 31 Aug 1839)

6-6. **Martha L. Tredway** (b. 22 Dec 1840)

6-7. **Daniel C. Tredway** (b. 29 Jan 1843)

6-8. **Elizabeth Tredway** (b. 10 Feb 1845)

6-9. **Aaron M. Tredway** (b. 27 Oct 1846)

6-10. **Nancy E. Tredway** (b. 16 Oct 1849)

6-11. **Charles R. Tredway** (22 Apr 1851 - 14 Jun 1872)

6-12. **William H. Tredway** (b. 25 Jan 1853)

6-13. **Resin B. Tredway** (b. 24 Sep 1855)

6-14. **Mary C. Tredway** (b. 18 Jun 1857)

7. **Sarah E. Tredway** (20 Feb 1817 - March, 1904) married **John Meredith** (21 Sep 1811 - 18 Sep 1876) and their children were as follows:

7-1. **Elizabeth Jane Meredith**

7-2. **Margaret Ellen Meredith**

7-3. **Crispen Tredway Meredith**

192

7-4. **Benjamin Wheeler Meredith**
7-5. **Mary Louise Meredith** (b. 13 Aug 1849)
7-6. **Hannah Jerusha Meredith**
7-7. **John Lyman Meredith**
7-8. **James Louis Meredith**
{Ref: *History of the Tredway Family*, by William T. Tredway (1930), pp. 99-108}

JAMES TRIMBLE

James Trimble requested a certificate of removal on the 12th day of the 2nd month, 1807, from the Baltimore Monthly Meeting, Western District, to the Waynesville Monthly Meeting in Ohio, having already moved there. {Ref: Baltimore Quaker Monthly Meeting Minutes}

RILEY TRUITT

Riley Truitt moved from Worcester Co., MD in 1817 to Sparta Township, Dearborn Co., IN and died there in 1818. See "Elijah Dorman," *q.v.* {Ref: *History of Dearborn and Ohio Counties, Indiana* (1885), p. 559}

ALEXANDER TRUMAN

Alexander Truman, son of **Henry Truman** and **Ann Magruder**, was born in 1750 or 1751 in Prince George's Co., MD and served as a captain in the 2nd and 6th MD Regiments during the Revolutionary War. He married in 1781 to **Margaret Reynolds**, daughter of **William Reynolds** and **Mary Howell**, of Annapolis, MD, and they had three children: **Alexander Magruder Truman, Thomas Truman, and Mary Ann Truman** (married **Byrd Rogers, Jr.** of Barren Co., KY and died in 1822). **Alexander Truman** (sometimes spelled Trueman) received a commission as a captain in the U. S. Army in 1790 and was subsequently promoted to the rank of major. In 1792 he was sent on a peace mission by the Secretary of War to visit the Miami Indians in the Ohio Territory and in April of that year he was shot and killed about 5 miles west of what is now Sidney, OH. {Ref: *Truman and Related Families of Early Maryland*, by Henry C. Peden, Jr. (1987), pp. 29-34; *Revolutionary Patriots of Prince George's County, Maryland, 1775-1783*, by Henry C. Peden, Jr. (1997), pp. 300-301}

BENJAMIN TURNER

Benjamin Turner was born in Frederick Co., MD on 12 Nov 1762 and lived there at the time of his enlistment in the Revolutionary War. He afterwards moved to Salisbury, NC for 12 years, returned to Frederick Co., MD, and then in 1802 moved to Ohio. He applied for a pension in Fairfield County on 5 Mar 1833. {Ref: *Genealogical Abstracts of Revolutionary War Pension Files*, by Virgil D. White (1990), Application S7769}

JAMES TURNER

James Turner was born on 27 Oct 1755 at Baltimore, MD and lived at Hagerstown, MD at the time of his enlistment in the Revolutionary War. He was a private in the Washington Co., MD militia company of Capt. **Henry Boteler** in 1776-1777. He married (wife's name not given) in 1777 and settled in Washington Co., MD for 4 years. He then moved to Washington Co., PA for 2 years, then to Mason Co., KY for 20 years, and then to Champaign Co., OH for 16 years. James applied for a pension on 18 Aug 1832 in Allen Co., OH. {Ref: *Genealogical Abstracts of Revolutionary War Pension Files*, by Virgil D. White (1990), Application S3841; *The Maryland Militia in the Revolutionary War*, by S. Eugene Clements & F. Edward Wright, p. 237; Revolutionary War Military Collection, Manuscript MS.1146, Maryland Historical Society}

WILLIAM TYIER

William Tyier was born in 1780 in Maryland (county not stated), married **Gertrude Davis** (b. 1789) and moved to Dearborn Co., IN *"in an early day."* Their children were as follows:

1. **Eliza A. Tyier** (died before 1885)
2. **John T. Tyier**
3. **Jane Tyier** (died before 1885)
4. **William S. Tyier** (see below)
5. **Amelia M. Tyier**

William Tyier died in 1843 and **Gertrude Tyier** died in 1866. Their son **William S. Tyier** was born on 6 Aug 1829 and married in Clay Township, Dearborn Co., IN on 31 Dec 1848 to **Martha E. Wills** (b. 16 Sep 1830, daughter of **Elliott Wills** and **Sarah Nelson**, of Ripley Co., IN). They settled on his father's farm and raised five orphan children to maturity, but had no children of their own. {Ref: *History of Dearborn and Ohio Counties, Indiana* (1885), p. 459}

JOHN TYLER

John Tyler (sometimes spelled Tylor) requested a certificate of removal from the Northwest Fork Monthly Meeting in Caroline Co., MD to the Milford Monthly Meeting in Wayne Co., IN on the 14th day of the 3rd month, 1832. The minutes of the Milford Monthly Meeting record a certificate of removal from Wilmington, DE for John Tyler. He joined the Hicksite branch of Quakers and, on the 25th day of the 5th month, 1837, **John Tyler**, son of **Thomas and Mary Tyler** (the mother being deceased), of Bethel, Wayne Co., IN, married **Phebe Middleton**, daughter of **John and Mary Middleton**, of Fall Creek, Madison Co., IN. {Ref: "Migration of Caroline County Quakers to Indiana," by F. Edward Wright, *Maryland Genealogical Society Bulletin*, Volume 34, No. 3 (1993), p. 285}

JOHN UNDERWOOD

On the 22nd day of the 6th month, 1814, the minutes of the Gunpowder Monthly Meeting in Baltimore Co., MD recorded that the marriage of **John Underwood** and **Mary Clark** (sometimes spelled Clerck) was accomplished in an orderly manner. In the 8th month of 1816 **John Underwood** produced a certificate of removal to the Baltimore Monthly Meeting, Eastern District, from the Deer Creek Monthly Meeting in Harford Co., MD, for himself, his wife **Mary**

Underwood, and their minor daughter **Amy Underwood**. On the 9th day of the 10th month, 1817 he requested a certificate of removal from the Baltimore Monthly Meeting, Eastern District, for himself, his wife **Mary Underwood**, and their two minor children, **Amy Underwood and Barclay Underwood**, to the White Water Monthly Meeting in Indiana. He again requested a certificate on the 6th day of the 11th month, 1817 to White Water Monthly Meeting, having already removed there. {Ref: Gunpowder and Baltimore Quaker Monthly Meeting Minutes}

GEORGE VALENTINE

George Valentine was born on 2 Jan 1752 in Lancaster Co., PA and lived there at the time of his enlistment in the Revolutionary War. He also enlisted as a private in the militia at Hagerstown, Washington Co., MD on 15 Aug 1781, served in the Continental Line, and was discharged on 30 Oct 1781. **Frederick Valentine**, in all likelihood a relative, also served as a private in the Washington Co., MD militia in 1776-1777. In 1803 George moved to Ohio and applied for a pension in Fairfield County on 1 Nov 1832. He died there on 27 Nov 1839. {Ref: *Genealogical Abstracts of Revolutionary War Pension Files*, by Virgil D. White (1990), Application S17171; *Archives of Maryland*, Volume 18, pp. 388, 412, and Volume 45, p. 657; *The Maryland Militia in the Revolutionary War*, by S. Eugene Clements & F. Edward Wright, p. 245; Revolutionary War Military Collection, Manuscript MS.1146, Maryland Historical Society}

SAMUEL VANCE

Samuel Vance was born in Bucks Co., PA on 18 Jun 1762 and lived in Harford Co., MD at the time of his enlistment in the Revolutionary War. He enrolled as a private in the company of Capt. **William Bradford** on 30 Sep 1775. He also signed the Association of Freemen at Gunpowder Neck in 1776 and took the Oath of Allegiance in 1778. Samuel subsequently moved to Ohio and applied for a pension in Clinton County in 26 Jun 1834, at which time and place **E. Vance** made an affidavit (relationship not given). {Ref: *Genealogical Abstracts of Revolutionary War Pension Files*, by Virgil D. White (1990), Application R10836}

NATHAN VEATCH

Nathan Veatch was born in Frederick Co., MD on 15 Aug 1752 and married **Elizabeth Cragg** on 24 Oct 1778, probably at Camden, SC. He served in North Carolina in 1780 during the Revolutionary War and subsequently moved to Ohio. Their children were as follows:

1. **Kinsey Veatch** (b. 4 Sep 1779)
2. **Martha Veatch** (b. 9 Mar 1781)
3. **Mary Veatch** (b. 27 Aug 1793)
4. **Isaac Veatch** (b. 18 Feb 1786) married first to **Lucinda Ramsey** in 1806 and second to **Mary Sprigg** in 1829
5. **Eleanor Veatch** probably married **Mr. Carpenter**
6. **Nathan Veatch, Jr.** (b. 7 Feb 1791)
7. **Elijah Veatch** (b. 23 Aug 1793)

8. **Elizabeth Veatch** (27 Dec 1796 - 1829) married **Nimrod Peyton** on 31 Oct 1819 in Harrison Co., IN

9. **Keziah Veatch** (b. 3 Jan 1803)

Nathan Veatch died in Harrison Co., IN on 5 Sep 1829 and **Elizabeth Veatch** died on 12 Oct 1833. {Ref: DAR Application 315960; *Index of Patriots, Revolutionary War Heroes and Their Families, Cincinnati Chapter DAR, 1893-1981*, by Jeraldyne Beets Clipson and Katherine Brewer Brinkdopke (1983), p. 264}

SILAS VEATCH

Silas Veatch, of Montgomery Co., MD, wrote his will on 30 Oct 1800 (probated 11 Jun 1806) and named his wife **Elizabeth Veatch** and children **Orlando Veatch, Kesiah Veatch** and **Susannah Veatch**, stating, in part, *"All of my children ... now reside out of the State of Maryland, some living in Kentucky and some on the northwest side of the Ohio ... "* He named **Hezekiah Veatch** as trustee. {Ref: *Abstract of Wills, Montgomery County, Maryland, 1776-1825*, by Mary G. Malloy, Jane C. Sween and Janet D. Manuel, pp. 138-139}

NOBLE VEAZEY

Noble Veazey, of Cecil Co., MD, served as a private during the War of 1812 under Capt. **Spencer Biddle** who initially commanded the company for 3 or 4 months in 1814, but being too old and infirm to continue his command, the company was placed under Capt. **John Sample** when it departed for Baltimore. Around 26 Oct 1814 Noble moved near Cincinnati, OH and applied for bounty land (warrant 55-160-54813) in Hamilton County on 17 Jan 1856, aged 67. Witnesses were **John L. Vattier** and **E. A. Ferguson**. {Ref: *Maryland Militia, War of 1812, Volume 3, Cecil & Harford Counties*, by F. Edward Wright, pp. 17, 70}

CHRISTOPHER WALKER

Christopher Walker was born in Baltimore, MD in 1757 and enlisted on 19 Jul 1776 in Frederick Co., MD during the Revolutionary War. He married **Patience Foster** on 8 Jun 1782 and their known children were as follows:

1. **John Walker** (b. 1786) married **Elizabeth Walker**
2. **Edward E. Walker** (b. 1 Nov 1799) married **Nancy Anna Foster**

Patience Walker died in Hamilton Co., OH by 1830 and **Christopher Walker** died in Cincinnati, OH on 6 May 1841. {Ref: DAR Application 538714; *Index of Patriots, Revolutionary War Heroes and Their Families, Cincinnati Chapter DAR, 1893-1981*, by Jeraldyne Beets Clipson and Katherine Brewer Brinkdopke (1983), p. 265; *Archives of Maryland*, Volume 18, p. 51}

MATTHEW WALKER

Matthew Walker served as a private during the War of 1812 in the company of Capt. **Andrew Baggs** in Caroline Co., MD from 23 Aug to 30 Aug 1813, having been drafted at Nine Bridges on or about 23 Aug 1813. He subsequently moved to Ohio and applied for bounty land at Warren in Trumbull County on 4 Jan 1856, aged 61. He stated that he was drafted for three months *"to repel an attack made by the British upon the village of St. Michaels ... and no attack being renewed he was then ordered to stand as a minute man during the remainder of said term of three months, and in that form was allowed to go home, but he was not finally discharged until the expiration of said term of three months ... draft was made at the time of the attack above mentioned, and his company marched with haste to meet the enemy, that they were drawn up prepared for instant engagement, and that the enemy retired after a short action with the portion of the army already upon the shore at the harbor of St. Michaels aforesaid ... "* **Matthew Walker** referred to **James McGuire** as his captain; however, McGuire was second in command under Capt. Bell in the other company of the Extra Battalion. Matthew subsequently moved to Ohio and applied for bounty land at Warren, Trumbull County, in December, 1850, aged 55. In 1857 **Robert Walker**, a resident of Warren, OH, aged 66 in December, 1856, and brother of **Matthew Walker**, stated that he had stood for the draft at the same time as Matthew, but he was not drafted. He stated that he remembered that the draft was made in great haste to repel an attack of the enemy at or near St. Michaels, MD, and that he well remembered the report of there being an attack and bloodshed at or about that time. All claims were rejected. {Ref: *Maryland Militia, War of 1812, Volume 1, Eastern Shore*, by F. Edward Wright, pp. 83, 115}

WILLIAM R. WANTON

William R. Wanton, a minor, requested a certificate of removal from the Baltimore Monthly Meeting, Western District, to the Alexandria Monthly Meeting on the 10th day of the 8th month, 1814, having already moved there. He subsequently returned to Baltimore and later requested a certificate of removal on the 9th day of the 7th month, 1824, to the Cincinnati Monthly Meeting in Ohio, having already removed there. {Ref: Baltimore Quaker Monthly Meeting Minutes}

EDWARD WARD

Edward Ward was born in 1757 in Charles Co., MD and moved with his parents when very young to Frederick Co., MD. He lived there at the time of his enlistment in the Revolutionary War and served in the company of Capt. **William Duvall** in the winter of 1776-1777, participated in the battle at Brunswick, NJ, and was discharged in June, 1777. He may have been the **Edward Ward** who took the Oath of Allegiance in Washington Co., MD in 1778. Edward married **Lucy Wilson** on 6 Aug 1779 and after the war they lived at Cumberland, MD until 1811 when they moved to Perry Co., OH. he applied for a pension on 14 Nov 1833 and died on 25 Aug 1840. **Lucy Ward** died on 27 May 1847, leaving these children:
1. **John Ward**
2. **James Ward**
3. **William Ward**
4. **Jeremiah Ward**
5. **Anna Ward** married **Mr. Burgess**

{Ref: *Genealogical Abstracts of Revolutionary War Pension Files*, by Virgil D. White (1990), Application R1115; *Revolutionary Patriots of Washington County*,

Maryland, 1776-1783, by Henry C. Peden, Jr. (1998), p. 395}

JAMES WARDEN

James Warden was born circa 1744 and enlisted at Baltimore, MD during the Revolutionary War. He subsequently moved to Ohio and applied for a pension in Butler County on 8 Jul 1819. In 1820 he had a wife aged 60 (name not given) and two granddaughters, **Sarah Warden**, aged 16, and **Mary Warden**, aged 14, lived with them. {Ref: *Genealogical Abstracts of Revolutionary War Pension Files*, by Virgil D. White (1990), Application S40631}

JAMES WATERS

James Waters (sometimes spelled Watters) was born circa 1756 and enlisted in St. Mary's Co., MD during the Revolutionary War. He subsequently moved to Ohio and applied for a pension in Fairfield County on 16 Sep 1818, aged 62. In 1820 he had a wife aged 61 (name not given) and a son **John Waters**, aged 16, living at home. In 1824 he stated his wife was aged 65 and also mentioned his son **James Waters, Jr.** from whom he had bought some wheat. James died on 10 May 1838 and his widow received his final payment on 25 Jun 1839. {Ref: *Genealogical Abstracts of Revolutionary War Pension Files*, by Virgil D. White (1990), Application S40642}

WAY

On the 27th day of the 5th month, 1802 the Women's Meeting of the Deer Creek Monthly Meeting in Harford Co., MD was informed that **Ann Way**, late **Ann Lukins**, had *"gone out in marriage with a man not of our society by the assistance of a Baptist teacher."* It was also reported that **Alse Lukins** had *"attended the disorderly marriage and partook in dancing."* On the 26th day of the 5th month, 1803, **Ann Way** was disowned. On the 7th day of the 4th month, 1817, the Deer Creek Monthly Meeting in Harford Co., MD received a communication from the Plymouth Monthly Meeting in Ohio, informing them that **Ann Way**, formerly of Deer Creek, had applied for reinstatement into the good order of Friends at Plymouth. {Ref: Deer Creek Quaker Monthly Meetings}

JOHN WEBB

John Webb, son of **James Webb** and **Mary Hurford**, of York Co., PA, was born about 1750 in Chester Co., PA and he moved with his parents to Baltimore (now Harford) Co., MD when he was nine years old. On 13 May 1780 he married **Elizabeth Montgomery**, daughter of **Thomas Montgomery**, and she died about 1802, leaving behind her husband and eleven children. **John Webb** moved his family to Salem, Columbiana Co., OH in 1803 and settled in what is now Perry Township (northeast quadrant of Section 30). The 11 children of **John and Elizabeth Webb** and the 3 children of **John and Leah Webb**, his second wife, were as follows:

1. **Thomas Webb** (26 Mar 1781, MD - 26 Mar 1847, OH) married **Naomi**

Smith (1784, VA - 14 Dec 1868, OH, daughter of **Samuel and Sally Smith**, founder of Smith's Ferry, OH) and their children were as follows:

    1-1. **Samuel Webb** (b. 10 Aug 1805) married **Jane Stevenson** (b. 1804) and lived in Wakeman, OH in 1882

    1-2. **John Webb** (married **Marie Gee** in 1829)

    1-3. **Elizabeth Webb** (died in infancy)

    1-4. **Sarah Webb** (married **William McKim** in 1836)

    1-5. **William Webb** (married **Mary Baker** in 1838)

    1-6. **Joseph Webb** (married **Susan Gee** in 1838)

    1-7. **Edith Webb** (married **Daniel Garwood** in 1837)

    1-8. **Thomas Smith Webb** (married **Sara Pennock** in 1840)

    1-9. **Asa Webb** (married **Sara Farquer** in 1844)

    1-10. **Isaac N. Webb** (married **Lyndia Whittle** in 1847)

    1-11. **George Washington Webb** (married **Catherine Pickering** in 1849)

    1-12. **Alice Ann Webb** (married **James Fetters** in 1848)

    1-13. **David Montgomery Webb** (married **Nancy Grant** in 1852)

  2. **James Webb** (Nov 1782, MD - 15 Apr 1863, OH) married **Keziah Bowman** (1789, PA - 2 Sep 1857, daughter of **Philip Casper Bowman** and **Katie Fast or Faust**) and their known children were as follows:

    2-1. **Joshua J. Webb** (18 Aug 1812, OH - 20 May 1888, IN)

    2-2. **Albert Webb**

    2-3. **Samantha Webb** (married **Mr. Lewis**)

    2-4. **Louervin B. Webb** (married **Sarah Hyatt**)

    2-5. **Elizabeth Webb** (married **Mr. Glass**)

    2-6. **Calvin Webb**

  3. **John Webb** (b. c1784, MD - 1827, OH) married **Phebe Smith** (29 Jul 1789, VA - June, 1822, OH, daughter of **Thomas Smith** and **Rachel Russell**, of Bucks Co., PA and founders of Smith's Ferry, OH in 1792); their children were as follows:

    3-1. **Thomas Smith Webb** (27 Jun 1810, OH - 30 Jan 1886, OH) married **Margaret Harbaugh** (27 Jun 1810, Hagerstown, MD - 30 Jan 1886, Massillion, OH, daughter of **Yost Harbaugh** and **Elizabeth Mong**)

    3-2. **Rachel Webb** (married **Thomas Jones**)

    3-3. **Sally Ann Webb** (10 Apr 1817 - 1886) married **William West** on 29 Mar 1839

    3-4. **Jesse Webb**

    3-5. **Richard Webb** (married **Lavisa Tollerton**)

    3-6. **Susan Webb** (married **Howell Bishop**)

  4. **Richard Webb** (b. c1786, d. 15 May 1857) married **Susannah Dillion** (1799-1882)

    4-1. **Elizabeth Webb** (married **Elisha Teeters**)

    4-2. **Polly Webb** (married **Jonathan Teeters**)

    4-3. **Martha Webb** (married **Mr. Bowman**)

    4-4. **Rebecca Webb** (married **Richard Vanzant**)

    4-5. **Stanton Webb** (married **Miss Bowman**)

4-6. **Isaac Webb** (married **Elizabeth Allen**)

4-7. **Minerva Webb** (married **William Dunn**)

4-8. **Abraham Webb**

4-9. **Susan Webb** (married **Mr. Bowman**)

4-10. **Lucinda Webb** (married **Mr. Williamson**)

5. **Ann Webb** (12 Jun 1787 - 6 May or 1 Jun 1867) married **David Painter** on 27 Oct 1813

5-1. **Mary Painter** (married first to **Ross Stratton** and second to **Mr. Starbuck**)

5-2. **Julia Painter** (married **Mr. Dean**)

5-3. **Elizabeth Painter** (married **Mr. Stratton**)

5-4. **Martha Painter** (married **Job Teeters**)

5-5. **William Painter** (unmarried)

5-6. **Phoebe Painter** (married **Mr. Dean**)

5-7. **Abraham Painter** (married **Alice Grenell?**)

6. **Martha Webb** (b. 1789) married **William Teeters** in 1810

6-1. **Phoebe Teeters**

6-2. **Rachel Teeters**

6-3. **Martha Teeters** (married **Mr. Shafter**)

6-4. **Elizabeth Teeters** (married **Mr. Jennings**)

6-4. **Samuel Teeters**

7. **Mary Webb** (b. 1790, twin of Elizabeth)

8. **Elizabeth Webb** (b. 1790, twin of Mary) married **William Hunt**

8-1. **Elizabeth Hunt** (married **Mr. Roller**)

8-2. **John Hunt**

8-3. **Martha Hunt** (married **Mr. Wall**)

8-4. **Seth Hunt**

9. **William Webb** (1791 - 1 Oct 1801) married **Betsy Walker**

9-1. **Lynda Ann Webb** (married **Gus Kingsbury**)

9-2. **Mary Webb**

9-3. **Mark A. Webb** (1822, OH - 1904, MO) married **Catherine Voothies** (1833, NY - 1917, MO)

10. **Abraham Webb** (15 Oct 1793, twin of Isaac - 15 Feb 1855) married first to **Margaret Shinn** and second to **Lea Wright**

10-1. **John Webb**

10-2. **Eliza Webb**

10-3. **Isaac Webb** (married **Mara Arter**)

10-4. **Rebecca Webb** (married **Mr. Teagarden**)

10-5. **Margaret Webb**

10-6. **William Webb**

10-7. **Emiline Webb** (married **Henry Phillips**)

10-8. **Julia Webb**

11. **Isaac Webb** (15 Oct 1793, twin of Abraham - 5 Jul 1886) married **Ann Jennings** (1805-1891) on 12 Jan 1824

11-1. **Simeon Webb** (married **Lyndia Ann Hiddleston**)

11-2. **Julia A. Webb** (married **Uriah Wilson**)
11-3. **Levi Webb** (died in infancy)
11-4. **Abraham Webb** (died in infancy)
11-5. **Eliza J. Webb** (married **Leonard Shilling**)
12. **Benjamin Webb**
13. **Polly Webb**
14. **Penina Webb**

John Webb died in Columbiana Co., OH in 1824. **Leah Webb** then moved to Illinois with her 3 children and later married **Mr. James**. {Ref: *A Genealogical and Historical Report of the Family of James Webb and Allied Lines, 1747-1970*, by Arthur P. Dows, Sr., of Lebanon, PA (1970); *History of Columbiana County, Ohio*, by Horace Mack (1879), p. 203; for additional information see *John Webb (c1754-1824) and Elizabeth Montgomery: Ancestors and Descendants*, by William Brooke Fetters, of Bowie, MD (1993)}

CHARLES D. WELLS

Charles D. Wells was born on 23 May 1758 in Baltimore Co., MD and lived there at the time of his enlistment in the Revolutionary War. In April, 1779 he moved to Brooke Co., VA (the part that later became Washington Co.) and in 1811 he moved to Harrison Co., OH. He applied for a pension on 12 Sep 1832 and mentioned that the children of his brothers (names were not given) lived near Chillicothe, OH. {Ref: *Genealogical Abstracts of Revolutionary War Pension Files*, by Virgil D. White (1990), Application S3493}

PETER WELLS

Peter Wells was born in 1759 in Bucks Co., PA and lived in Frederick Co., MD at the time of his enlistment in the Revolutionary War. He lived in Maryland after the war and then moved to Ross Co., OH (date not given). In 1831 he moved to Warren Co., IN where he applied for a pension on 3 Jul 1834. {Ref: *Genealogical Abstracts of Revolutionary War Pension Files*, by Virgil D. White (1990), Application R11317}

BENJAMIN WHEELER

Benjamin Wheeler was born in 1758 in Baltimore Co., MD and lived there at the time of his enlistment in the Revolutionary War. He served as a private in 1777 for 3 months in the company of Capt. **Thomas Marshall**. He later moved near Standing Stone, PA on the Juniata River (the part which later became Huntingdon Co.) and also enlisted there. After the war he moved to Bullitt Co., KY, then to Harrison Co., IN, and then to Clay Co., IN where he applied for a pension on 29 Oct 1833. His wife's name was not given, but his son **Thomas Wheeler** (b. 1779) married **Frances Thompson Boothe** (widow). Benjamin died in 1862. {Ref: *Genealogical Abstracts of Revolutionary War Pension Files*, by Virgil D. White (1990), Application S32585; DAR Application 352850; *A Roster of Revolutionary Ancestors of the Indiana Daughters of the American Revolution* (1976), p. 670}

DAVID WHETSTONE

David Whetstone was born in 1750 near Hagerstown, MD and lived at Funkstown, MD at the time of his enlistment in the Revolutionary War. Around 1820 or 1822 he moved to Ohio and applied for a pension on 12 Nov 1832. {Ref: *Genealogical Abstracts of Revolutionary War Pension Files*, by Virgil D. White (1990), Application S32591}

BENJAMIN WHIPS

Benjamin Whips was born in Anne Arundel Co., MD in August, 1753 and lived there at the time of his service in the Revolutionary War. He was enlisted by **Joseph Burgess** for the Flying Camp on 20 Jul 1776. After the war Benjamin moved to Ohio and applied for a pension in Perry County on 17 Jun 1836. He died between 1840 and 1845, and in 1853 he was referred to as late of Blackford Co., IN. His heirs were mentioned at that time, but no names were given. {Ref: *Genealogical Abstracts of Revolutionary War Pension Files*, by Virgil D. White (1990), Application R11391; **Archives of Maryland**, Volume 18, p. 40}

ABRAM WHITE

Abram White was born in Washington Co., MD on 21 Jun 1762, enlisted as a private in 1777 and served as an orderly sergeant in the company of Capt. **Zadoc Springer** in Fayette Co., PA during the Revolutionary War. He married three times: first to **Abigail ----** on 15 Jan 1800 in Shelby Co., KY; second wife's name unknown; and, third to **Millicent Hopewell**, who survived him. Their children were as follows:

1. **Abram White, Jr.** (b. 1811) married **Ada Marie Blakesley**
2. **John White**
3. **Enoch White** (b. 12 Jul 1814) married **Lydia Hollenbach**
4. **Alexander B. White** (b. 1825)
5. **Nancy White** married **Obed Blakesley**

Abram White died in Vermillion Co., IN on 22 Jun 1853. {Ref: DAR Application 450377; *A Roster of Revolutionary Ancestors of the Indiana Daughters of the American Revolution* (1976), p. 670}

JOHN WHITE

John White was born circa 1762 on the Eastern Shore of Maryland and was raised in Pennsylvania. In 1792 or 1793 he moved to North Bend on the Ohio River and from there he moved circa 1797 to what is now Miller Township in Ohio Co., IN. He died in 1852. {Ref: *History of Dearborn and Ohio Counties, Indiana* (1885), p. 459}

JOHN WHITE

On the 7th day of the 4th month, 1818, **John White**, by letter to the Little Falls Monthly Meeting in Harford Co., MD, requested a certificate of removal to White Water Monthly Meeting in Indiana. He again requested a certificate for himself and his family (names not given) on the 2nd day of the 6th month, 1818. {Ref: Little Falls Quaker Monthly Meeting Minutes}

THOMAS WHITE

Thomas White was born in 1756 in Middlesex Co., NJ and lived there at the time of his enlistment in the Revolutionary War. After the war he moved to Maryland (county not indicated) and lived there until 1823 when he moved to Ohio. He applied for a pension in Butler County on 2 Aug 1832 and on 8 Mar 1836 he had moved to Franklin Co., IN, having purchased land near Brookville in 1835. Thomas died on 16 Aug 1838 and left a widow **Mary White** who received his final payment in 1841. {Ref: *Genealogical Abstracts of Revolutionary War Pension Files*, by Virgil D. White (1990), Application S16291}

DANIEL WHITELEY

Daniel Whiteley (sometimes spelled Whitely and Wheatley) was born on the 24th day of the 9th month, 1788. A certificate of removal was requested by **Daniel and Celia Whiteley** from the Northwest Fork Monthly Meeting in Caroline Co., MD to the Milford Monthly Meeting in Wayne Co., IN for themselves and their five children (no date was given, but they were in Indiana by 1828 and Daniel was listed in the 1830 census of Fayette Co., IN). Their children were as follows:

1. **Mary C. Whiteley** (b. 6th day of 4th month, 1820) married **Benjamin Hiatt**, son of **Silas and Anna Hiatt**, at Milford Monthly Meeting on 28th day of 12th month, 1837

2. **Elizabeth A. Whiteley** (b. 5th day of 1st month, 1822, MD; d. 8th day of 11th month, 1826)

3. **Jane S. Whiteley** (b. 4th day of 1st month, 1824, MD) married **Elias Moore**, son of **Josiah and Elizabeth Moore**, of Richmond, IN, at the Milford Monthly Meeting on 2nd day of 11th month, 1843

4. **Sarah Ann Whiteley** (b. 12th day of 7th month, 1826, MD)

5. **Henry A. Whiteley** (b. 23rd day of 4th month, 1828, IN) married **Rachel W. Heacock**, daughter of **John and Christiana Heacock** (the mother being deceased), of Henry Co., IN, at Bethel Meeting House on 2nd day of 11th month, 1854

6. **Daniel Whiteley, Jr.** (b. 13th day of 3rd month, 1830, IN; d. 30th day of 4th month, 1882)

7. **Cecilia M. Whiteley** (b. 18th day of 5th month, 1832, IN)

8. **Elizabeth G. Whiteley** (b. 30th day of 8th month, 1834, IN)

9. **William P. Whiteley** (b. 27th day of 5th month, 1837, IN)

10. **Anna W. Whiteley** (b. 27th day of 5th month, 1837, IN) married **Uriah Woolman**, son of **Uriah and Mary Woolman** (the mother being deceased), of Preble Co., OH, at Milford Meeting House on 28th day of 11th month, 1860

11. **Martha Whiteley** (b. 19th day of 6th month, 1840, IN) married **James --- - [blank]**, of Wayne Co., IN, son of **Joseph and Rebecca ----**, of Clearfield Co., PA, at Milford Meeting House on 28th day of 11th month, 1861

12. **Ruth Whiteley** (b. 5th day of 8th month, 1842, d. 3rd day of 10th month,

1843)

Celia Whiteley died on the 5th day of the 3rd month, 1866 and Daniel Whiteley died on the 15th day of the 8th month, 1876. {Ref: "Migration of Caroline County Quakers to Indiana," by F. Edward Wright, *Maryland Genealogical Society Bulletin*, Volume 34, No. 3 (1993), pp. 285-286}

ISAAC WHITELEY

Isaac Whiteley (sometimes spelled Whitely and Wheatly) requested a certificate of removal from Northwest Fork Monthly Meeting in Caroline Co., MD to the Milford Monthly Meeting in Wayne Co., IN on the 12th day of the 3rd month, 1828, for himself, his wife Lydia, and their children James, Edward, and Francis. Isaac was listed in the 1830 census of Fayette Co., IN. All of the children of **Isaac and Lydia Whiteley** were as follows:

1. **James Anthony Whiteley** (b. 8th day of 10th month, 1821, MD; d. 4th day of 8th month, 1836, IN)
2. **Edward Hicks Whiteley** (b. 18th day of 12th month, 1823, MD) was reported on 19th day of 2nd month, 1857 for marrying contrary to discipline and was condemned for it, but allowed to retain his Quaker membership; he and wife **Anna Eliza Whiteley** (b. 7th day of 6th month, 1836) and their two children **William W. Whiteley** (b. 22nd day of 1st month, 1859) and **Lydia Whiteley** (b. 12th day of 9th month, 1861) were granted a certificate of removal to Maple Grove Monthly Meeting on the 20th day of the 2nd month, 1873
3. **Francis Henry Whiteley** (b. 13th day of 10th month, 1827, MD; d. 5th day of 11th month, 1862, IN)
4. **Isaac L. Whiteley** (b. 4th day of 4th month, 1830, IN)
5. **Lydia Ann Whiteley** (b. 23rd day of 8th month, 1832, IN) married **William Ferris**, son of **Joseph and Deborah Ferris**, of Milton, IN
6. **Peter A. Whiteley** (b. 23rd day of 10th month, 1834, d. 24th day of 2nd month, 1835)
7. **Mary Jane Whiteley** (b. 17th day of 1st month, 1836)

{Ref: "Migration of Caroline County Quakers to Indiana," by F. Edward Wright, *Maryland Genealogical Society Bulletin*, Volume 34, No. 3 (1993), p. 286}

WILLIS WHITELY

Willis Whitely (sometimes spelled Whiteley and Wheatley) claimed that he was drafted at Northwest Fork Bridge in Caroline Co., MD on or about August, 1813 and served as a private in the company of Capt. **Peter Willis** until discharged at St. Michaels, MD in September or October, 1813. He subsequently moved to Ohio and applied for bounty land in Fairfield County in 3 May 1856. His claim was rejected because he was not listed on the muster rolls, but **Willis Wheatley** did in fact serve on active duty for 10 days in August, 1813 in Capt. Willis' Company. {Ref: *Maryland Militia, War of 1812, Volume 1, Eastern Shore*, by F. Edward Wright, pp. 82, 116}

204

B. F. WILLIAMS

B. F. Williams, physician, of Ohio, married **Sally Dulaney Addison**, daughter of the late **Thomas G. Addison**, of Maryland, on 15 May 1836 in Cincinnati, OH. {Ref: *Baltimore American*, 25 May 1836, abstracted by Lorrie A. E. Erdman}

BENJAMIN WILLIAMS

Benjamin Williams was born circa 1759 and enlisted at Georgetown, MD during the Revolutionary War. He subsequently moved to Ohio and applied for a pension on 22 Nov 1819 in Hamilton County. In 1820 he was aged 61 with a wife (name not given) and 8 children, and 4 of his children lived with them, but not all of their names were given in his application:

1. ---- **Williams**
2. ---- **Williams**
3. ---- **Williams**
4. **Eliza Williams** (b. 1798)
5. **Joseph Williams** (b. 1800)
6. **William Williams** (b. 1803)
7. **Ezekiel Williams** (b. 1807)
8. ---- **Williams** (daughter, born 1809)

Benjamin Williams died on 7 Jan 1836. {Ref: *Genealogical Abstracts of Revolutionary War Pension Files*, by Virgil D. White (1990), Application S40691}

BENJAMIN WILLIAMS

Benjamin Williams enlisted at Hagerstown, MD during the Revolutionary War and served under Col. **Otho H. Williams** (no relationship was stated). He subsequently moved to Kentucky where he applied for a pension in Bourbon County on 12 Aug 1818, aged 56. In 1820 he had wife and one child living with him (no names were given). On 8 Jul 1834 he signed a power of attorney in Bourbon Co., KY to pursue a bounty land claim and on 27 Apr 1835 he had moved to Highland Co., OH to procure land for his children (no names were given). {Ref: *Genealogical Abstracts of Revolutionary War Pension Files*, by Virgil D. White (1990), Application S40693}

JAMES WILLIAMS

James Williams lived in Talbot Co., MD at the time of his enlistment in the Revolutionary War. He subsequently moved to Ohio and applied for a pension on 15 May 1818 in Pickaway County. In 1823 he had a wife aged about 60 (name not given) and 4 children lived with them, as follows:

1. **Esther Williams** (b. 1801)
2. **Mary Williams** (b. 1803)
3. **Charles Williams** (b. 1807)
4. **John Williams** (b. January, 1810)

{Ref: *Genealogical Abstracts of Revolutionary War Pension Files*, by Virgil D. White (1990), Application S40712}

205

JAMES WILLIAMS

James Williams was born on 22 Feb 1759 in Chester Co., PA and lived in Washington Co., MD at the time of his enlistment in the Revolutionary War. In 1778 he moved to Washington Co., PA and also enlisted there. By 1783 he was living in Ohio Co., VA and enlisted there as well. In 1793 he moved to Adams Co., OH and married **Elizabeth Miller** on 26 May 1805. James applied for a pension on 25 Oct 1832, a resident of Jefferson Township, and died on 11 Jul 1842. **Elizabeth Williams** applied for bounty land (warrant 55-160-26873) on 19 Apr 1855, aged 77. {Ref: *Genealogical Abstracts of Revolutionary War Pension Files*, by Virgil D. White (1990), Application S3590; *Maryland Revolutionary Records*, by Harry Wright Newman (1938), p. 125}

JEREMIAH WILLIAMS

Jeremiah Williams was born circa 1759 in Anne Arundel Co., MD and served in the Revolutionary War. He enlisted as a private in the 3rd MD Regiment on 15 Mar 1777 and was discharged on 15 Mar 1780. He married **Mary Gaither** in Anne Arundel County circa 15 Dec 1784 (date of license). They later moved to Ohio and Jeremiah applied for a pension in Fairfield County on 18 Oct 1819. By 1828 they moved to Seneca Co., OH, at which time he was aged 69 and his wife was aged 67. They had a son aged 22 (name not given) who lived them. **Reuben Williams** was Justice of the Peace in 1828, but no relationship was indicated. **Jeremiah Williams** died on 29 Aug 1842 and **Mary Williams** died on 25 Feb 1848. Their surviving children in 1851 were as follows:
1. **Jeremiah Williams** (of Fulton Co., OH)
2. **Susannah Egbert** (of Fulton Co., OH)
3. **Elisha Williams** (of Fulton Co., OH)
4. **Reuben Williams** (of Warsaw, IN)

{Ref: *Genealogical Abstracts of Revolutionary War Pension Files*, by Virgil D. White (1990), Application R11602; *Anne Arundel County, Maryland Marriage Records, 1777-1877*, by John W. Powell, p. 130; *Maryland Revolutionary Records*, by Harry Wright Newman (1938), pp. 55, 125}

WILLIAM WILLIAMS

William Williams was born on 20 Nov 1749 in Anne Arundel Co., MD and lived there at the time of his enlistment in the Revolutionary War. About 3 years after his service he moved to Frederick Co., MD and 9 years later he moved to Loudoun Co., VA. About 11 years later he moved to Ross Co., OH for 2 years and then moved to Pike Co., OH for 9 years before moving to Pickaway Co., OH where he applied for a pension on 19 Feb 1833. William's half-sisters were Mrs. **Elizabeth Findly**, aged 69 in September, 1833, and Mrs. **Mary Howard**, aged 66 in March, 1833, and his brother-in-law was **Cornelius Howard**, aged 64 in January, 1833, all living at that time in Pike Co., OH. The sisters stated they lived with their mother (name not given) during the Revolutionary War, but at that time she was married to a man named Howard (first name not given). **John Williams**, of Pickaway Co.,

OH, was also mentioned, but no relationship was given. {Ref: *Genealogical Abstracts of Revolutionary War Pension Files*, by Virgil D. White (1990), Application S3587}

WILLIAM WILLIAMS

William Williams was born on 24 Apr 1761 in Washington Co., MD and lived there at the time of his enlistment in the Revolutionary War. In the fall of 1778 he moved with his father (name not given) to Washington Co., PA, then to Brooke Co., VA, and in 1781 he moved to Ohio Co., VA and enlisted there. William applied for a pension on 16 Sep 1835 in Clermont Co., OH, having lived there over 33 years. In 1835 his brother **James Williams** (b. 1759) was a Justice of the Peace in Jefferson Township, Adams Co., OH, and in 1835 a **Zebina Williams** was a Justice of the Peace in Clermont Co., OH, but no relationship was indicated. In 1850 **Mary Williams**, widow of **William Williams**, lived at Gallipolis, OH. {Ref: *Genealogical Abstracts of Revolutionary War Pension Files*, by Virgil D. White (1990), Application S11627}

ISAAC WILSON

On the 10th day of the 1st month, 1805, **Isaac Wilson** requested a certificate of removal from the Baltimore Monthly Meeting, Western District, to the Middleton Monthly Meeting in Ohio for himself, his wife **Susanna Wilson**, and their three minor children, **Alizanna Wilson, David Wilson and John Webster Wilson**, having already removed there. {Ref: Baltimore Quaker Monthly Meeting Minutes}

Isaac Wilson, of Belmont Co., OH, son of **Samuel and Rebeckah Wilson**, of Bucks Co., PA (deceased), and **Ann McCoy**, of Baltimore, MD, widow of **Joseph McCoy** and daughter of **James Hicks**, late of Harford Co., MD, married in Baltimore City on the 14th day of the 4th month, 1819 at the Baltimore Monthly Meeting, Western District. {Ref: Baltimore Quaker Monthly Meeting Minutes}

MATTHEW WILSON

Matthew Wilson (sometimes spelled Willson) was born circa 1741 in Prince George's Co., MD and lived in Montgomery Co., MD at the time of his enlistment in the militia during the Revolutionary War. **Matthew Willson**, aged 35, lived in Sugarland Hundred, Montgomery Co., MD, in 1776 with his wife **Rachel Willson**. They subsequently moved to Ohio and he applied for a pension in Highland County on 23 Jul 1834, aged 93. {Ref: *Genealogical Abstracts of Revolutionary War Pension Files*, by Virgil D. White (1990), Application S11627; *Revolutionary Patriots of Montgomery County, Maryland, 1776-1783*, by Henry C. Peden, Jr. (1996), p. 362}

GEORGE WINDHAM

George Windham (sometimes spelled Winham and Wyndham) enlisted in Montgomery Co., MD during the Revolutionary War. He stated that he married **Mary Card** (b. 10 Dec 1764) on 11 Dec 1783, but her sister Mrs. **Ann Rowe** stated they were married in November, 1782 or 1783 in St. Mary's Co., MD. They subsequently moved to Ohio and he applied for a pension in Belmont County on 15 Aug 1818, aged 62; however, in 1820 he stated he was aged 60. Their children were as follows:

1. **Thomas Windham** (b. 28 Dec 1784)
2. **William Windham** (28 Jan 1787 - 7 Sep 1807)
3. **Harriot Windham** (b. 18 Jan 1789)
4. **Mary Windham** (b. 23 Apr 1791, twin)
5. **George Windham, Jr.** (b. 23 Apr 1791, twin)
6. **Ann Windham** (22 Jan 1794 - 6 Aug 1794)
7. **Elizabeth Windham** (b. 13 Jun 1795)
8. **Meriah Windham** (b. 25 May 1797, twin)
9. **Hezekiah Windham** (b. 25 May 1797, twin)
10. **Sarah Windham** (b. 18 Mar 1800)
11. **Benson Windham** (23 Nov 1804 - Oct 1805)

George Windham died on 2 Aug 1831 and **Mary Windham** applied for a widow's pension on 4 Dec 1838. She lived in Goshen Township and Smith Township in Belmont County before settling near St. Clairsville, OH in 1839. {Ref: *Genealogical Abstracts of Revolutionary War Pension Files*, by Virgil D. White (1990), Application W4535}

PETER WINGATE

Peter Wingate, of Cecil Co., MD, served as a private during the War of 1812 under Capt. **James Allen** who initially commanded the company until they marched to Baltimore and it was placed under Capt. **Thomas Patten** from 29 Aug to 27 Oct 1814. After the war he moved to Ohio and applied for bounty land in Clark County on 235 Jun 1851, aged 63. He applied again (warrant 55-120-56367) on 28 May 1855, aged 66. Witnesses were **Gabriel Prugh** and **Aquilla T. Prugh**. {Ref: *Maryland Militia, War of 1812, Volume 3, Cecil & Harford Counties*, by F. Edward Wright, pp. 2, 19, 70}

JACOB WISNER

Jacob Wisner was born in January, 1759 in Lancaster Co., PA and lived in Washington Co., MD at the time of his enlistment in the Revolutionary War. He served as a private in the militia companies of Capt. **Daniel Clapsaddle** and Capt. **Michael Fackler** in 1776 and 1777. Around 1824 he moved to Ohio and applied for a pension in Brown County on 1 Sep 1835. {Ref: *Genealogical Abstracts of Revolutionary War Pension Files*, by Virgil D. White (1990), Application R11743; *The Maryland Militia in the Revolutionary War*, by S. Eugene Clements & F. Edward Wright, p. 245; Revolutionary War Military Collection, Manuscript MS.1146, Maryland Historical Society}

MICHAEL WOLF

Michael Wolf served in the Maryland and Virginia Lines during the Revolutionary War and subsequently moved to Ohio. He applied for a pension in Pickaway County on 15 Jul 1818 and in 1820 he had no wife and was living with his children (no names were given). {Ref: *Genealogical Abstracts of Revolutionary War Pension Files*, by Virgil D. White (1990), Application S40726}

WILLIAM WOOD, JR.

William Wood, Jr. requested a certificate of removal on the 9th day of the 7th month, 1819, from the Baltimore Monthly Meeting, Western District, to the Smithfield Monthly Meeting in Ohio. {Ref: Baltimore Quaker Monthly Meeting Minutes}

DAVID WORLEY

David Worley was born in 1759 in Frederick Co., MD and lived in Washington Co., MD at the time of his enlistment in the Revolutionary War. He served at Fort Frederick and was also a substitute for **Thomas Worley**, but his relationship was not given. **Francis Worley** and **William Worley** also served in the Washington County militia. David later moved to Ohio and applied for a pension in Mill Creek Township, Union County, on 5 Apr 1833. {Ref: *Genealogical Abstracts of Revolutionary War Pension Files*, by Virgil D. White (1990), Application R11870; *Revolutionary Patriots of Washington County, Maryland, 1776-1783*, by Henry C. Peden, Jr., pp. 420-421}

HATFIELD WRIGHT

Hatfield Wright moved from Northwest Fork Monthly Meeting in Caroline Co., MD to the White Water Monthly Meeting in Wayne Co., IN around September, 1826. He was accompanied by his wife **Mary Wright** and their children **Isaac Wright, Hatfield Wright, Levin Wright, Mary Wright, Amelia Wright, and Lucretia Wright**. In their care was **Amelia Charles**, a minor. Their children were born in Maryland as follows:
1. **Mary Wright**, b. 1st day of 2nd month, 1801
2. **Cecelia Wright**, b. 28th day of 1st month, 1803
3. **Isaac Wright** (no date of birth was recorded)
4. **Hatfield V. Wright**, b. 27th day of 6th month, 1810
5. **Lucretia Wright**, b. 15th day of 2nd month, 1814
6. **Levin Wright**, b. 22nd day of 2nd month, 1818

Hatfield Wright died on the 3rd day of the 4th month, 1839 and in his will mentioned his children Ceily, Isaac, Hatfield, Amelia, Lucretia, and Levin, all of age. The executors were **Daniel Whitely** and **Isaac Whitely**, fellow natives of Caroline Co., MD. **Mary Wright** died on the 18th day of the 8th month, 1848. {Ref: "Migration of Caroline County Quakers to Indiana," by F. Edward Wright, *Maryland Genealogical Society Bulletin*, Volume 34, No. 3 (1993), p. 282}

JACOB WRIGHT

Jacob Wright, son of **Lemuel and Elizabeth Wright**, of Caroline Co., MD, lived in the Smithville area, just south of Houston Branch, and married **Rhoda Harris**, daughter of **James and Mary Harris**, in the Nicholite faith (a small sect which followed the same tenets as the Quakers). **Lemuel Wright** died in 1796 and

Jacob Wright died circa 1824. **Rhoda Wright** then moved with most of her children to Richmond, IN. Rhoda moved with her daughters Mary, Rhoda and Lydia in 1825 within the verge of White Water Monthly Meeting and in the same year another daughter Celia moved with her husband and children to Wayne Co., IN. Rhoda died at the home of her son Edward in 1852, aged 81. By that time she and most of her children were well settled in their new state of Indiana, as follows:

1. **Celia Wright** (b. 16 Oct 1790) married **William Wright** (16 May 1779 - 1854, son of **James and Sarah Wright**) on 19 Feb 1807 at the Northwest Fork Monthly Meeting, Caroline Co., MD. In 1825 they moved to Wayne Co., IN. Before they left Maryland, Marshy Creek Meeting reported on the 15th day of the 6th month, 1825 that *"William Wright, of James, had deviated from the principal of truth as to be guilty of taking that which was not his own, and much neglected the attendance of our religious meeting and also had taken some part in gambling and in strong drink."* The meeting noted that he had gone to another state by the time the letter of disownment had been prepared. By 1826 **William Wright** and his family seemed settled in their new environment and in the 25 Feb 1826 issue of the Richmond, IN newspaper *Public Ledger* he advertised he would receive on subscription *"produce of every description in Milton."*

2. **Ann Wright** (b. 11 Jun 1792) married **Daniel Wright** (1790-1820, son of **James and Ann Wright**) in 1817 in Caroline Co., MD. A widow at the time of the move of her mother and siblings to Wayne Co., IN, she nevertheless remained in the Smithville, MD area. Ann married second to **Wright Hubbard** in 1829. She had five children altogether, as follows:

    2-1. **Richard Henry Wright** (27 Mar 1818 - 20 Aug 1881)
    2-2. **Daniel Wright, Jr.** (born and died in 1820)
    2-3. **William E. Hubbard** (1 Feb 1830 - 16 Dec 1850)
    2-4. **James W. Hubbard** (7 Sep 1833 - 19 Jul 1863)
    2-5. **Sarah E. Hubbard** (b. circa 1837)

3. **Harris Wright** (b. 31 Aug 1794) married circa 10 Apr 1817 to **Anne Kimmey,** *"a person not a member of the Society of Friends,"* and he was disowned by the Northwest Fork Monthly Meeting. Nothing else is known about **Harris Wright** except for a reference to him in a letter in later years, sent by an agent or lawyer named **Edward Nichols** in Federalsburg, MD, sent to **John Brady** of Muncie, IN, husband of **Mary Wright**, Harris' younger sister, and in the letter Nichols inquired *"if Harriss is dead..."* (Information gleaned from one of about 15 letters written between 1830 and 1870 in manuscript collection at Ball State University. These letters are held by the university because one of Mary Wright's granddaughters married one of the Ball Brothers who became major industrialists of the area and benefactors of the school for whom it was named.)

4. **Lemuel Wright** (b. 2 Apr 1797, d. before 1846) was disowned by the Northwest Fork Monthly Meeting in 1818, for *"having much neglected the attendance of our meeting and keeps disorderly company, gambling, swearing ..."* There was a **Lemuel Wright** listed in the 1840 census of Park Co., IN.

5. **James H. Wright** (b. 7 Aug 1799) married **Rebeckah Evans** circa 11 Nov

210

1826 in Wayne Co., IN (marriage notice in *Public Ledger*). He was notified by the Northwest Fork Monthly Meeting in Caroline Co., MD of his disownment because of *"marrying contrary to the good order used among Friends"* (but he had already requested to be dropped from membership). He was listed in the 1830 census of Henry Co., IN.

6. **Edward Wright** (17 May 1801, Caroline Co., MD - 6 Feb 1866, buried in Beech Grove Cemetery, Muncie, IN) left the Northwest Fork Monthly Meeting for Wayne Co., IN circa 1825, perhaps at the same time as his mother and siblings, but his certificate of removal was not received by the White Water Monthly Meeting until 27 Jun 1827. Edward married **Rebecca Leverton** (possibly the daughter of **Moses and Rachel Leverton** and thus his first cousin) circa 1832-1833. She had been received by the Milford Monthly Meeting on the 17th day of the 6th month, 1830 and was reported on the 21st day of the 2nd month, 1833 for *"marrying out"* to Edward Wright. He owned a grocery store in Richmond, IN until 1848. Their children were as follows:

    6-1. **James Wright**
    6-2. **Isaac H. Wright** (1837-1856)
    6-3. **Edward Wright, Jr.** (1842-1845)
    6-4. **Joseph Wright**
    6-5. **Albert Wright**
    6-6. **Amelia Wright**

7. **Sarah H. Wright** married circa 1821 to **Daniel Ward** *"contrary to the good order of the Society"* and they moved to Wayne Co., IN circa 1830. Daniel operated a store in Marion, IN where he sold stoves, tinware, copperware and other items (1859 City Directory). Daniel and Sarah Ward (and other family members) are buried in the old cemetery adjoining Earlham College. Their children were as follows:

    7-1. **Eliza Ann Ward** (married **Abram Ernest**)
    7-2. **James W. Ward**
    7-3. **Mary Ellen Ward** (b. 9 Jul 1835, married **Mr. Buhl**)
    7-4. **Daniel Ward** (d. 1869)

8. **Mary Wright** (b. circa 1807, d. 30 Aug 1884) moved to Wayne Co., IN with her mother in 1825. She married **John Brady**, a harness maker, on 16 Mar 1825 *"contrary to the rules of discipline"* of the Society of Friends (Quakers), Northwest Fork Monthly Meeting. They moved from Caroline Co., MD to Muncie, IN where John became its first mayor. **John and Mary Brady** are buried in Beech Grove Cemetery in Muncie, IN. Their children were as follows:

    8-1. **William Fletcher Brady**
    8-2. **Samuel Franklin Brady**
    8-3. **John Brady, Jr.**
    8-4. **James Edgar Brady**
    8-5. **Mary Elizabeth Brady**
    8-6. **Thomas Jefferson Brady** (became a brigadier general (brevet) in the Civil War and his daughter married **George Ball** of the Ball Brothers who manufactured canning jars and other articles)

8-7. **Benjamin Brady**

8-8. **Edward Wright Brady**

9. **Rhoda Wright** moved to Wayne Co., IN with her mother in 1825. She was disowned on the 25th day of the 3rd month, 1829 by the White Water Monthly Meeting for having joined another society.

10. **Lydia Wright** moved to Wayne Co., IN with her mother in 1825, She married **James Ferguson** circa 9 Nov 1831 and had children **Clement Ferguson** and **Jane Ferguson. Lydia Ferguson** died in 1839. **Sarah Ward** wrote to her sister **Mary Brady** in Muncie, IN on 1 Dec 1839 to say *"Dear sister, we have met with an irreparable loss ... Lydia is no more."*

{Ref: "Migration of Caroline County Quakers to Indiana," by F. Edward Wright, *Maryland Genealogical Society Bulletin*, Volume 34, No. 3 (1993), pp. 279-284, citing his two books *Wrights of Bloomery* and *Descendants of Caleb Wright, 1760-1797*}

JOHN WRIGHT

John Wright, of Caroline Co., MD, married **Esther** ---- and later moved to Philadelphia. From there they moved to Wayne Co., IN where John began a business between Front and Pearl Streets in Richmond circa 1822. The business was continued by his son-in-law **Basil Brightwell**, who also built a flouring mill. Apprehensive of bankruptcy, Basil committed suicide and his son died a few years later (name and dates not given). **Esther Wright** died on the 6th day of the 3rd month, 1837. **John Wright, Sr.** died in Milton, IN on 31 Dec 1838 or the 1st day of the 1st month, 1839, aged 76 (both dates were given). {Ref: "Migration of Caroline County Quakers to Indiana," by F. Edward Wright, *Maryland Genealogical Society Bulletin*, Volume 34, No. 3 (1993), p. 282}

JONATHAN WRIGHT

Jonathan Wright (sometimes referred to as **Jonathan Wright, Jr.**) and his wife **Susanna Wright** requested a certificate of removal on the 28th day of the 8th month, 1805, from the Gunpowder Monthly Meeting in Baltimore Co., MD, for themselves and their three minor children, **Joel Wright, Susanna Wright, and Rebecca Wright**, to Miami Monthly Meeting in the State of Ohio. **Mary Wright** also requested a certificate to said meeting. {Ref: Gunpowder Quaker Monthly Meeting Minutes}

SAMUEL WYCKOFF

Samuel Wyckoff was born on 10 Jun 1760 in Hunterdon Co., NJ and lived in Washington (now Allegany) Co., MD at the time of his enlistment in the Revolutionary War. He is in all likelihood the **Samuel Wycoff, Jr.** who enlisted as a private in the Washington County militia on 5 Sep 1781 and served in the Continental Line. After the war he moved to Loudoun Co., VA, then to Hardy Co., VA, and then to Ohio. He applied for a pension in Licking County on 29 Oct 1832 and indicated that his youngest son (name not given) had the family bible. {Ref: *Genealogical Abstracts of Revolutionary War Pension Files*, by Virgil D. White

212

(1990), Application S4736; *Archives of Maryland*, Volume 18, p. 388}

BENJAMIN YEATS

Benjamin Yeats (sometimes spelled Yates) was born on 3 Apr 1745 in Baltimore Co., MD and lived in Frederick Co., MD at the time of his enlistment as a private in the Revolutionary War. He was a militia substitute, marched to Annapolis, and served from May to 10 Dec 1781. After the war he moved to Westmoreland Co., PA for 15 years and then moved to Adams Co., OH. About 14 years later he moved to Highland Co., OH and there he applied for a pension on 10 Mar 1834 as **Benjamin Yeats, Sr.** He was married twice, but his first wife's name was not stated. Their children were as follows:
1. **Samuel Yeats** (b. 3 Jun 1776, married **Phebe Brion** on 10 Jun 1799)
2. **Benjamin Yeats, Jr.**
3. **Robert Yeats**
4. **James Yeats**
5. **William Yeats**

Benjamin Yeats married second to **Sarah Ann Robinson** on 16 Jul 1835 at Hillsboro or Hillsborough, Highland Co., OH and died on 30 Jan 1849 at Manchester, Adams Co., OH, aged nearly 104. **Sarah Yeats** applied for a widow's pension on 8 May 1854 at Fulton, Hamilton Co., OH and she also applied for bounty land (warrant 55-160-3134) in 1855 at Cincinnati, OH, aged 50 and upwards. {Ref: *Genealogical Abstracts of Revolutionary War Pension Files*, by Virgil D. White (1990), Application W8202; DAR Application 308478; *A Roster of Revolutionary Ancestors of the Indiana Daughters of the American Revolution* (1976), p. 674; *Revolutionary Patriots of Frederick County, Maryland, 1775-1783*, by Henry C. Peden, Jr. (1995), pp. 404-405}

MATTHIAS YOUNG

Matthias Young was born in 1760 in Frederick Co., MD and lived there at the time of his enlistment in the Revolutionary War. He married **Anna Barbara Christ** on 2 Nov 1783 at Frederick, MD. They lived there after the war and then moved to Warren Co., OH. In 1829 they moved to Clinton Co., IN where he applied for a pension on 25 Mar 1834, aged 74. Matthias died on 11 Aug 1838 and **Anna Barbara Young** died on 10 Apr 1848, aged 83. Their children were as follows:
1. **John Young** (lived in Warren Co., OH in 1852)
2. **Matthias Young, Jr.** married **Hannah Aughe** and both died before 1852; their children were as follows:
   2-1. **John Young** (of Tippecanoe Co., IN)
   2-2. **Abraham Young** (of Howard Co., IN)
   2-3. **Barbara Young** m. **Thomas Paris** (Clinton Co., IN)
   2-4. **Matthias Young III** (of Howard Co., IN)
   2-5. **Margaret Young** m. **George Grant** (Howard Co., IN)
   2-6. **Joseph Young** (of Howard Co., IN)
   2-7. **Peter Young** (of Howard Co., IN)
   2-8. **Hannah Catherine Young** (of Howard Co., IN)

2-9. **Jackson Young** (of Howard Co., IN)

3. **Daniel Young** married **Peggy Creiger** and died before 1852; she was then living in Clinton Co., OH; in 1852 all of their children lived in Clinton Co., IN, as follows:

    3-1. **Peggy Young**

    3-2. **Eliza Young**

    3-3. **Samuel Young**

    3-4. **John Young**

    3-5. **Mary Young**

4. **Polly Young** married **Edward Ryan** and in 1852 lived in Tippecanoe Co., IN

5. **Catherine Young** married **John B. Coleman** and both died before 1852; their children in 1852 all lived in Clinton Co., IN except James, as follows:

    5-1. **Elizabeth Coleman** married **William Sheppard**

    5-2. **Thomas Coleman**

    5-3. **Barbara Ann Coleman** married **John F. Bowen**

    5-4. **Catherine Coleman** married **Philip Bowen**

    5-5. **James Coleman** (of California in 1849)

6. **Susannah Young** married **Henry Kriser** and she died before 1852; he was then living near Potosi, WI; their children (both of Potosi, WI in 1852) were as follows:

    6-1. **Louvisa Kriser** married **Celestin Koltenach**)

    6-2. **Mary Kriser** married **Davis Gillihan**)

7. **Henry Young** married **Sally Kriser** and he died before 1852; she was then living in Clinton Co., IN; their children, all of Clinton Co., IN in 1852, were as follows:

    7-1. **Minerva Young** married **George Mash**

    7-2. **Sarah Young** married **Cornelius J. Miller**

    7-3. **Elizabeth Young** married **Joshua Byers**

    7-4. **Henry Young, Jr.**

    7-5. **Keziah Young**

    7-6. **Mary Ann Young**

    7-7. **John Young**

    7-8. **Perry Young**

8. **David Young** (b. 1800 and lived in Clinton Co., IN in 1852)

9. **Solomon Young** (lived in Tippecanoe Co., IN in 1852)

10. **Samuel Young** married **Debora Ann Hevlin or Hevelin** and he died before 1852; she married second to **William Thatcher** and they lived in Clinton Co., IN in 1852; his children, all of Clinton Co., IN in 1852, were as follows:

    10-1. **Jacob Young**

    10-2. **Martha Young**

    10-3. **Amos Young**

    10-4. **Mary Young**

    10-5. **Albert Young**

11. **Elizabeth Young** married **John McCain** (she was a widow before 1852

214

in Clinton Co., IN)
{Ref: *Genealogical Abstracts of Revolutionary War Pension Files*, by Virgil D. White (1990), Application R11949; *Maryland Revolutionary Records*, by Harry Wright Newman (1938), p. 126}

INDEX

ACKRIGHT, Isaac, 1; John, 1
ADAIR, John, 89
ADAMS, Celia, 1; Elizabeth, 1; John,
1; Josiah, 1; Sophia, 1
ADDISON, Sally Dulaney, 204;
Thomas G., 204
AGNEW, Anne, 182
ALBAUGH, Mr., 151; Susannah, 1;
Zachariah, 1
ALBERT, Thomas, 1
ALDERSON, Abel, 5; Naomi, 5
ALEXANDER, Elizabeth, 1; Mary
Margaretha, 23; Walter, 73;
William, 1
ALFORD, Robert P., 110
ALLBAUGH, Susannah, 1;
Zachariah, 1
ALLEN, David, 146; Elizabeth, 199;
Hutchins, 2; J. B., 4; James, 207;
John, 2; Martha, 2; Mary, 2;
Rhoda, 2; Robert, 2; Thomas, 2
ALSTOTT, John, 117; Robert, 117
ALTMAN, Catherine, 28
AMBROSE, Ann, 83; Mary, 83
AMOS, Abel B. M., 5; Abeth, 6;
Abraham "Abram", 7, 8; Albert
W., 8; Alonzo Aquila, 2;
Amanda, 4, 7; Ann, 5, 7; Anna
Morice, 127; Anne, 127; Aquila,
2; Aquilla, 3; Aquilla Ditto, 3;
Aquilla McComas, 127; Ariel, 7;
Asbury, 3; Benjamin, 5, 127;
Benjamin Franklin, 127; Bethia,
15; Caroline, 7; Caroline A., 5;
Caroline D., 6; Cassana, 5;
Cassander, 4; Charlotte, 7;
Charlotte M., 7; Christiana, 3;
Corbin Clark, 2; Darcus, 6; Ditto,
3, 4; Edwin M., 8; Eldridge
Gerry, 127; Elijah, 4; Elijah

Neale, 4; Elizabeth, 3, 6, 7, 33;
Elizabeth "Betsy", 5; Elizabeth
Jane, 2, 127; Ellen, 6; Emmaline
Conwell, 4; Fred T., 6; Frederick,
5; Frederick T., 10; Geo. Wash.
Benj. Franklin, 2; Granville, 4;
Harrison, 5; Henry, 7; Henry
Richardson, 6; Hester J., 5; Isaac
Neale, 3; James, 3, 6; James H.,
3; James M., 6; James
Montgomery, 2; James Oliver,
127; James R., 6; John Archer, 8;
John G., 6; John Mordecai, 6;
John Streett, 6; John Wayne, 7;
Joseph, 3; Joshua, 5, 10, 127,
144; Josie, 8; Louisa Ann, 7;
Lucinda, 3; Margaret, 3; Martha,
3, 7; Martha "Patsy", 4; Martha
Jane, 4; Mary, 7, 8; Mary A.
"Molly", 5; Mary Ann, 6; Mary
Cordelia, 7; Mary Louisa, 2;
Mary M., 8; Meranda Emaline, 2;
Mordecai, 6, 8; Mordecai Streett,
7; Nancy, 3; Nancy Jane, 3;
Nicholas D., 6; Nicholas Day, 3,
4, 15, 184; Olivia, 7; Orpha Ann,
2; Polly, 4; Rachel, 6; Rebecca,
4; Rebecca Jane, 4; Robert, 8;
Samuel, 3; Sarah, 4, 184; Sarah
Ann, 8; Sarah Catherine "Kate",
127; Sarah Louise, 2; Sarah
Margaret, 8; Sophia Maud, 7;
Susannah, 4; Thomas, 4, 6, 8;
Thomas Alderson, 5; Thomas D.,
3; Thomas J., 4; Thomas
Montgomery, 2; William, 2, 4, 5,
6, 7, 8; William Bradford, 2;
William H., 7; William Harrison,
4; William Hayden, 3; William

Rampley, 6; William Thomas, 127

AMOSS, Aquila, 2; Frederick T., 39; John M., 8; Martha, 64; Mordecai, 6; Susanna, 64; William, 2, 64

ANDERSON, Ann, 9; Cyrelda Belle, 50; Elizabeth, 189; James, 189; Jane, 9; John, 9; Margaret, 9; Mary Elizabeth, 9; Nancy, 189; Peter, 8; Sally, 165; Samuel T., 100; William, 8, 9; Wright, 9

ANDRES, Adamaners, 9; James, 9

ANDRES FAMILY, 134

ANDREW, Noble, 9

ANDREWS, Jonathan, 42; Mr., 42

ANNAN, Robert L., 132

APPABEL, Elizabeth, 124

ARMAND, Brig. General, 39

ARMSTRONG, R.W., 57; Rachel, 137

ARNETT, Nancy, 9, 57; Samuel, 9

ARNEY, John, 15

ARNOLD, Eve, 10; George, 9, 10; Rev., 55

ARRASMITH, Nancy, 152; William, 152

ARTER, Mara, 199

ASHLEY, Mariam, 158; Marion, 158

ASHTON, Chenowith, 10; Joseph, 10; Laura, 10; Thomas, 10; William, 10

ATHON, James S., 40

ATKINSON, Joseph, 62

AUGHE, Hannah, 212

AYERS, Levina, 157

AYRES, John, 10

BABBITT, Mr., 21

BABBS, Greenberry, 122

BAGGS, Andrew, 47, 195

BAGLEY, Catherine A., 11; Elizabeth H., 11; Ellen, 10; Ellen

S., 11; Ferdinand, 11; George W., 11; John O., 11; Samuel H., 11; Susan, 10; Susanna O., 10; William, 10, 11

BAGUN, Henry, 11

BAHAW, Maria, 190

BAILEY, Joseph M., 92

BAILY, Abraham, 11; Ann, 11; Elizabeth, 11; Emmor, 11; Ezra, 11; Hannah, 11; Henry, 11; Jacob, 11; Margaret, 11; Martha, 11; Mary, 11; Phebe, 11

BAKER, Alphus, 55; Daniel, 173; Mary, 198; Polly, 173

BALCH, Albinda Bloomer, 11; Amos P., 11; Ann Wilkes, 11; Calvin, 11; Elizabeth R., 11; Ethelinda, 11; James, 11, 12; John C., 11; Jonathan Edward, 11; Martha, 11; Mary, 11; Susanna, 12

BALDWIN, Ann, 12; Charles E., 12; Elijah, 12; Elizabeth, 12; James, 12; John, 12, 13; Joseph, 12; Keziah, 12; Mary, 12, 13; Matilda, 12; Rebecca, 12; Sarah, 12

BALITZ, George, 13; William, 13

BALL, Ann, 136, 138; George, 210; James, 136; Jarrett, 42; Lyde, 42; Nancy, 136, 138; Susan, 136

BALLINGER, Manerow, 186; Milton, 186; Rebecca, 186; Sarah, 186; William, 186

BANTHAM, John, 13; Rachel, 13

BANTZ, Cornelius, 70

BARBER, Aquila, 13; Ellen, 13; Sarah, 82

BARBOUR, Ann Eliza, 174; Oliver P., 174

BARCHLEY, Elizabeth, 114

BARCROFT, Lydia, 13, 14

BARECROFT, Lydia, 13

BARKER, Mary Curry, 12
BARKERS, James, 14
BARLOW, Miss, 86
BARNES, Absalom, 14; Adam, 14,
    24, 111, 113; Captain, 111;
    Catharine, 14; Dorsey, 14; Elijah,
    14; Ellis, 14; George, 77;
    Hannah, 65; Mary, 147; Nathan,
    14; Oliver, 65; Ruth, 14
BARNETT, John, 15; William A., 15
BARRA, Mordeca, 15; Mordica, 15
BARRET, John, 15, 49
BARRETT, Alexander, 190
BARROW, America, 68; Aquila D.,
    68; Bennett, 67; Harriet G., 67;
    Louisa Sydney, 67; Mary J., 68;
    Thomas L.H., 68
BARRY, Caleb, 15; Elisha, 15;
    James, 20; Joshua, 15; Mordecai,
    15; Peninah, 15; William, 21
BARTON, Andrew, 16; Ann, 16;
    Anna, 16; Edward, 16; Elizabeth,
    16; Levin, 16; Lydia, 16; Mary,
    16; William, 16
BASFORD, Benjamin, 16; Elijah, 16;
    Richard, 16; Robert, 16
BASSFORD, Benjamin, 16; James
    C., 16; Wallace, 16
BATCH, Martha, 82
BATEMAN, William, 17
BATES, John, 77
BATTEE, Richard H., 116, 117
BAUGHMAN, Elizabeth, 61
BAXTER, Sarah, 97
BAY, Robert, 148
BAYLES, Jesse, 17; John B., 84;
    Susan Jane, 17
BEACH, Stephen, 155
BEALL, Christiana, 17; James, 17;
    Jeremiah, 17; John, 17; Joseph,
    17; Lloyd, 139; Margaret, 17;

    Nathaniel, 17; Ninian, 17; Sarah,
    17; Thomas, 18; Zephaniah, 17
BEALMEAR, Francis, 15, 64;
    Thomas, 18
BEALS, Nathan, 10
BEAMAN, George, 18; Margaret, 18;
    Mary, 18; Moses, 18; Samuel,
    18; Thomas, 18; William, 18
BEARD, William, 18
BEATTY, Captain, 70
BEAVENS, William, 23
BECHER, John, 73
BECKETT, Alfred, 19; Ann, 19;
    Anna, 19; Benjamin H., 19;
    Carle, 19; Egbert, 19; Eliza, 19;
    Elizabeth, 19; Humphrey, 19;
    James, 19; Lucy, 19, 179; Maria,
    19, 157; Marie, 19; Mary, 19;
    Polly, 19; William, 19
BECKWITH, Benjamin, 19
BEECHER, Harriet, 20; Rev. Dr., 20
BEEDLE, Jacob, 148
BEELER, Christopher C., 174
BELL, Amy, 126; Ann, 23; Belinda,
    126; Benjamin, 126; Captain,
    196; Cary, 126; Eunice, 126;
    Henrietta, 126; Jacob, 126;
    James, 126; Lancelot, 79; Mary,
    79, 126; Nancy, 126; Sarah, 26,
    79
BELLMEAR, Captain, 122
BELLMERE, Francis, 15
BELT, Margaret, 29
BEMAN, William, 18
BENNET, John, 136
BENNETT, Jesse, 20
BENSHOOF, Eve Ann, 139
BERGET, Aaron, 20, 97; Samuel, 97
BERRY, Abraham, 21; Andrew, 21;
    Catharine, 21; Dulcibella, 50;
    Elizabeth, 21; Esther Ann, 21;
    Hannah, 21; Isaac, 21; James, 20,

21; John, 21; Lydia Ann, 21;
Margaret, 21; Mary, 21; Mary
Jane, 21; Purnell, 21; Sarah, 21;
Sarah C., 21; Seymour, 21;
Susan, 21; William, 21; William
H., 21
BEVAN, Jesse L., 181
BEVANS, William, 23
BEVARD, Charles, 22; Elizabeth, 22;
George, 22; Hester, 22; James,
22; James Madison, 22; John, 22;
Martha, 22; William, 22
BIDDLE, Spencer, 195
BIRCH, Jesse, 182
BISHOP, Howell, 198
BITESELE, Henry, 23
BITZELL, Catherine, 23; Elizabeth,
23; George, 23; Gustave, 23;
Henry, 23; John, 23; Joseph, 23;
Mary, 23; Peter, 23; Samuel, 23
BIVEN, Henrietta, 162
BIVINS, William, 23
BIXBY, Mr., 177
BLACK, David, 15; Gabriel, 24;
Hugh, 23; James K., 23; John,
24; Joshua, 24, 25; Samuel, 24,
25; Sarah, 23; William, 24;
William H., 24
BLACKBURN, James, 25; Martha,
25; Rebecca, 25; William, 25
BLACKER, Lydia, 80
BLACKFORD, John Milton, 49
BLACKMORE, Elizabeth, 175;
Samuel, 175
BLACKWELL, Hugh, 23, 24; Sarah,
23
BLADES, Eli, 25
BLADS, Eli, 25
BLAIR, Andrew, 25, 26; David, 26;
Elizabeth, 26; Frances, 26;
James, 26; Jesse, 26; John, 25,
26; Samuel, 26; Sarah, 26

BLAKE, Mr., 166
BLAKESLEY, Ada Marie, 201;
Obed, 201
BODENHAMMER, Joseph, 124
BOELL, John, 40
BOLING, Elijah, 5
BOND, Benjamin, 26, 27; Dennis,
26; Eli, 27; Elijah J., 26; Eliza,
26; Ely, 27; Frances, 26; Harriott,
26; Jane, 26; Mary, 26; Merriken,
26; Mordecai, 26; Nicholas W.,
26; Silas, 26, 27
BONFIELD, John, 27
BOONE, Mary A., 49
BOOTH, Erastus, 89; Florence, 90
BOOTHE, Frances Thompson, 200
BORDLEY, W., 150
BOROFF, Michael, 23
BOSS, Adam, 27; Harriet, 27; Jacob,
27
BOSWELL, Mary Ann, 37
BOTELER, Henry, 193
BOURNE, George, 55; Rebecca, 55
BOWEN, John F., 213; Philip, 213
BOWER, Anna, 27, 28; Barbara, 27,
28; Catharine, 27; Catherine, 28;
Christiana, 27; Conrad, 28;
Elizabeth, 27; Frederick, 27;
George, 28; Henry, 28; Jacob,
27, 28; John, 27, 28; Magdalen,
28; Mary, 28; Sarah, 28;
Susannah, 27, 28
BOWLBY, Donald, 33
BOWLES, Lucinda, 185
BOWMAN, Catharine, 28; Charlotte,
28; Christian, 28; Elizabeth, 28;
Isaac, 28; Joannah, 29; John
Jacob, 28; John Nicholas, 28;
Joshua, 28; Katie, 29; Kezia, 28;
Keziah, 28, 198; Miss, 198; Mr.,
198, 199; Philip, 29; Philip

Casper, 28, 198; Rachel, 29; Rebecca, 28; Sarah, 28
BOYD, John, 29
BOYED, John, 29
BOYER, John, 29
BOYLE, Mary, 29; Mary A., 29; Mary Ann, 3; Sarah, 91; Thomas, 29
BOYLES, Charity, 121; Peter, 121
BRADFIELD, John, 92; Nathan, 182
BRADFORD, George W., 143; Margaret, 29; Martha, 5; Samuel, 29; William, 162, 194
BRADLEY, Cornelius, 30; David, 30; John, 30; Mary, 30
BRADOCK, Rebecca, 50
BRADY, Benjamin, 211; Edward Wright, 211; James Edgar, 210; John, 209, 210; Mary, 210, 211; Mary Elizabeth, 210; Samuel Franklin, 210; Thomas Jefferson, 210; William Fletcher, 210
BRANDENBURG, Samuel, 30; William, 30
BRANDLINGER, Conrad, 31
BRATTEN, William, 30
BRATTON, William, 30
BRENDLINGER, Conrad, 31
BRENTLINGER, Conrad, 31; Frederick, 31
BREVETT, Cassandra, 31; Cassandra A., 31; Elizabeth Boraston, 31; Ellen Isolobo, 31; George Fox, 31; James M., 31; Joseph, 31; Joseph Plummer, 31
BRIGHT, Starling, 166
BRIGHTWELL, Basil, 211
BRILEY, John, 31; John Jefferson, 31; Nelson, 31; Sally, 31; Samuel, 31; Tite, 31
BRION, Phebe, 212
BRISCOE, Hannah, 157

BRITTINGHAM, Abner, 32; Betsy, 32; Celey, 32; Enoch, 32; Hampton, 32; Hester, 32; Jeremiah, 31; Leah, 32; Lotty, 32; Martha, 32; Nancy, 32; Polly, 32; Rieley, 32; Solomon, 31, 32
BROOKE, R.S., 32
BROOKOVER, John, 32
BROOKS, Mary, 90; Thomas, 90
BROTHERTON, Hugh, 26
BROWER, John, 14
BROWN, Aquilla P., 33; Asa, 34; Basil, 34; Bentley, 35; Betsy, 34; Cassandra, 33; Catharine, 34; Catherine, 34, 126; Christena, 33; Christiana, 151; Clemency, 33; Edward, 34; Elias, 98; Elizabeth, 33, 35; Esther, 33; Fanny, 35; George, 33; Hannah, 35; Henry P., 34; Isaac, 32, 33; James, 32, 35, 117; James T., 33; John, 33, 35, 100; John R., 56; Joseph, 33, 34; Leah, 31; Margaret, 38; Margaret "Peggy", 34; Mary, 32; Mary "Polly", 35; Mary Ann, 33; Matilda, 35; Nancy, 34; Nicholas, 34; Rachel, 33; Rezin, 34; Ruth, 33; Sally, 34; Samuel, 35; Sarah, 34, 35; Solomon, 34; Susannah, 35; Thomas, 33, 34, 35; Vincent, 2; William, 33, 35
BRUMBLAY, Anna, 105; David M., 105; Elizabeth, 105; John, 105; Mary, 105; Sarah, 105
BRUNBACK, John, 87
BRYAN, Thomas, 35
BRYANT, Gilman, 64; Greenberry, 35
BUCHANAN, Alexander, 176; Lieutenant, 57; Lloyd, 17; Thomas R., 143
BUCKALEW, Ann, 22

BUCKINGHAM, John, 126; William, 126
BUHL, Mr., 210
BULL, E. P., 10; Sephrona, 10
BURBAGE, John, 84
BURCHFIELD, Betsy, 36; Elizabeth, 36; John, 36; Kitty, 36; Mary, 36; Nancy, 36; Robert, 35, 36; Sally, 36
BURDSAL, Aaron, 67; Aquila D., 67; Belle, 67; Charley H., 67; Elizabeth, 67; Harriet, 67; John D., 67; Laura, 67; Leander G., 67; Riley G., 67; Uriah, 67
BURGAN, Prescocia, 81
BURGES, Ann, 36; Daniel, 36; Deborah, 36; John, 36; Joseph, 36; Martha, 36; Tacey, 36
BURGESS, Joseph, 201; Mr., 196; Roderick, 24, 34, 70
BURGOON, Jacob, 36; John, 36; Robert, 36
BURGOONE, Jacob, 36; John, 36
BURKE, Nicholas, 114; Richard, 37
BURROUGH, Jeanette, 35
BURROWS, Jeremiah, 37
BURTON, Joshua, 37; Rosey, 84
BUSH, Elizabeth, 143
BUSKIRK, Abram, 37; Alfred, 37; George, 37; Hannah, 37; Isaac, 37; John, 37; Joseph, 37; Mary, 45; Michael, 45
BUSSEY, Bennett, 97
BUTLER, Henry, 38; John, 151; Richard, 116; Samuel, 38; Thomas, 44; William, 119
BUTT, Aaron, 177; Abram S., 177; Alexander, 178; Elizabeth, 177; John B., 177; Mary Ann, 177; Nancy, 177; Pitcherd, 178; Rebecca, 178; Samuel A., 177; Sarah Jane, 178

BUXTON, Anna Brittia, 107
BYCOURT, Martha J., 184
BYERS, Joshua, 213
BYRAM, Elizabeth, 147
CAHILL, James, 38
CALLAHAN, Dennis, 38; George, 38; John, 34, 38; Mary, 38
CALVERT, George, 38
CAMPBELL, David, 104; Elizabeth, 104; Joseph, 39
CARD, Mary, 206
CAREL, George, 39; William, 39
CARES, Rhoda, 2
CAREY, Solomon, 41
CARL, Sarah Jane, 127
CARLISLE, Benedict, 39; Benjamin, 39; Sarah, 39
CARMICHAEL, Rhoda Ann, 61
CARPENTER, Mr., 194
CARR, Absolom, 40; Elisha, 40; Elizabeth, 40; Grenberry, 39; Hannah, 40; Jefferson, 40; John, 40; Joseph, 40; Mary, 3; Mary Caroline, 40; Nancy, 40; Rachel, 39, 40; Rebecca, 40; Thomas, 40
CARRILL, William, 39
CARROL, Rachel, 40; William, 39
CARROLL, Rachel, 40
CARSON, Miss, 184
CARTER, Abigail, 185; Ruth, 41; William, 41
CARVER, John H., 41
CARY, Saul, 41; Solomon, 41
CASE, William, 149
CASEY, Jacob, 41; John B., 184; Philip, 134
CASH, John, 41; William, 41
CAVENDER, Alexander, 42; Ann, 95; Easter, 42; Eliza, 42; James, 42; John, 42; Margaret, 42; Polly, 42; Robert, 42
CAVINDER, John, 42

CAZIER, Captain, 80
CECIL, Adin, 43; Ann, 42; Brice
    Berry, 42; Elizabeth, 42; Hazel,
    42; Jeremiah, 42; Joshua, 42;
    Kinsey, 42; Levi, 42; Mary, 42;
    Melinda, 42
CHALK, Julia H., 2; Leonard, 2
CHAMBERS, Martha, 98
CHANCE, Amelia, 22
CHANDLER, E.C., 43; Unit, 43;
    William J., 65
CHANEY, John, 43; Lewis, 43
CHAPLINE, Alitha, 44; Atlas, 44;
    Cyrus, 44; Heros, 44; James, 44;
    Joseph, 44; Romena, 44; William
    Williams, 44
CHARLES, Amelia, 44, 45, 208;
    Henry, 44, 45; Levin, 44; Mary,
    44, 45
CHATHAM, Sarah, 5
CHENEY, John, 43; Lewis, 43
CHENOWETH, Isaac, 45; John, 45;
    Mary, 45
CHERRY, Mary, 5
CHEW, Ann J., 173; John, 92
CHIPMAN, Hannah, 99
CHISLEY, Elizabeth, 49
CHRIST, Anna Barbara, 212
CLANCEY, John, 45
CLAPSADDLE, Daniel, 207
CLARK, Anthony, 45; Asa, 147;
    Catherine, 46; Champ, 16;
    Elizabeth, 46; Ellen, 96; Hannah,
    6, 191; Jacob N., 45; James, 45,
    46; Jane, 46; Joannah, 46; John,
    46; Joseph, 46; Mary, 190, 193;
    Mr., 16, 181; Nancy, 46; Nancy
    Ann, 46; Sarah, 46, 48
CLARKE, Elisha, 46; John, 46
CLAYTON, Charlotte, 155; William,
    155

CLEMENTS, Emily, 185; Joshua, 46;
    Malvina, 170
CLERCK, Mary, 193
CLEVINGER, John, 65
CLIFTON, Thomas, 47
CLINE, Betsy, 183
CLINGON, Jane, 149
CLOSE, Henry, 47
CLOWDSLEY, Jane, 119
CLUTTER, Caspar, 47; Gasper, 47
COALE, Elizabeth, 163; William,
    163
COBB, E., 148; James, 47
COCHRAN, John, 37; Sarah, 46;
    Simeon, 46; Simon, 46, 48
COCKERAL, Abner, 132
COCKRELL, Enoch, 132
COE, Milburn, 157; Samuel, 119
COEN, Edward, 48; James, 48
COFFMAN, John, 103; Paul, 103
COLBERT, John William, 48
COLE, Betsy, 49; Cassandra, 83;
    Charles, 49; Elijah, 49; Ezekiel,
    48; Juliana, 49; Meshac, 49;
    Samuel, 48; Sarah, 15, 49; Tensa,
    49; Teresa, 187; Tersa, 187;
    Thomas, 48, 49
COLEMAN, Barbara Ann, 213;
    Catherine, 213; Elizabeth, 213;
    James, 213; John B., 213;
    Thomas, 213
COLLINS, Alpha, 49; Anna Maria,
    49; Charles, 49; Dearmond
    Leborn, 49; Ebenezer Van Buren,
    49; Edwill David Perkins, 49;
    Elizabeth, 147; Howard J., 49;
    John Ogden, 49; Melzena Jane,
    49; Robert C., 49; Stephen A., 49
COLVIN, Mr., 178
COMLY, Hannah, 34
CONAWAY, Charles, 50; Michael,
    50

CONLEY, Michael, 50
CONN, Thomas, 50
CONNOLLY, Mary, 120
CONOVER, Eliza, 3; Sarah A., 3
CONWAY, Charles, 50; Jeremiah,
    50; Michael, 50; Miles, 50;
    Richard, 50
COOK, Betsy, 113; Eliza, 156; Julia
    Ann, 156; William B., 156
COOMBS, Hannah, 40
COOPER, Elizabeth, 53; Nancy, 53
COPLIN, Martin V., 191
CORDRY, Annie E., 81
CORNTHWAIT, Mr., 16
CORNWALLIS, Lord, 86
CORRY, Mr., 78; Thomas H., 78;
    William, 78
CORY, Ann, 123; Dorothy, 123;
    Jeremiah, 123; Mr., 123
COSLER, Frances E., 3
COSNER, Sarah, 124
COTTINGHAM, Priscilla, 84;
    Thomas, 51
COURTNEY, Catharine, 51; Thomas,
    74
COVINGTON, Eunice, 51; George
    N., 51; John B., 51; Mary, 51;
    Polly, 51; Robert, 51; Robert E.,
    51; S.F., 51; Thomas, 51
COVINGTON FAMILY, 51
COWAN, Huldah A., 3
COX, Captain, 118; Daniel, 52;
    Elmer H., 52; Isaac, 51; Jacob,
    52; Lydia, 137; Nathaniel, 52;
    Pamelia Louise Tetree, 49;
    Susanna, 120
COY, Ann, 52; Elizabeth, 52; Esther,
    52; Frances, 52; Mary, 52;
    Nancy, 52; Samuel, 52; Sarah,
    52; Seely, 52; Susannah, 52;
    Thomas, 52; William, 52
CRABTREE, Mr., 90; W.T., 90

CRAFT, Eliza Ann, 4
CRAGG, Elizabeth, 194
CRAIG, Nancy J., 127; William, 53
CRAIGE, William, 53
CRAIN, Maria E., 46
CRANFORD, George, 116
CRAWFORD, Abel, 53; Benedict,
    53; Cassandra, 53; Cynthia, 53;
    Elijah, 53; Elizabeth, 53;
    Greenberry, 53; James, 53; John,
    53; Josiah, 53; Ruth, 53, 130;
    Sarah, 53
CREAGER, Valentine, 89
CREIGER, Peggy, 213
CREIGHTON, Mary, 179
CREPS, Saville, 23
CRESTMORE, George, 165; Lotty,
    165
CRIDER, John, 59
CRISTMORE, George, 165; Lotty,
    165
CRITCHFIELD, John, 54; William,
    54
CROFT, John, 54; Margaret, 54;
    Stacy, 54; William, 54
CROSBY, James, 54
CROSELY, Moses, 54; William, 55
CROSLEY, Anna, 55; Catharine, 55;
    Cynthia, 55; Elizabeth, 55, 170;
    George, 55; Mary, 55; Moses,
    54, 55; Rachel, 54, 55; Sarah, 55;
    William, 54, 55
CROSS, Adderson, 55; David, 55;
    Delilah, 55; George H., 55;
    Jeremiah, 55; Jerry, 55; John, 55,
    56; Jonathan, 55; Leonard, 55;
    Lydia, 56; Nancy Ann, 55;
    Rachel, 55; Rebecca, 56;
    William, 56
CROSSLEY, Moses, 54; William, 55
CROUCH, William, 56
CROW, Nelson, 174

CROWDY, Archibald, 97
CRULL, William, 8
CRUM, Adam, 56; David, 56; Henry, 56; Mary, 56; Willilam, 56
CRUMP, Rebecca, 4; Susannah, 4
CRUTHERS, Elizabeth, 1
CULBERTSON, William B., 137
CULL, Hugh, 56
CULLISON, Cassander, 4; Elizabeth, 80; Joseph, 190; Mary, 190
CULVER, Solomon, 9, 57
CUMMINGS, Jane, 42
DALE, Campbell, 57; Josiah, 57, 98
DALRYMPLE, J., 166
DAMSEL, Captain, 57
DAMSELL, Katharine, 57; William, 57
DANNER, David, 57; Jacob, 58; Samuel, 58
DANNOR, David, 57
DARBY, Augustus, 58; Ruth, 88
DARMER, Eveline, 49; Sarah Ann, 49
DASHIELL, Elizabeth, 142; Sarah, 105
DAVIDSON, Patrick, 132
DAVIS, Amos, 58; David, 25; Ebenezer, 59; Effee, 59; Eliza, 188; Enos, 58; Gertrude, 193; H.M., 60; Hannah, 59; Henrietta, 85, 105; Ichabod, 58; Irena, 59; Isaac, 60; Isaac R., 58; James, 58, 59; Jane, 59; Johannah, 60; John, 58; John W., 60; Jonathan, 3; Julia, 58; Levi, 59; Manloff, 150; Margaret, 59; Mariah A., 150; Martha, 25; Mary, 58; Mr., 46; Nancy, 59; Nancy Ann, 46; Noah, 105; Rachael, 59; Rebecca, 59; Rezin, 59; Ruth, 58; Samuel, 158; Sarah, 59; Stephen,

59; Thomas, 60, 88; William F.R., 60
DAWSON, Celia Ann, 60; Charles, 103; Deborah H., 79; Elisha, 60, 79; James H., 60; John, 60, 103; Lydia, 60; Margaret, 79; Rhoda A., 79; Sarah, 60; Sarah Ann, 60; W.H., 61; William D., 79
DAYHOFF, Lithia, 37
DE LA ROUERIE, Marquis, 39
DEAL, Henry, 61; Noble, 61; Rhoda A., 61
DEALE, Henry, 61
DEAN, Charles, 61; Mr., 199
DEAVER, Abraham, 61, 62; Ann, 62; Basel, 62; Eli, 62; Henry J., 62; James, 62; Levi, 62; Miscal, 62; Nancy, 62; Reuben, 62; Sarah Ann, 62; Susannah, 62; Walter, 62
DEFENBAUGH, Josiah, 70
DEFORD, Thomas, 62
DEFORD, Thomas, 62
DELASHMUTT, Elias, 62; Elias N., 63; Elizabeth, 63; Peter, 63; Sarah Ann, 63; William Waugh, 62
DELOUGHERY, Thomas, 63
DENNIS, Mary Ann, 52
DENNISTON, Robert, 26
DENUNE, Nancy, 118
DEVANN, James, 63; Lydia, 63
DIBBLE, Mary A., 152
DICK, Sarah, 104
DICKINSON, Braman, 29; Elizabeth, 166; George, 63; Thomas, 166; William R., 130
DICKSON, Joseph, 63
DIEHL, Armintha Jane, 119
DILLIAN, Noah, 82
DILLION, Moses, 64; Susannah, 198

DILLON, Elizabeth, 64; Hannah, 64; Isaac, 64; Moses, 63, 64; Peter, 64; Rebecca, 99
DIMMITT, Mary, 82
DION, Mr., 4
DISNEY, Amelia, 64; Richard D., 64; Richard J., 64; Thomas, 64; William, 116; William A., 64; William J., 64
DITTO, Christiana, 3, 4, 184; Christina, 15
DOBSON, Henry, 30, 145
DORMAN, America A., 64; Charles W., 64; Elijah, 64; Frank R., 64; H.J., 64; Jane, 64; John, 64; John S., 64
DORNECK, John, 64
DORNICK, John, 64
DORSEY, Amelia, 88; Anna, 88; Charles, 34; John, 36; John Worthington, 36; Mary, 65; Mary N., 88; Ruth, 182
DOUGLAS, Joseph, 142; Mr., 151
DOWDEN, Indiana R., 138; Mr., 138; Samuel, 138; Virgil, 103
DOWNEY, Alexander C., 65; John, 65; Thomas, 65
DOWNS, Mr., 177
DOYLE, Matthew, 77
DRAKE, Aaron, 191; Joseph, 65; Nancy, 80; Rachel Davis, 2
DRIGGS, Asa, 65; Daniel, 66; Elias, 66; Joseph, 66; Nathaniel, 65, 66; Sarah, 65, 66; Seth, 66
DRIGGS FAMILY, 65
DRUMMOND, Nancy, 40
DUDLEY, Lydia, 114
DUKES, Davis, 66; Elizabeth, 66; Isaac, 66; James, 66; Katharine, 66; Mary, 66; Samuel, 66; Spencer, 66; William, 66

DUMFORD, Nancy, 112; Solomon, 112
DUNBAR, Andrew, 82; Elizabeth, 82
DUNCAN, Catherine, 84; James, 69
DUNN, Elizabeth Temple, 170; Richardson, 66; Sarah, 66; William, 199; Williamson, 78
DUPONT, Reni, 100
DURHAM, Alazanah, 67; Alice I., 68; Aliceanna, 67; Aquila, 67, 68; Benjamin, 67; Charles, 68; Clemency, 67; Daniel, 67; Edward, 68; Eliza, 68; Elizabeth, 67; Ellen, 68; Emma, 68; Hannah, 67; Harriet, 68; Harriet E., 67; Hattie A., 68; James B., 68; John, 67; Joseph D., 67; Joshua, 66, 67, 68; Leander, 67, 68; Manford, 68; Martha, 67; Mary A., 68; Nellie, 68; Prescilla, 67; Samuel, 66, 68; Sarah, 67, 68; Sarah B., 67; Solon, 68; Thompson, 68; Warren, 68; William, 68; William B., 68; Winfield S., 68
DUVALL, William, 196
DYER, Edward, 69; Elizabeth, 69; Elizabeth "Betsy", 69; George Swann, 69; Mary "Polly", 69; Nancy, 69; Samuel, 69; Sarah, 69; Thomas, 69; William, 69
EAGON, Mary, 104
EBERHARD, Mary Ann, 62
ECCLESTON, John, 61
EDGELL, Henry, 69
EDWARDS, Thomas, 69
EGAN, James, 69
EGBERT, Susannah, 205
ELDER, John, 70; L.G., 70
ELDREDGE, H.E., 25
ELKINS, William, 70
ELLETT, Samuel, 70

ELLIOT, James, 116
ELLIOTT, Amelia, 64; Catharine, 70; David M., 126; Harrison, 126; John, 70; Keziah, 70; Mary, 81; Samuel, 70
ELLIS, Abraham, 71; Abraham F., 144; Christina, 71; Elizabeth, 71; India Ann, 71; James, 71; John, 70; Mary, 71; Mary Eliza, 68; Matilda, 71; Nancy, 71; Noah, 71; Rebecca, 71; Samuel, 71; Sarah, 71
ELLWELL, Thomas, 72
ELSEY, Edward, 71; Patrick, 71; Thomas, 71
ELWELL, David, 72; Elizabeth, 72; Hannah, 72; Jonathan, 72; Mary, 72; Sary, 72; Susannah, 72; Thomas, 72
ELY, Isaiah, 72
EMBREE, Hannah, 72; Israel, 72; Jesse, 72; John, 72; Joseph, 72; Lydia, 72; Phebe, 72; Samuel, 72
EMMETT, John, 72
EMMITT, Abraham, 73; Abram, 73; Anna, 73; Daniel Decatur, 73; David, 73; James, 73; John, 72, 73; Lafayette, 73; Margaret, 73; Margaret B., 73; Mary, 73; Rebecca, 73; William Yates, 73
EMORY, Captain, 38
ENDALY, William H., 3
ENDICOTT, Henrietta, 184
ENGLISH, William H., 21
ENOCH, Isaac, 73
ENYART, Mr., 146
EPPERSON, Lydia B., 4
ERNEST, Abram, 210
ESSIG, Adam, 74; Catherine, 74; Elizabeth, 73; George, 74; Jacob, 74; John, 73; Julia, 74; Juliana, 74; Polly, 73; Rebecca, 74; Sally,

74; Samuel, 74; Simon, 73, 74; William, 74
EUBANK, Herrington, 178
EVANS, Edward, 74; Jeremiah, 74; John, 74, 101; John R., 110; Nancy, 74, 126; Philip, 74; Rebeckah, 209; Walter, 74
EWELL, Alfred, 150; Mariah A., 150
FACKLER, Michael, 207
FAIR, Polly, 124
FAIRALL, Dorathea, 74; Horace, 74; Levi, 74
FARMER, Nathaniel, 75
FARQUER, Sara, 198
FARQUHAR, Allen, 75; Edward Andrew, 75; Elizabeth, 152; Mahlon, 75; Malen, 75
FARROW, Hulda D., 5
FAST, Ann Barbara, 76; Ann C. Margret, 76; Ann Catrine Margret, 75; Ann Elizabeth, 76; Barbara, 75; Christeany, 76; Christian, 75, 76; Clemmer, 76; David, 75, 76; Elizabeth, 76; Francis, 75; George, 76; Isaac, 76; Jacob, 75; Jeremiah, 76; John, 76; Katie, 28, 198; Levina, 76; Martin, 75, 76; Nancy, 76; Nicholas, 75; William, 75
FAUST, Katie, 28, 198
FEE, William, 164
FERGUSON, Clement, 211; E.A., 195; Isaac, 165; James, 127, 211; Jane, 211; Lotty, 165; Lydia, 211
FERRILL, Charlotte, 67
FERRIS, Anna, 76; Deborah, 203; Jane M., 85; John, 76; Joseph, 76, 203; Matthew, 76; William, 76, 203
FETTERS, James, 198
FILES, Mary Ann Railey, 49
FINDLY, Elizabeth, 205

FINE, Peter, 76
FINNEY, Agnes Ann, 127
FISCUS, Mr., 2
FISHER, Basil, 77; Bazzel, 77; Eliza
    Ann, 4; John, 77
FITZGERALD, Amanda, 89;
    Eleanor, 90
FITZWATER, Mary, 33; Samuel, 33
FLACK, George, 77
FLAKE, George, 77
FLECK, Anna Christena, 175;
    Christena, 175; George, 77
FLEMING, Alexander P., 78; Alice,
    78; Arthur, 78; David, 78;
    Eleanor, 78; Harriet, 78; Mary,
    78; Nancy, 78; Samuel, 78;
    Thomas, 78
FLEMMING, Thomas, 78
FLICK, George, 77
FLINT, John, 78
FOARD, Hezekiah, 101; Joseph R.,
    79
FOCKLER, Jacob, 15
FORMAN, Aaron, 79
FORSHAY, Obadiah, 138
FORWOOD, Jacob, 114; Mary, 114
FOSTER, Nancy Anna, 195;
    Patience, 195
FOULKE, Ann Eliza, 174;
    Cassandra, 174; Thomas D., 174
FOUTS, Ann (Nancy), 182
FOWLER, William, 43
FRAMPTON, Deborah, 79; Isaac, 79
FRANCIS, Elizabeth, 184
FRANKLIN, Jacob, 61
FRANKS, Abigail, 80; Abraham, 80;
    Catharine, 80; Christiana, 79, 80;
    Elizabeth, 80; Henry, 79, 80;
    John, 79; Michael, 80; Phebby,
    80; Sarah, 80; Uriah, 80
FRAZIER, George, 157; Rebecca,
    157; William, 157

FREE, Polly, 121
FREELAND, Frisby, 129
FRENCH, Mary Ann Railey, 49
FRESHOUR, Adam, 80; Jacob, 80;
    John, 80; Margaret, 80
FRIZELLE, J., 147
FROSHOUR, John, 80
FRY, Mary, 71, 191
FUDGE, Mr., 151
FULLER, Isabella, 162
FULLERTON, Mary, 6
FULTON, David, 80, 100; Julia Ann,
    149; Mary, 51; Samuel, 51, 126;
    William, 80; William T., 100
FUNKHOUSER, Margaret, 80
FURGESON, Isaac, 165; Lotty, 165
FYFFE, William H., 13
GADD, Absalom, 80; William, 80
GAITHER, Mary, 205
GALBRAITH, A.M., 180
GALLOWAY, Elihue, 81; Elijah, 81;
    Elisha, 81; Ephraim, 81; George
    W., 81; Harriet, 81; John, 81;
    Joseph, 81; Martha, 81; Mary,
    81; Robert, 81; Samuel, 81;
    Sarah A., 81; William, 81
GARBER, Anna, 151
GARLAND, James, 82; Perry, 176
GARRETT, Captain, 80; Harry, 39;
    William, 50, 57
GARRISON, Susanna Lavinia, 11
GARWOOD, Daniel, 198
GASKILL, Josiah, 58
GASSAWAY, Rachel, 161
GATCH, Conduce, 81, 82, 130;
    Elizabeth, 82; George, 82;
    Godfrey, 81; James D., 81;
    Lewis, 81; Philip, 81, 82;
    Prescocia, 82; Ruth, 82; Thomas,
    82
GATCHELL, Elisha, 82; Elizabeth,
    82; Hannah, 82; Jacob, 82;

Jeremiah, 82; Mary, 82; Nancy, 82; Nathan, 82
GATES, Nancy, 143
GAULT, Robert, 28
GAUNCE, Ann, 145; Mary Ann, 145; Nancy, 145
GEARHART, Eliza, 126
GEE, Job, 82; Marie, 198; Parker, 82; Susan, 198
GELSTRAP, Aaron, 59
GENTLE, Rebecca, 177
GEORGE, Phoebe, 147
GERLINGER, Catharine, 113
GERRY, James, 64, 165, 169
GEST, John, 82, 130
GIBBS, Sarah, 182
GIBSON, Robert, 7
GILBERT, Martin Taylor, 189; Sarah Ann, 189
GILES, William, 101
GILL, Ambrose, 83; Ann O., 83; Barbara, 83; Didymus, 83; Edward, 83, 84; Elizabeth, 83; Ezekiel C., 83; George T., 83; John, 83; John C., 83; John Price, 83; Joseph, 83; Joshua N., 83; Laurence, 83; Lou Ella, 83; Mary E., 83, 84; Mordecai, 83; Nettie, 83; Nicholas, 83; R. Stephen, 83; Sarah, 83; Stephen, 83; Sylvanus, 83; Tabitha, 83, 84; Thomas, 83; Thomas E., 83; William Carpenter, 83; William George, 83
GILLESPIE, Lucy, 49
GILLIHAN, Davis, 213
GILMOR, William, 84
GILMORE, William, 84
GIVAN, Adoniran J., 85; Albert G., 84; Alfred B., 85; Alfred M., 85; Catherine, 84; Charles M., 85; Cora A., 85; Elizabeth, 84;

Elizabeth A., 84; Ella J., 85; Eva A., 85; George, 85; George M., 85; Gilbert T., 84, 85; Harriet J., 85; Harry R., 85; Henrietta, 85; Hetty, 84; Irving P., 85; John F., 85; John W., 84; Joshua, 85; Margaret, 84; Margaret M., 84; Maria J., 84; Martha, 85; Mary, 85; Mary B., 85; Matilda, 84; Nancy, 84; Noah S., 85; Peter M., 85; Robert, 84, 85; Robert H., 84; Rosey, 84; Ruth, 84; Sallie, 84; Sanford E., 85; Sanford G., 85; Sarah, 84; Sarah C., 85; Sarah E., 85; Sarah R., 85; William L.H., 85
GLADDEN, Jacob, 85; James, 85; James W., 85
GLASS, Mr., 198
GLAZE, John, 34
GLAZIER, A.B., 55
GLENN, Isabella, 127; Mary Jane, 8
GLICK, Katherine, 83
GLOVER, William, 134
GOMBER, Jacob, 85, 86
GOMBIER, Jacob, 86
GOOD, Jacob, 12
GOODIE, Jacob, 12
GOODLIN, Nancy, 164
GOODMAN, Henry, 29
GORSUCH, Benjamin, 14
GOSNELL, Alexander, 86; Benjamin, 86; Delilah, 86; Dorcas, 86; Edith, 86; George, 86; John, 86; Nancy, 86; Patience, 86; Peter, 86; Thomas B., 86; Washington, 86
GRAFTON, Aquila, 86; Corbin, 86; Daniel, 86; William, 86, 87
GRAHAM, Deborah, 87; Elizabeth Ann, 87; James, 87; Michael, 87; Patience, 87

GRANT, Cassia, 123; George, 212; Mr., 123; Nancy, 198
GRASHAW, Madison, 163
GRAY, Elizabeth, 88, 115; Elizabeth Ann, 88; George, 87; James, 88; Joseph, 87, 88; Josephine, 88; Lydia, 115; Lydia Ann, 88; Mary, 87, 88; Peter, 88; William, 88, 115
GRAYBILL, Captain, 167
GRAYLESS, Elizabeth, 88
GRAYSON, Sarah, 66; Wesley, 88
GREEN, Allen, 88; Isaac, 34; Lewis, 88; Lewis H., 88; Mr., 102; Nathaniel, 147; Richard, 88; Sarah, 184
GREENWOOD, Philip, 88, 89; Sarah, 89
GREER, James, 190
GRENELL, Alice, 199
GREYLESS, Elizabeth, 88
GRIFFIN, Elizabeth, 69
GRIFFITH, Ann Moore, 89; Elizabeth, 88, 89; Keturah, 89; Mary, 89; Rebecca, 89; Reuben, 89; Sophia, 62
GRIMES, Henry, 126; J.J., 150; James J., 150
GROVE, Blanche, 127
GROVES, Elizabeth, 46; Mr., 46
GROWDY, William, 53
GRUBB, Electra, 5
GRUWELL, Sarah, 170
GUNION, Hugh, 89
GUYTON, Abraham, 90; Adeline Amanda, 89; Augustus, 90; Benjamin, 90; Catherine, 89, 90; Elisha, 89, 90; Elisha S., 90; Elizabeth, 90; Ellen Ann, 89; Frances, 89; John, 89; Margaret Catherine, 90; Mary, 90; Mary

Elizabeth, 89; Thomas Elisha, 90; William Fitzgerald, 90
GWYNN, Joseph, 39
HACKATHORN, James R., 26
HACKNEY, Mr., 62
HAGUE, S.M., 116
HAILEY, Thomas, 90
HALES, Anna, 90; Mary, 90; Randall, 90
HALEY, Anna, 90; Cassander, 90; Edward, 90; Rachel, 90; Thomas, 90
HALL, Aquila, 121; David, 20; Ellen, 15; J. Carvil, 148; John, 29; Sabrina Jane, 85; Thomas, 116; Thomas H., 15
HAMBLETON, Benjamin, 91; Charles, 90, 91; James, 90, 91; Joseph, 91; Martha, 91; Mary, 90, 91; Rachel, 91; William, 90
HAMBLETON FAMILY, 90
HAMILTON, Margaret, 154; William, 91, 122
HAMMER, George, 91; Jacob, 91; Tobias, 91
HAMMOND, Larkin, 102; Sarah, 91; Thomas, 91
HANCE, Benjamin, 92; John, 91, 92
HANDLEY, Handy, 92
HANDY, Ebenezer, 78; Robert, 78
HANGER, S.W., 126
HANNAH, Margaret, 184
HANNER, Jacob, 29
HANWAY, Amos, 25
HARBAUGH, Margaret, 198; Yost, 198
HARDACRE, George, 92; Leonard, 92
HARDESTY, Richard, 92
HARDING, Barton, 93; Nicholas, 93; Ruth, 93; Thomas, 92, 93

HARDMAN, Elias, 61; Henry, 111, 159
HARE, Elizabeth, 122
HARGROVE, Richard, 137; Ruth, 137; Sarah, 53
HARLAND, Nancy, 182
HARNEY, Shelby, 59
HARPER, Amanda, 7; James, 7; Lecky, 7; Mary Catherine, 7
HARRIS, Elizabeth A., 137; James, 208; Mary, 208; Rhoda, 208
HARRISON, Mr., 53
HARRISS, Harriet, 93; John, 93; Ruth, 93; Samuel, 93
HARTSHORN, Mary, 93; Patience, 93
HARVEY, Lieutenant, 57
HARWOOD, Benjamin, 93; Elizabeth, 145; Sarah G., 184
HASH, Elizabeth, 95
HASLETT, Eliza, 134; James, 134
HATTON, Rebecca, 94
HAUGH, Paul, 99
HAUL, Anna M., 74
HAWKINS, Ann, 94; Philip, 94; Richard, 53; Thomas, 53, 94
HAYES, Malinda C., 171
HAYMAN, Henry, 51; James, 51
HAYNE, William C., 84
HEACOCK, Christiana, 9, 202; Jesse, 9; John, 9, 202; Rachel W., 202
HEADLEY, Ellen, 155
HEALEY, Thomas, 90
HEARN, Mary Caroline, 40
HEATON, Eben, 96; Mary, 96
HECKLER, Polly, 79
HEDGES, Andrew, 86
HEFFNER, David, 94; Elizabeth, 94; Felts, 94; Jacob, 94; Valentine, 94
HEFLEY, Anna, 115
HEFNER, Jacob, 94

HEIFFNER, Jacob, 94
HEIFNER, Jacob, 94
HEISTER, Joseph, 34
HEIZEN, Edward, 25
HELVEY, Luvana, 42
HENDERSON, William, 3
HENDRICKSON, William, 95
HENDRIX, John, 59
HERCHING, Mr., 18
HERRINGTON, Mr., 177
HEVELIN, Debora Ann, 213
HEVLIN, Debora Ann, 213
HEWITT, Elinor, 53
HEWS, Gideon, 99
HEYSER, William, 47, 94
HIATT, Anna, 202; Benjamin, 202; Isabelle, 142; Silas, 202
HIBBERD, Phebe, 75
HICK, Giles, 142
HICKS, Ann, 96; James, 206
HIDDLESTON, Lyndia Ann, 199
HIGGENS, Sarah, 119
HIGGINS, Major, 93; Samuel, 80
HILL, Elizabeth, 36, 121; James, 95; William, 95
HILLIARD, Charles, 92
HINDS, Ann, 95; Benjamin, 95; Elizabeth, 95; Emily, 96; Henry, 96; Jacob, 96; Jacobus, 96; James, 95; Jane, 96; John, 95; Mary, 95; Reizen, 96; Sarah, 95
HINES, Nathaniel, 148
HIRST, William D., 180
HITCHCOCK, Asael, 96; Asel, 96; Isaac, 96; John, 96; Josias, 96; Nicholas, 96, 97; Rachel, 97; Sarah, 96; William, 96
HITE, Alexander, 97; George, 97; Jacob, 97; John, 97; Polly, 97; William, 97
HOAGLAND, Mr., 21
HOAGLIN, Mr., 155

HOBBS, Mary Ann, 168; Rachel, 39
HOBSON, Ann, 97; Joseph, 97
HODGKINS, Dora, 43; Elizabeth, 20, 97; Hannah, 97; Lydia, 97; Samuel, 97
HODGSKIN, Mary, 170, 172
HOGAN, Mary, 30
HOGG, John, 98; John W., 98; Martha Ann, 98; Sarah Jane, 98
HOLLENBACH, Lydia, 201
HOLLINGSWORTH, Joseph, 98; William, 101, 110
HOLLISTER, Jeremiah, 14
HOLLOWAY, Levi, 98
HOLMAN, Benjamin, 98; Catharine, 99; Edward, 98; George, 98; Greenup, 99; Henry, 98; Isaac, 99; Jesse, 99; Joel, 98; John, 98; Joseph, 98; Patsey, 98; Rebecca, 98; Sarah, 98; William, 98
HOLMES, Eli, 34
HOLTZ, Susan, 73
HONNELL, Rebecca, 23
HOOD, John, 122; Thomas, 107, 111, 113
HOOEY, Thomas, 87
HOOSIER, Peter, 106; Phillip, 106
HOOVER, Captain, 169; Rebecca, 108
HOPEWELL, Millicent, 201
HOPKINS, Martha, 33
HORNEY, William, 99
HOSKINSON, Emma, 38
HOTZ, Adam, 90
HOUGH, Hannah, 99; John, 99
HOUSE, Nancy, 62
HOUSH, Mr., 117
HOUSTON, Sarah, 184
HOWARD, Cornelius, 205; John Eager, 140, 147; Mary, 205; Ruth, 168
HOWELL, Mary, 192; Samuel, 99

HUBBARD, Bemont, 183; Elizabeth, 147; Wright, 209
HUES, Gideon, 99
HUFFMAN, John, 173; Mary, 163; Rosannah, 136
HUGH, Gideon, 99
HUGHES, Gideon, 99, 100; Jacob, 89; Mr., 93; Rebecca, 100; Sarah, 126
HULL, Ann, 100; John C., 100, 101
HUNT, Elizabeth, 199; James, 101; John, 199; Martha, 199; Mary H., 174; P.S.C., 25; Philip, 43; Rebecca, 174; Seth, 199; Strange, 171; William, 199
HUNTER, Isaac, 102; John, 101, 102; Joseph, 102
HUNTINGTON, Hannah, 171
HURFORD, Mary, 197
HURT, Thomas, 142
HUSBAND, Joseph, 150; Mary, 82, 150; Susanna, 150
HUSE, Gideon, 99
HUSSEY, George, 102
HUTCHESON, Maria, 114
HYATT, Sarah, 198; Whitfield, 143
IGLEHART, Ellen P., 102; Jane, 102; John S., 102; Margaret A., 102; Mary Ann, 102; Nicholas P., 102; Richard, 102; William, 102
IRELAND, Richard, 43
IRVIN, Elisha, 2
IRVING, Thomas, 149
ISGRIG, Daniel, 118; Michael, 118
ISRAEL, Mary, 88
JACKSON, Enoch, 103; Ezekiel, 103; John, 102, 103; Margaret, 103; Markey, 61; Sally, 103; Susan, 103
JACOBS, Catharine, 103; Elizabeth, 103; Sarah, 103; William, 103

JAMES, Basil, 103; Benjamin, 183; Henry, 103; John, 103; Melvina, 190; Mr., 200; Pinkney, 103; Thomas, 103
JAQUITH, Ann E., 85
JEAN, Ruth, 41
JENKINS, Coleman, 124
JENNINGS, Ann, 104, 199; David, 104; Deborah, 104; Elizabeth, 104; Isaac, 104; James, 104; Lydia, 172; Mr., 199; Rebecca A., 104; Samuel G., 104; Sarah, 104; Sarah L., 104; Susan, 104; Thomas, 104; Thomas A., 104; Thomas W., 104
JOHN, Mary, 104, 105; William, 104
JOHNS, Martha, 8
JOHNSON, Abijah, 65; Anna, 105, 106; Barret, 10; Benjamin, 105; Benjamin F., 106; Charles J., 106; Chloe, 65; Christopher, 106; Edward K., 105; Edward P., 106; Elizabeth, 78, 105; Francis M., 105; Griffith, 138; J.B., 124; James B., 124, 125; John D., 105; John W., 105; Joseph S., 105; Mahala J., 106; Margaret, 105; Mary Ann, 114; Mary J., 106; Morgan, 124; Samuel J., 105; Sarah, 105; Sarah E., 105; William, 106; William G., 106; William P., 105
JOHNSTON, Benjamin, 106; Bennett, 51; James, 106
JOHNSTONE, Martha, 130
JOLLY, Albert, 183; Henry, 183; Larisa, 12
JONES, Ann Buxton, 107; Anna, 107; Captain, 80; Cassandra, 107; Charlotte, 107; Elijah, 5; Eliza, 107; Emeline L.S., 104; Frederick, 29; Hannah, 5;

Harrison, 5; Isaiah, 126; Jacob, 107; James, 107; Jane, 107; John, 5, 53; Louise, 5; Lovina, 28; Mary Ann, 5; Melissa, 5; Nancy, 3; Nathan, 107; Rebecca, 5; Rose Ann, 107; Sarah, 5, 53, 83, 107; Sarah Virginia, 82; Thomas, 43, 107, 198; Thomas S., 4; William, 107
JORDAN, William, 59
JOURNEY, John, 164
JULIAN, Isaac, 107, 108
KALB, Susanna, 83
KANE, Daniel, 107
KEARNS, Polly, 4
KEETS, William, 108
KEEVER, John, 108; Mary, 108; William, 108
KELBRETH, James, 108
KELLEY, Jacob, 109; John, 109; Joshua, 108, 109; Moses, 108, 109; Nicholas, 108; William, 108, 109; William J., 109
KELLY, Fielden, 156; Mr., 36
KENDALL, Barbary, 119
KENNARD, Ann, 109; Elizabeth, 26, 72, 109; Ely, 26; Hannah, 26; Levi, 109; Levy, 109; Mary, 109; Thomas, 109, 133
KENNARD FAMILY, 109
KEPHART, Martin, 109
KERCHEVALL, Benjamin, 110
KERN, Catherine, 23; Jacob, 23; Sarah, 23
KERR, Ellen, 13; Harriet, 184; Mr., 1
KESSLER, Mr., 151
KESTLING, Elizabeth, 151
KETNER, Sarah, 83
KEYS, John, 126
KILGORE, William, 110
KIMBER, Isaac, 2
KIMMEY, Anne, 209

KING, Captain, 57; Elizabeth, 66; Elizabeth Angeline, 184; Gerrard, 110; John, 57; Kesiah C., 110; Maria, 111
KINGSBURY, Gus, 199
KINKEAD, George, 110
KINKEID, George, 110
KINNEY, Louis, 154
KIRBY, Eliza, 155; Elizabeth, 111; Elizabeth Brazer, 30
KIRK, John, 111
KIRKBRIDE, Hannah, 2
KITTLE, William, 111
KLINE, Peggy, 173
KLINHAUTZ, Frederick, 73
KNIGHT, Jacob, 112; James, 80
KNOTT, Elizabeth, 112; Hannah, 112; Ignatius, 112; John, 112; Susan, 112; William, 112
KNOX, Mary, 126
KOFFEL, Samuel, 58
KOLTENACH, Celestin, 213
KOYE, William, 52
KREAGER, Elizabeth, 28
KREBS, John, 28
KRISER, Henry, 213; Louvisa, 213; Mary, 213; Sally, 213
KUHNS, George, 173; John George, 173; Katharine, 173
LACEY, Amos, 112
LAFOLLETTE, Margaret, 49
LAIN, Jacob, 181
LAKIN, Ann, 62
LAMBERTSON, Thomas, 112
LANDON, Theron R., 28
LANE, N., 102; Uriah, 3
LANHAM, Robert, 148
LARKINGS, John, 113
LARKINS, Catharine, 113; James, 113
LASHLEY, George, 113
LASY, Amos, 112

LAWHEAD, John, 182
LAWRENCE, William, 113
LAWTON, Thomas, 114
LAZENBY, Susan Agnes, 49
LEACH, Edmond R., 113; John, 147; Joshua, 113; Priscilla, 114
LEAR, Jacob, 26
LEATHERBURY, Caroline, 114; Eli, 114; Elizabeth, 114; Jacob Forwood, 114; John T., 114; Martha, 114; Mary, 114; Parthenia, 114; Thomas, 114
LEATHERS, Mary, 151
LEAVITT, Humphrey H., 130
LEE, Charles G., 114; Joseph, 116; Lorenz, 92
LEECH, Edmond R., 113
LEEDS, Elizabeth, 114; George, 114; Lodowick, 114
LEGORE, Mary, 121
LEITCH, Benjamin, 43
LEMMON, George, 87
LEMON, Airy, 161; George, 188; Margaret, 161; William, 161
LETTER, Maria, 115
LETTS, Rachel, 126
LEVERTON, Ann J., 115; Arthur, 115; Charles, 115; John Edward, 115; Lemuel, 115; Louisa, 115; Moses, 115, 210; Oliver, 115; Rachel, 115, 210; Rebecca, 210; Thomas F., 115; Willis, 115
LEWIS, Clarissa, 174; Malinda, 148; Mr., 117, 198; Thomas J., 171
LICHENWALTER, Catherine, 74
LIGHTNER, George W., 69
LINE, John, 23
LINES, Mary Ann, 3
LINN, A.M., 116; Aaron, 115; Adam, 115; Andrew F., 115; Anna, 115; George, 115; John, 115; Joseph, 115; Samuel, 115

LINTHICUM, Aquila, 116; Aquilla, 117; Carrie, 116; Carrie Rachel, 116; John, 117; Jonathan, 117; Larkin, 116; Slingsbury, 39
LINTON, Elizabeth, 117; Esther, 117; Hannah, 117; William, 117
LITTELL, Frances, 117
LITTEN, James, 26; Sarah, 26
LITTLE, Frances, 117
LIVINGSTON, Thamer, 149
LLOYD, Nancy, 130
LOAR, Henry, 118; John, 118
LONG, Anna, 117; Elizabeth, 117; Jacob, 117; John, 117; Joseph, 117; Margrett, 117; Mary, 117; Nancy, 117; Sarah, 117; Susannah, 117
LONGNECKER, Nancy, 151
LOOFBURROW, Polly, 121
LOPEZ, J.M., 118
LORAH, Henry, 118
LOSTUTTER, Cynthia A., 152
LOUDEN, Sarah, 46
LOWE, Harrison, 92; John H., 42
LOWERY, Mary Ann, 97
LOWNES, Charles, 118
LOY, Hiram, 118
LOZIER, Fannie M., 81
LUCAS, Basil, 119; Cassandra, 119; Charles, 119; James, 119; Jane, 119; Jesse, 119; John, 118, 119; John B., 122; Richard, 119; Samuel, 119; Thomas, 119; William, 118, 119
LUDWICK, Jacob, 173; Peggy, 173
LUDWIG, George, 173; Nancy, 173; Rebecca, 173
LUKINS, Alse, 197; Ann, 197
LUSBY, Joseph, 119
LUTHER, Jacob, 119; Sarah, 119
LYNN, Captain, 74
LYON, James, 119

MCBRIDE, Mr., 180
MCBURNEY, Mary, 29
MCCAIN, John, 213
MCCANN, D.W., 126; Joanna, 170
MCCENEY, Benjamin, 61
MCCHORD, Mr., 58
MCCHRISTAL, Patrick, 128
MCCLAIN, Betsy, 125; Hannah, 125; Martha, 125; Matilda, 125; Rachel, 125; Seth, 191; William, 125
MCCLALLAN, Lieut., 57
MCCLELLAND, Ann, 130; Asa, 126; Cary, 125, 126; Eliza, 126; Elizabeth, 126; Ellen, 126; Hannah, 126; Jane, 126; John, 126; Margaret, 126; Mariah, 126; Marinda, 126; Mary, 126; Michael M., 126; Nancy, 126; William, 126
MCCLENNAN, Captain, 118
MCCLURE, Hiram, 171
MCCOMAS, Amanda, 127; Amos, 127; Aquila, 127; Augustus, 127; Elizabeth Ann, 127; Franklin, 127; James, 127; John, 127; John W., 127; Orpah Ellen, 127; Sarah A., 128; Sarah J., 127; Sarah Jane, 127; Sophia, 137; William Glenn, 127
MCCONKEY, Captain, 128; James, 128
MCCONNAUGHEY, Mary, 184
MCCONNELL, Elizabeth, 49
MCCORMICK, John, 128; Lavina, 124; Lucinda, 82; Tabitha, 124
MCCOY, Ann, 128, 206; Joseph, 206
MCCRACKEN, Sophia, 138
MCCRISTAL, Patrick, 128
MCCRISTEL, Patrick, 128
MCCULLOCK, Elizabeth, 159
MCCULLOH, Sarah, 32

MCCULLOUGH, Samuel, 163
MCDANIEL, Edward, 129; Walter,
128, 129; William, 128, 129
MCDERMUT, James, 129; Mark,
129
MCDONALD, Mr., 107
MCDONOUGH, Hugh, 129
MCDOUGAL, Joseph, 129
MCDOWELL, Alexander, 130;
Anna, 130; Jane, 155; John, 130;
Maria Antoinette, 130; Nancy,
156
MCDUGAL, Joseph, 129
MCFADIN, Hannah, 30
MCFANN, Mr., 126
MCFARLAND, Lydia, 33
MCGAUCHEY, Alexander, 46
MCGEE, Alexander, 182; Elizabeth,
105
MCGINLEY, Margaret, 33
MCGRATH, Margaret, 187
MCGREW, Andrew, 130; Anna, 130;
Charles, 130; Isaac, 130;
Jonathan, 130; Joseph, 130;
Margaret, 82, 130; Paul, 130;
William, 130
MCGRUE, Andrew, 130
MCGUIRE, James, 196; Sarah R., 3
MCINTYRE, Dorcas, 182
MACKALL, John G., 91
MCKAY, James, 130; William, 130
MCKEAN, Rebecca, 189
MCKENSEY, Bennett, 131
MCKENZIE, A.B., 131, 132;
Bennett, 131, 132; Catharine,
131; Elenor, 131; Jesse, 131;
John, 131; Joshua, 131; Moses,
131
MCKENZIE FAMILY, 131
MACKEY, William, 181
MCKIM, William, 198

MCKINSEY, Benjamin, 131;
Bennett, 131; Elizabeth, 131
MCKINZEY, Bennett, 131, 132;
Elenor, 132; Jesse, 132; John,
132; Joshua, 132; Moses, 132
MCKINZEY FAMILY, 131
MCKISSAN, John, 59
MCKNIGHT, John, 132; Rachel, 132
MCMEEKEN, William, 132
MCMILLAN, William, 163
MCMILLEN, Daniel, 132; Franklin,
132; Jane, 133; John W., 132;
Julia Ann, 132; Margaret, 132;
Stephen, 132; Susan Agnes, 49
MCMULLEN, Daniel James, 133
MCMUNN, Eliza Smith, 182
MCNAMEE, George, 173; Nancy,
173; Polly, 173; Thomas, 173
MCNEELEY, Isaac, 59; John, 59;
Levi, 59
MCQUEEN, Dugal, 133; Joshua,
133; Thomas, 133
MCVAY, Miss, 125
MCWILLIAMS, John, 116
MAGIN, Charles, 119; Sarah, 119
MAGNESS, Hannah, 189
MAGRUDER, Ann, 192
MAJOR, Anna C., 15
MALLINCOTT, John, 117
MALONEY, J.V., 131; Mildred Pratt,
131
MALOTT, Dory, 120; Elizabeth, 120;
John, 119, 120; Theodore, 120;
Thomas, 120
MANKER, Eleanor Jane, 171
MANLEY, John, 120; Susanna, 120
MANLY, Jesse, 120; John, 120;
Thomas, 120
MANSFIELD, Anna, 121; Charity,
121; Esther, 121; Martin, 121;
Samuel, 121; Thomas, 121;
Thomas W., 121

MANTZ, Peter, 76, 95
MAPES, Fanny, 155
MARK, Elizabeth, 121; George, 121;
Henry, 121; Jacob, 121; John,
121; Jonathan, 122; Joseph, 121,
122; Mary, 121; Peter, 121;
Samuel, 122; Susan, 122
MARRIOTT, Edith, 122; Thomas,
122; William, 122
MARSH, Ann, 123; John, 122, 123;
Jonathan, 122; Leviney, 122;
Margaret, 122; Margarett, 123;
Mary, 122; Susanna Morthlin,
123; William, 123
MARSHALL, Allen, 191; Captain,
147; Crispen, 191; Elizabeth,
191; Irwin, 191; Malona, 191;
Mary, 191; Nancy, 191; Owen,
191; Susannah, 5; Thomas, 191,
200; Tilson Wheeler, 5; William,
114
MARTAIN, Robert, 123
MARTIN, Ann, 123; Cassia, 123;
Dorothy, 123; Elizabeth, 123;
George, 123; John, 163; John P.,
123; Lloyd, 10; Luther, 123;
Mary, 85; Mr., 145; Nancy, 123;
Robert, 123; Samuel, 123; Sarah,
144
MARTS, Isaac, 124; Moses, 124
MASH, George, 213
MASON, Ann Barbara, 75, 76; Anna
Barbary, 75; Christiana, 79;
Elizabeth, 166; Jacob, 79;
Martin, 76
MASTEN, Charlotte, 124; Darius,
124; David, 124; Hezekiah, 124;
John, 124; Mary, 124; Mathias,
124; Sarah, 124
MASTERS, Ezekiel, 124; George,
124; Mary, 124, 125; Sarah, 124
MATSON, Aaron, 82

MATTHEWS, Ann, 125; Joel, 125;
Margaret, 62; Mary, 125;
Newgent, 163; Oliver, 125;
Phebe, 125; William, 125
MAXWELL, John, 125
MEADS, Elisha, 87, 188
MEDCALF, Abraham, 133; David,
133; Elizabeth, 109, 133; Jesse,
133; Jessy, 133; Joseph, 133;
Mary, 133; Moses, 109, 133;
Rachel, 133; Rebecca, 133;
Rebeckah, 133; Susannah, 109,
133
MEDLEY, William, 133, 134;
William Glover, 133
MEEK, Barbara Ann, 183; Rachel, 56
MEEKS, Joseph, 75
MEGRUE, Andrew, 130
MEHOLLIN, Elizabeth, 182
MELOTT, Thomas, 120
MENTZER, David, 87; Mary, 87
MEREDITH, Benjamin Wheeler,
192; Crispen Tredway, 191;
Elizabeth, 36; Elizabeth Jane,
191; Hannah Jerusha, 192; James
Louis, 192; John, 191; John
Lyman, 192; Margaret Ellen,
191; Mary Louise, 192
MERONEY, Philip, 41, 103
MERRILL, Charlotte, 84; George,
84; Sarah C., 84
METER, Andrew, 134
METTLER, Elizabeth, 126; Isaac,
134
METTLER FAMILY, 9
MICHAELS, Margaret, 49
MIDDLETON, Hannah, 72; John,
193; Mary, 193; Phebe, 193
MIDKELF, Moses, 133
MIKESELL, Andrew, 134; George,
134; Jacob, 134; John, 134;

Martin, 134; Michael, 134; Peter, 134
MILES, John, 134; Levin, 149
MILLEND, Samuel, 15
MILLER, Abraham, 181; Ann, 136; Cornelius J., 213; Deborah, 136; Edith, 135; Elizabeth, 94, 205; Ephraim G., 181; George, 135; Hannah R., 99; John, 70, 135; John M., 136; Josias, 135; Lidia, 135; Mary, 167, 181; Rachel, 135; Samuel, 117, 136; Samuel T., 136; Susanna, 153; Thomas, 136; William, 135, 143; William John, 135
MILLIKEN, Benjamin, 116, 117
MILLS, Daniel, 136; Elijah, 136; Jacob, 136; Joseph, 136; Michael, 136
MINOR, William, 119
MINSHALL, Enoch, 62
MISER, John, 44
MISNER, Phoebe, 157
MITCHELL, Mary W., 127; Sarah, 87
MOLEN, Bartin, 148
MOLETT, John, 120; Thomas, 120
MONDAY, John, 136; Susanna, 171
MONDY, Balser, 136; John, 136; Rosannah, 137
MONG, Elizabeth, 198
MONSARRAT, David T., 163
MONTGOMERY, Alexander, 137; Elizabeth, 2, 197; George, 137; Isaac, 137; John, 137; Lydia, 137; Margaret, 110; Mary, 137; Michael, 126; Nancy, 126; Polly, 137; Richard, 137; Ruth, 137; Sarah, 105, 127; Thomas, 137, 197; William, 137

MOODY, A., 62; Granville, 137; Louisa Brooks, 137; William, 137; William M., 137
MOOMAW, Mr., 1
MOORE, Adam, 138; Asa, 138; Elias, 202; Elizabeth, 138, 202; George, 138; George W., 3; Henrietta, 184; John, 138; John C., 138; Josiah, 202; Lucy, 138; Mahala, 138; Mary, 138; Nancy, 138, 139; Peter, 4; Phoebe, 138; Sanford, 184; William, 12, 138
MOPPS, Edwin S., 98
MORFORD, Elizabeth, 144; Robinson, 144
MORGAN, Aaron C., 190; Ann, 36; Armfield, 36; Drusilla, 36; Hugh, 36; John, 36
MORRIS, Aaron, 76, 79; Cornelius, 139; Cornelius (Neel), 139; Daniel, 139; Elizabeth, 76, 139; George, 79; Harriet, 139; Jane, 139; Lydia, 76, 79; Sarah, 139; William, 140
MORRISON, Alexander, 139; Anna, 139; Anny, 139; Daniel, 139, 140; George, 138; John, 139; Margaret, 139, 140; Mordecai, 139, 140; Nancy, 139; William, 139
MORTON, Delilah, 55
MOSS, Elizabeth, 49
MOTSINGER, Sarah, 33
MOUNTS, Mr., 181
MULHOLLAND, Elizabeth, 182
MULLIKEN, Rev., 59
MUMMEY, Jacob, 140; Samuel, 140
MURPHY, Benjamin, 140; Darby, 140; James, 140; Thomas, 140
MURRAY, Therissa Jane, 149
MUTERS, Elizabeth, 42

MYERS, Benjamin H., 81; Christopher, 77, 141; Henrietta, 125; Katherine, 2; Rosealtha M., 81; William, 77

NAGLE, Jacob, 141

NASH, Lewis, 171

NAYLOR, Abraham, 141; Ann, 141; Charles, 141; James, 141; John, 70, 141; Joseph, 141; Levinia, 122; Margaret, 141; Mary, 141; Rebecca, 141; Samuel, 141; William, 142

NEAL, Mary, 40

NEALE, Mahala, 184; Martha "Patsy", 3; Rebecca, 4

NEFF, Mr., 151

NEGLEY, Eve, 85

NEIGHKIRK, Henry, 44

NELSON, Elizabeth, 62; Sarah, 193

NEWELL, William, 12

NEWTON, Mariah, 81; Nancy, 130; Rachel, 130

NICHOLS, Edward, 209; George, 51; Polly, 51

NICHOLSON, Alice, 142; Charles L., 142; Eliza, 142; James, 30; John, 142; William L., 142

NIXON, Charles, 20

NOBLE, Caleb, 142; Charity, 142; Elizabeth, 142; John H., 142; Jonathan, 142; Levin, 142; Mr., 166; Nancy, 142; Nathan, 142; Summers, 143; Tamsey, 142; William, 142, 143

NORMAN, Rebecca, 88

NORRIS, Ann Mariah, 144; Aquila, 143; Aquilla, 144; Arnold, 143; Bazel, 144; Benjamin, 143, 144; Elijah, 143; Eliza, 144; Elizabeth, 143, 144; Ellen, 144; Gabriel, 144; Gibson, 144; Gilbert, 144; Hannah, 144; Isaac, 143; James,

143; John, 144; Luther, 144; Martha, 143; Mary, 144; Mary Ann, 144; Naomi, 143; Nathan, 143, 144; Otho, 144; Priscilla, 143; Priscilla Temperance, 143; Richard, 144; Ruth, 143; Sarah, 189; Temperance, 143; William, 143, 144

NORTH, Levi, 152; Lucinda, 152

NOTESTINE, Polly, 180

OARD, Jesse, 145; William, 145

OGBORN, Ann E., 149

O'HARRA, Elizabeth, 63

OLDACRES, Hannah, 21

OLDHAM, Cyrus, 80

OLMSTED, Maria L., 105

O'NEAL, Mr., 36

O'NEALE, David, 134; John, 145; Margaret, 145; Phoebe, 145

ORD, Jesse, 145; William, 145

ORME, Charles, 145

ORNDORFF, Christian, 77

O'ROUKE, Mary, 117

O'ROURKE, James, 116; Mary, 116; Thomas, 117

ORR, Eleanor, 170; James, 170; John, 28; William, 190

OSBURN, David, 82

OTT, Adam, 77; Barbara, 99, 167

OWEN, Elmira "Myra", 34; Stephen, 145

OWENS, Jane, 49; Nancy, 145; Richard, 93; Stephen, 145; Thomas, 93

OWINGS, Thomas, 77, 93, 111

OWINS, Thomas, 111

OZIAS, Mr., 151

PACK, Ann, 145; Elizabeth, 145, 146; Enos, 145; John O'Neale, 145; Mary, 145; Phoebe, 146; Rachel, 146; Thomas, 145; William, 145, 146

PADGETT, Nancy, 87
PAINE, Elizabeth, 143; William, 146
PAINTER, Abraham, 199; David, 199; Elizabeth, 199; Julia, 199; Martha, 199; Mary, 199; Phoebe, 199; William, 199
PALMER, Elizabeth, 95; Richard, 146
PANNELL, Edward, 32
PARIS, Thomas, 212
PARKER, Aquilla, 33; Mary, 33; Samuel B., 7
PARKINSON, Elizabeth, 146; John S., 146; Polly, 146; Thomas, 146
PARR, Enoch, 40; John, 40
PARRIS, Nicholas, 147
PARRISH, Jacob, 147
PARSONS, Ganer, 147
PATRICK, John, 22
PATTEN, Thomas, 207
PATTERSON, James, 65; Joshua S., 86; Katharine, 57
PAUL, Daniel, 126; Matilda Isabella, 4; Sarah, 4
PEACOCK, Neal, 147; Neale, 147
PEARCE, Andrew, 148; Elizabeth, 147; Hugh, 149, 150; James, 147; Jane, 148; Jesse, 148; John, 148, 150; Joseph, 147; Louis, 147; Mary, 148; Sarah, 17; Thomas, 147, 148
PECK, Elenor, 138
PEEK, Elenor, 138
PELL, William, 148
PELTIER, Jane, 46; Mr., 46
PENN, Benjamin, 148; Eleanor, 148; Elijah Taylor, 148; Elizabeth, 148; Joseph, 122, 148; Mary, 148; Nackey, 148; Nancy Ann, 148; Rachel, 148; Rebecca, 148; Rhoda, 148; Sophia, 148
PENNINGTON, George, 4

PENNOCK, Sara, 198
PERDRIZET, Eugenie, 68
PERKINS, Matthew, 176
PERRY, John, 117; Rachel, 12; William G., 14
PERSONETT, John, 149; Joseph, 149; Joseph H., 149; Lavina, 149; Lorenzo D., 149; Rolla, 149; Susannah, 149; William, 149
PETEET, Elizabeth, 190
PEYTON, Nimrod, 195
PHEBUS, George, 149; Nancy, 123; Samuel, 149
PHELPS, Epapheras, 117
PHILIPS, Samuel, 149; William, 149
PHILLIPS, Ann, 148; Henry, 199; Robert, 53
PHOEBUS, George, 149
PICKER, Mary, 181
PICKERING, Catherine, 198
PIERCE, Hugh, 149
PIERSE, Hugh, 149
PIGMAN, Joshua, 148; Philena, 164
PINKERTON, Robert A., 12
PIXLEY, Lydia, 154
PLATTENBURGH, A.U., 131; E.A., 131
PLAUGHER, Catherine, 121; Susannah, 122
PLOUGHER, Catherine, 121; Susannah, 122
PLUMB, Eve, 10; Jacob, 10
PLUMMER, Ann E., 150; Ann Eliza, 150; Benjamin, 150; Eleanor, 151; Frances W., 150; Francis William, 150; George, 121; Joanna, 151; Johannah, 150; John, 150; John R., 150; John T., 151; Joseph P., 150, 151; Mariah A., 150; Mary, 150; Mary M., 151; Mary Mifflin, 151; Phoebe,

151; Samuel, 59; Sarah C., 151;
Sarah Cresson, 150; Susanna,
152; Susannah, 150; Thomas,
151
POINTS, Nancy Jane, 15
PONTENAY, James, 155
PONTIUS, Jacob, 74; Peter, 74
PONTON, Polly, 4
PORTER, Agnes, 78; Andrew, 61,
169; Andy, 66; Dorcas Fornash,
86; Hetty, 86; Mr., 126
POTEE, Elizabeth, 190
POTEET, Elizabeth, 190
POTTERF, Caspar, 151
POTTORF, Anna, 151; Caspar, 151;
Casper, 152; Casper T., 151;
David, 151; Elizabeth, 151;
Jacob, 151; James, 151, 152;
James S., 151; Jefferson, 151;
John, 151; Joseph, 151; Nancy,
151, 152; Nancy Jane, 151, 152;
Polly, 151; Rosanna, 151;
Samuel, 151; Sarah, 151;
Susanna, 151
POTTORFF, Caspar, 151
POULTNEY, Anthony, 152; Samuel,
152
POUNDSTONE, Alfred M., 5
POWELL, George W., 25, 152; John
H., 152; Marcus L., 152; Mary
E., 152; Rachel, 54; Rosanna,
152; Sarah J., 152; William H.,
152; William J., 152
PRATHER, Bazil, 152; James, 148;
John Garret, 164; Thomas, 152
PRATZMAN, Joseph, 121
PREWITT, Wesley, 127
PRICE, Ann, 153; Benjamin, 2;
Elizabeth, 153; Frances, 153;
Hannah, 153; Isaac, 113, 153;
Israel, 153; John H., 153; Leah,
83; Nathaniel, 153; Stephen R.,

153; Susanna, 153; Warrick, 153;
William, 44, 153
PRIEST, Elizabeth, 94; Hankey, 95
PRITCHARD, James, 153, 154;
Kezia, 154; Margaret, 59
PROVIDENCE, Kirby, 83
PRUGH, Aquilla T., 207; Gabriel,
207
PRY, Jesse, 154
PUCKETT, Henry, 79
PUMPHREY, Charles, 13, 56, 128;
Greenbury, 64; Milo, 87
PUNTENNEY, Ann, 155; Aquilla,
155; Eliza, 156; Elizabeth, 155;
George H., 154; George
Hollingsworth, 154, 155; James,
155; James Guffy, 155; Jane,
155; John, 155; Joseph, 154, 155,
156; Lucinda, 156; Margaret,
154; Mary, 154; Matilda, 155;
McDowell, 156; Nelson, 155;
Nelson Hollingsworth, 155;
Pamelia, 155; Prisilia, 155;
Reason Gamble, 156; Samuel,
156; Sarah, 154, 155, 156;
William Hamilton, 154
PURNELL, Elisha, 140; Elizabeth,
131; G., 131; James S., 131
PUTERBAUGH, Joseph, 156
PUTTEE, Elizabeth, 190
QUARRY, Catherine, 104
QUIGG, Benjamin, 8
RADINGER, Mrs., 154
RAILSBACK, David, 174
RAINSBURG, John, 156
RALPH, Joseph, 49
RAMPLEY, Elizabeth, 6; James, 85,
86, 87, 96, 144, 188
RAMSBERG, John, 156
RAMSBERG FAMILY, 156
RAMSBURG, John, 156
RAMSBURGH, John, 156

RAMSEY, Allen, 156; Ann, 11; Lucinda, 194
RAMSOWER, John, 111
RANDALL, Bethiah, 157; Isaac, 157; John, 157; John T., 14; Sarah, 157; William, 157
RANEY, Benjamin F., 157; Maria, 19
RANK, Salome, 74
RANKIN, Daniel, 157; Eleanor, 157; James, 157; John, 157; Nancy, 157
RANKINS, Daniel, 157
RANNESPERGER, John, 156
RANSBERG, John, 156
RANSDELL, Harriet, 27
RAVEN, Isaac, 147
RAY, Cinthia, 50; George, 158; Jonathan, 158; Mary, 50
REARDON, Mary, 42
RECORD, Labon, 176
REED, Charles, 158; John, 158; Joseph H., 158; Mariam, 158; Marion, 158
REEVES, John Lewis, 3; Josias, 158; Levi, 107
REILLEY, Elizabeth, 159; John, 159; Robert, 159
REILLY, John, 159
REIMENSPERGER, John, 156
REINSBERGER, George, 156
REMSBURG, John, 156
REYNOLDS, John, 24, 77; Margaret, 192; Robert, 159; Thomas, 92; William, 192
RHODES, Henry, 77; Mary A., 62
RHUFF, Margaret, 159; Peter, 159
RICHARDS, Gabriel, 159; George, 148; John, 148; Parson, 12; Samuel, 29
RICHARDSON, Colonel, 38; Joshua, 101; Martha Ann, 6; Samuel,

159; Susannah, 8; William T., 159
RICKETTS, Edward, 160; John, 160; Nathan, 160; Reson, 160; Robert, 160; Thomas, 160
RIDENOUR, Jonathan, 151; Susanna, 151
RIDER, Catharine, 34
RIDGELY, Richard, 102
RIDGEWAY, Jonathan, 160
RIGBY, Ara, 161; James, 161; William, 161; William L., 161; William Lemon, 161
RIGGS, Eleanor, 33
RILEY, John, 159; Nicholas, 161
RINEHART, Levi, 126
RINGER, Frederick, 179; Joseph, 179; Sarah, 179
RITCHEY, Solomon, 59
ROAFF, Peter, 159
ROBE, David, 12
ROBERTS, Azel, 161; Hazel, 161; Mr., 36; Rachel, 113; Samuel, 163; Sarah, 163
ROBERTSON, Elizabeth, 40; James, 86; Martha, 107; Polly, 40; Rice W., 5; William D., 5
ROBINSON, John, 161; Mary, 163; Nancy A., 81; Rowena, 126; Ruth, 84, 163; Sarah Ann, 212
ROBY, Mary, 108
ROCK, Andrew, 161; Edward, 162; John, 162; Oliver, 162; William, 162
RODGERS, John, 100
ROGERS, Byrd, 192; Thomas, 82
ROHRER, Anna, 27; John, 27
ROLLER, Mr., 199
ROLLINS, Lucinda, 56; Nancy, 73; Selah, 162
ROOS, Martin, 162
ROOSS, Martin, 162

ROSE, Gottlieb, 162; Martin, 162; Reuben, 162; Thompson, 77

ROSS, Abner, 126; Ignatius, 162; Nancy, 147; Reuben, 162

ROUTH, Susan O., 11

ROUTZEN, John, 80

ROWE, Ann, 206

RUBLE, Elizabeth, 109

RUE, Richard, 98

RUFF, Henry P., 35

RUFFIN, Harriet Olive, 163; William, 163

RUNYON, Philip, 107

RUSSELL, Jesse, 163; Martha, 154; Rachel, 198; Thomas, 163; William, 154

RUST, Hannah, 130

RUTH, Mary, 11

RUTLEDGE, Abraham W., 163; America, 164; America Ann, 163; Benjamin, 163, 164; Eliza, 163, 164; Elizabeth, 163; Isaac, 163; Jacob, 163; Mary, 163; Miriam, 163; Nancy, 163; Peter, 163; Ruth, 163, 164; Sarah, 164; Sarah (Matilda), 163

RYAN, Edward, 213; James, 164; William, 164

ST. CLAIR, William, 169

ST. JULIAN, Rene, 107

SAMPLE, John, 100, 106, 110, 181, 195

SANDS, Alexander, 164

SANFORD, Miriam, 163

SAPPINGTON, Richard, 11

SARGENT, Anna, 164; Edward, 164; Eleanor, 164; James, 164; Mary, 148; Mary Ann, 164; Nelly, 164; Philena, 164; Sarah, 143, 164; Silas, 164

SATTERFIELD, Elijah, 69

SAULSBURY, Matthew, 183

SAUNDERS, Christiana, 189; David, 165; Edward, 189; Mary "Polly", 176

SAWENS, Edward, 34

SAXTON, Peninah, 15

SAYLOR, Catherine, 1

SCHNARIN, Juliana, 73

SCHNEIDER, George, 175

SCHOLLENBERGER, Catherine, 74

SCONCE, Jane, 132, 133; John C., 133

SCOTT, A., 100; A.C., 61; Benjamin, 165; Isaac, 165; James, 165; John, 165; Lotty, 165; Matthew, 165; Rev., 122

SEAMAN, Milton, 12

SEARGENT, James, 164

SEAWRIGHT, Samuel, 4

SEDERBORG, Andrew F., 166

SEDGWICK, Mary, 174

SEELY, Elizabeth Jane, 5

SELBY, Ann Wilson, 138; Henrietta, 140; Richard, 138

SELLERS, John Crawford, 35

SELWOOD, Susannah, 65

SERGEANT, Elijah, 164; James, 164; John, 164; Richard, 164; Snowden, 164; William, 164

SERJEANT, Elijah, 166

SEVER, George, 122

SEVERNS, Almeda, 191; Christine, 191; Elizabeth, 190; Hannah, 190; James, 190; Joseph, 190, 191; Leonard, 190; Malona, 190; Mary, 190, 191; Olive, 190; Ransom L., 191; Robert, 191; Samuel, 191; Sarah, 191; William, 190

SEWALL, James, 57

SEWARD, Elijah, 166; Elizabeth, 166; Jennie, 166; Matilda, 166;

Rea, 166; Samuel, 166; Sherman, 166; Starling, 166; Stephen, 166
SHAFER, Adam, 166; Andrew, 166; John, 163; Margaret, 6
SHAFTER, Mr., 199
SHARPLEY, John, 131
SHAVER, John, 163
SHAW, John, 110, 167
SHAWN, Frederick, 167
SHAYS, Mr., 102
SHEELER, Abraham, 167; Mary, 167
SHEETS, Mary, 183
SHELTON, Mary, 130; Thomas, 49
SHEPPARD, William, 213
SHERIFF, James, 147
SHERWOOD, Thomas, 167
SHICK, George, 155
SHIDELER, Susanna, 151
SHIDLE, Mary, 22
SHIELDS, Andrew Jackson, 139; Emma J., 3; John H., 139; John Henry, 139; William Van Buren, 139
SHILLING, Leonard, 200
SHIMER, Isaac, 63
SHINER, Catherine, 97; John, 169
SHINN, Margaret, 199
SHINNER, John, 169
SHION, Alpha, 49; Ebenezer, 49
SHIPLEY, Aaron, 168; Adam, 168; Amanmaseene, 168; Benedict, 168; Betsey, 168; Catharine, 14; Henry, 168; Mary, 168; Nansey, 168; Rachel, 168; Ruth, 168; Susan R., 18
SHLIFE, John, 167
SHOCKLEY, Elizabeth, 64
SHOEMAKER, Elizabeth, 89; John, 169
SHREVES, Mary "Polly", 19
SHRINER, Barbary, 169; John, 169
SHRIVER, Abraham, 86

SHULTZ, Catherine, 89; Elizabeth, 89; George, 89
SIMMONS, Thomas T., 16; William, 169
SIMPSON, Captain, 80; Catharine, 168; Mary, 168; Thomas, 168; Thompson, 168
SIMS, James, 61, 169
SINCLAIR, Mary, 2
SIPE, Daniel, 170
SIPES, Daniel, 170; Paul, 170
SISSILL, Joshua, 42
SKELTON, P., 170
SKINNER, Frederick, 129
SLADE, Alice, 171; Charles, 171; Charlotte, 171; Eleanor, 170; Ezekiel, 170, 171, 172; George Washington, 171; Isaac Newton, 171; James, 170, 171; John, 170; John Strange, 171; John W., 171; Lemuel Alexander, 171; Lemuel W., 171; Mary A., 171; Powell, 171; Samuel, 172; Sarah Ann, 171; Wayland, 171; William, 170; William Crosley, 170
SLUTS, Catharine, 172; John, 172
SLY, William, 172
SLYE, William, 172
SMALLWOOD, General, 38; William, 60
SMISER, David, 33; Emma, 34; Philip, 34
SMISSEN, Eleanor, 66
SMITH, Amanda F., 174; Ann J., 174; Ann M., 174; Anna, 179; Anne, 102; Anthony, 102; Barbara, 174; Benjamin C., 174; Cassandra, 174; Charles, 12; Elizabeth, 81; Francis D., 174; George H., 174; Hannah, 2; Hester, 22; Irvin, 174; James, 112, 120, 174; James S., 4; Jane,

102; John, 174; John P., 174; Joseph, 172, 183; Joseph W., 174; Judith, 138; Katharine, 173; Kosciouski C., 174; Kozciouski, 174; Louisa, 174; Margaret, 174; Mary, 174; Mary Helen, 90; Michael, 173; Mr., 36; Naomi, 198; Nathan, 173, 174; Nathan C., 174; Nicholas, 174; Oren E., 184; Peter, 174; Phebe, 198; Philip, 40; Pulaski, 174; Pulaski K., 174; Rebecca, 173; Rev., 15; S.C., 174; Sally, 198; Samuel, 198; Sarah Ann Catherine, 171; Sophia, 1; Thomas, 174, 198; William C., 174; William P., 174; Winston, 174

SMITHSON, John, 26, 84

SMYTH, Philip D., 175; Rebecca, 157

SNOOK, John, 175

SNOWDEN, Henry, 41

SNOWDENBERGER, Jacob, 134

SNYDER, Elizabeth, 34; George, 175; Peter, 175

SOLLADAY, Christena, 175; George, 175; Philip, 175

SOLLARS, Isaac, 175

SOLLERS, Eleanor, 176; Elizabeth, 176; Isaac, 175, 176; Nancy Ann, 176; Ruth, 176; Samuel, 176

SOULE, Jane, 176; Maria, 176; Sarah, 176

SOULE FAMILY, 176

SOUTH, Benjamin, 176; Hannah, 176; Hiram, 33; James, 176; John, 176; Mary, 176; Peter, 176; Sarah, 176; William, 176; Zedekiah, 176

SPARKLING, Mr., 16

SPARKS, Sarah, 22

SPIRES, Richard, 177

SPRAGE, Mr., 103

SPRIGG, Mary, 194; Thomas, 77, 159

SPRINGER, Zadoc, 201

SPRY, Catharine, 177; Elizabeth, 177; Mary, 177; Nathan, 177; Perry, 177; Ruth, 177; Samuel, 177; Thomas, 177; William, 177

SPYERS, Dorcus, 178; Elizabeth, 177; Henry, 178; Jane Miller, 178; John, 178; Martin, 178; Nancy, 178; Rebecca, 178; Richard, 177, 178; William, 177

STAMP, S., 43

STANDAGE, Mr., 138

STANDIFORD, Benjamin, 6; James Adolphus, 6; Sarah H., 6; William (Amos), 6

STANELY, Sarah, 124

STANTON, Ann M., 178; Celia, 178; Edward, 178; Isaac W., 178; James B., 178; Lucrecia, 178; Mary E., 178; Peter, 178

STAPLETON, Henrietta, 114

STARBUCK, Mr., 199

STARR, Samuel, 59

STENTZ, Daniel, 28

STERRET, Jane Eliza, 179

STERRIT, James, 178, 179; Rebecca, 179; Stewart, 178; William, 179

STEVENS, Hester, 159; Samuel, 58; William, 61

STEVENSON, Jane, 198; John, 71

STEWARD, Elizabeth, 148

STEWART, J.D., 107; Walter, 125; William L., 179

STIF, Elizabeth, 146

STIFFLER, Mary, 124

STONE, Sylvester, 19, 179

STONER, Andrew, 179; Joseph, 179; Philip, 179; Sarah, 179

STORTS, Jacob, 180

STOUDER, Joseph, 112; Samuel, 112
STOUGH, Elizabeth, 28
STRATTON, Mr., 199; Ross, 199
STREETER, Sarah, 96
STRETT, Mary M., 6
STRICKER, George, 110
STROUDER, Sarah, 33
STRUTHERS, Ann, 180; Ebenezer, 180; John, 180; Mary, 180; Matilda, 180; Thomas, 180
STUART, Elizabeth D., 43; William R., 43
STULL, Christiana, 17
STUTSON, Amelia, 180; Bethiah, 180; Genett, 180; Gennett, 180; James, 180; Jennet, 180; Jernet, 180; Sidney, 180
STUTSON FAMILY, 180
SULLIVAN, Caleb J., 93; Daniel, 180, 181; H.H., 93; John, 181; Sarah, 180, 181
SUMWALT, Dorcas, 181; Jacob, 181; Jemima, 181; Maria, 181
SWAIN, Adaline, 181; Charlotte, 7; George, 7; Henry, 181; James, 181; Jeremiah, 181; John, 181; Mary M., 7; Otha, 181; Samuel, 181; Thomas, 181; William, 181; Zachariah, 181
SWAMSTEDT, Sidney, 180
SWAN, Laura, 10
SWEENEY, Samuel B., 185
SWIFT, Richard, 181
SWIGGETT, Euphemia, 182; Jane, 182; Solomon, 182
SWING, Michael, 82
SWORMSTEDT, Sidney, 180
TALBOTT, Absalom, 182; Achsah, 183; Anna, 163; Basil Dorsey, 183; Benjamin, 182; Charles, 182; Charles Wells, 182;

Elizabeth, 182; Ephraim, 183; Ethelinda, 183; James, 182; John, 97; John Dorsey, 183; Joseph, 108, 183; Joshua Owen, 183; Mary, 97; Michal, 183; Nancy, 182; Providence, 182; Rebeckah, 97; Richard, 182, 183; Ruth, 182; Temperance, 182; Wells, 183
TALMADGE, Martha A., 49
TANEY, Colonel, 91
TANNEYHILL, Mordecai, 43
TAPLEY, Sophia J., 65
TAYLOR, Ann, 183; Anna, 53; Edward, 53; Eleanor, 164; James, 183; Rachel, 96; Richard, 183
TEAGARDEN, Mr., 199
TEDRICK, John, 89
TEETERS, Elisha, 198; Elizabeth, 199; Job, 199; Jonathan, 198; Martha, 199; Phoebe, 199; Rachel, 199; Samuel, 199; William, 199
TERRY, Susan Ulrey, 82
TETERICK, John M., 90
TETMAN, Emily, 56
THARP, Thomas, 183, 184
THATCHER, William, 213
THICKSTON, Rebecca, 162
THISSEL, Clarissa, 62
THOMAS, Alice, 186; Amanda, 185; Amos, 185; Ann M., 185; Anna Rebecca, 184; Benjamin, 184; Clement, 185; Cynthia, 186; Daniel, 184, 185; Eli Bird, 184; Elias Bird, 184; Elijah, 185; Eliza J., 185; Elizabeth, 138; Eva, 184; Francis M., 186; Franklin, 185; Harriet, 185; Henry Parker, 184; Jacob, 70; James B., 186; James M., 185; James S., 185; Jesse, 185; John, 55, 93, 185; Joseph, 185; Joseph M., 185; Laura, 185;

Lola, 185; Martha, 184, 185;
Martha Jane, 185; Mary Frances,
185; Mary N., 184; Melinda,
184; Miriam Sarah, 184; Nathan,
185; Oliver A., 185; Oscar, 186;
Priscilla, 185, 186; Rachel, 186;
Ransom A., 184; Rebecca, 185,
186; Rebecca A., 186; Richard
Symmes, 186; Robert, 185;
Samuel C., 185; Sarah, 60, 184,
185; Sarah Ann, 185; Sarah M.,
185; Susan, 185; Sylvester H.,
184; Wesley, 184, 185; William,
184, 185; William M., 185;
William S., 186; Zenith, 186
THOMPSON, Andrew, 67; Ann, 186;
Charles T., 5; Elizabeth, 67, 104;
George, 191; Harriet, 67; James,
186, 187; Martha, 80; Mary, 186;
Sarah, 67, 68
THOMSON, Jane, 101
THRASHER, Benjamin, 148
THUKSTON, Rebecca, 162
THURMAN, Demarue C., 4
TILGHMAN, Frisby, 12, 29
TILLARD, Edward, 135; William S.,
43
TILLISON, James Madison, 5
TIMANUS, Jacob, 187; John, 187;
Martha, 187; Mary, 187
TIPTEN, Luke, 187
TIPTON, Abijah, 187; Bebeckah,
187; David, 187; Elihu, 187;
Esther, 187; Hannah, 187;
Hester, 187; John, 187, 188;
Luke, 49, 187; Mary, 187;
Meshac, 187; Priscilla, 187;
Rachel, 187; Thomas, 188;
William, 188
TOLAND, Aquilla, 188
TOLLERTON, Lavisa, 198
TOMAR, Christopher, 188

TOMER, Christopher, 188; John,
188; Moses, 133
TOMLINSON, Sarah, 21
TOMPKINS, Cynthiana, 185; Mary,
185
TONGUES, Eleanor, 157; Ellender,
157
TOOLE, Martha, 42; Sarah, 43
TOWNSEND, Elizabeth, 188;
Thomas, 188
TRAIN, Elizabeth, 176
TREADWAY, Ann, 189; Aquila,
189; Charity, 189; Christiana,
189; Crispin, 190; Daniel, 189;
Edward, 189; Elizabeth, 189;
John Norris, 189; Mary, 189;
Sarah, 189; Thomas, 189, 190
TREDWAY, Aaron M., 191;
Abraham F., 191; Calvin S., 191;
Charles R., 191; Corbin, 191;
Crispen, 190, 191; Crispin, 190;
Daniel C., 191; Elijah L., 191;
Elizabeth, 190, 191; Garret S.,
190; Hannah, 190; James H.,
190; John, 190; Joseph, 190;
Mahala, 190; Martha L., 191;
Mary, 190, 191; Mary C., 191;
Nancy E., 191; Resin B., 191;
Resin Hammond, 190; Sarah E.,
191; Thomas, 190; Thomas B.,
191; Thomas Franklin, 190;
William H., 190, 191
TREES, Mary Ann, 5
TRIMBLE, James, 192
TROXEL, Jacob, 74
TROY, Caroline, 68
TRUEMAN, Alexander, 192
TRUITT, Elizabeth, 64; Jane, 64;
Rhoda, 155; Riley, 64, 192
TRULOCK, Mary, 96
TRUMAN, Alexander, 192;
Alexander Magruder, 192;

Henry, 192; Mary Ann, 192;
Thomas, 192
TRUMP, John, 74
TUCKER, Richard, 148
TURNER, Abigail, 34; Benjamin,
192; James, 192; John, 26; Mary
A., 171
TYIER, Amelia M., 193; Eliza A.,
193; Gertrude, 193; Jane, 193;
John T., 193; William, 193;
William S., 193
TYLER, John, 193; Mary, 193;
Thomas, 193
TYLOR, John, 193
UMBARGER, John, 117
UNDERWOOD, Amy, 194; Barclay,
194; John, 193; Mary, 194
VAIL, Asa, 102
VALENTINE, Frederick, 194;
George, 194; Mary, 134
VAN BUSKIRK, John, 37
VANCE, E., 194; Samuel, 194
VANZANT, Richard, 198
VATTIER, John L., 195
VEATCH, Eleanor, 194; Elijah, 194;
Elizabeth, 195; Hezekiah, 195;
Isaac, 194; Kesiah, 195; Keziah,
195; Kinsey, 194; Martha, 194;
Mary, 194; Nathan, 194, 195;
Orlando, 195; Silas, 195;
Susannah, 195
VEAZEY, Colonel, 100; John, 53;
Noble, 195
VERMILLION, John, 84
VICKERS, Clement, 59
VOOTHIES, Catherine, 199
WADDLE, John, 29
WADE, Joseph, 12
WAGONER, Sarah Catherine, 5;
William A., 5
WAITE, Martha, 155
WAITS, Charles, 176

WALKER, Betsy, 199; Christopher,
195; Edward E., 195; Elizabeth,
195; John, 195; Julia Catherine,
4; Matthew, 195, 196; Patience,
195; Robert, 196
WALL, Elizabeth, 187; Mr., 199
WALLACE, George William, 49;
Robert, 179; William, 44
WALLING, James, 65; William, 63
WALLIS, Mary, 22
WALLS, Elizabeth, 80
WALRAVEN, Philomena, 148;
Samuel, 164
WALTER, Mariah L., 132
WALTON, Mary, 143
WANN, Henry L., 4
WANTON, William R., 196
WARD, Ann, 142; Anna, 196;
Daniel, 210; Edward, 196; Eliza
Ann, 210; James, 2, 196; James
W., 210; Jeremiah, 196; John,
196; Lucy, 196; Mary Ellen, 210;
Mary White, 142; Sarah, 210,
211; William, 196
WARDEN, James, 197; Mary, 197;
Sarah, 197
WARFIELD, Charles A., 12; Charles
D., 111
WARNER, Martha, 114
WARREN, Amos T., 189; Bailey,
189; Benjamin, 189; Eliza, 2;
Elizabeth, 189; Evan, 189; James
Madison, 189; Levi, 189;
Wrightson Jackson, 189
WASHBURN, Eleanor, 157; George,
157
WASSON, Mr., 16
WATERMAN, Eleanor, 170
WATERS, Edith, 122; James, 197;
John, 197
WATHEN, Mary, 126

WATKINS, Gassaway, 24; Thomas, 168

WATT, Ann E., 7; Caroline, 7; Charlotte, 7; David T., 7; John, 7; John H., 7; Mary, 8; Mary M., 7; Nancy Isabella, 7; William O., 7

WATTERS, James, 197

WATTS, Rachel, 13

WAUGH, Anne, 63; Catherine, 62

WAY, Ann, 197

WAYNE, General, 13; Lucy Ann, 7; Sarah Ann, 8

WEAVER, Elizabeth, 74; Lewis, 29; Margaret, 6

WEBB, Abraham, 199, 200; Albert, 198; Alice Ann, 198; Alvin C., 68; Ann, 199; Anna, 68; Asa, 198; Benjamin, 200; Calvin, 198; Catharine, 70; David Montgomery, 198; Edith, 198; Eliza, 199; Eliza J., 200; Elizabeth, 197, 198, 199; Emiline, 199; Ferdinand, 68; George Washington, 198; Harriet, 68; Howard, 68; Isaac, 199; Isaac N., 198; James, 28, 197, 198; Jesse, 198; John, 197, 198, 199, 200; Joseph, 198; Joshua J., 198; Julia, 199; Julia A., 200; Keziah, 70; Leah, 197, 200; Levi, 200; Louervin B., 198; Louise, 67; Lucinda, 199; Lynda Ann, 199; Margaret, 199; Mark A., 199; Martha, 198, 199; Mary, 199; Minerva, 199; Mr., 68; Penina, 200; Polly, 198, 200; Rachel, 198; Rebecca, 198, 199; Richard, 198; Sally Ann, 198; Samantha, 198; Samuel, 198; Sarah, 68, 198; Simeon, 199; Stanton, 198; Susan, 198, 199;

Thomas, 197; Thomas Smith, 198; William, 70, 198, 199

WEEMS, Jesse E., 150

WEIR, Jane, 40; Mr., 107

WELCH, Augustus A., 29; Harry, 66; John, 66; Sarah, 66

WELLING, Mary Elizabeth, 190

WELLS, Achsah, 182; Catherine, 130; Charles D., 200; Dorinda, 182; Martin, 43; Mary, 38; Peter, 200; Temperance, 182

WELSH, Catharine, 172; James, 111

WELTNER, Ludwick, 47, 94

WEST, William, 198

WHANN, Adam, 101, 110

WHEATLEY, Daniel, 202; Willis, 203

WHEATLY, Isaac, 203

WHEELER, Benjamin, 200; Thomas, 200

WHETSTONE, David, 201

WHIPS, Benjamin, 201; Ruth, 93

WHITAKER, Sarah, 34

WHITE, Abram, 201; Alexander B., 201; Elizabeth, 12; Enoch, 201; John, 201; Mary, 202; Nancy, 201; Nancy A., 2; Tabitha, 154; Thomas, 12, 202

WHITEHEAD, Elizabeth, 38

WHITELEY, Anna Eliza, 203; Anna W., 202; Cecilia M., 202; Celia, 202, 203; Daniel, 202, 203; Edward, 203; Edward Hicks, 203; Elizabeth A., 202; Elizabeth G., 202; Francis, 203; Francis Henry, 203; Henry A., 202; Isaac, 203; Isaac L., 203; James, 203; James Anthony, 203; Jane S., 202; Lydia, 203; Lydia Ann, 203; Martha, 202; Mary C., 202; Mary Jane, 203; Peter A., 203; Ruth, 202; Sarah Ann, 202;

William P., 202; William W.,
203; Willis, 203
WHITELY, Daniel, 202, 208; Isaac,
203, 208; Willis, 203
WHITLER, Johanna, 60
WHITTAM, Mr., 36
WHITTEN, Johannah, 60
WHITTLE, Lyndia, 198
WILEY, Catherine, 127
WILKE, George, 73
WILKINSON, Anna, 121; George,
43; Priscilla, 113; Robert B., 114
WILLIAMS, Abram, 155; Agness,
136; Ann, 171; Anna, 45; B.F.,
204; Benjamin, 204; Catherine,
170; Charles, 204; David, 33;
Elisha, 205; Eliza, 204;
Elizabeth, 205; Ellen, 68; Esther,
32, 204; Ezekiel, 204; Hannah,
45; James, 204, 205, 206;
Jeremiah, 205; John, 204, 205;
Joseph, 204; Mary, 204, 205,
206; Nancy, 35, 148; Otho H.,
204; Reuben, 205; William, 45,
116, 142, 204, 205, 206; William
Alfred, 4; Zebina, 206
WILLIAMSON, Adeline, 183; Airy
"Ara", 161; David, 161;
Elizabeth, 161; Joseph M., 29;
Mary, 161; Mercy, 161; Mr.,
199; Olive, 161; Sarah, 161
WILLIS, Mary Malvina, 171; Peter,
9, 58, 69, 136, 203
WILLS, Elliott, 193; Martha E., 193
WILLSON, Matthew, 206; Rachel,
206
WILMINGTON, Narcissa, 68
WILSON, Alizanna, 206; David, 206;
Hillary, 43, 92; Isaac, 206; John
Webster, 206; Lucy, 196;
Matthew, 206; Nancy, 74;
Rebeckah, 206; Sally, 152;

Samuel, 206; Stephen, 43;
Susanna, 206; Uriah, 200;
William, 59
WILT, Mary, 188
WINDER, General, 122
WINDHAM, Ann, 207; Benson, 207;
Elizabeth, 207; George, 206, 207;
Harriot, 207; Hezekiah, 207;
Mary, 207; Meriah, 207; Sarah,
207; Thomas, 207; William, 207
WINGATE, Peter, 207
WINHAM, George, 206
WINPOUGH, Adam, 113
WINTERS, Mary, 53; Rhoda, 53
WISNER, Jacob, 207
WITHERS, Elizabeth, 183
WOLF, Michael, 207
WOLFE, Lydia, 3
WONN, Bethia, 180
WOOD, Achsah, 155; John, 122;
Mary, 5; William, 208
WOODFIELD, Mr., 138
WOODS, George, 130
WOODSON, Mary, 40
WOODWARD, Henry, 39
WOOLEN, Henry, 189
WOOLLEN, William W., 25; Wilson
A., 25
WOOLMAN, Mary, 202; Uriah, 202
WORKING, Maria C., 140
WORLEY, Bruce, 147; David, 208;
Francis, 208; Thomas, 208;
William, 208
WORN, Bethia, 180
WORTHINGTON, James, 8
WRIGHT, Albert, 210; Amelia, 208,
210; Ann, 60, 209; Aramintah,
155; Cecelia, 208; Celia, 60, 209;
Daniel, 209; Edward, 209, 210;
Elizabeth, 152, 208; Esther, 211;
Harris, 209; Hatfield, 44, 208;
Hatfield V., 208; Isaac, 208;

Isaac H., 210; Jacob, 208, 209; James, 209, 210; James H., 209; James W., 209; Joel, 152, 211; John, 211; Jonathan, 211; Joseph, 210; Joshua, 33; Lea, 199; Lemuel, 208, 209; Levin, 208; Lucretia, 208; Lydia, 97, 209, 211; Margaret, 163; Mary, 44, 208, 209, 210, 211; Mr., 49; Phoebe J., 126; Rebecca, 211; Rhoda, 209, 211; Richard Henry, 209; Sarah, 209; Sarah E., 209; Sarah H., 210; Susanna, 211; Thomas, 12; William, 60, 163, 209; William E., 209
WRITSON, Joseph, 159

WYATT, John L., 186; Oliver M., 186; William S., 186
WYCKOFF, Samuel, 211
WYNDHAM, George, 206
YATES, Benjamin, 212
YEATS, Benjamin, 212; James, 212; Robert, 212; Samuel, 212; Sarah, 212; William, 212
YONDISS, John, 175
YOUNG, Abraham, 212; Albert, 213; Amos, 213; Anna Barbara, 212; Barbara, 212; Catherine, 213; Daniel, 213; David, 213; Eliza, 213; Elizabeth, 213; Hannah Catherine, 212; Henry, 178, 213; Jackson, 213; Jacob, 213; John, 212, 213; Joseph, 212; Keziah, 213; Margaret, 212; Martha, 213; Mary, 213; Mary Ann, 213; Matthias, 212; Minerva, 213; Peggy, 213; Perry, 213; Peter, 212; Polly, 213; Samuel, 213; Sarah, 213; Solomon, 213; Susannah, 213; William, 163

Heritage Books by Henry C. Peden, Jr.:

A Closer Look at St. John's Parish Registers [Baltimore County, Maryland], 1701–1801

A Collection of Maryland Church Records

A Guide to Genealogical Research in Maryland: 5th Edition, Revised and Enlarged

*Abstracts of Marriages and Deaths in
Harford County, Maryland, Newspapers, 1837–1871*

Abstracts of the Ledgers and Accounts of the Bush Store and Rock Run Store, 1759–1771

Abstracts of the Orphans Court Proceedings of Harford County, 1778–1800

Abstracts of Wills, Harford County, Maryland, 1800–1805

Anne Arundel County, Maryland, Marriage References 1658–1800
Henry C. Peden, Jr. and Veronica Clarke Peden

Baltimore City [Maryland] Deaths and Burials, 1834–1840

Baltimore County, Maryland, Overseers of Roads, 1693–1793

Bastardy Cases in Baltimore County, Maryland, 1673–1783

Bastardy Cases in Harford County, Maryland, 1774–1844

Bible and Family Records of Harford County, Maryland, Families: Volume V

Cecil County, Maryland Marriage References, 1674–1824
Henry C. Peden, Jr. and Veronica Clarke Peden

Children of Harford County: Indentures and Guardianships, 1801–1830

Colonial Delaware Soldiers and Sailors, 1638–1776

*Colonial Families of the Eastern Shore of Maryland
Volumes 5, 6, 7, 8, 9, 11, 12, 13, 14, 16, and 19*
Henry C. Peden, Jr. and F. Edward Wright

*Colonial Families of the Eastern Shore of Maryland
Volume 21 and Volume 23*

Colonial Maryland Soldiers and Sailors, 1634–1734

Colonial Tavern Keepers of Maryland and Delaware, 1634–1776

Dorchester County, Maryland, Marriage References, 1669–1800
Henry C. Peden, Jr. and Veronica Clarke Peden

Dr. John Archer's First Medical Ledger, 1767–1769, Annotated Abstracts

Early Anglican Records of Cecil County

*Early Harford Countians, Individuals Living in
Harford County, Maryland in Its Formative Years
Volume 1: A to K, Volume 2: L to Z, and Volume 3: Supplement*

Family Cemeteries and Grave Sites in Harford County, Maryland

First Presbyterian Church Records, Baltimore, Maryland, 1840–1879

Frederick County, Maryland, Marriage References and Family Relationships, 1748–1800
Henry C. Peden, Jr. and Veronica Clarke Peden

Genealogical Gleanings from Harford County, Maryland, Medical Records, 1772–1852
Winner of the Norris Harris Prize from MHS for
the best genealogical reference book in 2016!

Harford County Taxpayers in 1870, 1872 and 1883

Harford County, Maryland Death Records, 1849–1899

Harford County, Maryland Deponents, 1775–1835

Harford County, Maryland Divorces and Separations, 1823–1923

Harford County, Maryland, Death Certificates, 1898–1918: An Annotated Index

Harford County, Maryland, Divorce Cases, 1827–1912: An Annotated Index

Harford County, Maryland, Inventories, 1774–1804

Harford County, Maryland, Marriage References and Family Relationships, 1774–1824
Henry C. Peden, Jr. and Veronica Clarke Peden

Harford County, Maryland, Marriage References and Family Relationships, 1825–1850

Harford County, Maryland, Marriage References and Family Relationships, 1851–1860
Henry C. Peden, Jr. and Veronica Clarke Peden

Harford County, Maryland, Marriage References and Family Relationships, 1861–1870
Henry C. Peden, Jr. and Veronica Clarke Peden

Harford County, Maryland, Marriage References and Family Relationships, 1871–1875

*Harford (Maryland) Homicides: Cases of Murder and Attempted Murder:
Committed by Men and Women Who Were "Seduced by the Instigation of the Devil"
in Harford County, Maryland During the 18th and 19th Centuries*

*Harford (Maryland) Suicides: Cases of Self-killings and Attempted Suicides
Committed by Men and Women Who Suffered from an "Aberration of the Mind"
in Harford County, Maryland, 1817–1947*

*Harford (Old Brick Baptist) Church,
Harford County, Maryland, Records and Members (1742–1974),
Tombstones, Burials (1775–2009) and Family Relationships*

Heirs and Legatees of Harford County, Maryland, 1774–1802

Heirs and Legatees of Harford County, Maryland, 1802–1846

Inhabitants of Baltimore County, Maryland, 1763–1774

Inhabitants of Cecil County, Maryland 1774–1800

Inhabitants of Cecil County, Maryland, 1649–1774

Inhabitants of Harford County, Maryland, 1791–1800

Inhabitants of Kent County, Maryland, 1637–1787

*Insolvent Debtors in 19th Century Harford County, Maryland:
A Legal and Genealogical Digest*

*Joseph A. Pennington & Co., Havre De Grace, Maryland, Funeral Home Records:
Volume II, 1877–1882, 1893–1900*

Kent County, Maryland Marriage References, 1642–1800
Henry C. Peden, Jr. and Veronica Clarke Peden

Marriages and Deaths from Baltimore Newspapers, 1817–1824

Maryland Bible Records, Volume 1: Baltimore and Harford Counties

Maryland Bible Records, Volume 2: Baltimore and Harford Counties

Maryland Bible Records, Volume 3: Carroll County

Maryland Bible Records, Volume 4: Eastern Shore

Maryland Bible Records, Volume 5: Harford, Baltimore and Carroll Counties

Maryland Bible Records, Volume 7: Baltimore, Harford and Frederick Counties

Maryland Deponents, 1634–1799

Maryland Deponents: Volume 3, 1634–1776

Maryland Prisoners Languishing in Goal, Volume 1: 1635–1765

Maryland Prisoners Languishing in Goal, Volume 2: 1766–1800

*Maryland Public Service Records, 1775–1783: A Compendium of Men and Women
of Maryland Who Rendered Aid in Support of the American Cause
against Great Britain during the Revolutionary War*

Marylanders and Delawareans in the French and Indian War, 1756–1763

*Marylanders to Carolina: Migration of Marylanders to
North Carolina and South Carolina prior to 1800*

Marylanders to Kentucky, 1775–1825

Marylanders to Ohio and Indiana, Migration Prior to 1835

Marylanders to Tennessee

Methodist Records of Baltimore City, Maryland: Volume 1, 1799–1829

Methodist Records of Baltimore City, Maryland: Volume 2, 1830–1839

*Methodist Records of Baltimore City, Maryland: Volume 3, 1840–1850
(East City Station)*

More Maryland Deponents, 1716–1799

*More Marylanders to Carolina:
Migration of Marylanders to North Carolina and South Carolina prior to 1800*

More Marylanders to Kentucky, 1778–1828

More Marylanders to Ohio and Indiana: Migrations Prior to 1835

Orphans and Indentured Children of Baltimore County, Maryland, 1777–1797

Outpensioners of Harford County, Maryland, 1856–1896

Presbyterian Records of Baltimore City, Maryland, 1765–1840

Quaker Records of Baltimore and Harford Counties, Maryland, 1801–1825

Quaker Records of Northern Maryland, 1716–1800

Quaker Records of Southern Maryland, 1658–1800

Revolutionary Patriots of Anne Arundel County, Maryland, 1775–1783

Revolutionary Patriots of Baltimore Town and Baltimore County, 1775–1783

Revolutionary Patriots of Calvert and St. Mary's Counties, Maryland, 1775–1783

Revolutionary Patriots of Caroline County, Maryland, 1775–1783

Revolutionary Patriots of Cecil County, Maryland, 1775–1783

Revolutionary Patriots of Charles County, Maryland, 1775–1783

Revolutionary Patriots of Delaware, 1775–1783

Revolutionary Patriots of Dorchester County, Maryland, 1775–1783

Revolutionary Patriots of Frederick County, Maryland, 1775–1783

Revolutionary Patriots of Harford County, Maryland, 1775–1783

Revolutionary Patriots of Kent and Queen Anne's Counties, 1775–1783

Revolutionary Patriots of Lancaster County, Pennsylvania, 1775–1783

Revolutionary Patriots of Maryland, 1775–1783: A Supplement

Revolutionary Patriots of Maryland, 1775–1783: Second Supplement

Revolutionary Patriots of Montgomery County, Maryland, 1776–1783

Revolutionary Patriots of Prince George's County, Maryland, 1775–1783

Revolutionary Patriots of Talbot County, Maryland, 1775–1783

Revolutionary Patriots of Washington County, Maryland, 1776–1783

Revolutionary Patriots of Worcester and Somerset Counties, Maryland, 1775–1783

*St. George's (Old Spesutia) Parish
Harford County, Maryland Church and Cemetery Records, 1820–1920*

St. John's and St. George's Parish Registers, 1696–1851

Survey Field Book of David and William Clark in Harford County, Maryland, 1770–1812

Talbot County, Maryland Marriage References, 1662–1800
Henry C. Peden, Jr. and Veronica Clarke Peden

The Crenshaws of Kentucky, 1800–1995

The Delaware Militia in the War of 1812

*Union Chapel United Methodist Church Cemetery Tombstone Inscriptions,
Wilna, Harford County, Maryland*